*Mis*Reading America

*Mis*Reading America

Scriptures and Difference

Edited by VINCENT L. WIMBUSH

with the Assistance of LALRUATKIMA AND
MELISSA RENEE REID

OXFORD
UNIVERSITY PRESS

OXFORD
UNIVERSITY PRESS

Oxford University Press is a department of the University of Oxford.
It furthers the University's objective of excellence in research, scholarship,
and education by publishing worldwide.

Oxford   New York
Auckland   Cape Town   Dar es Salaam   Hong Kong   Karachi
Kuala Lumpur   Madrid   Melbourne   Mexico City   Nairobi
New Delhi   Shanghai   Taipei   Toronto

With offices in
Argentina   Austria   Brazil   Chile   Czech Republic   France   Greece
Guatemala   Hungary   Italy   Japan   Poland   Portugal   Singapore
South Korea   Switzerland   Thailand   Turkey   Ukraine   Vietnam

Oxford is a registered trademark of Oxford University Press
in the UK and certain other countries.

Published in the United States of America by
Oxford University Press
198 Madison Avenue, New York, NY 10016

Library of Congress Cataloging-in-Publication Data
Misreading America : scriptures and difference / edited by Vincent L. Wimbush
with the assistance of Lalruatkima and Melissa Renee Reid.
pages cm
ISBN 978–0–19–997542–6 (pbk.) – ISBN 978–0–19–997541–9
1. Ethnicity–Religious aspects.   2. Ethnicity–United States.   3. Identification (Religion)
4. Minorities–Religious life–United States.   5. Minorities–United States–Social conditions.
6. Assimilation (Sociology)–United States.   7. United States–Ethnic relations.   I. Wimbush,
Vincent L.
BL65.E75M574 2013
277.30089–dc23
2013012868

9 8 7 6 5 4 3 2 1
Printed in the United States of America
on acid-free paper

In gratitude to
all the associates, assistants, and friends of
the academic-intellectual-political
transgression
also known as
the
Institute for Signifying Scriptures
(est. 2003)

CONTENTS

ACKNOWLEDGMENTS

Thanks are due to:

The Henry W. Luce Foundation and the Ford Foundation, for their support of the Institute for Signifying Scriptures (ISS) during the period that the project behind this volume was running. I shall always be grateful for the encouragement that officers of these foundations gave my work during the past several years.

ISS Research Assistants—graduate students—for their support with the initial planning and conceptualization meetings, the national conference and meetings, communications and logistics; and subsequent research and editorial work: Kenzie Grubitz; Jacqueline Hidalgo; Robin Owens; Brent Smith; Wendell C. Miller; Ryan Carhart; Thomas Crawford; Ian Fowles; Robert Mason; Kevin McGinnis; Richard W. Newton; Quynh-Hoa Nguyen; Sana Tayyen; Emmanuel Ukaegbu-Onuoha; and David Olali.

Research Group directors, the writers of chapters of the book, for their years of patience, support; engagement; and hard work and cooperation through the years of changes and challenges that made the project a success.

Interviewees, for their openness of mind and generosity of time.

Cynthia Read, editor at Oxford University Press for her belief in this somewhat odd project; to her assistant Sasha Grossman for her responsiveness and good offices; and to Molly Morrison and the production staff for their diligence.

Readers of the manuscript, especially Grey Gundaker, for her years of friendship and support and encouragement, and for her generosity of mind in the careful reading of the manuscript and offer of extensive and incisive, critical comments, and suggestions (most of which have been accepted for the sake of the improvement of the book).

Lalruatkima and Melissa Reid, advanced graduate students and ISS assistants, for their dedication and hard work in all areas of the project. They are enormously capable professionals. I am pleased to call them scholar-colleagues.

Rosamond C. Rodman, for her friendship, love, support, and wisdom about things that matter most.

Institute for Signifying Scriptures
Claremont, California
2013

CONTRIBUTORS

Efrain Agosto is professor of New Testament Studies at the New York Theological Seminary. He is the author of *Servant Leadership: Jesus and Paul* (2005); and *1 y 2 Corintios* (2008).

Tat-siong Benny Liew is a professor of New Testament at the Pacific School of Religion. He is the author of *What Is Asian American Biblical Hermeneutics? Reading the New Testament* (2008); and editor of *Reading Ideologies: Essays on the Bible and Interpretation in Honor of Mary Ann Tolbert* (2011).

Velma E. Love is Project Director of the Study of Black Congregational Life at Howard University School of Divinity. She is the author of *Divining the Self: A Study in Yoruba Myth and Human Consciousness* (2012).

Nadine Naber is an associate professor in the Program in American Culture and the Department of Women's Studies and an adjunct associate professor in the Department of Anthropology at the University of Michigan, Ann Arbor. She is author of *Arab America: Gender, Cultural Politics and Activism* (2012). She is co-editor of *Arab and American Feminisms* (2011) and co-editor of *Race and Arab Americans* (2008).

Andrea Smith is an associate professor in the Department of Media and Cultural Studies at the University of California, Riverside. She is the author of *Conquest: Sexual Violence and American Indian Genocide* (2005); and *Native Americans and the Christian Right: The Gendered Politics of Unlikely Alliances* (2008).

Matthew Stiffler is Researcher at the Arab American National Museum in Dearborn, MI. He is the author of "Orthodox, Arab, American: The

Flexibility of Christian Arabness in Detroit," in *Arab Detroit 9/11: Life in the Terror Decade* (2011).

Vincent L. Wimbush is professor of Religion and Director of the Institute for Signifying Scriptures at the Claremont Graduate University. He is the author of *White Men's Magic: Scripturalization as Slavery* (2012); and *The Bible and African Americans: A Brief History* (2003); and editor of *Theorizing Scriptures: New Critical Orientations to a Cultural Phenomenon* (2008); *African Americans and the Bible: Sacred Texts and Social Textures* (1999); and *The Bible and the American Myth: A Symposium on the Bible and the Constructions of Meaning* (1993).

*Mis*Reading America

Introduction

Knowing Ex-centrics/Ex-centric Knowing

VINCENT L WIMBUSH

THE ESSAYS INCLUDED IN this book are revisions of reports on research projects that were presented to a national conference organized by the Institute for Signifying Scriptures and convened in Claremont, California, in October 2009. The conference was the culmination of a three-year collaborative multidisciplinary ethnographic/ethnological research project on US communities of color as reading formations, especially in relationship to scriptures, with the latter understood as freighted but elastic shorthand for types of expressivity, representations, and social relations. The project took up such practices, representations, and relations as windows onto the self-understandings, politics, and orientations of selected complexly minoritized communities. These communities have in common the context that is the United States, with the challenges it holds for all regarding: pressures to conform to conventional-canonical forms of communication, representation, and embodiment (mimicry); opportunities to speak back to, confront, and overturn conventionality in all domains (interruptions); and the need to experience ongoing meaningful relationships ([re]orientation) to the dominant or centering politics, practices, ideologies, and myths that define "America." The project began with a focus on "fundamentalism," with the assumption that such a phenomenon would reflect the most problematic and persistent aspect of scriptural practices for all concerned and thereby provide an especially wide and pertinent window onto formations of dominant and minority formations. As the project developed and conversation and debate ensued, this focus was not so much abandoned as it was reconceptualized and reformulated—into the more broadly and analytically capacious categories and issues listed above and summarized in the subtitle of the book. So "scriptural fundamentalism" we came to understand as a complex phenomenon that subtends Western and now especially intensely US ideological-political-cultural formation. The effort to attach the phenomenon to and therewith overdetermine sub-cultural groups—the southern Bible Belt; peoples of color as the hyper-religious—is rejected and turned on its head. In different respects and to different degrees, "minoritized" communities, insofar as they in ongoing terms *mimic*, *resist*, and *(re)orient* themselves to the formation that is the United States in particular, and the West in general, signify (on) it as scrip-tural formation, the historical re-presentations and forms of expression which are refractions of what has come to be associated with fundamental-ism. The peoples with differently complex relationships with the dominant formation—the minoritized—do not allow the nature and historical and ongoing consequences of the formation to be easily veiled. There is no need to isolate fundamentalism from the history of orientations that define the West and which the minoritized signify on.

This signifying I term here "*mis*readings." With this term, which is also part of the title of this book, I have in mind Harold Bloom's usage and concept, having to do with an alternate individualist reading ("misreading"/"misprision") of a "text" of some sort that is understood to be a sign of a dynamic of "influence" and assertion ("strong" reading of "strong" reading . . .).[1] But for me and for this book project there is more—much more—at issue and at stake. Bloom's "strong" readers seem to be all in a/the family: one larger empire of willful, playful readers, little involved in the dynamics and griminess always played out on the (colonial/racial-ized) fringes.

What I have in mind in using the term here are the serious ludics (and rituals and organizational and institution-building work) of (re-)significa-tion that are part of the history of responses to a social-cultural-political syndrome—race-isms—in the latter-day empire that is the United States in which the views, sentiments, passions, testimonies, and interpretations of nonwhites, especially black peoples, are devalued. Their "readings" within this racialized society are always necessarily understood by the "white" mind/ear/eyes—in the complex effects of empire, attached to any color of body!—as a "lack," a "*mis*reading" of a different kind. In such a situation the problem is not a matter of simply engaging a precursor's (strong) text so as to find a (strong) alternate meaning. What is most problematic for the nonwhite communities of the United States is always (to different degrees and in different respects, to be sure) having voice or mind or language unacknowledged, understood as babble. Lest the reader begin to raise the furried apolitical academic brow in response to this argument, assuming that we are currently beyond this state of affairs, I remind him or her of the (2012) national political campaign climate that is raging as I am writing the first draft of this chapter. It was a climate in which the current sitting president—a historic figure who on account of his mixed-race background is, in the United States of America, identified among the not white, or "black"—was being called among many other things one who "does not *get* us," "does not *understand* our values," advances policies that are "*foreign*." The clamor was to "take back" "America." (Reader alert: you know what must follow: Who constitutes "us"? How inclusive is "our"? Who exactly is "foreign"? "Take back" what from whom?) In short, Barack Obama was assailed as one who "fundamentally"(!) *mis*reads "America." This is why fundamentalism *must* be recast. (How overdetermined is this charge? Is his misreading understood to be on account of what he lacks, what does or does not do, how he speaks? Or is it on account of who/what he is—not white? Does not the fact that these questions are asked or must be asked represent a problem?)

Of course, like so much that must be confronted in such a world constructed as white, some among nonwhite communities have reconceptualized and embraced the association of being black or brown or... with some sort of "lack." Such "*mis*readings" are far more profound, more poignant, more tragic, certainly, embracing of wider and deeper consequences and power dynamics than were those broached by Bloom.

With the project's orientation to the ethnographic, and given the backgrounds of the research participants, there was understandable awareness and wariness—of the history of pernicious uses and consequences of the ethnographic gaze—on the part of participants. But we came to a point of some resolution and commitment, if not total peace, about going forward. This was based on recognition that it is not simply the ethnographic gaze that warrants special scrutiny and wariness and skepticism but all of Western "science"—including exegesis, history, and literary and cultural and social criticism. In the face of such a situation, we resolved that we cannot and should not be paralyzed, but should instead, in the tradition of so many of our tribesmen and women, learn to use the "master's tools" and then hold forth with honesty and as much sensitivity as possible.

Furthermore—although the final verdict is up to readers—I make here the claim that this book and the project behind it is critical and compelling as a contribution to the lack of critical, sensitive, layered, and fulsome excavation work on communities of color in the United States. ("What shall we do with, how should we classify/categorize, those people?") The essayists and their teams of researchers would likely agree with me in claiming that academic programs and scholarship represent at best ongoing inattention to the communities to which we belong and which they studied and, at worst, very problematic construals of such. We still find in commentary and scholarship the all-too-easy reference to the hyper-religiousity of this group, the exotic nature of the other, the radical extremism or fundamentalism of another, the view of the silent "model minority" of yet another, and so forth. What we are confronted with is a profound and unfortunate legacy of *mis*education—on the part of the entire culture, including those of us who are part of the project that results in this book, about these several *sub*cultures.

With the focus on scripture/scripturalizing practices, the project is also unique and compelling insofar as it models ways to study the religious dimensions of the selected communities as ongoing dynamics, gestures/performances, expressions, and textures. This orientation is a marked departure from the usual hackneyed conceptualizations and old assumptions that characterize studies even within ethnic studies programs and discourses. ("Must we touch on, what shall we do with, how do we construe, religion?") The book represents collaborative comparative research as a window onto selected contemporary communities as they continue shaping themselves as reading formations—by focusing on scriptures, narrowly and broadly, elastically construed. And so researchers also learned from the communities they studied that scriptures have to do with more than text/textuality; they learned to view "scriptures" as shorthand for a complex cross-cultural phenomena, as performance, discourse, power dynamics, and social relations.

So a project of the sort represented by this book is very much needed. It models sensitive yet critical excavation of differently and complexly minoritized communities by those with roots in, or certainly identification with, parts of the communities studied. Insiders of a sort, to be sure, but the researchers are also part of the critical studies wings of their different sectors/fields of the academy. This means that they positioned themselves to be empathetic but also questioning at the most basic level; they also made themselves open to being surprised, to learning new things—about parts or aspects of themselves, even as they investigated others.

The essays are organized around the reporting and analysis of implications and ramifications of historical, ethnographic, and ethnological research covering the contemporary scripturalizing practices of five communities of color—Native, African, Asian, Arab, and Latino/a Americans. The purpose of the research projects was not only to contribute to excavations of these five contemporary communities (or at least one or more of their subgroups) by using "scriptures" and scripturalizing practices as an analytical wedge, but also to model and propose different orientations to and expansive understandings of the category and concept of scriptures as part of modern social formation and discourse. The primary focus is placed on contemporaries, but interpretive frameworks and perspectives are informed by historical as well as comparative research.

To make the project and the communication about its results as coherent and as compelling as possible, the essays are presented as responses of a sort—not necessarily in terms of a narrow explicitness or directness or in strict numeration and ordering, but in terms of general participation and investment in, and advancement of, a conversation—to the following overlapping but poignant questions and issues:

1) How does the community name and understand itself today? What are its origins in the United States? How has its self-naming/-understanding changed over time? What are some of the traditions and locations that mark this community?

2) What are the scripturalizing practices/rituals in evidence in this community? What are their origins? Influences? What are the typical settings, situations, dynamics of these practices? Who are the principal actors, performers, authority figures in relationship to these practices?

3) What are some of the material/physical objects and forms of expressiveness—past and present—through which, in relationship to which, the scripturalizing practices are carried out? What are their forms, shapes, sounds, colors, textures?

4) Why do some in this community persist in relating to scriptures? What work do they make scriptures do for them? What are some specific psychosocial and social-cultural needs and benefits that are reflected in connection with the phenomenon of scripturalizing?

5) What are the special themes and issues and problems that have historically been associated with this community and communicated through its scripturalizing?

6) Signifying on the questions: What are the pitfalls, risks, opportunities reflected in these questions and the approaches and assumptions behind them? What are the larger implications—overdetermination,

limitation, distortion, and so forth—of all the questions and issues mentioned above for an understanding of modern discourses, social formation, and power relations?

The chapters address these questions in different ways, with sensitive but persistent self-reflexive and sometimes disturbing questioning, investigation, and reporting and analysis. They are arranged as follows:

Chapter 1, Native Americans: "Native Peoples, Evangelical Christianity, and the Bible." Research Director Andrea Smith (University of California, Riverside), along with collaborator Terry LeBlanc (North American Institute for Indigenous Theological Studies, Toronto) focused research on Native evangelicals from diverse geographic and tribal backgrounds in the United States (and Canada). The chapter stresses the complexity of native peoples' perspectives on and adoptions of Christianity. Through interviews, conversations, and debates captured on film, the research team positioned native peoples themselves as theorists. Individuals are featured who wrestle with the fraught histories and perduring effects of the Christian mission and European colonialism. This wrestling featured a wide range of emotions and sentiment, including humor, thereby reflecting how weighty matters are negotiated and interpreted.

Chapter 2, African Americans: "Scriptures as Sundials in African American Lives." Research Director Velma Love (Howard University School of Divinity) and collaborators John L. Jackson, Jr. (University of Pennsylvania), and Renee K. Harrison (now at Howard University School of Divinity) studied African American seminary students at the Candler School of Theology, Emory University, in Atlanta, Georgia. These students included: a 55-year-old African American woman who embraced various religious traditions throughout her adult life in order to develop a system of meaning that would affirm her self-worth; a member of the African American Hebrew Israelites; and a Yoruba/Orisha priest. Through an examination of the self-reported life stories of these persons the research team discovered dominant themes related to worldview, self-understandings, and the dynamics of meaning-making in connection with the engagement of selected texts. Their analysis suggested that a fundamentalist orientation may meet a psychosocial need for certainty and stability when faced with change and uncertainty and represent a form of agency and self-empowerment, a redemptive strategy and form of rejection of mainstream society. In other words, the group found that the "texts" that constitute scriptures were used to sustain these students and help them reconfigure their world when necessary.

Chapter 3, Latino/a Communities: "Reading the Word in America: US Latino/a Religious Communities and Their Scriptures." Research Director Efrain Agosto (New York Theological Seminary) and collaborators Brian C. Clark (Hartford Seminary), Jacqueline Hidalgo (Williams College), and Elizabeth Conde-Frazier (Esperanza College) examined Latino/a treatments of scriptures in five communities—the Los Angeles Latino Muslim Association; the Latin American Bible Institute; two small Roman Catholic parishes in Connecticut; and the House of Restoration, a Pentecostal church in Hartford, Connecticut. The project stressed Latino/a Americans' uses of scriptures as part of Latino/a efforts to construct identities and epistemologies of opposition within and adjustment to the United States. Researchers found that for the Latino/a groups studied, authoritative texts form reading communities and, as guidance for life, scriptural readings provide the symbols and narratives that make experience readable.

Chapter 4, Asian Americans: "Asian Americans, Bible Believers: An Ethnological Study." Research Director Tat-siong Benny Liew (Pacific School of Religion), along with collaborators Brett Esaki (University of California, Santa Barbara), Russell Jeung (San Francisco State University), Helen Kim (Harvard Divinity School), Lalruatkima (Claremont Graduate University), James Kyung-Jin Lee (University of California, Irvine), and Quynh-Hoa Nguyen (CGU) investigated scriptural readings of multiple generations of Vietnamese Christians in Anaheim, California, and a variety of Asian American college students in Southern California and Boston, Massachusetts. The research team addressed the ambivalence(s) that Asian American Bible believers experience and express as both Asian Americans and Bible believers. Out of that double ambivalence, they adopt ideologies and practices representing complex negotiations with the Bible, including ideologies of biblical inerrancy and authority, and Asian American cultural orientations.

Chapter 5, Arab Americans: "Maronite Catholics, Orthodox Christians, and Sunni Muslims from the Arab Region: Between Empire, Racialization, and Assimilation." Research Director Nadine Naber (University of Michigan, Ann Arbor) and collaborators Matthew Stiffler (University of Michigan, Ann Arbor) and Sana Tayyen (CGU) focused on how Arab Americans—Sunni Muslims in Pomona, California, and Maronite and Orthodox Christians in metropolitan Detroit, Michigan—attempt to respond to the pressures and challenges, especially poignant after 9/11, of homogenization and domestication in the context of the United States, while facing the cultural, ethnic, and regional particularities that are part of the complex world of Arabs. Among such peoples, religious identities and practices, including engagements of scriptures, are entangled in a range of historical realities, including: the networks of social relationships that link Arab immigrant communities in the United States to their homelands; US empire building and the US-led wars in regions of the world that include Arab populations; the related internal histories and politics of their nations of origin; and the pressures of anti-Arab racism, immigration, and assimilation in the United States. The report illuminates how scriptures function within the communities studied as a tool to negotiate the tensions inherent in living in a diaspora while being deeply invested in respective homelands.

The uses of scriptures among the selected modern and contemporary minoritized communities as analytical wedges has forced attention to a number of issues and problems, including those having to do with discourse/knowledge/performance/center/power. I should like with this brief introductory chapter to attempt to provide some general perspectives on aspects of these issues and problems that cut across the five different communities that were the focus of the research project so that readers may get a larger sense of what is compelling about the project as collaboration.

I begin by referencing one of the famous passages from Frederick Douglass's *Narrative of the Life of Frederick Douglass, An American Slave, Written by Himself* (1845).[2] Although the slightly older, writerly Douglass thinking back in this passage on an incident in his life experience makes it a singularly pointed one for narratological effect, the incident may very well have been a recurring one. It is an incident that Douglass, still the relatively young but emerging lion-voiced abolitionist, remembers and recounts for the (assumed abolitionist-minded) reader with the poignant glosses of one who had been a slave. What he touches upon and opens up are several issues that provide perspective and challenge for all moderns, especially those interested and invested in thinking about critical thinking and interpretation.

The home plantation of Colonel Lloyd wore the appearance of a country village....It was called by the slaves the *Great House Farm*. ...The slaves selected to go to the Great House Farm, for the monthly allowance for themselves and their fellow-slaves, were peculiarly enthusiastic. While on their way, they would make the dense woods, for miles around, reverberate with their wild songs, revealing at once the highest joy and the deepest sadness. They would compose and sing as they went along, consulting neither time nor tune. The thought that came up, came out—if not in the word, in the sound; and—as frequently in the one as in the other. They would sometimes sing the most pathetic sentiment in the most rapturous tone, and the most rapturous sentiment in the most pathetic tone. Into all of their songs they would manage to weave something of the Great House Farm. Especially would they do this, when leaving home. They would then sing most exultingly...

"I am going away to the Great House Farm!

O, yea! O, yea! O!"

This they would sing, as a chorus, to words which to many would seem unmeaning jargon, but which, nevertheless, were full of meaning to themselves....I did not, when a slave, understand the deep meaning of those rude and apparently incoherent songs. I was myself within the circle; so that I neither saw nor hear as those without might see and hear. They told a tale of woe which was then altogether beyond my feeble comprehension; they were tones loud, long and deep; they breathed the prayer and complaint of souls boiling over with the bitterest anguish. Every tone was a testimony against slavery, and a prayer to God for deliverance from chains. The hearing of those wild notes always depressed my spirit, and filled me with ineffable sadness. I have frequently found myself in tears while hearing them. The mere recurrence [of] those songs, even now, afflicts me; and while I am writing these lines, an expression of feeling has already found its way down my cheek. To those songs I trace my first glimmering conception of the dehumanizing character of slavery.[3]

In this recounting Douglass names (for his narratological purposes) many issues for consideration—subjectivity and consciousness, collective and individual; discourse and power; power and knowledge; knowledge and positionality, or situatedness within a circle; knowledge and the center; knowledge and centers. He identifies at least three different categories of knowers: slave singers, as those who through their songs provide evidence that they have knowledge (but are not necessarily invested in or skilled at translation work beyond themselves); those outside (that is, being outside the circle—of singers—and beyond the narrative), as those who hear the songs only as jargon and so are also ignorant, cannot know; and Douglass himself, as the one in the fraught middle, the one who though technically at first "within the circle" and did not/could not know, later, as reflected in his writerly self—ironically, outside the circle of slavery—comes to know. Douglass here makes the point, almost totally lost in the Western Enlightenment/post-Enlightenment world, that the subalterns, in this case African slaves, were always knowers, always possessed knowledge. That he, a complex, layered, miscegenated self in consciousness, could not, and that others—the outside white world, represented by the Great House Farm—could not fathom was a matter begging analysis. It suggested, at the very least and in obvious but disturbing respects under the circumstances, the reality of multiple and conflicting forms of consciousness, knowledge, centers.

Douglass's recounting of the incident raises issues about the problematics of the center: long before Foucault, he reflects awareness that power is structured primarily through knowledge that is produced and apprehended and communicated in relationships. Obviously, the Great House Farm was the center around which the slaves' lives turned; it was a sign of dominance—of whiteness, of racialist and racist colonial slavocracy. Douglass made it clear that the slaves were necessarily oriented toward, and creatively wove into their singing, some things about the Great House Farm; there was simply no way not to reflect the Farm as center. But Douglass also seemed to recognize other different centers/circles—including that center/circle the slaves made among themselves for themselves, with its own discourses, gestures, performances, and epistemologies. This raised the question about the relationships between centers and of the phenomenon of the center itself.

Psychologist and theorist of art Rudolf Arnheim has taught us to think of the center most generally as "a focus of energy from which vectors radiate into the environment."[4] He has reminded us that across cultures the position of the center has been used to give perceivable expression to the divine or some exalted power—the gods, the saint, the monarch, and so forth. These symbols of the center were understood to "dwell above the pushes and pulls of the milling throng...outside the dimension of time, immobile, unshakable..."; they were thought of as the only elements "at rest," whereas everything else must "strain in some specific direction."[5] This squares with what historian of religion and culture Mircea Eliade advanced as an important theme in almost all his works: "Every microcosm, every inhabited region," he argued in *Images and Symbols,* has what may be called a "'Centre'... a place that is sacred above all."[6]

With focus on modern world social-political formation, but with attention actually paid mainly to Europe, comparative sociologist Shmuel Eisenstadt suggested that social-political centers were "the major foci and frameworks of charismatic orientations" through which the modern social and cultural orders were defined and identities constructed. He also thought that in the first (read: European) stages of the modern era, most movements of social protest revolved around "the broadening of the scope of participation [in] and channels of access to the centres," and were almost always a reflection of and response to social-class distinctions.[7]

Social scientists have argued that in comparison to Europe, participation in and access to the center or centers in the United States did not revolve around class/status distinctions. Historical sociologist Adam Seligman sums up this view:

> As an immigrant society, of diverse religious faiths and with divergent cultural backgrounds[,] the American conception of membership and collective identity [was] based on its political ideals[,] not "primordial criteria." The result of this has been that [quoting L. Sampson, "American as Surrogate Socialism," in *Failure of a Dream*] "Americanism is to the American not a tradition, or a territory, not what France is to a Frenchman or England to an Englishman, but a doctrine—what socialism is to a socialist." Adherence to this doctrine and its codes of civil religion and to the political ideals articulated and instituted in the republic, set the parameters of American collective identity. Thus...becoming an American has meant becoming a believer in this civil religion.[8]

Like every "religion," at least since the invention of writing and printing, this American "civil religion" has its foundational texts, its scriptures—among which in the earliest period were the Declaration of Independence, the Constitution, and Washington's Farewell Address. These texts reflected roots in the English tradition of common law and natural rights as well as in dissenting Puritanism. These civic texts as canonical texts reflected and helped to produce a nationalism that in turn promoted what Americanist François Furstenberg in his book *In the Name of the Father: Washington's Legacy, Slavery, and the Making of a Nation* called "consent...and a sense of mutual obligation."[9] Furstenberg argued that the civic texts were made to help create in what has become the United States "a powerful mythology" of the Founding Fathers, centered chiefly around George Washington as the "Father of the Nation," the "national patriarch." These civic texts thereby "bound Americans into members of a single nation."[10]

In Protestant Christian America, the civic texts were made to parallel the phenomenon of the reading of the Bible, not just in the scope (or universality) of their readership, but also in the types of practices by which they were engaged.[11] "Citizens" were told to read and interpret these civic texts as "sacred practice." They were taught to " 'engrave' Washington's words on their hearts just as they had been taught to internalize passages from the bible...to take Washington into their hearts just as they took

FIGURE I *Allegory of America.* "Frontispiece" in Rev. John Brown, *The Self-interpreting Bible. Containing the Old and New Testaments with References and Illustrations.* New York: Printed for T. Allen, and sold at his book and stationary store, 1792. Image courtesy of Claremont School of Theology Library, Claremont, California.

Jesus into their hearts...to read the Constitution as they read the Ten Commandments."[12] One cleric, in eulogizing Washington as he referenced Washington's Farewell Address, is recorded as having exhorted mourners to take a rather amazing psycho-cultural and hermeneutical step: "[B]ind [the Address] in your Bible next to the Sermon on the Mount that the lessons of your two Saviors may be read together."[13]

Juxtapositions of, and identifications between, the nation, the Constitution, the Bible, and the texts of the founders were strong to the point of being at fever pitch in some places. The force of the phenomenon is made clear in the frontispiece to a Bible, the first to be printed in New York, in 1792 (see figure 1).[14] The center of the image is an allegorical representation of "America" as a woman in a headdress, her elbow resting on a plinth with the names of Revolutionary "fathers" listed, Washington first. In one hand, she holds a scroll of the US Constitution; her other hand reaches forward to accept the Bible from a kneeling woman. A third woman holds a pole atop which is the liberty cap. Washington's life had become, in effect, a sacred text, needing to be read in order for citizenship to be secured, for American-ness to be confirmed.[15] The skill and practice of reading these civic texts were made the requirement for and registration of civic engagement. Like the situation in ancient Athens or Alexandria or India or China or Calvin's early modern Geneva, citizens in the society that was becoming the United States were understood to be scripture readers who through their reading could continually affirm their consent to the fathers.

Such practices in the United States were also complexly intertwined with the problem of slavery. The reading of civic texts promoted a paternalist understanding of slavery supposedly grounded in "bonds of affection"; and slavery itself seemed to make more plausible the social-political myth of tacit consent. Insofar as the paternalist image of slavery—to some degree, for some—masked the brutal violence upon which it was established, it helped make easier the acceptance of the lesser forms of coercion involved in persuading "free" Americans to "consent" to their nation.[16] The notion that had obtained in the oratory and writings of Jefferson and Madison (to a lesser degree) that citizenship for "all" was a matter of consent of the living in ongoing dynamic relationship with the living was quite powerful.[17] But by making allegiance to the nation "in the name of the fathers," in connection with the use of civic texts, some forces had betrayed at least one vision of a nation grounded in the consent of the living. The exaltation of the Founding Fathers and the founding documents turned them into objects of uncritical veneration and genuflection. Furstenberg leaves us with a haunting question: "By persuading future generations to live by the will of dead fathers, and to do so *by their own choice*, had civic texts ultimately turned Americans—this people so proud of its individual achievements, so prepared to live free or die—into slaves?"[18]

To put the matter as plainly and as bluntly as does Furstenburg but with respect to the irony of building a box into which one forces oneself to fit, it needs to be said that it was, of course, white folks—those who first named themselves as such on the basis of their first contact with, including their eventual violent domination of, the Other, who was red and black and brown; and then those other Europeans who, having been previously dominated and not considered white, but as a result of later social changes over the decades and centuries, including a coarsening of racialist ideologies and the ratcheting up of racial violence, were later grafted into whiteness—it was these folks who were identified with and participated in this center-ing formation that involved reading civic texts and scriptures, civic texts as scriptures.[19] As the late critic and theorist in whiteness studies Ruth Frankenberg helped us to understand, these were the folk who were and remain to this day, as a result of a remarkable trick of strategic discourses, "unmarked," referred to in categories not needing to be hyphenated, those whose very existence, language use, style, looks, tastes, sentiments, and feelings are assumed to be standard or conventional.[20]

The new white formation that was to be called "America" was made so primarily on the basis of scripture-reading. And the "scriptures"—in consonance with the arguments made earlier and in conversation with W. C. Smith and other theorists of the phenomenology of scriptures[21]—were (and still are) understood to be quite elastic and tensive, including both "sacred" and "civic" texts. All such texts, notwithstanding their tendencies to include rhapsodic paeans regarding the "all," regarding radical inclusivity, were (and still are) understood, according to the terms of Euro-American canonical-ideological construction and activation, not to have included any but white peoples. The "scriptures" were white—they were presumed to be: written *by* white folk, written *about* white folk, written *for* white folk. But by making the culturalist foundation texts into white scriptures those who made themselves white ironically made themselves slaves—ideological-discursive slaves, slaves to white texted-ness and canonicity, to the Weberian "iron cage," of scripture-reading.[22] This is in my view the root and baseline of fundamentalisms—religious, social, legal, and so forth—in the United States (and beyond).

But for this trick regarding whiteness in connection with scriptures to work at all, the Other, the nonwhite person, was supposed to be made invisible and rendered silent. Just as in Robert Penn Warren's famous poem "Pondy Woods" in which the black male character Big Jim, overdetermined by the Buzzard (a figure of American Philological Association/Modern Language Association/Society of Biblical Literature–like authority) was kept silent by the remark: "Nigger, your breed ain't hermeneutical"! Or like the astounding almost ex-officio pronouncement "That's not scriptural!" made during the 2008 presidential campaign by conservative movement leader Tony Perkins on CNN in response to Rev. Jeremiah Wright's recorded jeremiads against the history of domination and exploitation in the United States. Or like South Carolina congressman Joe Wilson's unprecedented outburst ("You lie!") at the first black president during his 2009 special address to Congress, which represented, according to Emory political scientist Andra Gillespie, an effort to keep Obama from holding forth in authoritative mode and was a refusal to see him as occupant of office that is our symbol of the center.[23] Notwithstanding these acts of violence and exclusion, which have a rather long history, nonwhite peoples, who were from the beginning either written out of or never presumed to be an appropriate presence in the scriptures and their mythic histories, and who were considered beyond the possibility of registering legitimate and authoritative interpretation of scriptures—these peoples have not kept silent and have not remained invisible.

As Douglass's account makes clear, ex-centric peoples—Natives and Africans, and the other Others, different still, those who have of their own free will come to this place, from various places at various times, through various means—have not only not remained silent and invisible, they have not been un-knowing, have not been in-adept at reading and interpreting scriptures, have not gone without inventing and using their own scriptures. Their "unmeaning jargon" has always "been full of meaning." Not only have they created their own "texts," as writer Ishmael Reed helps us to see they must,[24] they have also "read," signified on, and thus decentered and destabilized—as W. E. B. Du Bois, Zora Neale Hurston, Henry Louis Gates, Jr., and Houston Baker and Toni Morrison and many other critics have helped us understand—the nationalist white scriptures and the white readings of white scriptures.[25]

Scripturalizing and scripture readings from the peripheries may seem at first to represent, as W. E. B. Du Bois first indicated in *Souls of Black Folk,* and as later theorized by Houston Baker in *Afro-American Poetics: Revisions of Harlem and the Black Aesthetic,* only "omissions and silences."[26] But with deeper excavation of what Baker calls the "frenzied, laconic, and fragmented discursive "lowgrounds and inaudible valleys," we can hear the songs of the sort sung by the slaves Douglass heard.[27] On the peripheries, the silence is really code, like Zora Neale Hurston's "hidden meanin'" and its strategic off-stage double-voicing.[28]

From the positions off-center things look different and require different sensibilities and practices, including sensibilities and apprehensions about centers and peripheries themselves. This may be what Krister Stendahl in his 1983 Society of Biblical Literature presidential address was getting at when he seemingly nervously acknowledged that the apparent scribal guild penchant (as he perceived it in the 1980s) for story and language play, away from history, may reflect a social happiness index:

> Could it be that preoccupation with history comes natural when one is part of a culture which feels happy and hopeful about the historical process? Hegel's pan-historic philosophy belongs, after all, to the ascendancy of

Western imperialism—it was even said that other parts of the world were lifted "into history" when they were conquered, colonized, or converted by the West. Now the Western world is not so sure or so optimistic about where history—that is, "our" history—is going. So the glamour, the glory, the Shekinah has moved away from history.[29]

Ex-centric situations, where the oppressed and subaltern are concentrated, reflect that truth that according to Walter Benjamin "the 'state of emergency' in which we live is not the exception but the rule."[30] Physician-trained turned transgressive anthropologist and social critic Michael Taussig helps us to understand that Benjamin's unsettling statement was intended to provoke us to come to "a radically different way" of knowing through the positionality of the outliers:

> [I]n a state of siege order is frozen, yet disorder boils beneath the surface. Like a giant spring slowly compressed and ready to burst at any moment, immense tension lies in strange repose...we are required to rethink our notions of order, of center, and base.[31]

In a fascinating essay in 1991 entitled "Deforming Mirror of Truth: Slavery and the Master Narrative of American History," the late Americanist Nathan Huggins argued that the times—the state of emergency defined by a history of brutalization and marginalization of blacks and other non-whites in the United States—call for a new "narrative" that would force us to face "the deforming mirror of truth,"[32] that is, how our narratives have been woven in relationship to but at the high expense of the enslaved. Toni Morrison has called for something similar in her book *Playing in the Dark: Whiteness and the Literary Imagination*.[33] She challenged writers and critics, actually, all of us, to "avert the critical gaze from the racial object to the racial subject; from the described and imagined to the describers and imaginers; from the serving to the served."[34] Critical studies, she argued,

> should be investigations of the ways in which a nonwhite, Africanist presence and personae have been constructed—invented—in the United States, and of the literary uses this fabricated presence has served....All of us, readers and writers are bereft when criticism remains too polite or too fearful to notice a disrupting darkness before its eyes.[35]

The averted critical gaze about which Morrison writes should mean more not less focus on the ex-centrics who have always addressed the "disrupting darkness" that they were.

In *Aircraft Stories: Decentering the Object in Technoscience,*[36] British scholar John Law addresses these same matters but as sociologist of technology. He argues the need for a different epistemology that would reflect the truth about the multi-dimensionality and fractional nature of reality. Using the pinboard as metaphor for the "object" that was the British aircraft called TSR2 and the approach to studying it, Law offered a generalizable argument for an approach to knowledge of objects that goes beyond the "singularities and multiplicities of modernism and postmodernism."[37] The mere juxtaposition of images and the making of pastiches raises for him the notion that the world is "not a singular place," that objects in the world—an object like an aircraft—are both multiple and singular. This in turn suggests the importance of the "ordering logics of the fractionally coherent object," the prospect that there are different and valid knowledges that can be neither entirely reconciled nor dismissed, that knowing may be a process that is "decentered, distributed, but also partially connected."[38]

Then John Law makes a claim that is astounding: "[I]t requires fractional subjects to know...fractional objects."[39] His "logic of the pinboard" is understood as epistemology and methodology, ways of knowing that escape the possibilities of a single narrative that performs "denial of the conditions of its possibility," that makes it possible to know about features of the world that deny themselves when everything is drawn together into a single story.[40] Law's logic of the pinboard salutes "noncoherence, the play of the fractional."[41]

But who are the "fractional objects"? Who or what might model such knowing for us? Law ends his book with a sigh, despairing of the world of which he is part to orient itself in the direction he thinks important. He seems oblivious to the knowledge-making experiences of others as possible historical refractions of the orientation for which he sighs.

In *Mimesis and Alterity: A Particular History of the Senses,*[42] Michael Taussig, ironically, one of the theorists from whom Law draws some of his arguments, suggests a bridge that would take us back to the haunting scene that Frederick Douglass paints for us as a way forward. Taussig challenges readers to consider the mimetic faculty, especially that as performed by the "Third and Other worlds" as a result their being forced into contact with the "First World." The mirroring that is mimetic excess—"mimetic self-awareness...turned on itself, on its colonial endowment..."[43]—ruptures and destabilizes all identities and all knowledges. In this situation "mastery," canonical knowledge, is no longer possible. In the ongoing fraught histories of contact dominance is "mirrored in the eyes and handiwork of its Others."[44] This is, of course, an "unsettled" and "unsettling" situation,

FIGURE 2 *A white man.* Mud sculpture that was part of a sacred Mbari house, made by Owerri Ibo of Biafra. Situated in Umuedi Ofkelem, Nigeria. Photograph by Herbert M. Cole, 1967.

"a Nervous System—because the interpreting self is itself grafted into the object of study. The self enters into the alter against which the self is defined and sustained."[45]

Taussig betrayed just what the "Nervous System" meant in his poignant reflection on an image (see figure 2) of an Ibo mbari shrine that he discovered and that was included in Julia Blackburn's book *The White Man: First Responses of Aboriginal Peoples to the White Man* (1979):

> He frightens me, this African white man. He unsettles. He makes me wonder without end. Was the world historical power of whiteness achieved, then, through its being sacred as well as profane power? It makes me wonder about the constitution of whiteness as global colonial work and also as a minutely psychic one involving powers invisible to my senses but all too obvious, as reflected...by this strange artifact. I know next to nothing of the "context" of ritual, belief, or of social practice in which an older anthropology...would enmesh this African white man, "explain" him (away), "Africanize" him (as opposed to "whitenize" him). All I have is the image and its brief caption, and I am my own gaping subject of analysis, for it is precisely this fractured plane of visibility and invisibility that constitutes the impact of the image on

an uncomprehending West now face to face with it-self, bursting the earth. For the white man, to read this face means facing himself as Others read him, and the "natives' point of view" can never substitute for the fact that now the native is the white man himself and that suddenly, woefully, it dawns that the natives' point of view is endless and myriad. The white man as viewer is here virtually forced to interrogate himself, to interrogate the Other in and partially constitutive of his many and conflicting selves.... Such face-to-faceness no doubt brings its quotient of self-congratulation. "They think we are gods." But being a god is okay as long as it isn't excessive. After all, who knows—in imaging us as gods, might they not take our power?[46]

Taussig here helps to explain the power of Douglass's account: the latter is an example of "mimetic excess"—Douglass the writer is as removed from the slave singers as he is removed from Great House Farm. He thinks about the singers and their mimetics and about the discourse of Great House Farm: he is our window, our way out, our way forward in knowing ex-centric peoples and in ex-centric knowing. And ex-centric knowing is nothing if not marked, that is, self-reflexive, fractional, decentered.

So ex-centric knowing must now mean reading the center reading itself scripturally and singing all the while doing so. In the context we all share, it means reading America reading itself scripturally, all the while (as Amiri Baraka suggests) "per-forming"[47] texts.

Insofar as Douglass thinks about the singing of the slaves and its meaning, insofar as he thinks about his thinking and others' thinking and about his positionality and other positionalities within the larger regime that was the Great House Farm, to this extent he presents himself as the self-reflexive, free-thinking agent. Such presentation comes out of complex ex-centricity.

But take caution here: not all ex-centrics even know that they can read in this way. Not all flip their reading back in mimetic excess (the lack of such flipping is mimetics of the fundamentalist sort). Not all know how to read themselves (and others) reading America. An aspect of the power of the project—and its orientation and questions—behind this book is that it forces re-discovery and engagement of critical readers the likes of Lance Jeffers, a not very well known but inspiring member of the New Black Arts movement. He knew how to "per-form" in that way to which Douglass points. Consider Jeffers's poem, how he reflected the ex-centric soul reading the center. Consider the alternation of voice—the ex-centric grandmother, on the one hand; then the center-ed voice representing America, on the other; tune in to the scriptures she (representing all ex-centrics) sings; note the scriptures America wields. Read Jeffers "reading" America as an American! As one who would in our time squarely face the Tea Party revelers shouting about taking *their* country back. Read his phenomenal *mis*reading of American scriptures and of scriptures reading America, in his poem "My Blackness is the Beauty of this Land":[48]

My blackness is the beauty of this Land,
My blackness,
Tender and strong, wounded and wise,
My blackness:
I, drawling black grandmother, smile muscular and sweet,
Unstraightened white hair soon to grow in earth,
Work-thickened hand thoughtful and gentle on grandson's head,
My heart is bloody-razored by a million memories' thrall:
Remembering the crook-necked cracker who spat
On my naked body,
Remembering the splintering of my son's spirit
Because he remembered to be proud
Remembering the tragic eyes in my daughter's
Dark face when she learned her color's meaning,
   And my own dark rage a rusty knife with teeth to gnaw
My bowels,
   My agony ripped loose by anguished shouts in Sunday's
Humble church,
   My agony rainbowed to ecstasy when my feet oversoared
Montgomery's slime,
   Ah, this hurt, this hate, this ecstasy before I die,
   And all my love a strong cathedral!
   My blackness is the beauty of this land!
   Lay against this my whiteness, this land!
   Lay me, young Brutus stamping hard on the cat's tail,
   Gutting the Indian, gouging the nigger,
   Booting Little rock's Minnejean Brown in the buttocks and boast,
My sharp white teeth derision-bared as I the conqueror crush!
   Skyscraper-I, white hands burying God's human clouds beneath
The dust!
   Skyscraper-I, slim blond young Empire
Thrusting up my loveless bayonet to rape the sky,
   Then shrink all my long body with filth and in the gutter lie
   As lie I will to perfume this armpit garbage,

While I here standing black beside
Wrench tears from which the lies would suck the salt
To make me more American than America...
But yet my love and yet my hate shall civilize this land,
This land's salvation.

Notes

1. See his *A Map of Misreading* and *Anxiety of Influence*.
2. Found in Andrews, *Oxford Frederick Douglass Reader*.
3. Douglass, *Narrative of the Life*, ibid., 37–38.
4. Arnheim, *Power of the Center*, 13.
5. Ibid., 109.
6. Eliade, *Images and Symbols*, 39.
7. Eisenstadt, Roniger, and Seligman, *Centre-Formation*, 19.
8. Seligman, "American System of Stratification," in Eisenstadt et al., *Centre Formation,* 171–72.
9. Furstenberg, *In the Name of the Father*, 10–11, 14, 16–17, 19–20, 220. That such a phenomenon is not unique to the United States, and should be understood in terms of a comparative history of religions and culture is reflected in several works, including the work of Buddhism scholar Alan Cole. See his *Text as Father*.
10. Furstenberg, *In the Name of the Father*, 21.
11. Ibid., 51.
12. Ibid., 52.
13. Ibid.
14. See *The Self-Interpreting Bible: Containing the Sacred Text of the Old and New Testaments*, by Scottish cleric-theologian Rev. John Brown (New York: Hodge and Campbell, [1778] 1792), available in a scanned version on ElectricScotland, http://www.electricscotland.com/bible/brown/index.htm. See Furstenburg, *In the Name of the Father,* 60.
15. Furstenburg, *In the Name of the Father,* 61.
16. Ibid., 103.
17. Ibid., 220.
18. Ibid., 230–31.
19. For general and broad historical perspective see Marty, *Religion and Republic* and *Righteous Empire*; and Ahlstrom, *Religious History of the American People*.
20. Frankenberg, "Miracle of an Unmarked Whiteness," 72f.
21. See W. C. Smith, *What Is Scripture?*; Levering, *Rethinking Scripture*; and Wimbush, *Theorizing Scriptures*.
22. See Max Weber's *Protestant Ethic and the Spirit of Capitalism*, and, of course, the different arguments and controversies among his many interpreters, including the issue about how best to translate "*stahlhartes Gehaeuse.*"
23. For Warren, see "Pondy Woods," in his *New and Selected Poems: 1923-1985* (New York: Random House, 1985), 319–21. See Tony Perkins, religious conservative and head of Family Research Council, on CNN's *Anderson Cooper 360 Degrees*, March 14, 2008, re: Rev. Jeremiah Wright's prophetic words against the United States: "But, clearly, his message was unscriptural. I mean, as Christians, we're instructed in the New Testament

to pray for the well-being of our government, so that we might live a peaceful and quiet life. It's—it's hard to imagine how praying for the damnation of one's own country could lead to tranquility, and clearly an un-American message." Given his worldview and assumptions, Perkins's almost apodictic assertion that Wright was "unscriptural" was supposed to discredit his words and essentially end the debate, end Wright's legitimacy as public religious figure. And, re: challenges to Obama's leadership and the attempt to silence him, see Emory political science professor Andra Gillespie at http://shared.web.emory.edu/emory/news/releases/2009/09/obama-vulnerable-leadership-gillespie.html.

24. See Reed's fascinating work *Mumbo Jumbo*.

25. These writers do not address these matters in direct terms regarding scriptures in the traditional or narrow terms, but their theorizing and argumentation do address scriptures in broad and expansive terms argued for in this essay. The work of making connections between such critics and scriptures and setting forth some implications of their projects for the critical study of scriptures remains to be done.

26. Du Bois, *Souls*, and Baker, *Afro-American Poetics*.

27. See his essay "Lowground and Inaudible Valleys: Reflections on Afro-American Spirit Work," in Baker, *Afro-American Poetics,* chap. 3, especially 106, 109.

28. Hurston, *Mules and Men*. See also Gundaker, *Signs of Diaspora*; and Scott, *Domination*, for social scientific development of this theme.

29. Stendahl, "Bible as a Classic and the Bible as Holy Scripture," 3.

30. Statement is from Benjamin's "Theses on the Philosophy of History," in *Illuminations*, ed. Hannah Arendt, trans. Harry Zahn (New York: Schocken, 1969), 253–64. See Taussig's engagement of it in *Nervous System*, 10.

31. Taussig, *Nervous System*, 10.

32. Huggins, "Deforming Mirror of Truth, 44.

33. Morrison, *Playing in the Dark*, 3–28.

34. Ibid., 90.

35. Ibid., 90–91.

36. Law, *Aircraft Stories*.

37. Ibid., 203.

38. Ibid., 193–94.

39. Ibid., 197.

40. Ibid., 197–98.

41. Ibid., 203.

42. Taussig, *Mimesis and Alterity*.

43. Ibid., 252.

44. Ibid., xv, 236.

45. Ibid., 237.

46. Ibid., 238, 240.

47. Re: Baraka, see Benston, *Enactments of African-American Modernism*, 13.

48. Jeffers, *My Blackness*.

CHAPTER 1 | Native Evangelicals and Scriptural
Ethnologies

ANDREA SMITH

NATIVE SPIRITUALITIES ARE OFTEN presented in an orthogonal relationship with Christianity; that is, to be truly "Native" is to be traditional.
Native peoples who are Christian are then deemed less "authentic," more
"assimilated," and often traitors to the well-being of Native communities
by Natives and non-Natives alike. Native evangelicals, then, are particularly problematic within this schema. And yet, there are flourishing communities of Native evangelicals who not only claim a relationship with
rather than a disavowal of traditional spirituality, but also are organizing in
defense of Native sovereignty and determination.

Most studies of Native peoples and religion have focused on either
traditional spiritualities or more mainline forms of Christianity. Very few
have focused on Native peoples and evangelicalism. This chapter will
fill this gap by focusing on Native evangelicalism specifically. In doing
so, it will shed light on the intellectual and cultural production of Native
evangelicals as well as trouble simplistic notions of Native spirituality and
Native identity.

How does the community name and understand itself today?
What are its origins in the United States? How has its
self-naming/-understanding changed over time?

More than 400 independent indigenous nations were prospering in what is
now known as the United States when Europeans first arrived. Estimates

of the indigenous population prior to colonization range from 6 million to 40 million. More than 90 percent of the indigenous population was exterminated through the process of colonization. Today there are more than 300 Native reservations in the United States, covering 52.4 million acres of land. Most Native peoples live west of the Mississippi River, but 25 percent live in the Northeast, and North Carolina has the fifth largest Native population of any state. There are more than 200 Native villages in Alaska. Because of the federal policies of relocation in the 1950s that encouraged Native peoples to leave their land bases, over half of Native peoples currently live off-reservation.

To understand the relationship between Native peoples' theologies and their political commitments, it is necessary first to understand their distinct legal status in the United States. Native peoples understand themselves as belonging to indigenous nations that are distinct from the US government. As such, their relationship to the larger society is often articulated through the lens of colonization rather than racialization (although obviously these two logics intersect).

When the United States first emerged as an entity, it was not in a position to militarily conquer Native nations. In addition, the legitimacy of the US government was also in question at the time. One way to establish the legitimacy of a nation is to have itself recognized by other nations through treaties. Thus, the United States legitimized itself as an entity through the establishment of treaties with Indian nations. This process then creates a paradox for the United States. Only through treaties can the United States argue that there has ever been any legal transfer of land from Indian nations to itself. On the other hand, treaties imply relationships between two sovereign nations, and the United States has not wanted to recognize the complete sovereignty of Native nations. The US Constitution states that "all Treaties made, or which shall be made, under the Authority of the United States, shall be the supreme Law of the Land" (article VI, clause 2). Nevertheless, of the 350-plus treaties that the United States has signed with Native nations, none have been fully honored.

As a result of the particular legal status of Native peoples, virtually every aspect of Native life today falls under the supervision of some federal agency. Congress has created a bureaucracy so vast that in 1977, there was one government official for every nineteen Native people. Most of the government's Indian programs are administered by the Bureau of Indian Affairs (BIA). The BIA has about 13,500 employees nationwide and administers most of the federal Indian programs, with the exception of health and housing. The 1977 Senate Commission on Indian affairs reported that the federal agencies administering the government's Indian programs are inefficient, unnecessarily complex, patronizing, insensitive, and antagonistic to tribal self-government.

Today, Native peoples are at the bottom on all socioeconomic indicators. Because Native peoples are generally not accurately accounted for in most statistics, it is difficult to obtain accurate information on them. However, it is estimated that Native peoples living on reservations have a life expectancy of forty-seven years and a tuberculosis rate 425 percent greater, an alcoholism rate 579 percent greater, and a suicide rate 70 percent greater than the national average. One in three American Indians has diabetes. The unemployment rate on many reservations is over 90 percent and the high school dropout rate is 80 percent. This political and social context shapes how Native evangelicals theologize the relationship between the status of Native people and the Bible.

What are the special themes and issues and problems that have historically been associated with this community and communicated through its scripturalizing?

Native peoples have been subjected to long-standing colonial ethnographic interest in their spiritual traditions. Consequently, many Native communities are becoming increasingly vocal in speaking out against academic studies of their traditions. One reason for this trend is that Native spiritualities are land based—they are generally tied to the land base from which they originate (Deloria Jr. 1992). For this reason, Native religions are generally not proselytizing. They are generally seen by Native peoples as relevant only to the particular land base from which they originate; they are not necessarily applicable to peoples coming from different land bases. In addition, as many scholars have noted, Native religions are practice centered rather than belief centered. That is, Christianity, for instance, is generally defined by belief in a certain set of doctrinal principles about Jesus, the Bible, and so on. Evangelical Christianity, for instance, holds that one is "saved" when one professes belief in Jesus Christ as one's Lord and Savior. Native traditions, by contrast, are practice centered. That is, what is of primary importance is not so much the ability to articulate belief in a certain set of doctrines but to take part in the spiritual practice of one's community. Thus, it may be more important that a ceremony be done correctly than it is for everyone in that ceremony to know exactly *why* everything must be done in a certain way. As Vine Deloria Jr. notes, from a Native context, religion is "a way of life" rather than "a matter of the proper exposition of doctrines" (Deloria Jr. 1999). Even if Christians do not have access to a church, they continue to be Christians as long as they believe in Jesus. Native spiritualities, by contrast, may die if the people do not practice the ceremonies, even if the people continue to believe in their power. In addition, the efficacy of many practices is dependent on their remaining secret. Knowledge about these practices is not necessarily even available to all members of the community. But because these traditions are communal rather than individual based, it is understood that those who do have the relevant spiritual knowledge are praying for the entire community. Consequently, when knowledge about traditions is transmitted to outsiders who in turn try to practice it own their own, they may practice them incorrectly in a manner that can have spiritually negative consequences for the participants.

In their never-ending quest to "know" the Other, hordes of social scientists have plagued Native communities in an effort to procure their "tribal secrets" (Warrior 1994). To fully understand, to "know" Native peoples, is the manner in which the dominant society gains a sense of mastery and control over them. As a result, researchers have not often asked the questions, do Native people want others to know about them? Or, do Native communities find this research helpful?

As Linda Tuhiwai Smith notes, the heart of the issue is that the research done on indigenous peoples has historically never benefited indigenous peoples themselves; rather, Native communities are seen as "laboratories" in which research is conducted that will benefit the dominant society.

> The belief, for example, that research will "benefit mankind" conveys a strong sense of social responsibility. The problem with that particular term, as outlined in previous chapters, is that indigenous peoples are deeply cynical about the capacity, motives or methodologies of Western research to deliver any benefits to indigenous peoples whom science has long regarded, indeed has classified, as being "not human." (Smith 1999, 118)

In addition, the academic study of Native religious traditions has fueled a continued assault on indigenous knowledge by multinational corporations. Because current intellectual property rights law only respects individual ownership and not community ownership of intellectual or cultural property, nonindigenous entrepreneurs have been able to go into indigenous communities, gather knowledge about indigenous plants, medicines, music, or other cultural knowledge, take it because it is understood as "public" property, and then apply for individual patents for it and hence seize control over this knowledge in order to profit from it. As Laurie Whitt describes in the case of indigenous music:

> While others are free to copy the original indigenous song with impunity, were someone to attempt to copy the "original" copy (now transformed into the legally protected individual property of a composer who has "borrowed" it from the indigenous "public domain"), he or she would be subject to prosecution for copyright infringement. This includes any members of the indigenous community of the song's origin who cannot meet the requirement of "fair use." (Whitt 1998)

Entrepreneurs (and sometimes academics themselves) utilize academic studies to procure knowledge about Native communities that they can capitalize on. Native communities have no legal defense against these forms of cultural and intellectual theft.

Indigenous peoples have increasingly gained access to Western academic institutions and have increasing ability to talk back to those who attempt to study them. Tired of these colonial practices, tribal communities increasingly place restrictions on what research they will allow. They also regularly engage in other practices of resistance, such as deliberately giving anthropologists and other academics false information about their traditions in order to protect their communities. In light of the colonial context in which Native communities live, it makes sense to leave the study of Native traditional spiritualities to Native communities, which have the ability to do their own research projects as they see fit. Thus, this chapter does not focus on traditional spiritual practices, although information about them can be gleaned from the words of the interviewees.

Instead, this chapter focuses on Native evangelicalism, with some reference to Native Christians from the more mainline denominations. Because Native evangelicalisms are virtually invisible within the current scholarship, even on Native communities and Christianity, this chapter aims to further complicate our analyses of how Native peoples engage various religious and spiritual traditions.

Since evangelicals as a whole, then, are socially and politically essentialized with respect to their relationship to the Bible, Native evangelicals are often caught between two contradictory essentializing discourses. On one hand, Native peoples are often stereotyped as all-resistant traditional warriors who reject the trappings of Christian civilization. Therefore, Native peoples who are not only Christian but also evangelical Christian must be dupes for white supremacy, complicit in their own oppression.

In this intellectual ethnography, however, the tremendous political, intellectual, and theological diversity among Native peoples in general, and Native evangelicals in particular, becomes clear.

My methodological approach emerges from the current trend in Native studies of "decolonizing methodology" (Smith 1999). In particular, I employ what I term an "intellectual ethnography" to analyze the intellectual production of Native peoples Christian evangelicalism (Smith 2008).

Native studies forces us to problematize the role of the academic and of academic research in general. Rather than render Native people as objects of my study, I wish to position them as subjects of intellectual discourse about the relationships among spirituality, the Bible, and social/political engagement. Robert Warrior describes this project as "intellectual sovereignty." He notes that Native communities are seldom seen by non-Native scholars as sites of intellectual discourse, and his work uncovers long-standing Native intellectual traditions (Warrior 1994). I seek to build on the work of Warrior, broadening the application of intellectual sovereignty by identifying nonacademic activists as intellectuals. This work might, then, be described as an "intellectual ethnography." Rather than study Native people so that we can know more about them, I wish to illustrate what Native theorists have to tell us about the world we live in.

I believe an intellectual ethnography, besides positioning Native peoples as theologians and intellectuals in their own right, also helps to challenge the manner in which Native peoples are homogenized in mainstream ethnographic practice. As Anna Tsing notes, Native peoples are generally depicted "in a timeless, archaic condition outside modern history" (Tsing 1993). Similarly, I feel it is important to resist the homogenizing, essentializing tendency to stereotype all Native peoples' theories as represented by the few who are able to publish books and, instead, to attempt to depict them with as much complexity as possible. Thus, my approach is to reflect the diversity, complexities, and tensions within Native evangelical thought.

This impulse actually coincides with the concerns among Native evangelicals themselves, who are also calling for decolonized methodologies and pedagogies. For instance, at the 2004 North American Institute for Indigenous Theological Studies (NAIITS) conference, Tite Tiénou was a featured speaker who contended that while the church is becoming less Western, the theological and intellectual production of the church is still centered in the West.

> I contend that Christian theology and scholarship will remain "provincial" as long as some major challenges continue unaddressed [such as] the perception of indigenous Christian scholars as "purveyors of exotic raw intellectual

material"...Indigenous theologians are...relegated to the museums of theological curiosity just like their cultures. We are then left with this: the West claiming to produce universal theology and the rest writing "to articulate fundamental theology that will make [them] equal partners in the theological circles that determine what is theologically normative." (Tiénou 2005, 16–17)

This chapter, then, is not primarily concerned with making broad claims about Native evangelicals. Rather, I hope to present some of the intellectual and theological trends that are being produced in Native Bible-believing communities. Consequently, the chapter relies primarily on the words of the interviewees themselves. In this respect, it can be seen as creating a Native evangelical archive of social, religious, and political thought. By focusing less on my summary and critique of their perspectives and providing more space for evangelicals to speak for themselves, I aim to work against the processes of ethnographic entrapment in which Native studies becomes trapped in ethnographic multiculturalism, what da Silva describes as a "neoliberal multicultural" representation that "includes never-before-heard languages that speak of never-before-heard things that actualize a never-before-known consciousness" (da Silva 2007, 169). I do not claim that these trends are representative, but I hope that a glimpse at the ideas Native evangelicals have about their relationship to the Bible will destabilize mainstream essentialist notions about both evangelical and Native communities. In this way, the not easily encapsulated presentation of these perspectives mirrors the complexity of Native communities themselves.

My primary sources come from archival material, participant observation, and interviews. My analysis of the Christian Right relies upon an extensive survey of conservative Christian periodical literature listed in the Christian Periodical Index on relevant subject headings from the years 1991 to 2008, when Native evangelicals became more prominent in mainstream evangelicalism as a result of the rise of the race reconciliation movement. In addition, I surveyed all the articles published in *Christianity Today, Charisma,* and *World* from 1991 to 2008, to cover articles that might address these issues but might be indexed under other subjects. *Christianity Today* provides the widest coverage of issues covered in conservative evangelicalism generally, although it is rooted within neo-evangelism. *Charisma* provides coverage of issues rooted in Pentecostal/Charismatic Christianity. *World* provides coverage from an explicitly right-wing political perspective. My work is informed as well by the literature produced by a variety of evangelical Native organizations that are gaining greater prominence within white evangelical circles, such as Wiconi International, CHIEF, Indian Life, and My Daily Frybread.

In addition, my research team conducted twenty-six interviews with Native evangelicals at different sites: Wiconi International's Family Gathering of 2007; NAIITS 2007 conference; Envision 2008 conference; in the Oklahoma City area; and in the Washington state area. The first two sites provided an opportunity to talk with Native evangelicals from diverse geographic and tribal backgrounds. However, a limitation of these sites is that they generally attract Native evangelicals who support contextual ministries (that is, Christian ministries that also explicitly engage to some degree Native cultural traditions). Consequently, I supplemented these two sites with interviews from Native people involved in local churches in Oklahoma and Washington who may not necessarily support contextual ministries in order to diversify the representation of various theological positions Native evangelicals might hold. Appendix 1 at the end of the book indicates the sites of each interview. The goal of the interviews is not to tell the interviewees' "life stories." My hope is to present the interviews, not as narratives, but as primary texts for the development of Native evangelical theory. Because I am not focusing on the interviewees as ethnographic objects but as theorists in their own right, I do not focus on biographical information (just as I would cite Foucault or Derrida without telling their biographies). Rather, in the appendix I present what each interviewee wanted readers to know about her or him in order to contextualize her or his analysis.

Because Native peoples often see themselves as belonging to sovereign nations irrespective of the settler state that colonizes them, they engage in frequent exchanges with other indigenous nations across nation-state boundaries. Consequently, many of the peoples featured in this chapter live in Canada. Because the circuits of Native evangelical thought do not particularly respect US and Canadian boundaries, it did not make sense to exclude their analyses from this chapter.

What are the scripturalizing practices/rituals in evidence in this community? What are their origins? Influences? What are the typical settings, situations, dynamics of these practices? Who are the principal actors, performers, authority figures in relationship to these practices?

Native peoples scripturalizing practices are influenced by their subjection to a long history of Christian colonization. When Europeans came to conquer these lands, they were accompanied by missionaries who provided the theological rationale for conquest. Albert Cave, H. C. Porter, and others have demonstrated that Christian colonizers often envisioned Native peoples as Canaanites, worthy of mass destruction (Cave 1988; Kadir 1992; Sanders 1978). As an example, George Henry Lokei wrote in 1794:

> The human behavior of the governor at Pittsburgh greatly incensed those people, who according to the account given in the former Part of this history, represented the Indians as Canaanites, who without mercy ought to be destroyed from the face of the earth, and considered America as the land of promise given to the Christians. (Wrone and Nelson 1982, 68)

The policy of Christianization that had the most devastating impact on Native communities was the introduction of Native boarding schools.[1] During the nineteenth century and into the twentieth century, American Indian children were forcibly abducted from their homes to attend Christian and US government–run boarding schools as a matter of state policy. This system had its beginnings in the 1600s when John Eliot erected "praying towns" for American Indians in which he separated them out from their communities to receive Christian "civilizing" instruction. However, colonists soon concluded that such practices should be targeted toward children because they believed adults were too set in their ways to become Christianized. Jesuit priests began developing schools for Indian children along the St. Lawrence River in the 1600s.

However, the boarding school system became more formalized under Grant's peace policy of 1869–1870. The goal of this policy was to turn over the administration of Indian reservations to Christian denominations. As part of this policy, Congress set aside funds to erect school facilities to be run by churches and missionary societies. These facilities were a combination of day and boarding schools erected on Indian reservations.

Then, in 1879, the first off-reservation boarding school, Carlisle, was founded by Richard Pratt. He argued that as long as boarding schools were primarily situated on reservations, (1) it was too easy for children to run away from school, and (2) the efforts to assimilate Indian children into boarding schools would be reversed when children went back home to their families during the summer. He proposed a policy where children would be taken far from their homes at an early age and not returned to their homes until they were young adults. By 1909, there were twenty-five off-reservation boarding schools, 157 on-reservation boarding schools, and 307 day schools in operation. The stated rationale of the policy was to "kill the Indian and save the man." Over 100,000 Native children were forced into attending these schools.

Attendance at the boarding schools was mandatory, and children were forcibly taken from their homes for the majority of the year. They were forced to worship as Christians and speak English (Native traditions and languages were prohibited). Sexual, physical, and emotional violence was rampant. Even when teachers were charged with abuse, boarding schools refused to investigate. In the case of just one teacher, John Boone at the Hopi school, FBI investigations in 1987 found that he had sexually abused over 142 boys, but that the principal of that school had not investigated any allegations of abuse. Despite the epidemic of sexual abuse in boarding schools, the BIA did not issue a policy on reporting sexual abuse until 1987, and did not issue a policy to strengthen the background checks of potential teachers until 1989. These policies were not implemented. While not all Native peoples see their boarding school experiences as negative, it is generally the case that much if not most of the current dysfunctionality in Native communities can be traced to the boarding school era. As will become clear later in the chapter, the boarding school system has profoundly impacted the relationship between Native peoples and Christianity.

At the same time, as Homer Noley notes, Native peoples were never simply objects of Christian mission, but often redeployed missionary activities for their own purposes (Noley 2000). A case study can be found in the example of the Cherokee peoples. The Moravians, who were the first missionaries given permission by the Cherokee council to establish a permanent mission in 1801, were allowed to do so *only on the express condition* that they open a school to educate Cherokee children (Malone 1956, 93). As treaty making intensified during the late eighteenth century, Cherokee leaders felt the need to better their negotiating power by learning the language in which the treaties were written, English. Since it was common for white translators to alter the meaning of treaty language unbeknownst to Cherokees, the council decided in 1800 to support schools within the nation's boundaries that would teach its citizens the English language. The stress on the English language is important because the first missionaries, the Moravians, conducted their affairs in German for the most part. Recognizing this, the Cherokee council advised the Moravians that since treaties were not written in German, they were not to teach Cherokees German, but English (McLoughlin 1995, 48). Thus, it would appear that the Cherokee council allowed missionaries into its territory only insofar as their work furthered the aims and interests of the Cherokee Nation. This expression of Cherokee sovereignty is an example of Native self-determination that frequently passes unnoticed by scholars.

Because of this long history of Christian missionization, there have been Native Christians who hold the Bible as authoritative for hundreds of years. However, within mainstream evangelical discourse, Native peoples have been generally relegated to the status of object of the evangelical mission (Smith 2008). However, a shift began in the early 1990s with the development of the race reconciliation movement that sought to establish racial harmony and unity within evangelical churches. While this movement initially targeted African American communities, the Promise Keepers, a prominent evangelical men's ministry, began an effort to reach Native peoples in particular. Promise Keepers rallies have consistently featured Native speakers, and a contingent of Native men opened Promise Keeper's 1997 national gathering, the Stand in the Gap rally, with a blessing. According to Jon Lansa, the former liaison between Native communities and the Promise Keepers, over 18,000 Native men were formally associated with Promise Keepers as of 2000. The work of Promise Keepers in turn sparked the growing visibility of Native peoples and organizations, particularly—but not exclusively—within the charismatic movements in which Promise Keepers is rooted. As is discussed later, these groups coalesced around contextual ministries, which strive to preach the Gospel message within the context of Native traditions and cultures. Examples include Red Sea Ministries, Wiconi International (Richard Twiss), Warriors for Christ (Art Begay), Wesleyan Native American Ministries, Inuit Ministries International (Dr. Suuqiina), Eagle's Wings Ministry, the World Christian Gathering of Indigenous Peoples, *Native Wind*, Two Rivers Native American Training Center, and many others. It is important, however, not to overestimate the influence of Promise Keepers. Many of these groups that had previous affiliations with Promise Keepers no longer do, and some never did affiliate with Promise Keepers. But the point is that its popularity as a movement rooted in new charismatic Christianity provided a space for increased visibility for many Native groups interested in indigenous contextual ministry.

Of course, there are many Native conservative Christians within the Southern Baptist and other noncharismatic evangelical/fundamentalist denominations. However, they figure much less prominently in white-dominated fundamentalist or neo-evangelical venues, and they are often much less supportive of contextual ministries. Native peoples have also broken into the world of televangelism. God's Learning Channel features a Native-oriented show hosted by Jay Swallow and Negiel Bigpond from the Two Rivers Native American Training Center. Together, they have begun a project to put a Direct-to-Home satellite broadcast system in every Native American community center on every reservation in the United States and Canada. Within the more charismatic venues especially, Native peoples have recently begun to figure much more prominently as spokespersons rather than simply as objects of mission. However, as James Treat's *Around the Sacred Fire* demonstrates, this movement has precursors, such as the organizing of Native Christians to work with tribal tradition- als to stimulate cultural revival and unity among Native nations through the Indian Ecumenical Conference of the 1970s (Treat 2003). Tom Claus, for instance, began preaching in the 1940s and collaborating with Billy Graham in the 1960s. He wrote books in the 1970s, including *On Eagles' Wings* (Claus 1976), and founded CHIEF in 1975. Yet the new charismatic movement today has given him greater prominence that ever before.

An intellectual arm of the indigenous contextual movement devel- oped with the founding of the North American Institute for Indigenous Theological Studies (NAIITS) to provide master and doctoral graduate degrees for Native leaders in the area of contextualized evangelical mis- sions. In addition, NAIITS creates forums for dialogue and engagement with other emerging indigenous theological streams including the vari- ety which are emerging in Native North America. NAIITS has developed partnerships with Asbury Theological Seminary in Wilmore, Kentucky, as well as several denominational and nondenominational organizations, col- leges, and seminaries.

Before examining the theoretical production of Native peoples in con- servative evangelicalism, including the indigenous contextual ministry movement, it is important to stress the diversity of thought within this movement. In fact, many of these ministries are in conflict with each other. While these evangelical leaders often espouse common positions, one can- not assume that they all hold the same position. Thus, in this intellec- tual ethnography, I am presenting many of the ideas that circulate broadly within this movement without attempting to assess the work of any par- ticular individual or ministry.

Within this movement, Native evangelicals theorize their relationship to the Bible with respect to many critical issues. In this chapter, I focus on some of the key debates and concerns that center much of Native evangeli- cal thought.

Why do some in this community persist in relating
to scriptures? What work do they make scriptures do for them?

Donald Miller sheds some light on why Native peoples are prominent
within the new charismatic denominations in particular. He notes that a
defining feature of these movements is the adaption of Christianity to the
surrounding culture. He quotes prominent charismatic leader Greg Laurie,
who explains the strategy: "If they [nonbelievers] are going to reject the
message I preach, let them reject it, but let them reject the message and not
all the peripheral things that are secondary" (Miller 1997, 66). Thus, music
at church services tends to feature popular rock music rather than old-time
hymns. Congregants and even pastors wear casual clothing rather than
their "Sunday best." These movements attempt to distinguish between
what they see as the central message of Christianity and the outward forms
Christianity might take.

   This strategy has provoked much criticism from other evangelical/fun-
damentalist denominations, which charge that New Charismatics have
sold out the gospel message to secular culture. Many Native evangelicals,
however, see an opportunity for intervention in these new charismatic
movements. If it is legitimate to incorporate the secular "white" culture
into worship, then it must also be acceptable to incorporate Native culture as well. Leaders attempt such incorporation in a variety of ways—by
holding Christian powwows, adapting ceremonial songs with Christian
words, using the drum in services, wearing regalia during services, and
so on (Dixon 2006; Francis 1997; Grady 2004; Gruszka 1997; Huckins
2000; Steinken 1998; Stewart 2000; Suuqiina 2000; Twiss 2000a; Twiss
2000b; Woodley 2000). Their argument is that these Native "forms" do
not alter the basic "message" of Christianity (Twiss 1996). This movement in turn is critiqued not only by some mainstream evangelicals but
by Native evangelicals as well. Some Native traditionals and evangelicals argue that traditionalism and Christianity should not be intermixed.
And of those who think they should not be mixed, some reject one form
of spiritual expression over the other, while others may engage both but
argue that they should be engaged separately. Those who support traditionalism over Christianity or who engage in both independently are not
as prevalent in more evangelical circles (or at least not openly so), and
hence this chapter does not primarily focus their theorization. An exception was the analysis proffered by Marcus Briggs-Cloud, who identifies
some seemingly irreconcilable differences between Native traditions

and Christianity but argues for the prioritization of Native tradition over Christianity.

> An elder said to me, you are born a Muskogee first by blood....He said, you were born an Indian first, Christianity is something that you acquired, and I guess I try to reflect on that a lot because there are so few of us Indians left and quite a few Christians, and so my Native side needs a little more help perpetuating the culture and ceremonial life. (Interview, 2007)

While, as is discussed later, many evangelicals see the Creator in Native traditions as the same God worshiped in Christianity, Briggs-Cloud points to some differences in their conceptualization, even as he affirms a fundamental unity between the two.

> When Christians in my tribe start their prayers, they start "Our Father, up in Heaven." And so my dad says, "Why do they say 'Our Father'? How can you call this sacred being the same word that you call your earthly father. This is so bizarre."
>
> And I even remember reading when missionaries first came to the Choctaw people. It was so weird to them that the Creator would send their son. How could anyone give up their son for people who don't even care? It's not a direct purpose. People aren't going to grasp it all over this world. I'm kind of sorting through, what is distinctly indigenous, what is distinctly Muskogee, and what else has been influenced by European aspects of life. It's a very sticky situation.
>
> There's so many differences. My grandma always told me that Christianity and Traditionalism is the same thing, one Creator, and I believe that on the fundamental level if we break it down to simplicity. It is the same, it's both spiritual knowledge, both spiritual paths. (Interview, 2007)

Margaret McKane Mauldin mentions how her father practiced both Christianity and traditional spirituality, but did not necessarily bring the two together:

> He was a church and grounds person simultaneously, as a young man he was very active with grounds activities, but he also went to several churches, he was very acquainted with old time preachers and contemporary people, and so it's hard for me to say he was only a grounds person or a church person....My father was a medicine man, and today he is looked at the way

doctors in the white world are regarded because he was for healing. There are people in the church who looked at it as [if] it had witchcraft involved in this medicine, but he did not. (Interview, 2007)

But the more prevalent strand within Native evangelical discourse seems to revolve around the debate of whether evangelicals should practice Christianity in conjunction with or separate from Native traditional practices. Many evangelicals do not support engaging Native traditional practices at all. Exemplifying those who think traditionalism must be rejected for Christianity, Art Begay of Warriors for Christ says that his use of Native dance in worship contributed to "one pastor's wife ask[ing] if she could cast an Indian spirit out of him" (Grady 2000, 22). *Faith Today* ran an article that proclaimed: "Accommodation to the native belief system is not the answer. It will not bring Native people to a total commitment to Jesus Christ. When people are fully liberated from the old ways, they don't want to go back" (Barnes 1989, 59). *Charisma* reports that at one Native Christian conference in Branson, Missouri, the brochure announced "no drums or feathers" (Grady 2000, 22). *World* magazine features a Yanamomo Christian declaring: "The other foreigners tell us to reject the missionaries and go back to our old ways....But they do not have Christ in their hearts. Our old ways were evil. We will never go back" (Bomer 1996, 21).

Dicey Barnett and Shaunday Little explain that traditionalism is completely separate from Christianity.

Dicey Barnett:

I believe traditional ways is another denomination, because they have their ways of believing, and I do believe that we have one God, and traditional people have their ways of believing. (Interview, 2007)

Shaunday Little (in response to question, do you see any relationship between Christianity and the traditional cultural practices of your tribe?):

No, I see no relationship, I feel it's two different religions and it cannot be mixed...I think it's part of being raised that way, and once God has come into your life he sticks with you regardless, and just, I have been to stomp dance before and stuff, and from when I went I didn't see any relationship between the two, so that's the last time I ever went. (Interview, 2007)

Lucy Ann Williams Harjo, while expressing similar sentiments regarding the separations between Christianity and traditional practices, also suggests that there may be some room for rapprochement.

So I have not grown up in that at all, that was almost considered taboo, powwows and carnivals were considered taboo, you just didn't go to those, so I never grew up in the atmosphere of dancing or powwows or a girls blessing, because it encompasses a visit with the medicine man and that was not what I was brought up in. But my in-laws, they are a church going family, and so that blended into what I believe today, and I continue to hold fast to what my mom and dad have taught me about being a child of God is separate and different of the Navajo way. My in-laws say the same thing, that when you accept Christ you come out of it. But as a coordinator in education, you see a different side of that, that I'm learning about, it's gonna be the second powwow that we're doing. I don't have any belief in it, but I know that's what our Indian people practice and so as coordinator I plan events like that and support it, but what happens in that realm of the powwow, I don't even know the significance really or the main goal for why people powwow. I was always uncomfortable in areas and arenas like that because it's just not how I grew up, but I'm beginning to appreciate the different cultures and have a better understanding of it. We hear a whole lot about how it's the same God, same biblical principles and practices in that realm. I'm just not comfortable in that area. (Interview, 2008)

Others who now support contextualized ministry, initially did not. According to Richard Twiss,

It was a journey to come from hating white people and Christianity to now being one, I had to reconcile that conflict which was most difficult initially. The ministry leaders said you sort of had to choose: Christian or Indian. These were irreconcilable; they were not mutually compatible realities. So being naive, young, being very sincere and ardent about my faith, I thought that must be what you do. So, I put the cultural way and all that on the shelf, cut my hair, bought a suit, and got my Christian uniform and thought—that's what you do. And I did that for about eight years. In the meantime I met my wife, we had our first child, I pastored a predominantly white church for about thirteen years in Vancouver, Washington. And since then until now, it's been a journey of internal reconciliation of how do you be both. (Interview, 2007)

Douglas MacDonald suggests that Native peoples be flexible with respect to tradition. If the primary goal is to share the gospel, then engaging Native tradition is good if it furthers that goal, but this is not always the case.

And I know there's a lot of open doors for us as Native people to be in our traditional dress and speaking in our traditional language and our traditional songs and to be able to share gospel message. But in some places, we're not going to be accepted because of those criteria, and people still need to hear the gospel message. So that's kind of my thinking anyways.

And even if a person is struggling, with like maybe he is a Christian who has gone through a lot of evil spiritual stuff, with Native dancing and songs and sweats and different practices whatever they may be, then he doesn't need to hear that stuff, because that sort of just brings him back there. Just because they are Native doesn't means that they have to be a "born again Indian," like they have to go and do these different practices in order to get healing. And that's something I don't agree with, but that's something I've seen taught—like if we're going to be free as Native people then we have to get back to our culture and I don't agree with that. I just think that Native people are so widespread in who they are and where their needs are at. (Interview, 2007)

Although some Native evangelicals do maintain the distinctness between Christianity and traditionalism, they do not necessarily wish to participate in non-Native churches. They may desire to hear the Bible in their language and appreciate the presence of Native culture even in churches that do not explicitly engage Native traditions. Margaret McKane Mauldin states:

The spirit in the Indian churches is so much warmer than the white churches, the white churches were very formal and stiff, and there is no way that Indians as a group can feel welcomed or warmly accepted in the white churches. And today we have Indian churches and white churches standing side by side in the same communities, but the Indians go to their churches and the white people go to their churches, and I don't see any sharing of the Bible and the teachings, and it's just so different. I don't see a time where the white churches will accept Indian people the way they are. I wish to be a Christian, but I like the feeling within the Indian churches because it's so warm and they do accept you.

Culturally I would say we are a friendlier people. The past politicians in the American government have pointed to this fact that we are like children, and I believe this is what they were talking about, we are trusting and we are friendly people, and this makes us also loving toward one another and toward other people. (Interview, 2007)

Those who do support bringing the two together frequently make the argument that Christianity is also transmitted through culture, but because it is transmitted through the dominant culture, we do not recognize this cultural mixing as such. The question, they propose, is not whether or not Christianity works through culture, but through *whose* culture. According to Cheryl Bear,

> In regards to Native people, those people who are Native, who are Christians and struggle with how to be Native and how to be Christian, I would say that we have to be authentically Native as Christians. We can't live a double life—on the one hand in church as Christians and on the other hand participating in ceremonies in traditions—without bringing them together. And I think it's possible to bring the two together because I really believe that God was working with us in culture, but I really do believe that most of our traditions are gifts from Creator, that God gave them to us. So when people say we shouldn't mix these things, it's a conversation that has been going on for a long time. Especially in the dominant culture here, we tend to think it's just "the church," but it's seeped with American culture, or perhaps Canadian culture, but we don't see that though because we're so used to being part of the dominant society. We always take it for granted....And for me personally, as a Native person, I have felt like I really became a Christian in the eyes of God when I started embracing who I was as a Native person. I don't think you can...hate who God made us and call us ourselves Christians because we're despising a gift Creator wants to give us. (Interview, 2007)

The presumption, then, behind supporting indigenous contextual ministries is that Native traditions are not wholly outside God. Rather than a set of demonic practices in need of redemption by God, Native cultures and traditions prepared the way for their eventual fulfillment in the gospel of Jesus. According to Cheryl Bear,

> Pro-Christian First Nations have always known of the "Creator." Sun Dance, Vision quests, all were about relating to the "Creator." Our people have always believed in the Creator but that is where our belief stops. We do not know or understand this Creator...we still need the Scriptures, the

teaching, the doctrine, and the theology....This Unknowable God is the same Being as our Great Mystery: it is none other than our Lord and Savior Jesus Christ. (Interview, 2007)

My People International produces Vacation Bible School curricula for Native youth that is founded on this philosophy. According to this curricula,

God was involved in the lives of Aboriginal people far before Europeans reached the shores of the America's. We have failed to see in their cultures, traditions and heritage, God's preparation of them for the Good News of Jesus Christ far before the "discovery" of this "New World." The story of Salvation through Jesus should have brought to Aboriginal people to complete what had already been started and correct where it had gone off track, not entirely devastate it. (My People International 2000, 7)

This series, then, is an attempt to affirm the values, cultures, and tradition of Aboriginal people while teaching the truth of the Savior, Jesus, from God's word—the Bible. It is one way that the church can assist Aboriginal people in regeneration and renewal of culture and, most importantly, their faith in and relationship with God. Aboriginal people want their children to know themselves as Aboriginal people while "walking the Jesus Trail" (My People International 2000, 6).

This curricula uses creation stories "which show how God was preparing the hearts of Aboriginal people before they received the good news of Jesus Christ" (My People International 2000, 10). These stories are then followed with biblical stories to show how the Bible completes the traditional story.

A central reason for contextualized ministries identified by many evangelicals is that it helps Native peoples both to see themselves in the biblical text and recognize that their identities are God-given rather than something they must reject. Edith Woodley describes the impact of her husband's (Randy Woodley) Eagle's Wings Ministry on her identity.

It was really hard because I really struggled with who I was as a Native person. I didn't like my skin color, my hair color, my reservation...I just didn't like being Indian...

But after Randy and I met, he was doing different things with different elders in Oklahoma. They were doing powwows and the sweat lodge, and different things like that, so it was kind of strange, because...you don't mix the two. But as I watched what he was doing and I watched the people respond to him, the whole time, I kept struggling the whole time, is the Christian side right? Because I knew Native Christians who were saying those things were wrong, they don't mix. And then I was struggling inside because of with my own Native identity. I just started really praying and saying: Ok God, if you created us, created me to be who I am, then you gave us these ceremonies, these prayer times, and stuff like that, so what's right? I never said anything to Randy or to anybody, I just prayed. Eventually, as I watched the young men, 15, 16, 17 [years old], boys who were coming in, who were first downcast and real negative, and from all of the country before they were brought to the boarding school, a lot from hard families. As a year went by, I started seeing a change in the boys; they were smiling; they were talking to me. It was almost like a second home for them, where they knew that Randy and what he was doing was bringing back to them a piece of what the Creator had given them. And as I saw their lives transformed, I just thought, ok something has to be here. (Interview, 2007)

Of concern for those who do support contextual ministry is the need to draw a line as to what aspects of Native culture can be mixed with Christianity. They do not all agree on what is acceptable—some condemn sweat lodges and naming ceremonies, for instance, while other do not. But most are clear on this principle: "a line must be drawn on what is permissible and what is clearly defined in Scripture as against the principles of the Kingdom of God" (Smith 1997, 124)

What are the principles for deciding what is acceptably within the bounds of Bible-based Christianity? Generally, proponents distinguish between cultural blending and syncretism: According to Richard Twiss,

> We must guard against syncretism and not allow the blending of Native religion and historical Christian faith. We must make a crystal clear distinction between theological and cultural blending or mixing. Theological syncretism is in direct contradiction of biblical truth, and cultural blending is a normal fact of everyday life. (Twiss 1998, 16)

According to Richard Twiss, the central issue is whether or not Scripture is the framework by which cultural practices are interpreted. Syncretism results "when people have adopted foreign forms but interpreted them largely within the context of their local tribal religious beliefs. They do not reinterpret their cultural forms in light of Scripture, they simply give their pagan deities Christian names or labels" (Twiss 1998, 10).

My People International explains how Native medicine can be used in a Christian context.

> There are aspects of traditional healing methods that are good....There was an elder who came from a long line of medicine men who became a Christian. He continued the traditional healing methods of using plants and roots, to take care of physical illnesses. Now however, he did so while praying to and, proclaiming his faith in Jesus Christ as the ultimate healer. (My People International 2000, 45)

According to Adrian Jacobs, "Other aspects of Aboriginal culture are not supported by Biblical teaching like; prayer to intermediary spirits, easy divorce, witchcraft, shamanism, and fortune telling" (Jacobs 1998, 23). Interestingly, while these various thinkers have clear guidelines for discerning which Native practices are biblical, they simultaneously point to the challenges of being able to do so. Jacobs, for instance, states that all theologizing happens within the context of "the worldview of a specific culture" and notes that on the most fundamental level, how we see "the way things are, [is] shaped by our culture" (Jacobs 1998, 11). In the context of his larger argument, Jacobs is contending that white Christians claim to make biblical judgments on what is culturally acceptable while disavowing the fact that what they see as biblical is shaped by their worldview. But it stands to reason that the same thing would also be true for Native evangelicals—that what they see as biblical is also shaped by their culture. Jacobs's argument leaves open the possibility for a more open-ended evangelicalism that might be less quick to judge which Native cultural practices are biblical and which are not.

Both those who support and those who oppose contextual ministry argue that there is a tendency to romanticize tradition or precolonial Native life. Thus, while many are critical of how Native traditions have been demonized within Christianity, they also hold that the Bible provides a measure to judge the godliness of Native cultural practices. Terry LeBlanc, while critical of colonialism, argues that Native peoples should not romanticize their precolonial histories.

> I think we fool ourselves into thinking that kind of thing [colonialism] didn't happen in the Native North American context. I just think of Micmac people who were part of a confederacy of four other tribes called the Wabanaki Confederacy for very specific purposes, trade and economics, and so forth, but also, for protection. Well, protection from whom? Well,

against the other tribes, well, specifically who? The Mohawks who were our bitter enemies? We like to make jokes that Mohawks stole our women and we went down and took their canoes. And Europeans didn't bring that animosity between us, it existed prior to Europeans coming here, and we needed protection and we created confederacies. The Iroquois confederacy was created because the Iroquois people were constantly at war with each other, and the great law and the treaty of peace were brought among them so that they could live well. So we fool ourselves into thinking that we were not colonial, we certainly were, so it doesn't necessarily require military might, it's just in what ways do we seek to coerce someone or some group of people to become like us. I think we sometimes like to idealize who we were, so I talk about these two myths that we live between, the one myth that said we lived in the Garden of Eden before the Europeans came here and we were wonderful and beautiful. The other myth that said we were Godless heathens, and neither of those are true. Somewhere in the middle is the reality. (Interview, 2007)

It should be noted that while Native evangelicals demonstrate concern about "drawing a line" between Christianity and traditionalism, some evangelicals critique the policing of this line as well. States Twiss,

As Native leaders it is we who must be careful that we do not allow Biblical ignorance to lead to an unfounded fear of "syncretism" among ourselves. We must counsel, pray and dialogue to prevent syncretism from being an emotionally defined standard for a type of modern day inquisition to root and burn out of Native Christians any tie to their culture and tradition. When we do this what we are doing is basically denying God's handiwork in us. (Twiss 1996, 52)

Anita Keith and David Bird also de-emphasize the need to draw lines between Native traditions and Christianity.
    Anita Keith:

So the traditional people, that's just another way that Creator is teaching us how to relate to him—here is my story and here is how you can love me. You can smudge, you can Sundance, and in that process I will communion with you. And some people can do the Sundance without integrity and God will not meet them. And others can do it with a very pure heart and God will meet them there. Some people study the Bible without integrity, and slam people with it, and try to have other people live it out, and God will not meet them. But if they read the word with integrity, God will meet them there. So it's a form, it's a function, it's just another vehicle. I think the panorama of worshiping is absolutely wonderful, and to say that you're way is wrong—that's not good...

I have no problem with moving from traditional way of worshiping, sweat, Sundance, or any of those ceremonies. There is no demonic in it, it's all about creator, and us connecting to him. (Interview, 2007)

In addressing the relationship between Native traditions and the Bible, many Native evangelicals who work in contextual ministries have dealt with Native traditionalists who argue they are following the "white man's religion" while simultaneously facing Native and non-Native evangelicals who argue that they are practicing pagan ways. Not all evangelicals, however, face these conflicts. Margie Yazzie, in response to a question about whether she has to address other Native Christians who have differing biblical interpretations, puts it this way:

No, I don't think so because we're all supposed to be the same mind and frame, and if they are going by the teachings of the Bible, then all the teaching should be the same. I don't think the[re] are differences. But if they happen to be wrong in the church then the brothers and sisters in the church can tell them quietly or inside the church without anyone being around. And that's what I tell my brothers and sisters, what's the right way and they appreciate that. (Interview, 2007)

Virginia Mason argues that Christianity comes from Native peoples rather than white people.

Whoever said that [Christianity is a white religion], is very mistaken. Number one, the Europeans came in here, thinking that they were bringing God to us, little did they know, we had God, we had our Creator, we had, they deemed us savages, dirty Indians, any name they could call us. No way, they never brought Christianity to us, in fact, I think later down the line, they still don't want to admit it, let's put it that way. We had God here all the time. We may not have done a lot of things we do now, like reading the holy bible, but I don't care, we had the Bible, in the nature around us. And I'll tell you what, we knew how to take care of it, we knew how to take care of everything, from the little tiniest plants to the biggest trees, and in Indian name, they say—that's "mother earth"—and we held it sacred. Oh no, nobody can tell me that only the white people brought it, no sir, no. (Interview, 2007)

But many do face conflicts in either or in both directions. Cheryl Bear describes tensions she has addressed on both sides:

One friend of mine confronted me when he found out I was going to seminary, he said, what are you doing?! Don't you know what they did to our people, and what about the residential schools? And that just stopped me in my tracks, this was years ago, and I thought, you're right you know, you're totally right. I totally know where you are coming from and I feel that pain. And at the same time I said to him, I have to tell you the truth about Jesus, who Jesus is, he is an ancient brown man who was part of a tribal people and he would come to us today if he could. He would come in a different way, not the way the early missionaries brought him, wrapped in European culture, but that's not how he came originally. So I talk in terms of that, I try to say, you know what there is a history that goes farther back, our history with Christianity started recently, but there is a history, the biblical record of who Jesus is, a couple thousands of years old, and let's look at who that was, specifically who Jesus was and what he means to us today. So I try to bring them a little farther back to the truth, and some people who didn't like culture, some Christians, they say we just wanted the pure gospel, not any of this other, additional stuff, like adding drums or regalia. And we're like, well the pure gospel is that Jesus entering a culture, completely immersed in a human culture. That is a pure gospel, so if we want to do that, what does that mean to us? Like Paul, one of his guys was going to minister to the Jews but he was a gentile man, and he had to get circumcised in order to minister to the Jews. He had to contextualize himself to a point of great pain, and so how should the early missionaries have contextualized themselves in order to minister to our people? But we can do that today, there is still hope, time, and our people are worth it. They are worth the conversation, to hear the truth of the gospel. (Interview, 2007)

Some, such as Marcus Briggs-Cloud, find particular challenges in dealing with the historic distrust between many Native peoples and Christianity.

I remember a couple of summers ago there was this girl I was really digging, and I was on fire for this chick and so we were talking, mostly about decolonization topics. But then she made a comment and she said, any Indian that practices Christianity is lost. And I said, "Scratch her off the list!" And I said I resent that statement for a number of reasons. This is rooted in what the definition of what an Indian is. If you look at the tribes on the East Coast, like the Mashpee or the Catawba, where they were colonized pretty quickly and received Christianity pretty quickly. They probably haven't had a Pequod ceremony in the couple hundred years, and their language died out a hundred seventy years ago. Mohicans, the last speaker died about eighty years ago. So they were left with Christianity. Christianity seems to be part of how they identify themselves. (Interview, 2007)

Vincent Yellow Old Woman states:

Simply because it was, who brought the Bible to us? If it was black, they would say black religion, if it was Koreans they would have said Korean, it's an Asian, if it was European they would say the same thing. But it just happens to be the white people so because of that they associate with that culture, with that group. You're always gonna have that. People who embrace the evangelical, like myself, the First Nation, we are considered white because of that. If it was Korean they would consider me Korean. But the opportunity for us is to set the record straight, it's a challenge, don't take as a setback, just an opportunity to say, hey, no group of people can claim God for themselves. (Interview, 2007)

Margaret McKane Mauldin points to criticism from other Native Christians for attending white churches.

Unfortunately, I must say that I have come up against people like this and it's always like a personal slap in the face to me. But, unfortunately again, the people that do this the most, or it seems that way, are people who call themselves Christians in the Indian churches. They'll be standing there with the King James Bible in their hand and they're pointing at me and questioning me why about I go to white churches. If I feel like I need to answer them, I say, well whose Bible are you holding? Is this an Indian Bible, or a white man's Bible? And if so, what Bible do you use and do you use the Bible? How did you become a Christian, and what do you use in your worship services? I have found this to be a very discouraging thing, for young people, to hear and to be around, this type of attitude, because I personally know that it is not a more enlightened attitude. (Interview, 2007)

Others suggest that they find acceptance with Native traditionals, but run into conflict with other Native Christians.
Chebon Kernell:

No one has ever come up to me directly and said it's a white religion. The ironic thing is that on one end, I've heard Native Christians demonize traditional ways, but on the other hand in traditional circles, only minimally have I ever heard something derogatorily said about the Christian church. So it's somewhat accepted to say that whatever that person's journey in life has taken with them, no one is going to take that away from them. Whether it's in the church or in ceremonial life, and that's something in my own personal story and own personal testimony was when I first experience authentic love was in that ceremony. (Interview, 2007)

Both Anita Keith and David Bird recount events in which conflicts with conservative evangelicals resulted in major disruptions of their ministries.
Anita Keith:

About two months ago we had in our city, there was Habitat for Humanity, and they built a whole slew of homes, and they rented a white mainstream church for a celebration, to have their banquet. A single mom and her daughters were getting a house and they invited them to powwow dance, and they were going to dance in this celebration. And this pastor said, absolutely not, and he said, pagan, and [took] great offense, and so the Habitat for Humanity were just heartbroken and so they couldn't even get out of the deal and so this thing had to go one. And this family was so crushed because the first time a single mom aboriginal woman gets a new home and this is what she has to remember it by, and this really leaves that sting. (Interview, 2007)

David Bird:

So what I do is that I make a brochure for a healing circle, and on the front is four colored circles and inside the circle is the logo of our church, and on the back page is the address of the church, and I put a scripture, blessed are our peacemakers, and I put a pipe just above, because the pipe is always recognized as a peace pipe. So I put the phone number of our church, my home, and our office. I was working in counseling center, [the] Healing through Christ Counseling Center, was what it was called. And it was a Pentecostal church overseeing this counseling center, a Native Pentecostal church. So it was an all Native organization, one hundred percent Native. So when I put the brochure I get called into this meeting. I'm the Office manager of this staff of seven, but my director of this center, who was also the pastor of this church, the president of the corporation, and his associate, we have a discussion and they say, we don't want our phone number or name on these brochures, we don't want our name to be associated with what you are doing at First Nation's alliance church, especially with this Native culture stuff. We don't like this Native culture, we think it's evil, it's of the devil. It's basically how they put it. And so that was probably in the summer. And then when my contract was done in January, and I had written the proposals for this healing foundation, for this organization, they were doing quite well financially and generally they just renew people's contract because they were doing a good job. And everyone's contract got renewed. But then I had a special meeting, that morning, they let me know they were not going to renew my contract. It wasn't personal they said, it was just business. And so I had no income for the next three months because there is not just much agreement with us over a simple thing, over a picture for a brochure. (Interview, 2007)

In Bird's account, it was specifically a Native group that opposed his attempt to do contextualized ministry. Chebon Kernell similarly points out that contextualized ministries are often more supported by non-Native Christians than by Native Christians.

One of the things I talk about when I go into non-Native churches, is when you talk about traditional issues such as bringing a drum or cedar into a church, that it's more commonly accepted in non-Native churches than in our own Native churches. And when I say that, people just can't believe that, and I believe that it's a direct result of that experience with those kind of first generation of missionaries....And so I've had a lot of encounters in different types of denominations, and pretty much the preacher would say the exact same thing the preacher after them would say. And that's pretty much the case even in revivals and things. And so the theology that you find, what I called our Native Southern Baptist and our Native United Methodist Churches is almost identical to each other. I think Native preachers want to learn and understand, but we haven't been given the tools to examine [the Bible] critically for ourselves. (Interview, 2007)

As mentioned in the beginning of the chapter, an assumption frequently made about Native evangelicals is that they are necessarily politically conservative and/or apolitical. It is frequently presumed that Native evangelicals, because they are Christian, necessarily support the colonization that went with Christianization. In surveying the political analysis of Native evangelicals, however, it is clear the there is really no singular perspective on the proper relationship between the Bible and political commitment.

Some evangelicals do not involve themselves directly in political struggle.

Shaunday Little:

Politically, I'm not involved, I don't get involved, it's not one of my interests, but I do believe the Bible does tell you what is going to happen politically and how they will end up. (Interview, 2007)

Casey Church:

I don't vote, I don't get involved in politics. But I have to live under a government and respect the government's ways. God says in the Bible, to respect the people over us, that he has given them authority in certain ways to govern, I totally understand that, but I haven't been a voter, only for five years, only because I had to move to a new part of the country, that I didn't want to make decisions for a state, a city, a people, a tribe, a peoples that I didn't understand. And I haven't been a real political person. The politics I am involved in are mostly spiritual aspects, theological ways. I realize people are going to be elected one way or the other whether 10 or 90 percent show up to vote. And I just pray God will use those people to govern us wisely. (Interview, 2007)

Others find that Christian faith guides them into political work.

Vincent Yellow Old Woman:

I've been in politics in a lot of years, been elected to my tribe's politics. So I had to be skilled in understanding what the federal government was saying, and for the most part it was very paternalistic; they broke our treaties, [have] taken our land away and that's a whole different component. And so how I use it, is to pray, in my personal relationship with God, just to exercise and to trust God to give me wisdom. And we have lawyers and legal counsel and consultants that work with us, and we have former tribal leaders that help us. So we have every kind of resource to help our band to be successful. And a big part, for me, is my prayer. Especially since the paternalistic federal government, I have to have a lot of patience and I don't have a lot of patience so I have to ask God for help with patience. (Interview, 2007)

Douglas MacDonald acknowledges the importance of political commitment and colonization, but contends that Jesus is concerned more with personal transformation than with political transformation.

Yes, the Bible I believe does inform my view of colonization. And it's interesting to me that Jesus himself was under the dominant Roman society, and the people who were part of his people group desperately wanted out from under that oppressive government, and they thought he might be king and take them out of that. And they were looking for a revolution, and it's interesting to me that Jesus was more interested in a revolution of their hearts than society, and I think that's what he's on about today as well. Although I appreciate our chiefs and all of the hard work that they do—and in Canada we have grand chiefs that go to Ottawa and speak on our behalf and I appreciate all of their work—but I know Jesus is more interested in our hearts than in politics. (Interview, 2007)

Richard Twiss also speaks to the problems of radical political activism when it becomes spiritually unmoored.

And during that time AIM was going strong and I joined the American Indian Movement and went to Washington, DC to participate in the takeover of the Bureau of Indian Affairs office building with that whole eight days of occupation and all that. And during that time I began to hate white people and hate Christianity, hearing all the stories of Catholic Boarding School and abuse. Although [boarding school was] positive for my mom, it was a horrible experience for my other five aunties and uncles. And so after AIM [American Indian Movement], I spent some time in jail, involved in drugs and alcohol. And I just felt that my life as a 19-year-old was not going in a good direction I did not know what else to do. I ended up in jail in Washington State on some drug and alcohol charges. The judge wanted me to go into this treatment program because of my blood alcohol content, but I didn't want to go. So I talked this friend into going to Hawaii with me, her brother was in the Army, in Honolulu. So we left and went to Hawaii and by that time, after my time at AIM, there would be times when I would watch our highly respected spiritual leaders, our medicine men, who were very much espousing a kind of life style, a set of values—respect and honor and all of that. And yet, there would be times during the height of the whole focus on spirituality, whether it be Lakota or First Nation, that these men would come out of the bar drunk as a skunk with a woman under each arm. And there was this whole phenomenon of this stud complex and so many of those guys have children all over the country today. Some guys a couple dozen babies. But there was this sort of hypocrisy, they would be espousing these values and holding us young guys to it, but meanwhile it was about drugs, it was about promiscuity, it was about drinking and carousing. So it created a bit of a disillusionment. (Interview, 2007)

On the other hand, Ray Aldred is suspicious of attempts to spiritualize concerns about social justice and colonization. He argues that reconciliation efforts need to have tangible outcomes.

> If you have a relationship with Christ, it should make you less of an ass. I just think you can't take people's land and somehow justify that. That's just wrong. I try not to spiritualize stuff too much. There are specific land claims dealing with this land right here. They need to give it back. When it comes to those reconciliation gatherings, the ones that have really been effective in helping the relationship move forward are talking about specific things. They aren't just talking airy fairy, it's about specific things. (Interview, 2008)

Randy Woodley similar ties a belief in Jesus with a political commitment to social justice.

> God has a preference for the poor and justice and so anything that reeks of corporate greed or anti-environmentalism, I would use the Bible to support and say, you can't say you follow Creator and follow the policies of George Bush, like war. I wouldn't say I'm a pacifist I guess I'm a wannabe pacifist, but I really do believe in peace. The Evangelical church has used the Bible to make it into the opposite of what it says and that's very sick. (Interview, 2007)

In Native Studies, many scholars propose decolonization as a guiding principle for Native scholarship and activism. This work generally presumes a non-Christian framework for decolonization. But interestingly, some Native evangelicals also support decolonization as a guiding principle for biblical faith. At the 2007 NAIITS conference, Robert Francis gave a keynote address centering on the need for decolonization.[2] According to Francis, colonization can be defined as

> what happens when one people invades the territory of another people, appropriating the territory as their own, asserting control over and actually or essentially destroying the original inhabitants through outright murder, hegemonic subjugation, enslavement, removal or absorption into the society and culture of the colonizers.... Colonization is violence and violation of the most extreme sort. Colonization is theft and rape and murder and cannibalism on the grandest scale. Colonization is genocide. There is nothing worse under the sun.

Francis began his talk with an adaption of Mark 5:1–20.

One day Jesus got into a fishing boat with his 12 disciples, and they all sailed out onto Lake Gennesaret, intending to picnic on the opposite shore. As they were about halfway across the lake, a sudden storm swept in. In keeping with his usual behavior during inclement weather, Jesus was fast asleep in the stern of the boat when a huge twister or whirlwind swept up the little craft, transporting the boat, along with all thirteen passengers through space and time to twenty-first-century North America. When the wind abated, Jesus and his disciples found themselves on dry land, somewhere in the midst of an Indian reservation. Jumping down from the boat, John and Peter looked around, shrugged their shoulders and spread a cloth on the ground for the picnic.

The boat had landed at the edge of a large cemetery where many graves were marked with make-shift stones or wooden crosses once painted white. In the center of the cemetery was a large mass grave, reminder of a massacre of not so long ago. As the others gathered round, taking seats on the sparse grass, Jesus distributed loaves and fishes for a meal.

Just then an automobile came roaring down the paved road not far from where the group sat eating. Having no prior experience with any such machine, the disciples were astonished and more than a bit frightened. The car slowed but did not stop, the passenger door flew open, and a woman, pushed by a hairy, masculine hand, tumbled out into the roadside ditch. She lay there for a moment, a seemingly lifeless heap of rags and flesh. Then leaping to her feet, the woman began to scream and cry in an alarming manner. She watched the automobile disappear over a distant hill; then turning, she suddenly noticed the disciples and Jesus at their picnic. Shaking her head with fury, the woman ran shrieking up to where they were, only to stop short, a look of shocked recognition in her eyes.

The woman's clothing was torn and filthy. Her hair was a mess, shortly cropped, yet matted and caked with greasy dirt and dried blood. There were bruises on her face and on other areas of her body that were visible. Her lower arms were a mass of scars and infected cuts, the result of years of self-mutilation. She stank with the combined smells of stale beer, urine, feces and vomit. The disciples were thoroughly disgusted, their appetites gone.

The woman stood there, hesitating, a hideously twisted expression on her face, but her astonished silence did not last long. "Jesus! What are you doing here?" screamed a voice from within the woman. "You're the last person I'd expect to see here!" This statement was followed with maniacal laughter.

Looking deeply into the woman's eyes, Jesus asked, "What is your name?"

"My name?" asked the voice. "What is my name? My name is... Cavalry... Infantry... Military Mega-Complex. My name is Trading-Company... Border-Town Liquor Store... Multi-National Corporation. My name is Proselytizing Missionary... Religious Order... Denominational Mission Board. My name is White Man's School... Historical Misrepresentation... Hollywood Stereotype. We are many. We are organized. We are in control. Our intentions are always and only for the very best."

"Get out of her," Jesus said.

With one last shriek, the evil spirits left the woman. The woman who had been healed also stood. "Jesus," she said, "may I go with you? I want to become a Christian."

With a weary smile and a shake of his head, Jesus replied, "No child, this is not my intent for you. Stay here, with your own people, and tell them what Creator has done."

This parable contains an implicit critique of not only past acts of colonization, but the current colonial world order. In addition, the last paragraph seems to suggest that for Native peoples to follow Jesus, they can best do so, not by becoming Christian, but by following their traditional ways. This implication was corroborated further by Francis's analysis of religion as a tool of colonization.

Francis then called for a project of decolonization; of total divestment from all colonial structures, including churches. If one must engage these colonial institutions, one should do so as a warrior going to battle, but one should never become invested in them.

We should understand that there are indeed people with a heart for decolonization in the churches, in business, even in the military as well as in schools, colleges and seminaries, even if most of these organizations, the systems themselves are broken or even malignant, delivered over to the enemy as tools or weapons of colonization.

Even so, it is not for us to somehow share power with the colonizers. Can you imagine Jesus saying this to his disciples? "Here's good news: I had a positive meeting with Lucifer in the wilderness. He shed light on several issues. Afterward, the two of us met with Caesar, Pilate, Herod and Caiaphas. They are expressing a willingness to share some of their power with us. All we have to do is, ahem, submit to their superior authority. What do you say, guys? 'If you can't beat 'em, join 'em!' Right?"

If we are called into church, into the economic system, into the military, into school, college or seminary, it is proper that we go in the way of a warrior entering the camp of the enemy, knowing the dangers that are there, knowing that we risk captivity and death at the hands of cannibals, knowing that at the very least we will sustain grievous wounds, the scars of which we will bear all our lives.

I am not saying the Spirit of Creator cannot be encountered in church. The Spirit of Creator is everywhere and may reach out to anyone anywhere—even in the most unlikely of settings.

What I am saying is inasmuch as churches theologically inspire, empower, encourage and drive all aspects of colonization while directly participating and occupying themselves in colonizing activities, churches are dancing to the devil's tune. There is no healing or wholeness to be found in that dance. Damage and death are found in that dance. Beware!

Jesus entered the seat of the colonizing power. He rode into Jerusalem. He stormed into the temple. He walked into the governor's own mansion and out of the city to the place of the skull. He will forever bear the scars. That is what Jesus did, and as surely as we choose to call ourselves Jesus' followers, we may do no less. We must live our lives and give our lives for the purpose of decolonization, that the People may live.

Francis seems to take the most radical stance of suggesting that evangelicals may even need to leave the church to follow a truly decolonized Christianity. But many other evangelicals also make strong stances against colonization historically as well as its contemporary manifestations. Roger Boyer speaks to the need to address colonization, but proposes that Native peoples need to reconcile rather than to simply separate from their oppressors.

I have a passion to reconcile, to get rid of the whole mentality of moving from victimization to healing is important, and I think that's honestly why Jesus came. That's the message of the Gospel, to move from being victims of this oppressive spirit that has come to destroy and kill and steal from us, and as people it's important to say enough is enough...

So this whole reconciliation and restoration, the Bible is very clear on how to do that, you know, if the brother offends you, seek that brother, sit down have coffee, smoke the peace pipe, talk about the problem, address the issues. If that does not work, the Bible says get a mediator, and someone who can stand on a neutral ground and say these are the issues we're having here, we need to come to a reconciliation. If we don't, it's like a disease that will eat us alive, and our well- being and our self-worth will be diminished or eroded because of this. And so for me, I definitely believe the scripture has a way, a message on reconciliation. (Interview, 2007)

Similarly, Dicey Barnett speaks to the need for all races to reconcile. "I believe the Bible stands for one race, and everybody being conformed to that race, that's all races" (interview, 2007).

Other evangelicals point to the need to address the continuing injustices against Native peoples and to support contemporary land struggles. Tom Bee's Red Sea Ministries website asserts "that Native Americans are God's chosen people on this continent; we are the landlords appointed by God" (http://www.redseaministries.org). Qaumaniq and Suuquinah contend:

Because of a history of *manifest destiny*, most Euro-Americans have an understanding that says they have a right to go anywhere, anytime, unhindered, and settle anywhere without opposition. This so-called *manifest destiny* was and is a lie that has been used to create unspeakable hardships for indigenous people everywhere, and to dishonor them in the most egregious ways possible. (Qaumaniq and Suuqiina 2007, 143)

Adrian Jacobs similarly address this theme. He argues that God uses nations to judge other nations. So he suggests that colonization may have been a judgment against Native nations. For instance, he considers the possibility that the colonization of the Iroquois may be a judgment for their role in the destruction of the Huron. He also postulates that the destruction of the Aztecs was a judgment against their human sacrifices (Jacobs 1998, 64). He does not think all Native nations are equally "guilty" but does think that Native nations that were less sinful may have escaped the harsher forms of genocide.

However, Jacobs does not place colonizers on the side of God. Rather he contends that they may face the same judgment. He evokes Saul's broken treaty with the Gibeonites to say "God really does care about broke treaties and will bring judgment eventually" (Jacobs 1998, 64). He suggests that the billion dollar damage to Hydro Quebec during an ice storm in January 1998 was perhaps a consequence of Quebec's destroying Cree lands by building a dam that flooded their territory. Jacobs states that he is not a prophet and thus cannot "declare the state of affairs in the North America to be His judgment on broken treaties," but concludes that "when there is a recounting concerning broken treaties, I do not want to be on the side of the violators" (Jacobs 1998, 66).

A *NAIITS* journal article by Debra Henry and Elizabeth Levesque calls on Canadian churches to make financial restitution as well as formal apologies for their complicity in residential school abuse. They argue that this abuse is the result of when " 'manifest destiny' is passed off as God's will" (Henry and Levesque 2004, 47). Nicole Yellow Old Woman similarly critiques Christian complicity in land theft.

> Yeah, of course the big Evangelical movement in the states says that they are gonna sway the vote. But I vote also as a Christian but also as a First Nation's person. Because what party that they're saying is the good party, the Christian party, is also the party that is taking away our land, right? That's what a "good Christian" does, right, under the lines of religion, right? That's what they do. They do things in the name of God, right? Just like when they came into our country, in the name of God, they tried to kill us indigenous people, right? Because that's what good Christians do, right? No, it's not. (Interview, 2007)

Besides these critiques of colonization, some evangelicals proffer visions of sovereignty based on biblical principles that echo some feminist and other more radical perspectives. Terry LeBlanc ties Native nationalism to an implicit critique of capitalism:

> The gap between rich and poor still exists In fact, it [is] widening at an increasing rate—despite the assurances of the World Bank and the G7 that there is overall improvement in the human condition worldwide. Sadly, those of us in the indigenous community seem to be buying it hook, line, and sinker! MBA's are being churned out in Indian country faster than the social work and legal degrees.... The battle against assimilation is being conceded on a selective front. We are buying into an economic worldview so foreign that it didn't even register as a remote possibility to our ancestor.... When, under the rubric of development, we disguise unchecked greed for bigger and better and more of Western free enterprise and big business we do a grave disservice to our fellow human beings (LeBlanc 2000).

He explains that traditional indigenous economic structures more closely emulate biblical principles than do contemporary capitalist ones:

> What I see, what I understand to be a traditional way of life for Micmac and Wabanaki Confederacy, and other tribes I am familiar with, I look at

the way of life, and the scriptures speak of some of those very qualities. For example, Second Corinthians chapter 8, says, let the one who has gathers little, share with the one who has gathered abundance, not by the way of hardship but by the way of equality, so that in a future time, their abundance will be a supply for your lack. And I think of our how communities have operated down through history, and people shared willingly with one another cared for sick, and there were certain ways in which that was undertaken, ensured that no one grows above others. It wasn't oppressive, it did allow for people to succeed according to their own skills and ability, but the greatest success was the degree to which they provided for others. And I see that in scriptures, in the Old Testament where they talked about the Year of Jubilee, so there is this period of time when one person or group of people might process over another, but at the end of this forty-ninth year in the fiftieth year in the year of Jubilee, everything was restored to the way it was at the beginning of the fifty-year period, and they started again so that there wasn't this multigenerational poverty and the despair and the inequity they brought. I think that affirms many of the principles we see that were historically part of tribal life. (Interview, 2007)

Meanwhile, Adrian Jacobs suggests an alternate model of both indigenous and church governance that echo some of the visions for indigenous nationhood found in anarchist and feminist indigents. Mohawk scholar Taiaiake Alfred contends that while the term "sovereignty is popular among Native scholars/activists, it is an inappropriate term to describe the political/spiritual/cultural aspirations of Native peoples. He contends that sovereignty is premised on the ability to exercise power through the state by means of coercion and domination. Traditional forms of indigenous governance by contrast are based on different understandings of power.

The Native concept of governance is based on...the "primacy of conscience." There is no central or coercive authority and decision-making is collective. Leaders rely on their persuasive abilities to achieve a consensus that respects the autonomy of individuals, each of whom is free to dissent from and remain unaffected by the collective decision....

A crucial feature of the indigenous concept of governance is its respect for individual autonomy. This respect precludes the notion of "sovereignty"—the idea that there can be a permanent transference of power or authority from the individual to an abstraction of the collective called "government."

In the indigenous tradition, there is no coercion, only the compelling force of conscience based on those inherited and collectively refined principles that structure the society. (Alfred 1999, 25)

As long as indigenous peoples frame their struggles in terms of sovereignty, Alfred argues, they inevitably find themselves co-opted by the state—reproducing forms of governance based on oppressive, Western forms of governance. In addition, the concept of sovereignty continues to affirm the legitimacy of the state: "To frame the struggle to achieve justice in terms of indigenous 'claims' against the state is implicitly to accept the fiction of state sovereignty" (Alfred 1999, 57). He generally juxtaposes nationhood and nationalism as terms preferable to sovereignty. Sovereignty is an exclusionary concept rooted in an adversarial and coercive Western notion of power. (Alfred 1999, 59)

It is with indigenous notions of power such as these that contemporary Native nationalism seeks to replace the dividing, alienating, and exploitative notions, based on fear, that drive politics inside and outside Native communities today. (Alfred 1999, 53)

Similarly, Adrian Jacob argues that both churches and society at large can model themselves over the principles of consensus and egalitarianism that Alfred outlines. He concurs that Iroquois leaders "derived their power from the people" (Jacobs 1998, 69). He then contends that this model is one that can be informative to all Christians.

I am suggesting that one of the greatest contributions that Iroquoian people can make toward reformation among Aboriginal people is assisting the return to the value of consensus decision-making and the inherent respect of that process. Abusive people find it very hard to work in an environment of open heartedness, respect trust, and group sharing. Hierarchical systems maintain their structures through the careful control of information. Closed-door meetings and in-camera sessions abound in this system emphasizing privileged information. Dictators know the value of propaganda. (Jacobs 1999, 25)

As I discuss in another work, the principles articulated by Jacobs resonate with Native feminist calls to envision nationhood based on principles of horizontal authority, interconnectedness with a larger global world and mutual respect and responsibility. These visions contrast sharply with nation-state forms of governance that are based on principles of domination, violence, and social hierarchy (Smith 2008).

What are some of the material/physical objects and forms of expressiveness—past and present—through which, in relationship to which, the scripturalizing practices are carried out? What are their forms, shapes, sounds, colors, and textures?

In the 1980s, mainstream evangelicalism was embroiled in a "Battle of the Bible" (Price 1986). Evangelicals argued over whether or not the Bible was inerrant (no errors of any kind),[4] infallible (no errors in teaching),[5] or neither.[6] Although this battle has since subsided, the differences of thought regarding biblical inerrancy are prevalent within Native evangelicalism.

Many Native evangelicals argue that the Bible is the inerrant word of God. Lucy Ann Williams Harjo states:

> Well, I am taking God's word for what it is, and that it's all truth, and because of how I see it I don't see any error in it, I don't see anything I would take out, because again it would be man determining what goes in and what goes out. I think it's truth and I wouldn't change it. (Interview, 2007)

Douglas MacDonald states (in response to question: Do you think there are any errors in the Bible?):

> No, I don't actually, and for me, I'd say, and I hope this is true across the board, if we do believe there are errors in the Bible, then it's a slippery slope of personalizing scripture....Yeah, I think the Bible is God's word. I do think I've done some research in seeing that it is, a valuable and true document, but I'm not really schooled in that area of research about why it would be factual, but I think we can get as much fact as possible, but it's more important about how we actually live what his words say in our lives. (Interview, 2007)

Margie Yazzie suggests that only the King James Version is inerrant: "Here we should read from the King James because it's the closest we can get to the Hebrew or Mosiac law, anything that's close to that we should believe it." In response to question, does the Bible have errors? she adds, "Well you gotta be careful how those words are used, different definitions and whatever. If you have to, go back to the original King James version" (interview, 2007).

Some evangelicals support inerrancy, but point to the importance of contextualizing biblical narratives in order to arrive at a correct understanding of the text. Casey Church demonstrates this practice by re-reading the biblical passages that seem to prohibit women from teaching (more discussion on biblical approaches to gender is forthcoming later in the chapter).

> It's God word, and I accept it as whole. It was meant for a culture at that time, so women teaching at that time was different. Women were not educated, so if they were educated, I believe they would be allowed to teach. Men were the only ones educated. So in our [Potawotami] instance, women were educated, matrilineal societies. They passed down the knowledge; women in our culture were educated along with men. We're more egalitarian. Everybody had something to teach, no one person had all the knowledge, so you go to who has the knowledge. My grandma was a medicine person. People would come to her to ask about how to handle children's sicknesses, and she would give them medicine. But if you went to a man who was not educated that way and didn't know those things, would you allow him to teach? No, in that context you wouldn't allow a man to teach. So that's how I see different aspects of the Bible. You have to look at the Bible as a whole. You can't get so much influenced by what other men are telling you to understand. We have the same Holy Spirit that is the same interpreter of the Bible. So if we take the time to study the scripture, the context, the culture, we too would interpret the Bible along with the educated person, as long as the Holy Spirit is guiding it. (Interview, 2007)

Others focus primarily on biblical infallibility—the Bible's truthfulness in regard to teaching or theology.
Lincoln Harjo:

> I would say as far as inaccuracies per se, saying that the Bible is teaching anything that is false, no. But I don't know how many different Bibles there are, but all of them have got different interpretations. But I wouldn't say there are any false teachings, anything that would lead a person astray to something that is wrong. But I give an example: one word that has been commonly misconstrued because the interpretation is wrong in the King James Version. You have heard of the word Beelzebub? One example, in the King James Version, it's interpreted as Lord of the Flies. That's wrong, the proper Hebrew interpretation of that word is Lord of Things that Fly, not Lord of the Flies, so the lonely fly has gotten the bad rap of being associated with Satan. But they are not evil. (Interview, 2007)

Margaret McKane Mauldin explains that all in the Bible that is meant as a lesson for us is valid, but not all in the Bible is meant to be lesson: "I think it teaches us everything. I know there are incidents in the Bible that are taken in a way that it isn't message to us today, and you study it carefully and that's not. So, there's not anything that I don't support, if it's given as a lesson to us" (interview, 2007).

Richard Twiss contends that while the Bible may be error free, it is never interpreted error-free.

> I think the Bible is perfect in all of its ways, free of any error. Is the Bible understood error free? No. Do human beings have within their own monocultural experience the capacity to fully comprehend the perfect truths contained in the scripture? No. So the scripture can only be understood within the multicultural, multiethnic context. So that as one culture views God in the Bible, and then as all these view points, or perspectives, sort of settle on the Bible, then revelation or truth is reflected back to them out of the Bible, then collectively, you have the best possible chance, I suppose, to understand what the Bible says, which is the perfect authoritative word of God. Do we understand it perfectly? Not even. Do we comprehend the fullness of it? Never can. So that's the problem, people believe their view of it is *the* authoritative view when only the Bible is authoritative. So the truth of scripture is far greater than our understanding of it. (Interview, 2007)

Meanwhile Terry LeBlanc suggests that while the Bible may or may not be inerrant, this issue is not of critical importance.

> I think you can create a position and support it. If people say verbal plenary inspiration, the entire thing, in every word, is exactly correct, I say, well, maybe but maybe not, and does it matter? I think it's a communication of God to us. It's a written format that was originally of an oral traditional people and it was committed to a text, and the text has been transmitted to us, and those who have gone before us in the faith have gathered those texts and said, these are authentic, and they gave them to us and I think they speak to us in an authoritative way. Are there errors? I don't think I want to think so much in terms of errors, so much as, as they create again, sort of a direction for us; that to me is consistent, down through the ages. (Interview, 2007)

In many cases, Native peoples could not and still do not necessarily read the Bible directly. In response to question, What's your relationship to the Bible? Barnett discusses her relationship to Scripture primarily in terms of hearing it: "I don't read a lot of it but I believe Jesus died for our sins. . . . I heard it many times and that's what I believe in" (interview, 2007).

Meanwhile, others speak of the need to aggressively studying the Bible and its many translations, regardless of their formal educational status.

Margaret McKane Mauldin:

I would say what I witnessed was the non-training of [Native peoples by] the white people that came into our world and set up Methodism. It wasn't just that our Indian preachers were only given certain tasks. Many couldn't read English yet they were made preachers and I saw that as so wrong. How in the world could we have real Christian training when very little of the Bible was used? When all the churches had Children's Sunday school where we learned a line or two of scripture? We didn't know what they were for, nobody taught us. Many of the preachers that stood before us behind the pulpit were in the same position as the children. We didn't know what scripture was, what it was for. Over a long period of time I took upon myself to read the entire Bible, most of what I read was just one word, but over time it started becoming clearer to me. (Interview, 2007)

Lincoln Harjo:

I like to get as many documents, as many concordances, try to get the originally Greek, Hebrew, or Aramaic writings, or even, the readings like from Josephus and other things that have accounts of Biblical importance. Those things are helpful in understanding what God's word is really saying. (Interview, 2007)

Nicole Yellow Old Woman:

My approach is the Holy Spirit. That's my approach. My first year in Bible school I made a pact to myself that I was gonna read Genesis to Revelation in each translation, because you've got the NIV, King James, just finished New Living Translation, North American Revised Standard Translation, because I wanted God to speak to me in a different way. (Interview, 2007)

Another important consideration for Native communities and the Bible is language. In the United States, the Bible is generally read in an English translation from Greek and Hebrew. But some Native communities read their Bibles in their Native languages. These translation projects are also quite diverse. Some are translations from the Greek and Hebrew, while others are translated from English. The result is that, depending on these diverse histories, Native peoples having varying degrees of interest in having the Bible translated in Native languages.

Missionaries have historically complained that indigenous languages were unable to communicate Christian concepts. From their perspective, Indians not only lack the Scripture, they lack the language that would allow them to comprehend God. Jonathan Edwards complained: "The Indian languages are extremely barbarous and barren, and very ill fitted for communicating things moral and divine, or even things speculative and abstract. In short, they are wholly unfit for a people possessed of civilization, knowledge, and refinement" (Edwards 1998, vol. 2, clxxx). Missionaries also complained that indigenous languages were unable to communicate the concepts of "Lord, Savior, salvation, sinner, justice, condemnation, faith, repentance, justification, adoption, sanctification, grace, glory, and heaven" (Edwards 1998, vol. 1, 426). It is not sufficient, therefore, simply to have Scriptures; the Scriptures must be in a suitable language—and that language happens to be English. After all, if Christianity couched in languages that do not have concepts of Lord, Savior, salvation, sinner, and so on, then are Native peoples practicing the Christianity of English-speaking cultures?

Noting these linguistic divides, Kernell advocates the translation of the Bible into Native languages:

I think it's very important that the Bible be translated into Native languages. You see so many instances where certain words have certain meanings. Nowadays, English is the dominant form of communication but in many ways our own tribal languages can give an understanding of what is more authentic to what was going on. This is a story I share with my church, is the whole concept of Jesus King, Jesus, and the word that originally had been interpreted, a missionary interpretation, *Mike* [in Muskogee], was one of King, but that interpretation is insufficient because in turn, *Mike* is almost like a servant is almost like the least of these, to put New Testament English into that. So to say Jesus is sort of like a servant leader who has showing the way, is something that is very much like him, so I think that language is the way that we have to begin to interpret in looking at that in a healthy way. (Interview, 2007)

Justine Smith notes in her analysis of the Cherokee Bible that because the Bible is a translation of the Greek and Hebrew versions rather than the English versions of the Bible, the Cherokee Bible is not simply a replication of the texts of the dominant culture; it can serve as an oppositional text to the English Bible (Smith 2000). Marcus Briggs-Cloud, by contrast, argues against the reading the Bible in his language (Muskogee) because it is translated from English.

> I don't like the Creek Bible because, I'm not anti-Protestant or anything; it was written by Protestants. I wish I was more well versed in Hebrew and Greek and Latin and even German, but I'm not. So I just acquired various translations over the years, and building upon that. But by the time it gets to English, with the cultural gaps included, I always think about how much I'm missing out on. When I'm reading it from English to Creek there's a whole bunch of things missing. The old timers, they don't know the difference, the ones that don't speak English that well, a lot of older ones now they speak English but their parents don't, so when they read the Creek Bible they were reading probably something more relative to their worldview, to their upbringing. But it's not the same thing as reading it in English, so I know it's not the same thing as if it was read in Hebrew. The Creek Bible is translated from English, and there were no Biblical scholars that helped in this translation, it was just missionaries and it was just about simplistic conversion and also only just the New Testament. It was not originally written to sustain a whole society of people to grow in Christian faith.
>
> So the Creek Bible was not something that was written to go on into the evolution of society, just for that group of people in that particular time period. And our people have changed drastically because of assimilation, acculturation, and our people would not read it the same way, just as English-speaking people would not read it the same now as 500 years ago.

In response to the question, if there was a translation from Greek and Hebrew directly to Creek would that be something valuable? Briggs-Cloud adds:

> Well that would be really difficult, I would want to be a part of it so the words would not be butchered and the meanings watered down, because that's like killing our own language. Christianity has done enough killing." (Interview, 2007).

Signifying on the questions: What are the pitfalls, risks, and opportunities reflected in these questions and the approaches and assumptions behind them? What are the larger implications—overdetermination, limitation, distortion, and so forth—of all the questions and issues discussed so far in this chapter for an understanding of modern discourses, social formation, and power relations?

While Native evangelicalism cannot be dismissed as simply politically and socially regressive, certainly its association with evangelicalism's traditionally conservative approaches toward gender and sexuality influences it. At the same time, many Native evangelicals also articulate more progressive stances on these often divisive issues.

The 1970s gave birth to the evangelical feminist movement with the founding of the Evangelical Women's Caucus (EWC). However, it was not until the 1980s, with the splintering of Christians for Biblical Equality (CBE) from the EWC over the issue of gay rights, that mainstream evangelicalism became particularly embroiled in a debate over gender egalitarianism (the position that supports gender equality in marriage and in the church) and gender complementarianism (the position that women and men have complementary roles; hence men should be the heads of the home, and pastoral positions should be reserved for men). Some complementarians, particularly Charismatic Christians, may support women as pastors but may still support male headship (men as head of the household and of the church) in marriage. Women feature prominently in the development of Pentecostal/Charismatic Christianity (Hyatt 2000, 121). These two positions became represented by CBE, which supports gender equality (although it makes a stand against homosexuality in its statement of faith), and the Council of Biblical Manhood and Womanhood (CBMW), which formed in 1987 specifically to counter CBE.

One does not generally see a Native presence within these organizations or Native evangelical thought specifically referencing complementarianism versus egalitarianism, but Native evangelical thought does reflect the differing positions on gender roles found in mainstream evangelicalism. Some Native evangelicals do support male headship. Dicey Barnett expresses support even as she demonstrates concern that headship can lead to abuse: "Yes, I believe that the male gender is supposed to be the background of the family. They are supposed to provide for the family. They were made with more physical strength so they could provide for the family. But in a lot of ways, you hear statistics about the men misusing their physical strength otherwise" (interview, 2007). Margaret McKane Mauldin echoes the complementarian philosophy that men and women do have distinct roles but is clear that both are equally valued: "Yes, women were assigned certain duties and men were assigned these things and I see nothing wrong with these assignments that we have strayed so far from [and] that we have created problems because of that, but I don't think God set us apart so that one could be superior over the other" (interview, 2007). Margie Yazzie and Shaunday Little express concern that men frequently do not fulfill their roles as leaders in the home.

Margie Yazzie:

The male is supposed to be strong because they are the ones that take care of the family, and the mothers take care of the kids. Women should be silent, at least not be argumentative, and take it as is. The women should not be able to overcome the man, because they have a part in this too. Man was created first, then the woman. You know God took care of that because he said Man needed a helper and women can and helped the men. When it comes to that, even children, the girls and the boys, should be able to know what they are doing, because the parents teach us that.

[Men] because they are stronger, should be able to take pressure more. But times have changed. Women have taken over because the men can't because, I guess it's because they take on so much these days, and the woman is more the peacemaker. (Interview, 2007)

Shaunday Little:

I believe [men] are more laid back. They'd rather stay home and women would rather work, and I think men are supposed to be more of the backbone of the family and provide. (Interview, 2007)

Douglas MacDonald notes that those who do not support male headship do not consider the fact that men are also supposed to resemble Christ. Women are to submit to their husbands, but husbands are also supposed to submit to Christ. This parallel obligation guards against abuse, and women's submission to their husbands provides men the opportunity to be Christ-like.

I don't want to use the word submissive, but I think that as a husband and wife they are working together, but ultimately, it comes to him to make the decision. If you are behind the husband and saying, I believe you and

I believe that you will make the right decision for our family, the best decision, then I think it takes some weight off his shoulders and makes him stand up as a man, to do what's best. I really think that's where God's Scripture comes in. There's so much about humbling ourselves and unique to him and I think what if men had that in their head, they are submitting to Christ and living up as he did for others. When people hear about, wives submit to their husbands; that's a hard one for people because they have all this other stuff they are thinking about—not what Christ is like. So if we had our minds on what Christ is like and that's what husbands should be, I think it's really comforting and that you know there is a man that is going to protect you and that he is going to be there for you. (Interview, 2007)

He also explains that while he is uncomfortable with women in pastoral positions, he has no problems with women exercising leadership in other societal roles.

I'm not exactly sure if there's a line to be drawn somewhere. An elder lady, I think I'm uncomfortable with in the church. Deaconess, I feel comfortable with. I'm starting to feel a little bit comfortable with the idea of having a youth pastor that's a girl....That is something that I've grown up [with] and I expect for a pastor to be a male pastor. But so as far as women in leadership as being a professor, or other things, I have no problem with that. (Interview, 2007)

Similar to the reading on male headship we saw in the previous section on biblical hermeneutics, Lucy Ann Williams and Lincoln Harjo, while not explicitly taking a position on the issue of male headship, do contend that these "problem passages" have been misused to mistreat women. Lincoln further postulates that these doctrinal boundaries on gender, as well as any other issue, hinder the working of God's spirit.
Lucy Ann Williams Harjo:

But as far as the female role, I think we as Christians have taken a lot of God's word and have made a lot of rules that maybe God did not intend. We have belittled women in a whole lot of ways throughout history. Throughout a lot of different cultures women are looked down upon, but if you look in his word you find women leading in a lot of different areas. But you still come back to these same Scriptures that talk of a women's role as married and stands behind her husband. But I think a lot of scripture from God's word is taken out of context, and Man has taken it according to his belief and what he is taught and he applies it to what he thinks it ought to be. But I don't think God has intended women to be dirt in some countries, to be beaten, killed, and still obey. I think that women have a previous calling and most women don't know that, because they bring a lot of emotion into whatever their gifts are, and they bring a lot of heart, their willingness to serve, and they bring a lot of traits that men don't have. (Interview, 2007)

Lincoln Harjo:

When God said he created us equally, I really think he meant that. And no one should treat another, whether female or male, any differently. We're all just as special to God as the next person. I think doctrine has gotten in the way. A lot of time, Paul is used to say the women should be silent and all that. But people take that out of context because they need to realize that was under the Jewish religion, under the Hebrew religion, that women could not speak in church. A lot of early churches back then, women were kind of formed under that context. That didn't mean they couldn't speak, but it had to be under the husband's covering to speak in a synagogue or whatever. And that's been blown out of context. Because if you look all through the Old and New Testament where women are featured well above what men would be normally featured as being a leader. Deborah, Esther, Rebecca, those are some big time leaders of Israel, and [in the] New Testament you see some of the most powerful testimonials. Mary Magdalene, Martha, Mary mother of Jesus—they had more faith than even the disciples because they were the first ones at the tomb, were two women because they believed that their master was important; they were the first ones to find out—it wasn't the men because they were back home afraid of what the religious crowds would do to them. Religion is vastly different than believe and knowing God, God is a person, and knowing him is a relationship, it's not a rule or a doctrine, because like I said all those things try to lock it into a box. (Interview, 2007)

It seems that, as in mainstream evangelicalism, there is a greater a tendency to support egalitarian positions among Natives rooted in Charismatic Christianity. What is distinct in Native evangelicalism, however, is that many evangelicals who do support more egalitarian positions often reference the fact that their Native traditions were generally more egalitarian prior to colonization. This reference point contributes to their position that gender inequality in the church is thus more a result of European patriarchal values than biblical values, as Cheryl Bear and David Bird state.

Cheryl Bear:

And way back, originally, women and men had much more of a partnership with our people historically, and so I think that part of the colonization
effect is that women have been subjected to same things that they have in
Western culture, and our Native women have been oppressed in our situation and sort of rules popped up that women are not equal or welcome in
certain places or whatever, and I don't think it was historically so. In some
instances, I was told by some elders that women were treated better, and
where I am from it's a matrilineal society so women tend to have a bit more
of a voice in the tribe. We don't have anything like [male headship] in the
marriage. (Interview, 2007)

David Bird:

I never had a problem; I always promoted equality. Where I'm from, we
always had women pastors, teachers; women always had a role in society.
It has changed. Even from what I understand of First Nation's traditional
understanding, women always had a place of honor; it wasn't a male dominated society. People needed to work together—especially to survive in
this land, you needed to work together. So we see how Jesus does relate to
women, a more healthy way than society around him was, so that should
make men who live in a male-dominated society to think. There needs to
be a mutual respect here and that women do have a place of respect and
honor and equality. Even in the creation story, Eve is created second but
she is created out of Adam's side. They are supposed to walk side by side,
be together and work together. And although it is translated that Eve is supposed to be the helper, I think that's a mistranslation. They are supposed to
work together to accomplish whatever there is to do together as a married
couple. So the thing is that God's most beautiful creation is not the man, it's
the woman, who is last of all his created order, that's the last one. (Interview,
2007)

Similarly, Ray Aldred argues that patriarchy is the result of mainstream
cultural values rather biblical values. "I think at this point in my life, men
and women are equal, but I also recognize that it is a male-dominated
world, and I'd be goofy if I didn't think that it's harder for my daughters
than it is for my sons, and it's harder for my wife then it is for me. So
I think a lot of times, the whole question about gender is more of a cultural
argument, not so much about what the Bible says" (interview, 2008).

Chebon Kernell and Marcus Briggs-Cloud concur that Native traditions were not patriarchal. However, rather than arguing that the Bible coincides with Native traditions on gender issues, they critique the Bible (or at least biblical interpretation) through the lens of Native traditions. Kernell seems to differentiate the Bible from God's will, at least in terms of how the Bible is classically interpreted.

The Bible does not instruct me on how to approach genders or my relationship with females. I think there has been an error in that interpretation. We really did not know what was going on then unless we were speaking Hebrew and living their lifetime. And so what I think has happened is that many people here today have misinterpreted those things such as relationship between man and woman, whether in marriage or in life. And also, in the letters of Paul where he instructs how to live life such as man should be the head of the household and things like that, I challenge every notion of that to its fullest and I use my Native ethos to challenge those ideas because one of the things that we are taught is to live in balance. The Creator would not want there to [be] an imbalance on earth and so there is supposed to be an equal balance between genders male and female, and that's something that permeated through our live[s] and ceremonies. And so I challenge some of those classical interpretations of men being in charge and controlling things when that's not, in my opinion, what God asks of the people. And so I think the Bible, it's been kind of hard to deconstruct what's already been constructed there through classical interpretation. (Interview, 2007)

Briggs-Cloud uses Native traditional values to critique the Bible, particularly Paul. In the end, however, he is not sure if the issue is Paul (who he says is not "indigenously friendly," or how Paul is interpreted.

So Paul writes, wives submit to your husbands—and most people build on that to say that men are the head of households and all that kind of stuff. But this is very contrary to Muskogee society where we are a matriarchal society where the women are the backbone of the community in the spiritual and political realm. Every clan seems to have a certain group of women they really look to for that kind of guidance. You can't have or achieve this sacredness without the male and the female coming together in a balanced sense. So when you look around in the world, men run the world, and this is why we are so out of balance. And you don't need a PhD to figure this out, my elders certainly don't. When I go to the churches and they talk about this, I say, just a friendly reminder, this isn't how we do things and they say—you pick, Christian or Indian way. It's all crap.

So the way that I see, you know, Paul, is not the most indigenously friendly person. (Interview, 2007)

Cheryl Bear suggests that following God's will requires that women not be closed off to particular positions in the church. Bear relates how her call to be a pastor shaped her understanding of the Bible's position on women's leadership.

I never knew that the Bible had anything to say about women. I had these preconceived ideas about what my job could be. I thought the highest I could attain to would be a pastor's wife, and then when I got married, my husband said you have to be a pastor with me. I think that would be a good thing, I have feeling you are called to this. I was interested but not sold on it, and when I started going to Bible school I went to Life Bible College of Canada. They were very big on encouraging women to be equal partners in the work of the kingdom, and so, that was exciting. I was very encouraged by the Bible specifically where Jesus elevates the status of women, almost every encounter where he meets with women, he speaks to her: when rabbis are not supposed to speak to women, he teaches women; when women are not supposed to be taught, and he forgives the adulterous women; and just all of these instances. Especially with Martha and Mary, I think we misinterpret that a lot and we think, oh we shouldn't be busybodies like Martha, we should be more attentive like Mary. But Mary was sitting in a position of a disciple at the feet of Jesus, and that was no place for a woman. So when Martha comes out and says, Jesus, Mary should be helping me in the kitchen, everyone in the room would have said yeah that's true, according to our culture. She shouldn't be on the floor at Jesus' feet; she should be in her place. And Jesus says, Mary has chosen the better way. And so he's teaching a woman, and it just goes on, the Bible just affirming the place of women in leadership. I think that can also inform some of our Native traditions. (Interview, 2007)

Anita Keith further argues that restricting women to particular roles in the church actually amounts to disobedience to God's will.

The Scripture doesn't teach us—here is your role, although we have some general roles—it's, be obedient and wait, you lay your whole life down and you press it into service. And when He commissions you, you go and do.

I love to live in that freedom, and a church environment that allows that. Because there is a lot of churches that don't allow women to be, so how could you ever listen to God and get a commission from him if the Church says only men in leadership and women are down here? How can the Spirit press you into service? You can't because you are chained. (Interview, 2007)

While many Native evangelicals support gender equality, they also often support the idea that there are distinct roles and characteristics of each gender. Roger Boyer, for instance, talks of the complementary nature of male and female roles, and notes that while he supports women's leadership in the church, he believes that in traditional ceremonial life, some roles are designated for men and some for women.

We are two halves before marriage, and then we leave mother and father and become one, I don't understand that mystery, but I do understand the importance of having my wife help me, because there are some areas of my life that are void without her input, compassion, empathy understanding, discernment, all those emotional aspects. Now I do believe that amongst First Nation traditions, that singing circles and drumming is for men, there are some rites of passage and rituals that we do that are for men only. But, as we've said in the past, those are for men only, but it doesn't hinder women from having their own ceremonies. They have their own stuff, but it doesn't mean that men can't help with that process, stand on the outside and watch and help with the experience. So some ceremonies are gender specific and some aren't. I respect that because I do believe that Christ deals with men differently then he would with women. And I guess what my meaning behind "deal with" is to walk or talk or communicate or correct with, I think it's different for men and for women and we need to understand that as well. But again, it's not to say men are from Mars or women are from Venus, but it's to say that we communicate differently. (Interview, 2007)

In this respect, he echoes the sentiments of some Native feminists who argue that having a separation of gender roles in Native ceremonial life is not patriarchal per se because both men's and women's gender roles are equally respected (Smith 2008).

As is discussed in the next section, the general consensus that women and men do have distinct roles, then, shapes Native evangelical discourse on homosexuality.

Much of the controversy around evangelicals within mainstream society has to do with the positions they typically hold on what Chebon Kernell terms "hot-button issues," such as abortion and homosexuality. On one hand, it seems generally to be the case that Native evangelicals, as with evangelicals as a whole, agree that homosexuality and abortion are contrary to biblical principles. As Shaunday Little states: "Abortions, I believe it's wrong. Once that seed is inserted into the egg, it's alive, and I believe with abortion you are killing a human being and that's not right. And homophobia [*sic*], I believe that's wrong; it's every man for women and women for man, not man for man or women for women" (interview, 2007). However, there is some dissent within evangelical circles, as can be seen in the growth of the evangelical LGBT movement. In addition, the 2008 presidential campaign of Barack Obama has begun to shed light on some of the shifts and variations even within anti-gay or pro-life evangelical communities. For instance, Frank Schaeffer, the son of Francis Shaeffer (who was one of the founders of the evangelical pro-life movement) endorsed Obama, arguing that Obama's economic policies would reduce poverty and thus lead to fewer abortions than would McCain's stated pro-life policy.

Within Native evangelicalism, we also see variations in analysis around these hot-button issues. Martin Yazzie suggests that the increased visibility of homosexuality is foretold in the Bible as a possible harbinger of the End Days.

> Everything is coming the way it was said it was going to come. For example, the gay people, everyone is gonna love their own sex, and you can't really judge them. Things that are happening now, that's been mentioned [in the Bible]—children killing their parents, children losing respect for their parents. It comes back to what the Bible says, what He said. He has all these prophecies that tell you exactly what is going to happen and to be prepared. (Interview, 2007)

Many Native evangelicals, while arguing that homosexuality and abortion are antibiblical, stress the importance of loving responses to these issues. MacDonald contends that in the case of abortion, it is important to provide support to women who have unwanted pregnancies rather than protest abortion clinics. He also suggests that many people may become entrenched in homosexuality either because of prior abuse or because they are ostracized if their demeanor does not match stereotypical gender performances. So he suggests that the best way to address what he sees as antibiblical behavior is to address the causes that give rise to these behaviors in the first place, by ending abuse and showing respect to peoples who might perform gender differently.

I don't really want to talk about it, this person became pregnant through their father or uncle or cousin, but that life that was created is something that was special. But a Biblical response would be to help support that mother, that orphan, as much as we possibly can. I do feel uncomfortable holding up signs that say abortion sucks, and all these people giving you the finger as they drive by. Instead, we should be saying, how can we help you and show the loving side of not agreeing with abortion.

Homosexuality is an unspoken thing on reserves. It's there, and I don't agree with that. But I suspect that a lot of people who have gotten into homosexuality have been abused. Also I know that there are a lot of people, like women that look manly and men who have delicate features. Sometimes, we make fun of those people and they think, that's probably who I should be anyways. And I really feel that God isn't someone who is just shaking their finger at us, and saying you shouldn't do this or do that. I feel that He is really wanting us to be free from the things that are going to hurt us and he's going to want us to really enjoy life to the full, and that's my perspective. (Interview, 2007)

Roger Boyer describes how his position has shifted in relationship to his aunt, who is gay. He has learned to stress being compassionate rather than judgmental on this issue.

In the area of homosexuality, that's really close to home. My aunty is two spirited, walking two paths. At first, it was really difficult for me as a young man to know that my aunt was walking this pathway. From what I've heard about from elders, there wasn't a whole lot of that going on before. From hearing her story, it's about abuse from men. And so when she says, I've tried to love men, and I've only been let down, abused, and beat up, and so that's part of her story. And before I would have just said that's just your excuse, but now I understand that's part of her story, that's turning on the light, that's real. So honestly I believe that the people who bash homosexuality, it's from lack of understanding, it's ignorance.

Now from my perspective, it is a chosen lifestyle. I do believe in the sanctity of marriage. I believe Creator meant for man to be with woman and no\where do I believe that woman should be with a woman in that way. But for my aunty it's been loving her from where she's at and saying I know you've chosen this path, but you're my aunty, and I'm ok with it. But you're still my aunty, you're my blood, the blood that runs in your veins is the same that runs in mine and I'm ok, and willing to walk with you on this. I don't agree with you; I don't validate this pathway because I don't believe that's the pathway of our people. But I will walk with you. When I see some of the things in the media about these pastors bashing these people, telling them they are going to hell, telling them that they are sinners and condemning them, I look at that and I go, that's not Jesus. That's the spirit of the oppressor or the colonizer, saying that because you are different you are damned. (Interview, 2007)

Similarly, Lucy Ann Williams Harjo's friendship with people who are gay contributes to her unwillingness to judge them.

But I grew up with homosexuals and they are good friends of mine, they are awfully funny, the ones from the reservation, I mean. When I think of a homosexual I think of the reservation, because they were so funny and I smile. But based on God's word, God loves them without even a second thought, and if God loves them, why should I judge them? God loves me even though I haven't had a perfect life, I've seen a lot and been through a lot, who am I to judge? I know that his word is teaching me to love people regardless, to be patient and treat people like how he would treat them. That's what I believe. (Interview, 2007)

David Bird similarly argues for treating women who have abortions with respect and compassion.

With abortion, it's another difficult issue. I always speak against abortion. Even in First Nation society, it's just not something we did. We always tried to give birth, pregnancy regardless. But treat people with respect. If they've gone through the abortion, you still got to treat them and help them walk through it because there is actually a loss, and there is a lot of grieving involved with that. A lot of condemnation comes on a person who has gone through an abortion, especially where I come from in Saskatchewan, it's a real conservative society. People make mistakes and errors in life. And maybe some people would do things differently if given different opportunities, a different chance. (Interview, 2007)

Adrian Jacobs, in his proposed constitution for Aboriginal churches, proposes the following language for prospective churches: Each member must

> 6) commit in writing to a Membership Covenant that declares:
>   a) Sex outside of marriage is sinful, including; fornication, adultery, homosexuality, and premarital. Members agree to live a holy life in this regard and agree that failure to do so accompanied with a non-repentant attitude or failure to be accountable can result in dismissal from membership. (Jacobs 1999, 34)

Others stress the importance of recognizing that, while homosexuality and abortion are sins, one should not elevate these sins over other sins.
Ray Aldred:

> Inevitably, evangelicals tend to reduce morality to abortion and gay marriage, but there are all these other moral issues they say nothing about, like unemployment. (Interview, 2008)

Terry LeBlanc:

> Whether it's taking of a life or whether sexual misconduct of any sort, I believe it is dishonoring the image of God in us. I don't think it's a good thing to create a hierarchy of sin. (Interview, 2007)

David Bird:

> Homosexuality, we always try to be very respectful of the person who has that lifestyle. I know there is some debate about how homosexual lifestyle begins. Even in Native traditions, these individuals like this would rise up every now and then, and they were considered people who walked in two worlds. So they were treated with a lot of respect and treated with a lot of hesitancy. I believe the Bible defines homosexuality as sin. But it also defines murder as sin. But we don't shun murderers as much as we would to a homosexual which is just so not right. (Interview, 2007)

Lincoln Harjo:

> To a certain degree, I believe that abortion is wrong, basically. I am not going to force my position onto someone, but I'm not going to judge them

and treat them like they are the worst person to ever be processed on this planet. But the way I look at it, once life has been started whether at conception or down the road, what right does anyone else have to destroy that life?

Homosexuality, I say it's wrong. A union between a man and a woman is natural. Personally I believe [homosexuality] is wrong, but I believe being fat is wrong too. I believe any sexually perverse activity of any kind, whether it's adult fornication. God says all sin is sin. (Interview, 2007)

David Bird notes that his approach was not always well accepted by other Christians. They wanted him to "just come down hard." His critics thought, " Preach it the way the Bible almost spells it out, homosexuality is sin and therefore sin means hell." Jennifer and Janine LeBlanc suggest that while homosexuality is a sin, it is not necessary to condemn people who are gay. Rather, it is important to demonstrate God's love to them, so that God can begin to act in their lives and show them how their lives need to change. Janine in particular does not think homosexuality precludes one from being a Christian, but both agree that if one begins to follow Christ, one's lifestyle will change in accordance with God's will. Consequently, condemnatory attitudes on the part of Christians can drive people away from the church, thereby making it more difficult for people who are gay to have their lifestyles challenged by God's spirit.

Jennifer LeBlanc:

And I think in regards to being a gay Christian, or a Christian that has an abortion, I think you will start to question things once you start getting into a deeper faith in Christ. In a community people can help you look at that through the lens of scripture; through community, Christ and Holy Spirit will speak to you. Janine and I in our early university years, we had lots of gay and lesbians friends; not my persuasion, but we had very good friends that I still hold dear and I still have a very few friends who I will never discard because of who they choose to be sexually. I don't agree with their lifestyle; I think there is a better way for them to live in community and be loved and I hope some time they come to Christ and that would be awesome. I'm never going to leave their life because I could be an instrument in their life, showing them the way of Christ. I think when we get into those exclusionist things; exclude people just because of sexuality, drugs, race or gender. Then you're also just choosing to just not to be the person Christ has made you to be in their life. (Interview, 2007)

Janine LeBlanc:

God will start to speak with you in that context in different things, may
start to challenge you, about your lifestyle, but I don't think that excludes
you from being a Christian and knowing Creator and God and having a
real relationship with Christ. I think God is going to work with you where
you're at, and if that's where you're at, then great. The whole issue, going
back to homosexuality, and women who have had abortions, we've othered
people so much in the Church, we've pushed people out, and I don't think
the church has a great theology of that. And we're missing out on an opportunity for Christ. And it's not like we're saying that people are defined by
these issues, like gay, but that these are people and we are missing having
relationships with people, because we are excluding and othering people.
The church, I see it very much that way. (Interview, 2007)

Interestingly, while arguing that homosexuality and abortions are unbibli-
cal, Jennifer states that she does not approve of using the Bible to support
public policies on these issues. She contends such strategies are unhelpful
and divisive.

I think when we make stance on those issues, especially in the United States,
it's so popular to use Scripture in those political ways. What I see especially
in the South, it's like no, I will not use scripture politically, because what
I see with these hot button issues, one stands on this side and one on the
other side, and it's divisive. (Interview, 2007)

On the issue of abortion specifically, many Native evangelicals uphold
that abortion is in as contrary to Native values as it is contrary to biblical
principles.
Douglas MacDonald:

Well abortion is a no-no in the Native community, life is important, however
it came, but life is really important. (Interview, 2007)

Roger Boyer:

I talk about what our people as Ojibwe say, that life is sacred, life is a gift
from Creator. So for me it's not scriptural, it's a traditional thing where
I stand on abortion and how I deal with it. (Interview, 2007)

Cheryl Bear states that abortion and homosexuality are not acceptable from a biblical perspective, but interestingly upholds the importance of "choice":

> As far as the abortion issue, I'd like to see children being born, raised, or given through adoption. That would be the highest goal for women. And I say that as well, as a woman, I do appreciate a need for a woman to have choice, and to have control over her own body and so I do understand that. I wish that we could somehow help and just have more information on the dangers of abortion and how traumatic it is, because I've never heard of a woman who had an abortion and said, I never thought about it again. I've heard the opposite; where it's just this haunting experience that never leaves them and causes depression and great emotional upheaval. And so I want to respect people's choices. With homosexuality, it is their choice. Everyone has the right to choose how they are going to live their life. I, as another human being, don't feel I have any right to tell them you cannot be what you want to be. And so that is a stand that I feel like I need to take as a human being. And the Bible talks about these things not being ok, and so I think that the way God created us was a man and a woman to be together. I think they are human beings and everyone needs love. (Interview, 2007)

Meanwhile, Chebon Kernell suggests that the Bible does not necessarily have clear positions on abortion or homosexuality. He contends that many political positions that are purportedly based on the Bible are shaped more by mainstream evangelical discourse than by what the Bible actually says. He suggests alternatively that these issues be addressed under a more general biblical hermeneutic of social justice.

> The Bible, probably, is I would say minimally helpful in determining political positions. I know I always laugh when I'm jogging down the road and I see a car that passes me that says "I vote by the Book" with a Bible on the back, and I'm just like, oh, ok. First of all we have to realize how we Native people have been taught to interpret the Bible. We were in essence told what to think about the Bible, we were in essence told, this is how it is, and this is how God wants you to view it and to not do that would be sinful. And that is something that is very prominent in Native churches today, so much so that we don't question what is going on in here.
>
> And so when we ask if that Bible is helpful, I think in certain contexts it is, when I think about the social justice nature of Jesus as the

Christ, I think it's very motivating. But when the hot button topics come up such as homosexuality, abortion, and things like that, I don't know if they would be helpful for myself. I would use the interpretation of social justice to approach those topics as opposed to classical ways of interpreting. (Interview, 2007)

And while Briggs-Cloud describes himself as "anti-abortion in all capacities," on the basis of his traditional as well as biblical beliefs, on the issue of homosexuality, his traditional values conflict with what he sees as the more evangelical biblical stance.

There is a verse that pretty bluntly states that homosexuality is wrong. For most fundamentalists, this is very wrong, but for my people, we call it "half man half woman." They can see a male and female side. They are blessings to our people; they are our medicine people. They are gifts to the creator that bring prophecy and revelation to the community. Our gay people are groomed from the time they are young. They recognize at a young age they are this way. They drink from their own cups, own utensils, they don't play with other boys, they are groomed to stay in touch with the sacred, just like any other medicine person. I know they are victims of this oppression of being part of a minority group and I can definitely relate to that, but in our society, it's not something that creates an imbalance in our community, it's a blessing. The problem is, Christianity has influenced our people in a fundamentalist way that this is very wrong.

There is an elder woman who pouring her heart out on how hard it is for her to accept that her son is gay. She bluntly told me that she knows that he'll burn in hell but while she is here with him she wants to love him and know him. So she can't turn her back. I'm like, what motivates you to form this conclusion about your son? Obviously, you're not following traditional ways. This is a woman who is full-blood and fluent speaking, raised at the ceremonial ground. But her grandmother said you have to pick, the ground or the church, and she chose the church but her sister chose the ground. And I just feel for her so much. She's been lied to, people took Scripture and they manipulated it to socially control the people how they felt was appropriate, and now it's created domestic problems. And this will affect his whole life psychologically. She couldn't accept him as a Muskogee, and he will never know his responsibility as a gay man in Muskogee society, because the only teaching he's been exposed to is Christianity. He doesn't even know that to be a gay person is a blessing. (Interview, 2007)

Conclusion

Within Native studies, Christianization has generally been equated with assimilation. The germinal works of Robert Warrior's previously mentioned essay, "Canaanites, Cowboys, and Indians," and Vine Deloria's *God is Red* both posited an absolute incommensurability between Native spiritual traditions and Christianity. These works have often taken an almost canonical status in religious studies, thereby reifying the notion that Native Christians are more assimilated than traditional ones. Of course, since these works were originally published, biblical and religious scholars have increasingly engaged poststructuralist and postcolonial theory which challenges notions of textual determinacy that seem to undergird Warrior's and Deloria's analysis. As Itumeleng Mosala argues, the Bible and other forms of theological discourse are never fixed and always subject to contestation. "It is not enough to recognize text as ideology. Interpretations of texts do alter the texts. Contrary to Warrior's argument, texts are signifying practices and therefore they exist ideologically and permanently problematically" (Mosala 1989, 158). Mosala's approach suggests that theological discourse is never simply liberatory or oppressive, but that oppressed groups can engage in to wrest it away from paradigms set up dominating classes in order to further liberatory struggles. Or, to quote African theologian Emmanuel Martey: "Unlike Audre Lorde, who might be wondering whether the master's tools could indeed be used to dismantle the master's house, African theologians are fully convinced that the gun, in efficient hands, could well kill its owner" (Martey 1994, 46).

Now, there are increasingly greater numbers of works that posit a more complicated relationship between Native peoples and Christianity, but still, relatively few of these focus on evangelical Christians, who are still seen as hopelessly reactionary. In fact, even though I myself am an evangelical, I often imagined that I (as do many of the interviewees in this chapter) must be one of the very few evangelicals who share my set of political and social views. Perhaps because I had learned to be quiet about my viewpoint in evangelical settings, I was not always able to find others who might agree with me. While I realized that evangelicals, like everyone else, are entirely more complicated than they are represented or than they may represent themselves, I was awakened to my own conceptual limitations when I begun this research.

Three individuals described in this chapter—Richard Twiss, Randy Woodley, and Terry LeBlanc—read an earlier article I wrote on the public writings of Native peoples in the Promise Keepers movement.

Although this chapter focused on the progressive sectors within Native evangelicalism, these individuals called me to account for minimizing their commitments to social and political justice. In other words, they were even more progressive than I had realized. Borrowing from James Scott, it is clear that when we only look at the public transcripts of Native evangelical discourse in which leaders are forced to make strategic interventions within landscapes not of their own choosing, we may miss what may be very radical politically that can be found only in the private transcripts. Stereotypes and assumptions can keep us (and I include myself in this category) from pursuing relationships with those that might actually share political visions that are more similar to ours than we might have guessed.

Thus, while adherence to the Bible has come to mean an unthinking reactionary position on political, social, and theological issues, this chapter demonstrates that because evangelicals having an ongoing relationship with what they see as the living word of God, the Bible can open up new ways of looking at the world as much as it may close them down. Many of the theological positions articulated in this chapter speak to how Native evangelicals have diverse perspectives on a variety of issues. But also, individuals shift as their faith grows and develops.

This chapter also calls into question the manner in which the Bible is singled out as a policing strategy or a rhetorical weapon against political or spiritual dissent. While the Bible frequently does serve in that function, it is clear that many other tropes do as well. For instance, while many evangelicals would oppose homosexuality on the basis of the Bible, it is also true that, for instance, the Navajo nation banned same-sex marriage, but used tradition as the basis for their ban. What this signals is that our attention should be drawn less to the particular object that gets used as a policing strategy, and more to the policing strategy itself. In addition, if we focus only on how the Bible is used as a weapon to support oppression, we fail to account for how diverse communities also use the Bible to resist oppression. As Ray Aldred argues, the Bible is only interpreted within the context of community—the community by definition being unstable and ever changing. Thus, regardless of the transcendence evangelicals attach to biblical meaning, this meaning cannot be discerned outside the immanence of a community with its ever-changing complexities and contradiction.

Hopefully, this chapter also makes an intervention into the "vanishing Indian" discourse that pervades mainstream scholarship and analysis. In particular, to cite Anne McClintock, Indigenous peoples are seen as occupying "anachronistic space" that is always a prior, primitive state to modernity (McClintock 1995). Because Native peoples within the colonial imaginary are always seen as necessarily anterior to civilization, when they engage in postcontact practices (like Christian evangelicalism), they are necessarily marked as inauthentic Natives. Any engagement with contemporary society marks Native peoples as somehow contaminated. Furthermore, within this colonial logic, Native primitiveness cannot engage modernity without fundamentally becoming inauthentic because Nativeness is fundamentally already constructed as the "other" of Western subjectivity. To use da Silva's phrase, Native peoples are thus inevitably positioned at the "horizon of death" (da Silva 2007, 27). This work seeks to intervene in this primitivizing discourse by demonstrating how Native identities are expansive and ever changing—they can be informed by and inform multiple theoretical perspectives while retaining their integrity.

Thus, this chapter engages in what Audra Simpson terms "ethnographic refusal." That is, within mainstream academia, Native Studies is in the position of what I term "ethnographic entrapment." That is, Native peoples are seen as the containers of "truth" which must be unveiled. They cannot be those who tell truths. In this chapter, I aim less to make generalizable claims about Native evangelicals, than to point to how they are theorizing their own truths. My goal is not to present Native evangelicals as an ethnographic community but to represent Native evangelicals as producers of theory and analyses in their own right. Their theorization is particularly important at this current historical juncture as the election of Barack Obama has highlighted the shifting political allegiances within evangelical communities, particularly communities of color. The analysis proffered by Native evangelicals can point to how allegiances can be created and reshaped, and how political, social, and religious boundaries can be reformed in the future, not just for Native peoples, but for everyone.

Notes

1. For sources on boarding schools, see www.boardingschoolhealingproject.org or see A. Smith, *Conquest.*

2. The text of Robert Francis's talk can be found on the Mid American Indian Fellowships website, http://www.midamericanindianfellowships.org/PDF/DCRS%20 1%20Colonization%20Weapons%20Gifts%20Diseases%20Medicine.pdf.

3. See Lindsell, *Battle of the Bible*; this was one of the most influential books espousing this point of view. Lindsell argues that the Bible "does not contain error of any kind, including scientific and historical facts." See also the Chicago Statement on Biblical Hermeneutics, in Earl Radmacher and Robert Preus (eds.), *Hermeneutics, Inerrancy and the Bible* (Grand Rapids, MI: Zondervan, 1984).

4. See Donald Bloesch, *Essentials of Evangelical Theology*; Fuller, "On Relevation and Biblical Authority"; and Hubbard, *What We Evangelicals Believe*.

5. See Beegle, *Scripture*.

CHAPTER 2 | Scriptures as Sundials in African American Lives

VELMA E. LOVE

Introduction

The sun cast a beam of light on the dial and created a shadow by which the ancients were able to tell the time of day and thereby order their lives. As we move about our contemporary worlds of lights and shadows, perhaps scriptures function in somewhat the same way, for the scriptures of a people reflect the social environment and register the emotional climate at any given moment. How, then, might a reading of scriptures in America also reflect a reading of America? What can the script(ure)s of a people tell us about who they are, where they have been, and where they are going? Wesley Kort reminds us that "because the texts that constitute a person's scriptures are primary for the world they support, those texts hold the potential to sustain or reconfigure that world when it has in part been disconfirmed or at points found to be unsatisfactory or unworkable."[1]

This chapter explores some of the ways in which the texts that have become scriptures in African American lives have functioned to sustain or reconfigure worlds. As part of a larger research report of scripturalizing practices of five communities of color, this chapter offers responses to six core questions:

1) How has the community's self-naming/understanding evolved over time from its historical origins?
2) What are the origins, influences, typical settings, dynamics, and principal performers of this community's scripturalizing practices?

3) What are some historical and current forms of expressiveness through which, and in relation to which, the scripturalizing practices are carried out?
4) What psychosocial and sociocultural benefits do practitioners derive from their persistent relating to scriptures?
5) What are the special themes and issues and problems that have historically been associated with this community and communicated through its scripturalizing?
6) What are the pitfalls, opportunities, and larger implications reflected in these questions and the approaches and assumptions behind them?

We crafted a framework for exploring responses to these questions within our research data with theoretical tools provided by Charles Long's three perspectives for the study of African American religion, that is, "Africa as historical reality and religious image, involuntary presence in America, and the experience and symbol of God." Our goal is to shed light on the social functions of scriptures in African American religious consciousness.[2] In pursuit of this goal we look at sacred story as expressed in personal and public narrative as well as the expressive arts, beginning with a historical overview that helps situate African American orientations to scripture. We continue with the weaving of a thematic tapestry that reflects an improvisational and adaptive response to the abrupt removal of a people from their cultural homeland. These diverse and intense efforts to repair a torn cultural landscape are informed by script(ure)s whether oral, written, or embodied in the lives of those whose *cultural* identity started as African and through various mutations became "colored," "negro," "black," and Afro-American and African American.

Methodology

The purpose of this study, to examine African American engagements of scriptures and the psychosocial and political consequences and implications of such engagements, dictated the methodology: a mixed-method qualitative research design, including qualitative interviews, focus groups, participant observation, and document analysis. Research sites included Tallahassee, Florida, and Atlanta, Georgia. The population sample included college and seminary students as well as members of local community religious organizations, including the Tallahassee and Atlanta chapters of the African Hebrew Israelites and several local churches. The ethnographic data collected included transcripts from fifteen interviews (eight men and seven women, ranging in age from 21 to 60) and four focus groups, each composed of 5–12 college and seminary students ranging in age from 19 to 40, for a total of 31 focus-group participants. Participant observer researchers also gathered data by attending study groups, meetings, and worship services and analyzing primary source documents available from the sponsoring organizations. These methods have proven to be effective and appropriate for a study of the "relationality" and "performativity" of scriptures in contemporary African American culture.

The life-story interview provided an opportunity for participants to tell their personal stories and by self-report provide a window into the ways in which they narrated the development of a religious conscious-ness that reflects worldview and self-understanding. The interview proto-col focused on questions related to birth and family of origin, education and culture, inner spiritual life, religious practices, and engagements with sacred texts. Placing the questions about sacred texts and religious orientation in the context of the participants' life stories enhanced the likelihood of authentic response and also provided a more textured and in-depth understanding of the elements related to the development of reli-gious consciousness. Telling one's life story is also of value to the indi-vidual, for the process of relaying the story and reporting the experience dictates a level of clarity and reflective attention.[3] The life story itself becomes a sacred text, and the researcher begins to see the archetypal patterns, themes, and motifs of a larger human story reflected in the indi-vidual life as lived and reported.

The focus group, as another qualitative tool, not only allows the researcher to hear several stories simultaneously but also to benefit from the interaction of members of the group. This strategy is particularly appropriate for the nature of this study because one's religious orientation is strongly impacted by social context. Community flourishes in similarity of religious belief. Observing focus-group members react to each other's ideas, though in a contrived setting, simulates some of the dynamics of religious community. Focus-group participants are often very aware of how they are perceived by other members of the group. This heightened level of self-consciousness likewise exists in religious communities. The focus group, then, provides an opportunity not only to collect a concen-trated amount of data on a specific topic but also to observe the interac-tive discussions on topics that often generate intense feelings and strong disagreements.

By the same token, participant observation is an intimate way of learning. The researcher in the midst of a worship service, a religious ritual, a group Bible study, or among the patrons in a local restaurant, has the benefit of a first-hand experience, which itself lends texture and thick description to the phenomenon under consideration. Participant observation provides the researcher with the sights, sounds, smells, and feelings from which sensory scholarship can emerge. Although some of what our researchers saw and heard may have stimulated diverse reactions, this intimate way of knowing provided a form of knowledge available no other way.

It also helped researchers recognize and acknowledge the subjective nature of the ethnographic gaze.

The "church of art" signs in Missionary Mary's yard, the Primitive Baptist Church preacher walking across the pews and grabbing the hands of congregants from the homeless shelter down the street, the group of African Hebrew Israelites meeting in the back of the vegetarian restaurant in Atlanta, the bowed heads of black college students gathered around "the flame of knowledge" for prayer, the stage actors performing "sweet father divine" scenes from the play *Crumbs From the Table of Joy*,[4] are powerful images that speak volumes about religious sensibilities and the social function of sacred texts in African American culture. These images come directly from participant observation activities. Document analysis rounds out the research design. We examined audio recordings, websites, and print materials from the African Hebrew Israelites and St. Mary's Primitive Baptist Church and coded these materials for scriptural references and prevalent themes reflecting worldview and self-understanding. Our examination of online sources included the African American Lectionary, a liturgical and special events calendar established in 2006, with relevant scriptural references, contextual commentaries, and cultural source materials for use by pastors and other religious leaders in preparing sermons, ceremonies, and special programs. Data gathered from the African American Lectionary helped shed light on preaching as a scripturalizing practice in contemporary African American culture.

How has the community's self-naming/-understanding evolved over time from its historical origins?

Any examination of the historical backdrop for contemporary African American engagements with scriptures must begin with Africa as the point of departure, as Vincent Wimbush and Charles Long, both historians of religion, suggest.[5] Helpful for this analysis are Wimbush's discussion of the Bible as a language world and his concentric circle schema of six "readings," beginning with Africa as the center of the circle and continuing with five additional "readings," each representing a broad social movement reflecting the social functions of the Bible in African American culture.[6] As Wimbush notes, how strange it must have seemed when the missionary invaders came with their holy book, insisting that it and it alone was the source of sacred knowledge. Scholars of African culture remind us that in the African mind sacred energy infuses all things. Wisdom is elemental and radiates from the one consciousness through all and in all, suggesting that the African worldview lends itself to expansive and multiple expressions of God.[7] In their thinking, the experience and symbol of God cannot be restricted to the words contained in one book. This is the lens through which the enslaved Africans began to view the Protestant scriptures. Reflecting on the long passage of the enslaved from an African homeland to an alien American land, Howard Thurman mused, "How does the human spirit accommodate itself to desolation? How did they? What tools of the spirit were in their hands with which to cut a path through the wilderness of their despair?"[8] Their bodily memories became tools of the spirit, and over time they fashioned new scriptures and new languages from which to create for themselves a world anew.

Wimbush's next circle, reading two, changes the focus from Africa to the New World, to the United States of America, in particular. He labels this period in the eighteenth century as the beginning of a kind of African American folk religious ethos, with Africans converting to Christianity in significant numbers. The Africans learned from the enslavers that each person had a degree of freedom in interpreting the Bible. They could embrace certain parts and ignore others; thus the Bible became a language world, a means of communicating about their experiences, their challenges, their hopes and dreams. The Bible became a centering point around which social solidarity was created. The interpretive lens was one of psychosocial and physical trauma. The people could identify with the heroic characters of the Hebrew scriptures and the long-suffering but victorious Christ of the New Testament scriptures, and with these scripts they could rewrite their own imaginative possibilities.[9]

As Wimbush notes, the third reading, covering the early to mid-nineteenth century is characterized by black folks engaged in public debate about the economy, morality, and the politics of slavery. Various readings of the Bible during this period reflected both integrationist and radical nationalist orientations and points in between. The use of a key passage from the New Testament (Gal. 3:28), "There is neither Jew nor Greek, there is neither slave nor free. There is neither male nor female; for you are all one in Christ Jesus," engaged the Bible as a means of taking the social consciousness of America to task.[10] By the same token, free blacks, such as David Walker, used the Christian scriptures to appeal to the conscience of America, calling for the abolition of slavery. David Walker's Appeal in 1829 reflects a "reading" of scripture as a simultaneous "reading" of America. Walker calls into question the moral consciousness of America and points to the inherent contradictions in the Christian precepts and the treatment of the enslaved Africans.[11] His observation is a recurring theme in later African American scriptural readings.

Moving forward to America's urban centers in the early twentieth century, we find new religious formations in response to the challenges of urban life. The Holiness and Pentecostal groups developed. The Garvey Movement, Father Divine, the Black Jews, and the Nation of Islam emerged. These groups remixed or reformulated traditional forms, consulting the holy books to solve their personal problems. They embraced an interest in esoteric knowledge and expressed disdain for the mainstream church organization. Their sacred texts functioned as mythic, ideological, building blocks, and fueled an empowered and reinvented self. If reading three was characterized by relative acceptance, then reading four was the opposite. It represented a radical psychosocial stance.[12] Miles Mark Fisher, Professor of History at Shaw University in Raleigh, North Carolina, and pastor of White Rock Baptist Church in Durham, noted the changing religious landscape, with non-mainstream groups, referred to as "cults," becoming more prominent during this time. These groups provided social services for the community, often included racially mixed congregations, and were accepting of women in leadership roles.

Although each historical period was marked by diversity in scriptural interpretations, all these "readings" reflect a religious consciousness clearly linked to the African American social and historical experience. But a different phenomenon appears in the 1940s and 1950s, Wimbush notes, and a fundamentalist orientation surfaces, reflecting a step outside the circle. How did this pivot point, this shift in consciousness come about and what does it mean? Wimbush suggests that this turn toward fundamentalism represents a "crisis of thinking, of security"; but why does this phenomenon continue to appear in contemporary African American religious sensibilities? Some have suggested that it is the psychological need for certainty. This sentiment is reflected in the following excerpt from literary giant Maya Angelou's memoir, *I Know Why the Caged Bird Sings*:

> Reverend Thomas took his text from Deuteronomy and I was stretched between loathing his voice and wanting to listen to the sermon. Deuteronomy was my favorite book in the Bible. The laws were so absolute, so clearly set down, that I knew if a person truly wanted to avoid hell and brimstone and being roasted forever in the devil's fire, all she had to do was memorize Deuteronomy and follow its teaching, word for word.[13]

This need for certainty also surfaces as a theme in the life stories of a number of individuals who participated in *this* study. One of the research associates, Renee K. Harrison, citing historical documents and contemporary narratives, argues that what Wimbush terms "a step outside the circle" is squarely within the circle and has existed from the earliest engagements with the Bible to the present day. The use of scriptures to commit violence against the self, psychologically damaging one's humanity and one's well-being, is a phenomenon that cannot be overlooked, and it has always existed, she insists, pointing to the following slave narrative excerpts as an example:

> Slavery in this country, taking everything into consideration, was a Godsend for the slaves. The twenty million Negroes are descended from four million sent over from Africa. If it had not been for the slave traffic, we would still be living in Africa. I would be a heathen and my children would be heathens. Out of bad comes good.[14]
>
> Now whether it is right, and lawful, in the sight of God for them to make slaves of us or not, I am certain that while we are slaves, it is our duty to obey our masters, in all their lawful commands, and mind them unless we are bid to do that which we know to be—sin, or forbidden in God's word. The apostle Paul says, "Servants be obedient to them that are your masters according to the flesh, with fear and trembling with singleness in our heart as unto Christ: Not with eye service, not as men pleasers, but as servants of Christ doing the will of God from the heart."[15]

These are but two of several examples cited by Harrison in support of her point that the fundamentalist interpretation was clearly in evidence in the nineteenth century, countering Wimbush's focus on the twentieth-century "step outside the circle." Additional citations come from the students she interviewed and are reported in subsequent discussions of current forms of scripturalizing practices.

Drawing special attention to the narratives of women, Wimbush asserts that "women have always made the circle true." Historically, African American women have called into question the true meaning of freedom in the context of religious practice, challenging those who denied women leadership positions and drawing upon their own knowledge of Spirit power to address social inequalities. We need only look at the contemporary writings of "womanist" scholars for evidence of this continued recognition of pain, suffering, and the engagement of scriptures to articulate the ongoing quest for a better life.[16]

African American naming and self-understanding are reflected in the ways in which the Bible has been interpreted and applied to everyday life experiences, from the earliest hearing/reading at the center of the circle through the period of enslavement in the nineteenth century and forward into the twenty-first century. There has always been diversity in interpretation, application, expression, practice, and affiliation. Not all African Americans embrace the biblical text, and those who do sometimes include it along with other sacred texts (verbal and written) that provide a scriptural function in their lives. A case in point is the First African Presbyterian Church in Atlanta, Georgia, where the pastor and many of the congregants have some level of initiation and affiliation with the Yoruba/Orisha tradition of West African origin. Along with the Christian and Hebrew scriptures, they also avail themselves of the Ifa/Odu, Yoruba scriptures, accessed through divinatory readings. They find no contradiction in embracing multiple religious identities.

What are the origins, influences, typical settings, dynamics, and principal performers of this community's scripturalizing practices?

African American scripturalizing practices grow out of African American life and, like the sundial, reflect the emotional climate, the light and shadows, of day-to-day existence. Settings may be private and personal, as in devotional readings, divinatory rituals, and reflective meditations, or public and communal, in open spaces such as the popular ritual space surrounding the flame of knowledge at a historically black college or university. Principal performers are everyday people in both informal and formal spaces; women, men, children, and youth of all ages. African American scripturalizing practices simply permeate life and are expressed in many forms, in songs, sermons, prayers, plays, stage productions, poetry, paintings, carvings, spoken word, and conversations. The following excerpt from the personal narrative of William B. McClain, Professor of Preaching and Worship, reflects a common narration of African American experience in relationship to the Bible:

> The Bible has a peculiar and particular authority in the black community and culture. In the town in Alabama in which I grew up, there was hardly a home that did not own a family bible. In fact, it was considered a shame and a disgrace, if not an outright sin, not to own and usually display a Bible. Not simply there to be read and digested, it was also the book in which was placed all the important events of the family....Our family Bible chronicled our family history.
>
> The Bible had a significance unparalleled by any other book. It was the sacred book, the source of truth, the textbook for living, the book of inspiration, the literary composition par excellence, and the final arbiter for any religious dispute. It was the Bible—and that was that!
>
> In my family you were expected to read it and memorize it. The test of whether you did came regularly and often: each day at mealtime.[17]

McClain's description of his early relationship with the Bible is not uncommon. Many of the African American college students who participated in the research reported similar experiences of reciting Bible verses during meal times and remembering the importance of the family Bible that was prominently displayed in their homes or the homes of grandparents. The memorization and recitation of Bible verses was an important scripturalizing practice as well as an aspect of spiritual development and socialization in African American Christian families.

The African American seminary and college students who participated in the research displayed a strong fundamentalist orientation toward the interpretation of scripture. They overwhelmingly viewed the Bible as a "rule book," the "infallible word of God," and "something to be feared." See, for example, the following excerpts from the seminary-student focus-group discussions:

> There's a church for everybody and nobody has an excuse to be un-churched...God has ordained the Bible or it would not have lasted for centuries.
>
> I think that it [the Bible] is a text that the Lord would have us to go back to time and time again because everything that you may want or desire or need answers for is pretty much in the Bible. Sometimes it is contradictory because it is situational.

The Bible says in Ephesians chapter 6 that we are to have the sword of the word. The Bible is just like a sword and the sword is a tool...And so the word of God I do believe should be taken literally, but it is based on how you see it, how you use that literal word that will determine whether or not it becomes empowering to you or whether it becomes a hindrance.

You need the Bible like you need the water to survive.[18]

These comments reflect the general perspectives of the participating seminary students. Though slightly older than the undergraduate students, the seminary students, male and female, seemed to have a fundamentalist religious orientation that was just as strong as that of the undergraduate students. It seems that both groups were fearful that their education might cause them to "lose" their faith. This could be interpreted as a psychological need for certainty, for grounding and for infallible answers, for "holding," as Holmes points out.[19]

Seminary students who participated in this study represent a unique demographic of the African American Christian community. They are at a cusp between layperson/lay leader and ordained clergy, between church and academy, and at a place where they feel "book learning" will cause them to "lose their burning" as they engage in dialogue and conversation with others from varying ethnic backgrounds and faith communities who do not share their views. The seminary students were at a juncture in their education where they enter professing to know "nearly everything about God" and soon discover and articulate that they "know nothing at all." The following activity reflects the sentiments of this group.

Four African American seminary students who had been part of an earlier focus group in Atlanta, Georgia, participated in a nonverbal activity to express their sentiments regarding the Bible. The four were affiliated with predominately black Baptist, nondenominational, African Methodist Episcopal (AME), and Pentecostal churches. The researcher asked them to imagine a line between two walls, at one end of which, on the far left, are the words "Strongly Agree," and on the far right are the words "Strongly Disagree." Students were advised to move along the pendulum and stand in the area that best represented their response to the questions. The middle represented a near-neutral or balanced point between the two, where they neither strongly agreed nor strongly disagreed. The students were assigned numbers for anonymity.

FACILITATOR: When I was growing up, I was taught that the Bible is the infallible Word of God.

RESPONSE: All participants stand beneath the "Strongly Agree" sign.

FACILITATOR: Neither the Bible nor any other sacred text had an influence on my life as I was growing up.

RESPONSE: All participants moved to the "Strongly Disagree" sign.

FACILITATOR: A literal interpretation of the Bible does not make sense in the modern world.

RESPONSE: No. 1 and no. 3 stand in the middle. No. 4 and no. 2 stand in the "Strongly Disagree" section.

FACILITATOR: College, seminary, theology school has had no impact on the way I read and interpret the Bible or any other sacred text.

RESPONSE: All participants stand in the middle.

FACILITATOR: I still believe, today, that the Bible is the infallible Word of God.

RESPONSE: No. 2 and no. 3 stand in the "Strongly Agree" section. No.4 stands midway between the "Strongly Agree" section and the middle section. No. 1 stands just outside the middle section, though close to the "Agree" section.

FACILITATOR: I agree with everything that's in the biblical text, and it is a sacred text.

RESPONSE: Student no. 2 and student no. 3 remain in the "Strongly Agree" section. Student no. 1 remains in the previous section (just outside the middle) and student no. 4 moves to the middle, then, decides to move midway between the "Strongly Agree" section and the middle section.

FACILITATOR: I believe that the Bible is the inspired Word of God.

RESPONSE: All participants stand in the "Strongly Agree" section.

FACILITATOR: I believe that the Bible is a sacred text.

RESPONSE: All participants stand in the "Strongly Agree" section.

FACILITATOR: What, if anything, do you find confusing about using the Bible or any other sacred text as a guide for living?

STUDENT NO. 2: I don't find anything confusing; I guess because I don't see other texts as being concerned with the salvation of those who choose to follow texts that aren't truth.

FACILITATOR: So, you do see the Bible as sacred?

STUDENT NO. 2: Yes.

FACILITATOR: But other texts, in your opinion, are not sacred.

STUDENT NO. 2: Yes.

The researcher reported that students continued the discussion reiterating that the Bible serves as a guide and the absolute truth for living. She asked them to consider their position and answer the question, How does one interpret the text in light of the social and historical realities around them? and before answering to consider a present-day dilemma facing the African American community. Student no. 1 raised her hand and said, "Let's take the issue of homosexuality and the church. Silence, in a way, is agreement. Homosexuality may be a sin, but it's also a sin to allow people to denigrate and harass, kill, maim people because of their sexual preferences." According to the researcher, this comment was followed by an awkward silence, and no one else spoke.

The facilitator asked if there were other comments, questions, or examples to which the group should direct its attention. Still no one spoke. She then asked, "What about the Curse of Ham? Are you familiar with the assertion that black people are the descendants of Ham and are therefore cursed?" The students nod. "How do you explain it?" she continues. No one speaks. She prods again with the question, "Is blackness a sin?" Student no. 2 immediately says, "No." Student no. 3 chimes in, saying the problem is in the interpretation, and not the biblical text. The other two students agree. Student no. 2 speaks again: "When Ezekiel was in exile, the people asked him if they were required to pay for the sins of their fathers and the prophet told them they weren't, once the new covenant was made . . . and so, as with the Hamite argument, if it was, supposedly, at one time, according to Ezekiel, that's been done away with once Christ came. [Some of the other participants join in agreement.] So, in the Hamite case [even if blackness was a sin], Christ came in and definitely did away with it." They all nod in agreement. "We do have to think about the interpreter's context," student no. 2 adds. The researcher noted that the four students appeared to find the conversation a bit unsettling.[20] This conversation indicates the important role the students' early teachings still played in their engagements with the biblical text, even though they were second- and third-year graduate students who were being encouraged to apply their critical thinking skills.

Just as the Bible historically played an important role in the African American family, it also played a role in the larger community. The black preacher, as teacher, interpreter, counselor, community advocate, and spiritual adviser has always been one of the principal performers of scripturalizing practices, by preaching to the needs and concerns of congregants.

The African American Lectionary Project directs attention to this practice. In a 2006 poll of 10,000 African American clergy, twelve issues were identified as important concerns facing the African American community: strengthening men and boys and women and girls; strengthening families; unemployment, poverty, and economic empowerment; violence in our communities; strengthening education; racism; AIDS and health issues; finding ways to welcome all to the church; drug recovery; incarceration; addressing the problem of greed; and the environment.[21] Of the fifty-nine calendar entries for 2008 on the website, twenty-five, or 42 percent, either directly or indirectly address one or more of these issues. The special-topic lectionary entries include the following:

January 1, 2008: Emancipation Proclamation Day and Juneteenth
January 13, 2008: A Service of Healing (for those suffering emotional distress, grief, divorce, and physical ailments)
January 20, 2008: Dr. Martin Luther King's Birthday (Beloved Community Day)
February 3, 2008: African Heritage Sunday
February 17, 2008: MAAFA Service
February 24, 2008: Contemporary Heroes and Heroines Day
March 2, 2008: Anti-Incarceration Day
March 9, 2008: Jesus and Women
March 30, 2008: Resurrection Remix: Strengthening the Community
April 6, 2008: Resurrection Remix: Strengthening the Family
April 13, 2008: Jesus and Economic Justice Sunday
April 20, 2008: Earth Day
April 27, 2008: Jesus and Hip Hop Culture (Young Adult Sunday)
May 4, 2008: Youth Day (Youth and Sex)
June 22, 2008: Graduation Day
June 29, 2008: Arts Day
August 10, 2008: Seniors, Elders, and Grandparents Day
August 13, 2008: Celebration of Vocations (Labor Day)
September 21, 2008: Homecoming (Family and Friends Day)
October 12, 2008: Cancer Awareness
October 26, 2008: Youth Day (Youth and Character)
October 9, 2008: A Day of Healing
November 16, 2008: Kinship and Singles Sunday
November 30, 2008 (World AIDS Day)
December 28, 2008 (Kwanzaa)[22]

Each entry includes one or more biblical passages, a description of the liturgical moment, and a two-part commentary: part I is an autobiographical description of the contemporary context of the African American interpreter, and part II is a relevant biblical commentary to assist the preacher or the liturgist in designing a message that is appropriate for the occasion. Some include sermonic outlines and a list of possible sermon titles and accompanying songs as well as other source materials, such as videos and books, to aid in preparation. The foregoing list of entries reflects the contemporary social issues that religious organizations address through the public scripturalizing practices of preaching and liturgy. Some of the concerns highlighted have historical counterparts. For example, in the early 1800s, Daniel Payne, an influential AME bishop, was a strong advocate of the church assuming responsibility in establishing schools and encouraging education and cultural development as a means to freedom.[23]

What are some historical and current forms of expressiveness through which, and in relation to which, the scripturalizing practices are carried out?

In both group and individual narratives, we find that scriptures often inspire as well as motivate action and movement, establishing boundaries and providing guidelines for social formation. Both discursive and active communities form around scriptures and their interpretative responses, just as Karin Barber notes in her reference to the Yoruba proverb about the role of the listener in bringing meaning to a text, "We say half a word to the wise, when it gets inside him or her it will become whole."[24] This saying suggests that scriptural meanings and functions depend to a large extent upon the interpreting community.

One example of a social grouping based on a specific interpretation of the biblical text is the religious group known as the African Hebrew Israelites of Jerusalem, based in Dimona, Israel with affiliated groups throughout the United States. Adherents believe that African Americans are descendants of the ancient Hebrew Israelites of the Hebrew Scriptures. Members from the Tallahassee and Atlanta chapters participated in this study.

The African Hebrew Israelites of Jerusalem seem to reflect the classic characteristics of what Yates and Hunter refer to as a "fundamentalist world-historical narrative." The world-history narrative unfolds in three steps: (1) history has gone awry, (2) what went wrong with history is "modernity" in its various guises (3) members of the fundamentalist group are called to make it right again.[25] We can identify these components in the following excerpts from the collective story of the African Hebrew

Israelites. This first excerpt comes from the philosophy section of "Our Story" on the Kingdom of Yah website.

> In today's world, man has created so many diversions from and substitutions for the true worship of God that the people have lost their way. We realized just how far we had been led away from God and were astounded by the drastic changes required for those of us who desired to fulfill our responsibility to God as Hebrew Israelites. Nonetheless, we have committed ourselves to the high degree of courage and discipline required to establish an alternative lifestyle that is in harmony with the cycles of God.[26]

The founder/leader of the African Hebrew Israelites of Jerusalem, Ben Ammi, cites the following scriptures in the movement's Platform of Righteousness: The Platform for the 21st century; the Millennial Sanctification and Separation:[27]

> The people have been virtually hypnotized, feigning contentment and acting as if they do not see the social and moral decay eating at the society around them. But the history recorded in the Holy Scriptures reminds us that we have seen these circumstances before, in the days of Noah.
>
> And Yah saw that the wickedness of man was great in the earth, and that every imagination of the thoughts of his heart was only evil continually. (Genesis 6:5)
>
> The earth also was corrupt before Yah, and the earth was filled with violence (Genesis 6:11)

Each plank of Ammi's platform of righteousness is "rooted in the timeless advice of the prophets of Israel, who when confronted with a society in turmoil and opposition to Yah, admonished our forefathers to seek the old paths—the every aspect of life."

> Thus saith the Law, Stand ye in the ways, and see, and ask for the old paths, where is the good way, and walk in it, and ye shall find rest for your souls. (Jeremiah 6:16)

The Movement's corporate narrative of turning back to the old way, a more righteous way is reflected in the following excerpt from a personal narrative of one member of the movement:

> After finding the truth about my heritage, and my cultural connection to the children of Israel, the Kingdom appeared to be the vehicle that was actually

living the complete fullness of what I found to be true Biblical prophecy. The kingdom was established officially in 1970 by His Excellency Ben Ammi. It was established in Northeast Africa in the land of Israel in a small city called Dimona. It was established by a group of ex-African Americans who left America in 1967 and moved into Liberia, West Africa, for two-and-a-half years, where they purged themselves of the negritudes acquired as captives in North America. After spending two and half years in the bush, a third of that population made the final journey home to Israel in 1967, and then when they were officially settled by 1970, the government or the Kingdom was established in its fullness.

...We suffered great persecution from those that were already there based on our claim to be descendants of the Biblical Israelites—naturally it was controversial and it was a struggle from that point on....But since then we lived in the land for twenty-two years on tourist visas and in 2004 we were granted permanent residence saying we would always be citizens in the land of Israel....We became the sons and daughters of the living God, human.[28]

These narratives are consistent with the redemptive self-narrative described by Dan P. McAdams in his exploration of the psychological and cultural dynamics of the stories Americans live by.[29] McAdams defines redemptive story as the general belief in deliverance from suffering and the movement into a better world. This theme is very prevalent in the story of the African Hebrew Israelites. The biblical scriptures cited earlier are used as an authoritative basis for developing a way of life based on a resistance to certain "evils" of modernity. The Kingdom of Yah communities are in the following locations: Dimona, Israel; Atlanta, Georgia; Tallahassee, Florida; Cleveland, Ohio; Chicago, Illinois; Washington, DC; St. Louis, Missouri; Vicksburg, Mississippi; and Houston, Texas.

In each location, members operate businesses known as "redemptive enterprises." These include vegetarian restaurants, beauty and barber shops, organic farms, tofu factories, schools and day-care centers, and bookstores, all of which are considered by members of the community to be vehicles for attaining the lifestyle ordained by Yah.

The African Hebrew Israelites of Jerusalem (the estimated 2,000 members in the home Village of Peace in Dimona, Israel) and the relatively small affiliate communities sprinkled throughout the United States provide a classic example of what Yates and Hunter refer to as a "world historical narrative" of a fundamentalist movement. Their redemption story is revealed through personal and corporate narrative as expressed in the life-story interviews, the Kingdom of Yah website, and print materials, music, and other cultural products of the organization. Unlike the fundamentalist "reading" that Wimbush referenced in his brief history of African American engagements with the Bible, this fundamentalist movement does not discard the cultural lens to embrace a "purity of doctrine," but instead places the history of oppression at the very center of their interpretation of scripture and their perceived mandate to resist the "evils" of modern society.

> And in the days of these kings shall the God of heaven set up a kingdom, which shall never be destroyed: and the kingdom shall not be left to other people, but it shall break in pieces and consume all these kingdoms, and it shall stand for ever. (Daniel 2:44)

Members of the Tallahassee and Atlanta communities report frequent visits to Israel and a strong sense of kinship with the Israeli community. This case study points to the use of sacred texts in the development of social identity. The founder, Ben Ammi, cites the Hebrew Scriptures as the basis for his call to venture forth and establish the Kingdom of Yah; that is, to begin a new community with a people of common racial ancestry willing to embrace the same philosophy and lifestyle. The group of 350 African Americans left Chicago, Illinois, in 1967, spent two-and-half years "purging themselves of the negritudes acquired as captives in North America."[30] This language, alone, points to an intentional effort to redefine and reinvent self and community. Establishing a new social identity linking with their African ancestry was a primary objective of the group. The fact that they wanted to "purge themselves of negritudes," suggests a desire to reclaim what they considered to be a more authentic self, the self origin, the African identity. This attitude reflects historian of religion Charles H. Long's assertion that African American religions are a definite outgrowth of the enslaved African's involuntary presence in America. Likewise, Vincent Wimbush also suggests that any study of the history of African American engagements with the Bible must begin with African sensibilities at the center.[31] The African Hebrew Israelites of Jerusalem, then, have returned to that center, defining themselves as descendants of the biblical Israelites.[32]

What psychosocial and sociocultural benefits do practitioners derive from their persistent relating to scriptures?

The grounded theory that emerged from the life-story narratives of the interviewees served as a guide in the interpretation and analysis that began with the first interview and continued to unfold throughout the process. Grounded theory suggests that every life story is a sacred story and as such is in some way connected to a larger communal/human story. Each story thus represents a view of self, a view of world, and something that connects the two, providing the individual with a sense of coherence.[33] Our sample of African American life-story narratives reflects a view of world as ranging from "harsh, unfriendly and corrupted," to an energy matrix of exciting possibilities; and a view of self ranging from "unworthy, and inadequate" to "divine expression of the one Infinite Source." In what ways might African American "readings of script(ure)s" reflect also a "reading of America?"

A quest for meaning, belonging, affirmation, and agency forms the backstory of all the data we gathered. The quest started early in life, for some as early as reciting Bible verses at the age of four or five, with no clue as to the meaning or the purpose. For others, it was the age of twelve or thirteen, when they were baptized and received into the "fellowship of Christ," still with little understanding of what it all meant. With each personal narrative we found themes, patterns, and motifs reflecting the psychological and social functions of the "sacred story" as lived out in the unique journey of the individual. Some of our narrators have experienced more than one cycle of the "call, initiation, return" pattern along the journey, and each of their stories reflects different aspects of the African American social and historical experience. The following pages provide a glimpse into this world through the voices of those who have lived in these inner and outer spaces of meaning-making. I use Cynthia's story as a thru line for this discussion and will weave a tapestry of other narrative segments, along with my analytical perspective. Cynthia, a fifty-five-year-old African American woman speaks:

> When I was about twelve or thirteen I went to church with my stepmother and they did an altar call. She told me to go up and tell them that I wanted to be baptized. I just did what she said. I really didn't even know what that meant, but I did it anyway. Then at some point later on this woman left my father I remember waking up one morning and she was gone. I guessed it was because they were not legally married and she had decided that they were living in sin.
>
> Since my father did not go to church, I didn't have any more exposure to it until I was about twenty. I was married then and my sister-in-law invited me to go with her to a tent revival. She always had her Bible, and she was talking about the love of God and the love of Jesus, and I thought maybe she

had found something that could help me. I didn't know what to do with my life. I was looking for direction and purpose and answers.[34]

The tent revival represented a call to adventure for Cynthia, a departure from her everyday life, a significant point in her search for purpose and direction. Her comments about looking for direction, purpose, and answers suggest that the stage was set for the embrace of a fundamentalist orientation toward the Bible. This orientation would fulfill a psychological need for clearly defined directives and a system of meaning that would affirm her self-worth.[35] This call to adventure started her on a journey filled with obstacles, challenges, and conflicts, a time that in biblical terminology would be defined as a "wilderness" experience. She describes her journey as an intense search for understanding and knowledge.

> So I went to this tent meeting, and, when they did the altar call, I went up there, and when they were talking about how much Jesus loved me, I thought surely this must be my answer. I cried uncontrollably because I felt like for the first time somebody really cared about me. My sister-in-law gave me a Bible and that was the beginning for me. I had dropped out of high school. I couldn't even read. I taught myself to read by reading the Bible and looking up words in the dictionary that I didn't know. I found a lot of answers in the book of Proverbs. I translated everything into do's and don'ts....Everything was black and white for me. I was reading and studying all the time. I was on a mission to learn the truth and to apply it to my life.

Cynthia's dependence on the Bible as the source for meaning is echoed by the focus-group participants as well other individuals whom we interviewed. Repeatedly, we heard that the Bible was a rule book and the ultimate authority for living. In Cynthia's story these sentiments are consistent with the voices coming from a social location defined by poverty, lack of education, and a life of pain and struggle. Cynthia was abandoned by her mother at an early age and raised partly by her grandmother, at times by a family friend, and at times by her father. The need for love was paramount in her life. But her sentiments in many ways are echoed in the comments of African American college students and seminarians. In spite of their education and the somewhat different socio-economic circumstances of their families of origin, many espoused the same belief in the Bible as the ultimate authority in life, the rule book, the infallible word of God, against which all else must be measured.

We continue with Cynthia's story:

My sister-in-law invited me to church with her, and I was so happy to see that so many people loved God, and I felt that I had found a place to go that lined up with what I felt inside. But after awhile I began to realize that they did not see the Bible the way I did.

I remember being very dogmatic because I wanted to do what was right. I had to stay right in order to continue to have God's love and to have a better life....I read the Bible. I prayed and fasted for weeks at a time. I saw visions and I became known as one with the gift of prophecy. I started telling people what I saw, that they were not living the way God wanted. If they did not line up with my thinking I didn't want to have anything to do with them. This did not go over too well....I went from the Baptist church to the holiness church because prophecy was accepted there. At first this felt like it was right for me. But I became a problem for them. I asked too many questions and I would not accept their indoctrination.[36]

Cynthia's journey and quest for knowledge continues. She encounters multiple challenges as she goes from church to church seeking a community that she can belong to and feel comfortable with. The social function of the fundamentalist religious orientation is an integral part of her quest. She moves from Baptist to Holiness to white charismatic in an effort to meet her need for certainty and stability, something that was not present in her personal life. By this time she was a single parent, raising two daughters alone and trying not to "sin against God," fearful of the consequences for herself and her children. Because she was taught that sex outside of marriage was an abomination before God, she entered into several short-lived, ill-advised marriages, twice to men in prison, because she believed so strongly in the power of forgiveness.

There was one period, she says, where she just stayed away from people because she was so afraid of "sin and corruption." She wanted to be the perfect Christian, and not be involved in "worldly" things, so much so that when she came home from work one day and saw that her daughters had decorated their bedroom with pictures of Smurfs (a playful cartoon character), she tore all the pictures off the wall and threw them in the trash, vowing that she would not have pictures of demons in her house.

After that experience where I was not accepted in that one church I looked around for a while and somehow ended up going to this non-denominational, charismatic, predominately white church. It was a teaching church and I liked that, but what I didn't know when I went there was that they did not think women could be called to the ministry. I had quite an experience there. I knew I had to be different, more orderly, more intellectual I guess, less emotional. Everything had to be done orderly. They tamed me. I was less radical in my expression, but I was still deep into studying the Bible. I wanted to teach other people because I wanted them to get it right too, so we all could have a better life. I had a Bible Study at my house and I was bringing in people from the street and teaching them. I would then take them to this church with me. This was the first time that there was a noticeable number of Black folk in the congregation. All of the folk I brought in I was teaching them at my own Bible Study. Then they would go and participate in the Bible Study at the church. Somehow one of the women in my group made a comment to someone that I was a better teacher than the pastor. The word got back to the pastor and he and his wife came to my house to meet with me. They wanted to know why I was saying that I was a better teacher. I had no idea what they were talking about. They were there to decide if I should continue to be a part of their church or if they should ask me to leave. After that I left and all of the Black folk that I had recruited followed me. I later heard that when the pastor realized how many people had followed me, he changed his mind about allowing women to be in ministry. I would see women in the street and they would come up to me and thank me for bringing about a change in that church. They had to explain to me what they were talking about. At first I didn't know.[37]

Cynthia's account of her experience in the white fundamentalist church suggests that she went looking for some ultimate truth. She knew the white environment required a different form of expression from her. She described it as more orderly, less radical, less emotional, and more intelligent. What she doesn't say, but implies, is that she had to be "less black, less of who she really was." She continued her passionate quest for truth and her ecstatic form of religious expression through the group Bible study in her home. She said they had some amazing experiences with Spirit. They prayed nightly, saw visions, and received prophetic messages. Her account confirms Charles Long's assertion that there is a direct correlation between the hardness of life and the ecstasy of worship. Cynthia's sincerity, commitment, and success as a teacher and evangelist were so impressive that the white pastor changed his mind about women as ministers. His change of heart came too late, though, for after he had suggested that Cynthia was out of order, she voluntarily moved on.

When I left there I had my own little house church in my apartment for a while. That didn't last long. Someone invited me to another church and I decide[d] I would try it. They had some sort of probationary membership where you would go to these study groups for three months and then they would decide if you met their qualifications to join the church. At the end of my three months they told me I could not continue because I had too much of my own mind and I was not willing to submit to the pastor who was the head of the church. I was happy when they told me that, because it just confirmed what God had already told me. This was not the place for me. As it turned out, later on I heard that the pastor was sleeping around with different women in the church, and it ended up being a huge sex scandal in the church. A number of people left.[38]

Questions related to the dynamics of gender, sexuality, power, and control surface here. These problematic issues are given little attention in the church, and congregants generally obey an unspoken vow to silence. Cynthia speaks to this later in her story. For her it becomes an issue of blatant hypocrisy and a definite turn off.

I was happy that I had already left that church. I was still searching for answers and I decided to go to Rhema Bible Training College in Tulsa, Oklahoma, but I did not find any answers there. In fact, it was just more of the same. They did not believe that anybody could have prophecy as a gift. Kenneth Hagin, the founder, was supposedly the only one with the gift of prophecy. About thirty, or 40%, of the students there were black. We were all searching for something that would make our lives better. They taught the fivefold ministry and that the Bible was the infallible word of God. By this time I was beginning to think something was terribly wrong. I found it very disappointing.

There were students there living in their cars, thinking they were doing the will of God. They didn't even have a place to live. When I told them they should consider that maybe God wanted them to get a job, they didn't want to hear what I had to say. When I left Rhema, I was just about through with the church, but I thought maybe if I learned more about the Hebrew culture I could get some answers.[39]

The quest continued.

I first learned about Ben Ammi's group through someone who knew I was searching for the truth of the scriptures from the Hebrew perspective.

I had been to a local Jewish synagogue and they couldn't understand why I was there, but I was there to learn how the Hebrew people thought, something about their culture, and how they looked at life, so I could get better answers and could see how the Bible was supposed to work for me. I was not so much interested in being a part of their community and they could see that. I tried a couple of different groups; then someone told me about a black man who came to town from Texas every week and he was teaching the scriptures from the Hebrew perspective. I thought that was the answer I had been seeking. They had some of the Hebrew stuff and a lot of the black stuff... the music, the drumming, the emotion. I connected on a certain level in a way that I had not connected in the white church. I was living in South Carolina at the time and I started attending a group that met in Charlotte, North Carolina. After awhile, it no longer spoke to my needs.

I left the church for good. I concluded that it was about power and control, money and sex. The church had not helped me be successful in life. I decided to find my own spiritual path. I invested twenty some years in the church. It didn't work for me. Now I'm about elevating my own consciousness, finding my inner truth and wisdom and living from that place.[40]

After a lengthy "wilderness experience" of muddling through, Cynthia has finally reached the third phase of her journey, the resolution. She has reached a point of self-actualization and self-reliance and in the process has altogether rejected the church but not the spiritual path. "My spiritual walk is as strong as ever," she explains. This aspect of her story is different from that of the other interviewees, but it is not atypical, for many are seeking a level of authenticity that leads them on an inner journey apart from the mainstream, institutional church.[41] Cynthia's story is one of instability and uncertainty, of fits and starts, and yet perseverance and strength. One year, she said, she moved seven times, meaning that she changed her personal residence every few weeks. She was running from a stalker. She experienced many personal hardships, even a period of homelessness. It is no wonder that the certainty of the fundamentalist doctrine appealed to her. But her mythic story did not end there. She slayed the dragons, found the allies, moved on, and finally came home with newly found wisdom and understanding. Ultimately, she says, she found what she was looking for within herself. Her story offers a window unto the psycho-spiritual benefits of persistent scripturalizing practices.

What are the special themes and issues and problems that have historically been associated with this community and communicated through its scripturalizing?

In the introduction to his collection of readings in African American religion, Larry G. Murphy notes that in addition to pursuing the religious quest to answer the ultimate questions of life related to origins, destiny, security, and meaning, African Americans throughout history have spent a great deal of religious energy on the quest for freedom and human dignity.[42] This energy has been directed at both countering biblical narratives used to authorize and legitimate oppression and embracing narratives that authorize actions for social justice. The Bible in many instances serves as a framework for individual and communal life. In this study, nearly all the participants reported having memories of preschool experiences that impressed upon them the importance of the Bible, not only as a sacred text, but also as the ultimate authority on life. They frowned upon the use of the term "fundamentalist" as a categorical description and expressed the belief that their perspective was simply the "truth." We learned that the "fundamentalist" perspective functions for African American adherents in many of the same ways that it functions for their Euro-American counterparts. It provides a unifying philosophy of life, a sense of security, encouragement, and certainty. But for African Americans there is a cost that has not been considered. This uncounted cost is what Wimbush describes as the "erasure" of self, and what Charles Long refers to as an "archaic religious consciousness."[43] Wimbush and Long view this as a high cost to pay, one that results in a kind of "stuckness," an inability to evolve as well as an inability to find a locus of power within the self as the basis from which to operate.

The adherents, by self-report, however, do not see it this way, for they keep their attention focused on the "infallible word of God." Their personal commitment to the faith dictates their behavior, enhances their sense of self-worth, and assures them of meaning and purpose in life even in a world that does not affirm their existence. The popular lyrics, "Give me Jesus. Give me Jesus. That's all I want...just give me Jesus" are not empty words, but deep-seated belief for many, as the following scene from the Tallahassee, Florida, field notes shows:

> As I sat at a table in the back corner of a Chinese restaurant I heard, "Sir, are you a registered voter?" I looked up and noticed that a middle-aged African American woman was speaking to a young African American man

who appeared to be a construction worker. He answered, "I don't vote." Her immediate response was "Why not?" He answered, "I don't believe in voting. They're going to put who they want in office any way." With a bewildered look on her face she replied, "You don't believe in the power of the vote?" The response, "No, they're going to put who they want in office anyway. You need to get the truth sister. I'm just waiting on Jesus. All we need is Jesus." To that the woman responded, "Oh, I know the truth." Then she turned and left. I wanted to run after her and to ask her what she was thinking. I wanted to know how many times she had encountered such responses in her effort to register new voters. I quickly finished eating and hurried outside, but she was gone. I got in my car and drove away. I couldn't shake the experience... and I found myself turning that conversation over and over in my head. It seemed to me to come from another time and place, a time when black people felt a pervasive sense of powerlessness and lack of agency, a place of resignation, a place where one's hope found no inner space to anchor.[44]

Is this the uncounted cost of African American religious fundamentalism? This theme is a recurring thread throughout the narratives highlighted in the data gathered. See, for example, the following excerpt below from one woman's story:

> I turned to the Bible seeking answers.... I wanted to be the best Christian, to do all that was required of me so I could feel the love of God and be blessed. I didn't know much about love and I didn't feel much love in my life... so when they told me about the love of Jesus I thought that was the answer to all my problems.[45]

What are the pitfalls, opportunities, and larger implications reflected in these questions and the approaches and assumptions behind them?

The scope of this study is its greatest pitfall. A study of "modern discourses, social formation, and power relations" in relationship to the scripture and scripturalizing practices of a diverse community of people is a project of huge proportions. It is by nature subjective. Each of the preceding five questions, with its own contours, problems, and subtexts is sufficient for the basis of a study in and of itself. The expansive and undefined time period (historical and contemporary) of the questions poses additional challenges. In spite of the limitations, though, this study of African American engagements with scriptures provides an opportunity to experiment with and develop the "signifying scriptures" model of studying sacred texts by focusing on the people and their self-narratives of engagement with scriptures, along with the cultural products resulting from such engagements, rather than or in addition to the deciphering and decoding of the text itself. It thus expands the notion of texts.

This study of African American engagements of scriptures showcases the value of a mixed-method design, qualitative methods in particular, for the study of scriptures in contemporary society. By examining the self-reported life stories of individuals, we were able to see the dominant themes related to worldview, self-understanding, and the dynamics of meaning-making through the engagement of selected texts. Focus-group discussions and participant observation provided additional data.

We interviewed individuals affiliated with the African Hebrew Israelites in Tallahassee, Florida, and Atlanta, Georgia, conducted focus-group discussions with seminary and college students in Atlanta and Tallahassee, and with members of local church congregations. We found the "fundamentalist orientation" to be prevalent among those involved in the study, regardless of age or gender. Our analysis of the data suggests that a fundamentalist orientation may meet a psychosocial need for certainty and stability when faced with change and uncertainty (seminary and college students). Such orientation could represent a form of agency and self-empowerment (Cynthia's story) or a redemptive strategy and form of rejection of mainstream society, as in the formation of the African Hebrew Israelites of Jerusalem and their satellite communities and redemptive enterprises. The stories we examined are diverse and warrant careful consideration, but they all speak to the "relationality" of scripture and what can be learned though an intimate study of the people and their relationships to their scriptures. The question continues to be a fascinating one: does the person interpret the scripture or does the scripture interpret the person?

This study also provided an opportunity to examine scriptural engagements through expressive culture. When this study was presented at the Institute for Signifying Scriptures Conference in Claremont, California, Renee K. Harrison, through a sensuous and evocative multimedia presentation, took the audience on a journey that transported us from present to past and back again. Her visual montage opened with the American flag waving in the breeze to the strains of Ray Charles singing, "God Bless America." Nothing unusual about that, but as the artist continued to belt out the lyrics, the image shifted and the symbol of Papa Legba, Yoruba god of the crossroads, appeared followed by the image of slave ships with their human cargo of enslaved Africans shackled and chained. More images bombarded the senses, images of Bibles and churches, baptisms and funerals, marches and demonstrations; Yoruba symbols, Catholic symbols, Islamic symbols, Jewish symbols; images of black people dancing and praying and singing, embodied expressions of their sacred stories. A total of seventy-five images flashed on the screen.

After the five-minute montage, Harrison directed the audience's attention to the complex irony of Ray Charles's beautiful America in contrast to the grotesque images of lynching in the nineteenth century and the striking images of black people falling to the ground under the pressure of water hoses during the civil rights movement in the twentieth century. She noted the irony of fluid religious expressions against the foregrounded photo of the Harmony Baptist Church marquee in Polk County, Georgia, proclaiming, "A free thinker is Satan's slave." Harrison reported that the photo was taken on August 23, 2008, and immediately placed on livejournal.com by a teenager conducting field research for a high school project. She noted that, within days, bloggers around the world responded, leaving two interpretations of the black evangelical church's marquee. One interpretation dominating the airwaves was "one is open to evil if one is open to new ideas" and the second was "if one does not accept or hold firm to biblical literalism one is bound for hell." Her reflection on these statements led Harrison to raise important questions:

> What happens when this fundamentalist ideology meets the systemic and historical realities of race, class, gender, and religio-cultural oppressions, heterosexism and homophobia? What happens when such ideology is faced with the pressing day-to-day socio-political and economic realities of poverty, unemployment, inadequate health care, HIV/AIDS, homelessness, domestic violence, divorce, teenage pregnancy, abortion, and so forth? In what ways is the Bible or any sacred text read literally interpreted in light of these realities?[46]

The questions Harrison posed in her dramatic and poetic presentation stimulated a lively discussion around the implications of African American scriptural interpretation as reflected in the slave narratives in comparison to that reflected in the contemporary narratives of college students. To what extent do both speak to the social function of scriptures in liberative as well as oppressive ways? Has the story changed? Is a new story emerging? The discussion moderator, T. Hasan Johnson, commented that the use of the sun and the river, metaphors from nature, was a creative and effective approach to discussing that elusive natural energy that religion attempts to account for. Scripturalizing practices grow out of such energies and as such are dynamic, powerful, evocative, and impactful, just as the blazing sun casting its shadows and the flowing river moving everything caught it its stream.

The narratives highlighted in this report speak to the impact of social and historical experiences and the use of scriptures in the construction of identity and sense of self. I am reminded here of bell hooks's discussion of black people and self-esteem in her book *Rock My Soul* (2003). She argues that in the world beyond slavery, over time the black church began to shift from the liberation theology that had been so necessary to survive, to a conservative faith and a fundamentalist interpretation of the Bible. She suggests that perhaps this came about as a result of black preachers being educated in conservative, status quo institutions. Regardless of the reason, she says, the consequences negatively impacted not only black people's self-esteem, but their health as well.

> Black people who embraced a more fundamentalist Christian doctrine, with its binary focus on good and evil, dark and light, chosen and un-chosen, could no longer look to religion to provide a healthy basis for self-esteem....And even when black people did not absorb all this thinking, it created confusion and contradictions that were and are emotionally stressful. That stress has been apparent in the arena of healthy self-esteem about the body and sexuality.[47]

The church has ceased to be the institution that supports the self-esteem of poor black people, hooks concludes, and they are thus left without a refuge for the wounded self. Applying theories of post-traumatic stress, she contends that the inner wounds of abuse and abandonment stem from the socio-historical experiences of slavery and oppression, which to this day have not been adequately addressed. Black folk are too interested in narratives of triumph, she suggests, arguing that the reality is much more complex and adding that "while some of us have managed to triumph, to endure, and overcome, many more black folks are struggling to achieve a small degree of psychological well-being."[48] In Cynthia's story we see both the triumph and the trauma, the relentless struggle and the emotional pain, from childhood abandonment to an unending quest for a place of spiritual grounding and acceptance; but she reports that she has "let the suffering go," to embrace a stronger sense of self and her own unique spiritual path. She could not find this self in the confines of the fundamentalist doctrine even within the institutional church.

The story of the African Hebrew Israelites is a different narrative altogether, but it, too, is a narrative of transformation and redemption and grows out of the historical experience of a collective trauma of slavery and oppression. Theirs is a radical story of separation and restoration, of a people leaving the only country they know to purge, cleanse, and heal themselves of a negative sense of self and to establish a village of peace and love. They turned to the Hebrew scriptures for source material for rewriting their story, but like their Protestant counterparts, they were in search of doctrinal certainty and, in the words of Cathy Caruth, "bearing witness to some forgotten wound."[49] Citing Freud's theory of trauma, Caruth contends that historical trauma is more than a psychic wound; it is also "the story of a wound that cries out, that addresses us in the attempt to tell us of a reality or truth not otherwise available and what remains unknown in our very actions and our language."[50]

What remains unknown, according to Barbara Holmes, is that "we [black folk] have forgotten how to pause and rest, how to care for and heal one another."[51] But the black church, she says, at one time knew how to collectively hold the people in a protective membrane of safety that offered a shield against communal oppression and individual angst. Citing cosmologist Brian Swimme, she notes the human need to be held, reminding us that the universe "holds" through physical phenomena such as the law of gravity, the pre-birth amniotic sac that holds the unborn child, and the ozone layer that cradles the earth, for, she says, in Swimme's words, "when we do not feel held, we create restrictions and rules to hold us and protect us from groundlessness."[52] Perhaps scriptures and scripturalizing practices provide one way of meeting this human need for a sense of security. In this sense the engagement of scriptures, like a sundial, reflects the emotional climate of the religious adherents.

Notes

1. Kort, *"Take, Read" Scripture, Textuality, and Cultural Practice*, 3.
2. Long, "Perspectives for the Study of African American Religion," 9–19.
3. Atkinson, *Life Story Interview*.
4. Nottage, *Crumbs from the Table of Joy*.
5. See Wimbush, *Bible and African Americans*, 2003; see also Long, "Perspectives for the Study of Afro-American Religion," 9–19.
6. Wimbush, *Bible and African Americans*.
7. See Mbiti, *Introduction to African Religion*; and Asante, *The Egyptian Philosophers*.
8. Thurman, "On Viewing the Coast of Africa," 301–302.

9. Wimbush, *Bible and African Americans*, 21–32.

10. Ibid., 33–45.

11. Walker, "Our Wretchedness in Consequence of the Preachers of Religion," 195.

12. Wimbush, *Bible and African Americans,* 47–62.

13. Angelou, *I Know Why the Caged Bird Sings*, 38.

14. Renee K. Harrison, Theorizing Scriptures Conference presentation, Claremont, CA, 2009, citing *Martin Jackson in Bullwhip Days: The Slave Remembers*, ed. James Melon (New York: Avon Books, 1989), 227.

15. Ibid., citing Hammon, "Address to the Negroes in the State of New York," 34–35.

16. See, for example, Townes, *Troubling in My Soul.*

17. William B. McClain, "African American Preaching and the Bible: Biblical Authority or Biblical Liberalism," 74.

18. Focus group conducted by Renee K. Harrison, Candler School of Theology, Atlanta, GA, April 2007.

19. Holmes, *Joy Unspeakable*, 186.

20. Renee K. Harrison, ISS Conference presentation at Claremont Graduate University, Claremont, CA 2009.

21. African American Lectionary, www.theafricanamericanlectionary.org/issues.asp.

22. African American Lectionary, calendar entries for 2008, www. theafricanamerican-lectionary.org/calender2008.asp..

23. Payne, "Education in the AME Church," 243–51.

24. Barber, *The Anthropology of Texts,* 137.

25. Yates and Hunter, "Fundamentalism: When History Goes Awry," 130.

26. http://africanhebrewisraelitesofjerusalem.com/?page_id=2.

27. Ammi, *Platform of Righteousness*, 1.

28. Interview with an African Hebrew Israelite of Jerusalem member in Tallahassee, FL, 2007.

29. McAdams, *Redemptive Self.*

30. African Hebrew Israelite of Jerusalem member, interview, 2007.

31. Wimbush, "Introduction: Reading Darkness, Reading Scriptures," 2–3.

32. John L. Jackson Jr., Professor of Anthropology and Communications, University of Pennsylvania, contributed to the African Hebrew Israelites section of this report and also participated in the panel presentation of the research at the Signifying Scriptures Conference, Claremont Graduate University, Claremont, CA, 2009.

33. Hood Jr., Hill, and Williamson, *Psychology of Religious Fundamentalism,* 14–15.

34. Cynthia Williams (fictitious name), name of interviewee withheld to protect anonymity. Interview conducted in Tallahassee, FL, by the author, August 2008.

35. Hood Jr., Hill, and Williamson. *Psychology of Religious Fundamentalism.*

36. Williams interview, August 2008.

37. Ibid.

38. Ibid.

39. Ibid.

40. Ibid.

41. Holmes, *Joy Unspeakable*, 109.

42. Murphy, *Down by the Riverside.*

43. Long, "Perspectives for the Study of African American Religion," 9–19.

44. From Tallahassee, FL, field notes by author, September 2008.

45. Williams interview, August 2008.

46. Renee K. Harrison presenting at the Institute for Signifying Scriptures Conference at Claremont Graduate University, Claremont, CA.

47. hooks, *Rock My Soul*, 146.

48. Ibid.

49. Caruth, *Unclaimed Experience*, 7.

50. Ibid., 5.

51. Holmes, *Joy Unspeakable*, 109.

52. Ibid.,186.

CHAPTER 3 | Reading the Word in America

US Latino/a Religious Communities and
Their Scriptures

EFRAIN AGOSTO

Introduction: Observing a Community Read Its Scriptures

To understand the increasingly large Latino/a community in the United
States, one must explore, among so many other dimensions, the religious expressions of this community. Even then, we are confronted with
a complex array of dynamics in terms of the various faith traditions, large
and small, old and new, to which Latinos and Latinas adhere, especially
in the United States, where the menu is large and the opportunities for
exploring new expressions are many. Of course, the major world religions
that Hispanics have brought with them from Latin America—Roman
Catholicism and Protestantism in particular—still hold sway here "in the
States." However, such twentieth-century and uniquely North American
religious expressions as Pentecostalism and, increasingly, a recovery
of age-old, old world Islamic expressions, have begun to make inroads
among Hispanics, especially among newer immigrants and the young.
Moreover, whatever the current state of religion among Latinos/as in
the United States, all pay a measure of attention to the phenomenon of
"scriptures" or "scripturalization." That is, they create, adapt, "read" and
interpret sacred texts, whether written or otherwise expressed. This chapter, based on research conducted by a team of Latino and Latina religion
scholars between 2007 and 2009,[1] will show that in a variety of local-
ized Latino/a religious communities, Catholic, Pentecostal, and Muslim
Latinos and Latinas tend to read and interpret their scriptures in ways that

help build their lives as newer "Americans;" newer because either they or their parents, or, in some cases, their grandparents made the fateful decision to "come to America." In fact, "crossing borders" is a major theme in the scriptures of some of these Latino/a religious adherents, and a major theme in their lives. How does the notion of having authorized writings as a guide for faith but also for life in general help or hinder these newer communities was an important question for the original researchers of this project. This chapter addresses this question as well.

Methods of Inquiry

First, let me say a word about how the research was conducted. Four researchers, including the author, explored four sites and conducted interviews with various groups of Latinos and Latinas, some connected to these sites; others not. One of the decisions the team made early was to approach the study of the use of scriptures among Latina/o religious communities in the United States by focusing on urban communities that had a high concentration of Latino/a constituencies to which we already had some access. So, with researchers already present in the Los Angeles area, with a total population close to 50 percent Latino/a, and in Hartford, Connecticut, a capital city that has the largest per capita population of Puerto Ricans on the US mainland, it was easy to make faith communities in those geographic areas the focus of our research. Moreover, both Los Angeles and Hartford have significant religious communities that serve these large Latino/a constituencies, both traditional Latino/a Roman Catholic and Protestant congregations, as well as emerging Latino/a Pentecostal and Muslim religious groups.

The team engaged several steps in investigating the scripturalizing practices of the US Latino/a religious communities we studied. First, we spent a significant amount of time visiting, observing, and participating with each of our research sites, taking extensive notes of what we saw and heard in terms of the re-presentation of the Bible or Qur'an as scripture, as well as other kinds of inscribed scripturalizations in the community. To what and whom did these communities give authority? What role did the Bible, the Qur'an, or other kinds of scriptures have in their midst, whether talked about or depicted in their songs, language, and physical surroundings? All these questions and more were explored as we visited, engaged, and talked to people informally at our sites from January 2007 through summer 2008. These observations also included content analyses of written material distributed at the sites, such as mission statements, brochures, songs, presentations, and websites hosted by these communities, as well as audiovisual materials, such as sermon tapes and DVDs of services, sermons, and lectures. How were scriptures depicted in these materials and how were these materials themselves a part of the communities' scripturalization?

Second, we conducted formal interviews with members of these communities, both leaders and participants, based on a questionnaire we designed to guide our interviews.[2] The questions included exploring the life and spiritual journeys of the folks we interviewed, their views on scriptures, the roles of scripture in their lives, the authority they attached to these scriptures, and what were some of the most important specific scriptural texts in their lives. For example, in one our of sites, the House of Restoration Church in Hartford, a Pentecostal Latino/a community, we interviewed, in separate sessions, the senior pastor of the church; the pastoral staff, including elders; a group of the church's Bible-school teachers; worship leaders; and choir members. These interviews were recorded, with the permission of the participants, and transcribed as texts and resources for our research study. Most of the names have been changed except when we were given express permission to disclose identities, usually among the leadership. We also had our personal notes and recollections of the interviews that were transcribed and discussed. A similar set of interviews with individual members of a second site, the Los Angeles Latino Muslim Association (LALMA) were also conducted and included recordings and transcriptions, along with notes from each interview as well as extensive notes from visits to LALMA meetings, informal teaching, prayer, and social gatherings on Sunday mornings and afternoons in various locations in the Los Angeles area. And so it went with the other sites included in this research study, as will be discussed.

A third step in the research process entailed applying the grounded theory method to our analysis of the materials that were collected. As described by Elizabeth Conde-Frazier, grounded theory involves analyzing data—interview transcriptions, observation notes, site content material, and so on—from the "ground-up" and in reflective conversation with the community itself, so that a theory emerges from connections with the data and the community being studied, rather than being imposed from the outside.[3] In other words, grounded theory generates the data first and then systematically approaches it to discover a theory based on the data generated, rather than starting with a theory and then trying to fit the data to that theory. Grounded theory is the notion of theory as *process*. It examines the interrelationships among conditions, meaning, and action. Grounded theory permits one to analyze information while generating theory that may help to study the areas of interest as well as others that may emerge in the course of the investigation. Thus, many of the themes that the group described in the previous research report, and which I revisit in this chapter, emerged from discussions with site members and the team's overall analysis.

These three steps, then—observation/participation, interviews, and grounded theory analysis—constituted the basic methods of inquiry that informed the research on scriptural practices in Latino/a religious communities of the United States. Further description of these methods will follow as this chapter unfolds. First, however, we need to understand something of the socioeconomic context in which Latinos and Latinas in the United States live out their lives, practice their faith, and exercise their scripturalizing practices.

Understanding the Larger Latino/a Context

How does the Latino/a community name and understand itself today? What are its origins in the United States? Before describing the various sites of the Latino/a scripturalizing project and discussing the themes that emerged about reading scriptures in the very different religious communities that were studied, it is important to consider, however briefly, the wider historical, socioeconomic and religious contexts of the Latino/a reality in the United States.

Who are Latinos/as in the United States?

Who are the Latinos and Latinas in the United States? First, it should be noted that the masculine and feminine terms, respectively, "Latino" and "Latina," represent a more current ascription of groups that include almost 50 million descendants of Spanish-speaking countries, especially Mexico, the Caribbean, and Latin America, living in the United States. In a recent essay, Fernando Segovia carefully studies the various permutations in how the Latino/a community in the United States names itself or is named. He concludes that while "Hispanic" and "Hispanic-Americans" are more apt names because of their broader application, "Latino/a" (a bilingual construction of "Latin" from "Latin America" and the addition of the Spanish gender vowels "a" for female and "o" for male) have become the most widely accepted usage in the United States, in particular by Latinos and Latinas themselves. This is so because the terms have come to be associated specifically with those groups of people descendant from Latin America and the Caribbean and living in the United States, and not any other part of the world. Those born in Spain, whether living in the United States or elsewhere, might still be "Spanish" or "Spaniards," but their descendants in Mexico, Cuba, or Puerto Rico, for example, while oftentimes still calling themselves Mexican Americans or Cubans or Puerto Ricans, increasingly also refer to themselves and are referred to as Latinos or Latinas. It is the ties to the United States and its hegemonic presence in the Western Hemisphere, including Latin America, that has pushed the unity of Latin American descendent groups, both those more recent immigrants and those who have lived in the United States for generations, to grab hold of the more politically charged term "Latino/a." Moreover, as a term, "Hispanics" was given to us by the US government in search of terms for its census in the 1980s. "Latino/a"—made popular by Latinos and Latinas from the world of politics and the arts—has become more widely adopted than not, especially in the last decade or so. It has been "scripturalized" into the acceptable terms of ascription and description for this large and diverse community.[4]

How did we get here?

Three brief vignettes bring some light to the question of the historical origins of the Latino/a community in the United States. The first vignette takes us to the Southwest in the 1840s, when the spoils of the Mexican-American War, determined by the Treaty of Guadalupe Hidalgo (1848), left Mexico with centuries-old territories now annexed by the United States, including California, New Mexico, Arizona, Nevada, Utah, part of Colorado, Wyoming, and Kansas (Texas had been annexed previously). The people living in those regions immediately became "Americans," even though they were Mexicans. The xenophobia against Mexican immigrants evident in the United States today, whether documented with legal papers or not, is the historical residue of those fateful land annexations over 160 years ago. Mexican Americans, of course, represent the largest Latina/o constituency, over 31 million strong according to the 2010 census, an increase of 54 percent over the 2000 census. Mexican Americans represent 63 percent of the total Latino/a population in the United States.[5] Moreover, the Mexican presence in regions other than the West and Southwest grew considerably since 2000. For example, the Latino/a population in eight southern states—Alabama, Arkansas, Kentucky, Maryland, Mississippi, North Carolina, South Carolina, and Tennessee—more than doubled between 2000 and 2010. South Carolina grew the fastest, increasing from 95,000 in 2000 to 236,000 in 2010 (a 148 percent increase). Alabama showed the second fastest rate of growth at 145 percent, increasing from 76,000 to 186,000.[6] The vast majority of this growth was the influx of Mexican and other Central American immigrants seeking agricultural work and warmer temperatures than they would find in the Northeast and Midwest.

A second historical vignette takes us to the Caribbean in the 1890s. There, the United States won another war against a Spanish-speaking nation, this time Spain, which had been the colonizer in the region for some 400 years. As the spoils of that war, the United States received Puerto Rico, Cuba, and the Philippines. It granted independence to Cuba and the Philippines, although not without exacting a price from those disparate cultures—such as commercial advantages in Cuba and military bases in the Philippines. Puerto Rico, however, remained a colony. English was instituted as the language of instruction in the schools, and fewer and fewer Puerto Rican children successfully completed primary and secondary education, exacerbating poverty on the island. By 1917, an act of Congress declared Puerto Ricans US citizens, and immediately Puerto Rican men were drafted to fight for their colonizers in World War I. By 1940, massive numbers of Puerto Ricans began to migrate to New York City, although places like Hartford, Connecticut, were also impacted by the Puerto Rican presence because of the recruitment of workers from the island for the tobacco fields of northern Connecticut. Puerto Ricans represent the second largest Latina/o constituency in the United States: 4.6 million according to the 2010 census, up from 3.4 million in 2000, an increase of almost 36 percent, although the percentage of total Latino/a population that is Puerto Rican decreased from 9.6 percent in 2000 to 9.2 percent in 2010.[7] There are another 3.7 million Puerto Ricans on the island of Puerto Rico, which since the 1950s has held an ambiguous hybrid status as *Estado Libre Asociado de Puerto Rico* (Associated Free State of Puerto Rico), officially known in English as the Commonwealth of Puerto Rico.

The other Caribbean "spoils" of the Spanish-American War in 1898 represent a third vignette. In 1959, after sixty years of US economic domination, Cuba expressed her self-determination by overthrowing the US-sponsored dictator Fulgencio Batista in favor of the socialist revolutionary Fidel Castro. When Castro aligned this small island nation ninety miles from the coast of Florida with Communist Russia, hundreds of thousands of mostly middle- and upper-middle-class Cubans fled the island in the 1960s. Two waves of poorer Cubans also immigrated in the decades that followed. As a result, Cubans became the third largest Latino/a constituency in the United States, numbering 1.78 million in the 2010 census, or 3.5 percent, of the total Latino/a population in the United States.[8] Most of the Cuban diaspora is centered in the Miami area, with enclaves in places like Union City, New Jersey, in the Northeast. Many of the generation of Cubans that came to the States in the 1960s expecting to return to Cuba very soon have begun to pass on, and a new generation of Cubans is feeling quite comfortable in the United States. Moreover, the future of Cuba and its relations with the United States hangs in the balance as the Castro regime has begun to show its age after over fifty years in power.

In the meantime, increasing numbers of Latinos and Latinas from other parts of Latin America have come to the States over the last two decades; it is projected, for example, that Dominicans will soon outnumber Puerto Ricans in New York.[9] Salvadorans, spurred by their own, internal political and economic upheavals in the 1980s, had already represented the largest Central American group in the United States (besides Mexicans, of course)—655,000, according to the 2000 census. In the 2010 census they showed an increase of 152 percent with a population of 1.6 million people of Salvadoran origin, which is 3 percent of the total Latina/o population in the United States. For a variety of geopolitical and economic reasons, many of them are concentrated in the Los Angeles and Washington, DC areas.[10]

Finally, the 2010 census indicates that there are 2.7 million Latinos and Latinas with origins in South American nations, up from 1.3 million South Americans in 2000. This represents an increase of almost 105 percent and an increase in the share of total US Latino/a population from 3.8 percent to 5.5 percent.[11] The city of Hartford, with a population of about 124,000, has over 49,000 Latinos/as, or about 40 percent of the city's population.[12] Historically, Puerto Ricans made up the vast majority of the city's Latino/a population. More recently, the percentage of Puerto Ricans has decreased, as the presence of other Latin Americans, such as Mexicans, Dominicans and Peruvians, has increased in the last decade. In 2001, Hartford elected the first Latino mayor of a capital city in the United States, Puerto Rican–born, Hartford-bred Eddie Perez. The election demonstrated not only the strong presence and impact of Latino/as in Hartford but also their ability to form strong coalitions across various racial, ethnic, and political groups. After Mayor Perez was forced to resign following corruption charges in 2009, another Puerto Rican, Pedro Segarra, president of the Hartford City

Council, took over the mayoralty to finish Perez's term and was elected to his own four-year term in November 2011.

Los Angeles, of course, also elected a Latino mayor, in 2005, Antonio Villaraigosa, a Mexican American, born and raised in East Los Angeles. Thus the two regions in which we studied religious sites are strongholds of Latino/a community presence. Mike Davis, in his study of the 2000 census and his projections beyond, reports on the rapid rise of a Latina/o plurality in Los Angeles:

> At the beginning of the Vietnam War, Los Angeles still had the highest percentage of native-born white Protestants of the ten biggest U.S. cities. But Latinos moved into the passing lane in the late 1970s when they achieved a plurality in the City of Los Angeles: by 1998 they outnumbered Anglos in Los Angeles County by more than a million.[13]

By 2005, Latino/as surpassed 50 percent of the population in both Los Angeles city and county, and it is projected that in forty years there will be close to 15 million Latino/as in the region, doubling the 2000 census numbers.[14] In fact, the 2010 census shows that there are 4.7 million Latino/as in Los Angeles County, a number well on the way toward the 15 million projected thirty years from now. Los Angeles County is among the eight counties in the country that account for more than 25 percent of total Latino/a population nationwide.[15]

Moreover, these trends of Latino/a growth are spreading throughout the country. "Among the counties with at least 10,000 or more Hispanics in 2010 (469 counties), the top five fastest-growing counties were Luzerne, Pennsylvania (479 percent change); Henry, Georgia (339 percent change); Kendall, Illinois (338 percent change); Douglas, Georgia (321 percent change); and Shelby, Alabama (297 percent change)."[16] Except for Illinois, these states do not represent traditional strongholds of Latino/a presence. As Mike Davis points out, US urban areas in particular have been impacted by increased Latina/o populations. "In seven of the ten biggest cities—New York, Los Angeles, Houston, San Diego, Phoenix, Dallas and San Antonio—Latinos now outnumber Blacks; and in Los Angeles, Houston, Dallas and San Antonio, non-Hispanic whites as well."[17] Adding up the population of the 100 largest cities in the United States, close to 25 percent of it is Latino/a. By the year 2025, Davis predicts that 17.6 percent of the US population will be Latino/a. In California, that number will be 43 percent; in New York State, almost 22 percent; and in Texas, more than 37.5 percent. Davis calls this the "Latinization" of the United

States.[18] The results of the 2010 census have begun to verify many of these projections: 16 percent of the US population is Latino/a; 37.6 million, or 75 percent, of Latino/as live in eight states with Latino/a populations of one million or more (California, Texas, Florida, New York, Illinois, Arizona, New Jersey, and Colorado). Latino/as in California accounted for 14 million (28 percent) of the total Latino/a population, while the Latino/a population in Texas accounted for 9.5 million (19 percent). Florida stands at 8.4 percent and New York, at almost 7 percent.[19] The "Latinization" of large segments of the US scene is well on its way.

Economic and Educational Realities in the Latino/a Context

These astounding population statistics, exploding numbers and expanding political clout have not eliminated some of the more serious economic and educational issues facing the Latino/a community. African Americans and Hispanics still make up the largest percentage of Americans below the poverty level: 24 percent and 22 percent, respectively, in 2002.[20] By 2007, those figures had not changed much: 21.5 percent of the Latino/a population in the United States was below the poverty level. Educational attainment, of course, impacts income levels, and in a study of school enrollments in 2006, it was noted that while high school dropout rates for the 18- to 21-year-old age group is 11 percent, in some regions of the country, particularly in the South and Southwest—the latter with states with many Latinas and Latinos (including Arizona, New Mexico and Texas)—that rate often exceeds 14 percent.[21] In Hartford, which we noted earlier has a high percentage of Latina/os, the high-school dropout rate among 16- to 18-year-olds is close to 50 percent. However, the size of the population of Latino/as in the earlier grades in many of these regions is significant. In the West, native-born, white non-Hispanics are a minority in grades K-12, while Latinas and Latinos make up 31 percent from nursery through grade 12. Yet Latina/os make up only 15 percent of the college students in these regions.

When engaging statistics about college enrollment, one must keep in mind that there are high dropout rates among Latino/as. Thus there is already a smaller pool of persons from which to draw for college enrollment. The 2006 census reports that while 79 percent of Asians who graduate from high school go on to college, and 61 percent of non-Latino/a whites attend at least a two- or four-year college program, only 49 percent of blacks and 45 percent of Latinos/as do so. However, there are several other mitigating factors, including the fact that the majority of Latinos and

Latinas that do go to college either delay the start of school (58 percent of Latina/o high-school graduates go to college directly, whereas 69 percent of whites do so) or go to two-year colleges initially (42 percent of whites who attend college, do so at a four-year institution in contrast to only 23 percent of Latina/as). The census report on 2006 student enrollment put it another way: "The percentage enrolled in a 2-year college was not statistically different among non-Hispanic, White-alone, Black-alone, Asian alone, and Hispanic 16- to 21-year old high school graduates. By contrast, enrollments in 4-year colleges differed among non-Hispanic White-alone students and each of the other groups." A similar phenomenon is evident when one considers the difference between foreign-born Latino/as and native-born Latinos/as. "Overall enrollment of native Hispanic 16- to 21-year olds in college was 52 percent, compared with a rate of 45 percent for all Hispanic 16- to 21-year olds."[22] Therefore, as with many dynamics related to recent immigrants in the United States, immigrant status has a negative impact on educational attainment.

This is further compounded when you consider the plight of young Latino/as born in their parents' Latin American country. The latter then immigrated to the United States without proper documentation while their children were young and raised them in the States as essentially "Americans." Yet these same children cannot get in-state tuition rates to attend local community and state colleges, even if they are otherwise outstanding students in high school, because of their lack of legal status. The out-of-state rates and lack of financial aid for so-called "international students" makes it prohibitive for these otherwise "average American kids" to attend college and launch their careers. The American Dream Act that has gone before Congress without success has been an attempt to right this wrong. One wonders how Latino/a young people impacted by this "glass ceiling" read the religious scriptures of their faith traditions when certain American "scriptures"—immigration laws—limit their progress in America. In the research at various religious sites, our team had the opportunity to engage some Bible college students who faced these dilemmas, as well as "undocumented" residents of our various locales and religious communities.

Thus, another dimension to the dynamics of Latino/as and their educational/economic status relates to the number of years that a person has been living in the United States. The levels of acculturation determine the different influences on a person as well as his or her life circumstances. Therefore, one brings different motivations and questions to reading scriptures, for example, based in part on how long they have experienced the larger influences of US society, including religious affiliation. These levels of acculturation are more easily determined by studying the different generations of Latinos/as. In the Latino/a team research report, the "first-generation" comprises persons who came from their country of origin after the age of 18 years; the "second-generation" comprises persons who were born in the United States to first-generation parents or who came to the United States between the ages of 0 and 5 years (like those young people being denied educational opportunity now because their parents came without the right "scriptures"). The "1.5" generation comprises persons who came between 5 and 17 years of age, who too could be affected in their educational opportunities depending on their parents' immigrant status.

All these factors can only lead to the conclusion that Latinas and Latinos in the United States tend to be poorer and less educated than most of their counterparts in other racial and ethnic groups. Latino/as tend to be at the bottom of most indicators of socioeconomic success in the United States. Yet, their numbers keep growing. Projections before the 2010 census determined that by the year 2025, there would be approximately 59 million Latinos/as in the United States. However, in 2010, we are already at over 50 million. So those earlier projections now seem low. Moreover, the presence of Latinos and Latinas in major US cities, for example, has helped many of those urban areas stay afloat after population losses due to "accelerated white flight." Mike Davis posits, "Latinos, with help from Asian immigrants, compensated for this exodus to the edge cities and exurbs."[23]

Religious Affiliation

One final factor should be considered in terms of the makeup of the Latino/a population in the United States—the matter of religion. In an extensive study entitled, "Changing Faiths: Latinos and the Transformation of American Religion," (2007), the Pew Charitable Trusts collected a wealth of data on Latino/a religious dimensions.[24] Most Latino/as continue to be Roman Catholic (68 percent), with significant growth of evangelicals among Puerto Ricans and Central Americans (which have proportions of 27 percent and 22 percent evangelicals, respectively).[25] The number of Latino/as among mainline Protestants remains relatively small in all national groups, even smaller than those who identify themselves as secular.

Smaller still are the numbers among Latino/a Muslims. The Pew study indicated that less than 1 percent of Latino/as identify with "other religions" besides Christianity, including Islam. However, the number of Latino/a Muslim adherents is rapidly changing. Although it is difficult to estimate actual numbers, estimates provided by the American Muslim Council in 1997 indicated that there were about 40,000 Latino/a Muslims in the United States. In 2006, Ali Khan of the American Muslim Council in Chicago put the US Latino/a Muslim population closer to 200,000. More conservative estimates since then suggest that US Latino/a Muslims number anywhere from 50,000 to 75,000. Like Latino/a constituencies in general, Muslim populations appear to concentrate in larger US cities, such as Chicago, New York, and Los Angeles. It is estimated that there are at least 1,000 Latino/a Muslims living in Southern California. Nationwide, Latino/a Muslims constitute a diverse group of people, with a wide range of ages, educational attainment, and socioeconomic status. They also tend to have a mixed set of relationships to their country of origin, or that of their parents, in Latin America or Puerto Rico.[26]

Some Implications for Our Study

What do these demographic realities teach us about the Latino/a community with regard to religion and scriptures? First, religious communities have invariably played a key role in helping the Latino/a community survive these difficult socioeconomic challenges, and indeed, to thrive in spite of them. Secondly, however, there is so much more to do to help Latina/o communities overcome the grim reality painted by these statistics. In part, this project looks to see how the process of scripturalization in Latino/a religious communities helps or does not help with the needed response to these challenging circumstances.

Scripturalizing Practices: Sites from East to West in Latino/a America

In this section, I describe the settings in which the Latino/a research team conducted its work in order to understand the scripturalizing practices and rituals evidenced in the US Latino/a community. Obviously, these settings are in no way exhaustive or even typical as much as they are illustrative of the kinds of both common and distinctive practices present in Latino/a religious communities throughout the country. We also note the principal actors, both authority figures and regular participants, in these settings, so that their views on the role of the scriptures in their communities and their lives may be voiced.

The House of Restoration Church, Hartford, Connecticut

House of Restoration Church was founded in 1957 as the *Iglesia Cristiana Pentecostal El Tabernaculo* (Tabernacle Pentecostal Christian Church). It is the oldest organized Latina/o Protestant church in Hartford. Its senior pastor at the time of our research, Bishop Jeremiah Torres, came to lead the church in 1994 and quickly built up the church membership, created a second service in English for English-dominant young adult Hispanics, and changed the name to reflect a more charismatic, independent flavor, rather than maintaining its classical Latino/a Pentecostal roots. In 2006, the church opened a beautiful new, state-of-the-art facility adjacent to the previous structure, which seated 500 members. The new sanctuary, equipped with an elaborate stage, choir lofts, and a balcony, seats 1500 people. The church has close to 1000 members and continues to grow.

The bulk of the research on House of Restoration Church was conducted from January to June 2007 and included regular Sunday morning visits, sometimes to both the 8 a.m. Spanish-language service and the 11 a.m. English-language service but most of the time to one or the other during the six-month period. Several visits were also conducted during the Wednesday-evening Bible study and worship service. In addition, group interviews were conducted with the elders of the church, Bible school teachers, and worship leaders, including choir members. In addition, the research team interviewed Bishop Torres, who is also the leader of the Christian Pentecostal Church, the indigenous Latina/o denomination for which House of Restoration is currently the flagship church. Thus, House of Restoration represents an interesting combination of old and new. The original church that started this denomination was established in 1932 in Brooklyn, New York. That church, now a large, almost "mega-church," no longer belongs to the denomination, and Bishop Torres is very interested in bringing it back into the fold. Most churches in the denomination, however, are more like the original church, small and struggling, serving mostly first-generation Latino/as, unlike House of Restoration, which is striving to serve both, and using what they deem to be appropriate understandings of the Christian scriptures to do so.[27]

Latin American Bible Institute, La Puente, California

In a 1988 study of Latino/a theological education in the United States, church historian Justo Gonzalez demonstrated the importance of local, grass-roots Bible institutes for the training of indigenous Latino/a pastors and lay leaders in Latino/a Protestant traditions.[28] The Latin American

Bible Institute (LABI) in La Puente, California, is one of the oldest of such Bible institutes, founded in 1920 to serve the needs of the emerging Spanish-speaking Pentecostals in the Assemblies of God movement on the West Coast. Today, the student body of LABI includes mostly Pentecostal groups, including those that are independent and nondenominational, and not just Assemblies of God (the oldest and largest officially Pentecostal denomination in the United States, founded in 1914). Culturally, LABI students and faculty are mostly Mexican American, Mexican, and Central American. They provided a good balance for the scriptural studies Latino/a research efforts that included Hartford Pentecostals from the Northeast (mostly Puerto Rican), as well as Roman Catholic Hispanics from the same region and Latino/a Muslims from Los Angeles that were also explored in the study.

LABI, with its eighty-plus years of providing theological education for the Latino/a community in the United States and Latin America, expects its students to complete three years of biblical, theological, and ministerial studies in order to be ordained with the Assemblies of God. Besides visiting classes and a chapel service, the research team conducted group interviews with a group of faculty members and administrators, many of whom were first-generation Hispanics (Spanish-dominant adults born in Mexico, Central America, or South America), and a group of students, many of them bilingual second-generation Latinos and Latinas (18 to 30 years old, some born in the United States and some who came here between the ages of 5 and 17).

Like many grassroots Bible institutes across the country, the curriculum of LABI includes a major focus on understanding the Bible, including courses in various books of the Bible and biblical hermeneutics. Except for courses in English for the bilingual US Latino/a students, courses are taught in Spanish, especially for the first-generation pastors and laypersons who are part of the student body and who take classes mostly in the evenings. Young-adult students who come from Latin America also take their courses in Spanish. Many of them will be returning to that context once they complete the program. Readings in the Spanish-language curriculum at LABI include translated works of North American theologians, most of whom are Pentecostal or evangelical in theological orientation. The curriculum, especially in English, also includes publications more recently emerging from US Latino/a Bible scholars and theologians that are in conversation with contextual and culturally attuned academic scholarship, such as Latin American liberation theology.[29] The curriculum in English is offered to a smaller number of second-generation young adults, who tend to live on campus. These students bring a different set of life experiences (including immigration, discrimination, and difficult home situations, both socially and economically), educational history (often with spotty academic records in poor urban schools) and questions of faith (who am I as Latino/a Christian youth living in the US?) to their formation for ministry and service to church and community. Their experiences and questions include how they view scriptures, as we shall see later. For some of these younger bilingual students, LABI, like other Latino Bible institutes, is a stepping stone to more formalized education in accredited institutions.[30]

A Women's Bible-Study Group in the West

Given the often marginalized voices of Latina Pentecostal women in such settings as a large Pentecostal church (although this was not the case in House of Restoration, where our observations and interviews showed many women in leadership positions, including the pastor who followed Bishop Torres, Rev. Miriam Torres, the bishop's wife) or a Pentecostal Bible institute (where women administrators seemed rather quiet and deferential to their male counterparts during group interviews), the research team decided to include interviews with groups of women leaders. One in particular stood out in our project report. During a conference of religious leaders on the topic of immigration in California, Elizabeth Conde-Frazier encountered a group of Latina lay and clergy women who decided to form a Bible discussion group, both to respond to the interview questions of our research study and to explore issues of call and ministry in light of traditional and not-so-traditional understandings of their scriptures. A fascinating feature of this group was that while Latinas all, they were more interdenominational than the other groups studied in our project. The group included a core of fourteen women who were Presbyterian, Assembly of God, *Iglesia de Dios Pentecostal* (Pentecostal Church of God, one of the largest Pentecostal groups in Puerto Rico), Methodist, Evangelical Covenant, American Baptist, and Catholic. Most of the women were first-generation Hispanics (they had come to the United States as young adults or adults), with one having come to the United States as a child (making her a "1.5-generation" Latina), and one born and raised here (and thus a "second-generation" Latina). Although other women visited the group once or twice, for the most part it was a unified cohort that stayed together for the six weeks, going through the original interview questions, and discussing and elaborating themes that emerged from the original questions.

The women read specific scriptural passages together and voiced concerns about these texts that they normally would not have expressed in their regular settings.

The Los Angeles Latino Muslim Association

LALMA was established by five Latino/a Muslims in September 1999 in response to the need for Spanish-language resources on Islam. The group's goals are to teach the basics of Islam to Latino/a Muslims, especially those who need such teaching to take place in Spanish with Spanish-language resources. Therefore, locating Spanish writings on Islam is another key goal of this group. As noted on the LALMA web-site (www.lalma.org), they wish to "provide spiritual support to the 'New Latino Muslim' during the transition from Christianity to Islam" and to do so with Latino/a culture and language in mind.[31] LALMA helps the Latino or Latina "revert"[32] to Islam prepare for the official confession of faith to Islam (the *shahadah*). More often than not they stay with the group beyond that moment in order to continue to grow in the practice of their newfound faith.

Jacqueline Hidalgo, who researched this group, noted in the research report that most of the Latinos and Latinas who attended regular LALMA meetings were recent reverts, while some had become Muslim twenty or more years ago. Latino/a Muslims who regularly attended LALMA meetings were a cross-section of first generation, with a couple from generation 1.5, and many second generation or later. One of the regular attendees was half Salvadoran and half African American. Most attendees were either from Mexico or were the children or grandchildren of Mexicans. One even traced his ancestry to New Mexico when it had been part of Mexico. Other attendees had roots, either directly or through their family ties, in Central and South America, especially Guatemala, Costa Rica, and Peru. Religiously, most LALMA members had been Roman Catholic, with varying levels of religiosity. There were also other religious traditions represented, including Church of God in Christ, evangelical, and Hindu (a previous convert to Hinduism and now a Muslim). Attendance at meetings usually consisted of more women than men, although the margins were slight enough that sometimes men outnumbered women.

Marta Khadija (whose birth name is Felicitas R. Galedary, and with whose permission we cite her by her Muslim name in this chapter) is one of the founders of LALMA and coordinates most of the group's meetings and activities. At the time of research, LALMA met on the first two Sundays of every month at the Islamic Center of Southern California, and on the last two Sundays of the month at the Masjid Omar ibn Al-Khattab, also in Los Angeles. These Sunday sessions offer Arabic classes, guest lectures on different aspects of Islam, and textual studies, including the Qur'an and such books as Martin Lings's *Muhammad: His Life Based on the Earliest Sources* and al-Ghazali's *On the Duty of Brotherhood.* The morning classes precede midday prayers at the mosque, which the Latinos/as often attend with other Muslims. Besides the Sunday meetings, LALMA also sponsors events such as conferences on the Islamic roots of Spain and activities in honor of Ramadan. Marta Khadija has traveled on LALMA's behalf to other countries in order to acquire Spanish-language materials on Islam. LALMA also tries to enhance the education of its constituencies through participation and collaboration with the other multiethnic Muslim communities in Los Angeles. LALMA leaders also offer workshops on the basics of Islam for Spanish-speaking, non-Muslim Latino/as. They maintain a good working relationship with the Roman Catholic Archdiocese of Los Angeles and, for example, Spanish-speaking Methodists. Such efforts are part of LALMA's interfaith outreach to the broader Latina/o community.

Although LALMA teaches that Islam does not promote ethnic or racial boundaries, some LALMA members appreciated the opportunity to study about Islam in a bilingual, Spanish-English context. Several members indicated their preference for studying with Latino/a Muslims, while others appreciated the connection to people of Middle Eastern, African, and Asian Muslim origins through exposure in larger-mosque activities, especially since LALMA participates in two different mosques with multiethnic constituencies. Nonetheless, there has been a comfort level achieved by having access to a Latino/a Islamic experience, including scriptural study, as exemplified by this comment from one LALMA participant: "It's a bunch of Latino people, I feel comfortable around them because I feel that, me as a Latino becoming a Muslim, it's hard because most of the people are either of Arab or Lebanese descent and it can throw you off where you feel like you don't fit in even though you believe what they believe....LALMA gives me a feeling where I feel welcomed and I feel in a place with the people that are of my ethnicity and you know from all Latin Americans, Latin America."[33] This comfort level with religious practice, including scriptural study, due to common culture and language was true for all the groups that participated in the Latino/a research study on scripturalizing practices.

St. Mary's Roman Catholic Church in New Britain, Connecticut

A fifth group for our study, researched by Brian Clark, involved a thriving community of Latino/a Catholics in New Britain, Connecticut. St. Mary's Roman Catholic Church, founded over 150 years ago, is considered the "mother church" for Catholics in central Connecticut. Since its founding St. Mary's has served the needs of newly arrived immigrants. In response to a growing Puerto Rican population in New Britain, the church established a Spanish-language mass in 1962, which has been ongoing for close to fifty years. In addition to the popular Sunday morning mass held in Spanish, the church sponsors a community outreach center that offers vocational training for more recent Latino/a immigrants, many of them from Mexico and Central America. Besides the mass, the church organizes various gatherings, including Bible studies and prayer services, to encourage the active participation of the Latino/a laity. These include a Thursday night Base Community Bible Study that meets in the homes of parishioners and is in many ways modeled after base communities in Latin American Catholic religious groups that focus on the socioeconomic well-being of their constituencies. The St. Mary Latino/a group uses a Bible-study curriculum keyed to the lectionary and prepared by Renew International, an organization that fosters the "spiritual renewal" of Catholics.

Father Carlos Zapata is a key figure in organizing mass, the Base Community Bible studies and other activities for these New Britain Latino/a Catholics. In addition to Sunday mass and Thursday Bible studies, he also conducts a Wednesday-evening Spanish-language mass that usually draws at least one hundred worshippers to the Chapel of Our Lady of Guadalupe, which is in the basement of St. Mary's and has an altar in honor of La Virgin de Guadalupe, the iconic figure of Mexican Catholicism. The mass is immediately followed by a much smaller prayer service that is associated with another international Catholic renewal organization, the *Escuela Evangelización, Juan Pablo II* (John Paul II School of Evangelization). This group began in Paraguay to fulfill a Vatican call for a "new evangelization" to be led by Catholic laity. The US branch of this group is headquartered in New Jersey, and St. Mary Latinos/as use materials and conducts spiritual retreats in accordance with the guidelines of the La Escuela Evangelización. These retreats immerse Catholic laity in Charismatic spirituality and train them to be lay evangelists who teach other Catholics the basic tenants of their faith, spiritual renewal within the faith, and sharing the faith with non-Catholics.

Much of the liturgical and organizational leadership of the Wednesday-evening Mass and prayer service lies in the hands of active laypeople of St. Mary's Church, most of whom are Latinas. This practice resonates with the purpose of the Pope John evangelization school to train and develop lay leadership. Analysis of this experience at St. Mary's Church, which involved attending meetings of both the Wednesday evening mass and prayer service during the summer of 2008, as well as conducting interviews with various members of the community, both individually and in groups, follows, along with that of the other groups.

Resonance and Resistance: Common Themes in Reading Scriptures

In this section, I explore several common areas that the various sites of the research on Latino/a scripturalizing practices demonstrated. In particular, themes that resonated in some shape or form with all the groups included reflection on the authority of scriptures, the life experience of the readers and how it was altered or altering in its encounter with scriptures, the resonance and meaning-making some readers found in their engagement with scriptures, and the guidance sought as a result of such engagement in terms of dealing with life as a Latino or Latina in the United States. Such an exploration will point toward the work that participants expect scriptures to do for them as well as the psychosocial and social-cultural needs and benefits connected with the phenomenon of scripturalizing.

The Authority of Scriptures in the Lives of Latino/a Readers

Given that we explored scripturalizing practices with a variety of Christian and Muslim voices, it is noteworthy that practically all the participants we interviewed for the study held their scriptures in high regard. Of the approximately sixty to seventy-five Latina/o persons we interviewed from the Christian traditions, all of them attested to the authority of the Bible in their lives. Now, they defined that authority in a variety of ways, such as: "the Bible is the inerrant word of God"; "the Bible is formational to our lives"; "the authority of the Bible lies in its power to transform our lives"; "it brings about a deep spiritual experience and a spiritual change in the person"; and "it has authority because it is the written expression of a moral code for humanity and a source of wisdom." Similar statements, though differently phrased, characterize

Muslim views of the Qur'an, such as "the word of God gives guidance to daily lives"; "it has transformational power"; and "it engages believers as rational and ethical human beings." The Qur'an, in part, proved its authority based on the recognition by Latino/a Muslim reverts of the ethical practices the Qur'an seemed to enable in their daily lives and the daily lives of others with whom they interacted. The Latino/a research study explored what belief about the authority of the Bible and the Qur'an meant to the Latina/o persons whom we encountered, and how they constructed or described this authority.

Only one of the interviewees in the research project employed this traditional fundamentalist language: "the Bible is the inerrant word of God." When this Latino pastor was asked what he meant by this claim, he replied "the Bible is inerrant because it does not have errors. It tells us the truth—the truth about God and the truth about ourselves. When I read the word it tells me who I really am. I cannot hide from the truth of the word."[34] This response is to be distinguished from fundamentalist positions that focus on the written text rather than the identity issues of the reader. When asked how we get at this truth that bears both meaning in the text and personal meaning for the reader, the pastor explained: "We need a relationship with the one who is the truth, Jesus. Without a relationship to him then the word means nothing to us. That truth can be touching us but we cannot let it into our hearts." Here the participant believes that the infallibility of the Bible cannot be experienced as real except through the reader's relationship to Jesus. He goes on to explain: "The Bible is inspired. It is not the part that pertains to us today. It is the full content. I have never bought that argument that not all parts of the Bible pertain to us but to those to whom it was originally written. If it is a part of the Bible today then it speaks to us today."[35] These statements seem more in line with fundamentalist principles that the entire Bible is the Word of God. For this pastor, to fall short of accepting the authority of the Christian scriptures in their entirety would lead to a false understanding of the Christian faith. Yet he allows himself some space to consider the human aspect of scriptural interpretation—the reader's relationship to Jesus and God, and how scriptures relate to one's own identity and status in the world. Other interlocutors in the study highlight this aspect of the importance of personal experience with scriptures, as we shall see.

However, some of our participants, across the faith traditions, wanted to emphasize the importance of the written word in their lives. One of the interviewees in LALMA, for example, named Juan, expressed a desire for a "strict" form of Islam. In fact, he contrasted the Qur'an and its reliability with the "less dependable" Christian Bible. He explained how the Qur'an was eternal. He distinguished the Qur'an from the Bible and Hadith (subsequent interpretations of the Qur'an by the immediate followers of Muhammad after his death). Juan felt that both the Bible and the Hadith were texts one could turn to for "comfort" or supplementary information, but that the Qur'an holds a special location that one turns to for definite guidance. Raised in the Church of God in Christ (the largest black Pentecostal denomination in the United States), Juan was always interested in finding ways to "gauge the person's religiosity," and was, therefore, especially interested in clear boundaries. He disliked Shi'ism as an expression of Islam because it reminded him too much of Catholicism, with its more ritualistic tendencies. Juan prefers a stricter Sunni Islam because he thinks it draws a clear, visible line around who is Muslim. Similar to the Pastor Jose's desire to create strict adherence to the written Word of God, Juan seeks "discipline" in his religious life. While advocating a strict approach to Islam and viewing the Qur'an as the perfect word of God, the Qur'an ultimately proved its worth for Juan, as well as others interviewed who held less strict views than he about the authority of the written words of their scripture, in terms of its role as a resource in the experience of everyday life.[36]

The Role of "Experience" in Relating to Scriptures

One church leader in our study made this telling statement about the role of experience in engaging scriptures: "The authority of the Bible lies in its power to transform our lives, it brings about a deep spiritual experience and a spiritual change in the person." For this person and others like her across the traditions studied in this project, it is the transformation of lives, not just the mere words of written scriptures that lend authority to their scriptures. There were different ways to understand the transformational power of the Bible in the lives of the participants of our study. One participant in the women's Bible study group suggested that "it takes place as our thoughts and then our way of living, our actions begin to change just like it says in Romans 12:1" (which reads, "Therefore, I urge you, brothers, in view of God's mercy, to offer your bodies as living sacrifices, holy and pleasing to God—this is your spiritual act of worship"). A willingness to experience change leads to actions that result in transformation. According to this woman, this is what her scriptures teach and how they function in one's life.

A second participant in the women's group cited some of the teaching from her church, another source of authority in these matters:

> It means that the Bible becomes *rhema*—it speaks into our lives; it orients. *Rhema* is not just a direction or meaning, which everyone seeks and that as immigrants it is easy for people to say that we read the Bible because we are lost in a new world. No, *rhema* means a word that is life giving; it becomes life itself within me. This is why it is illuminating and why it orients. It makes a path of life in me—this is my destiny. It speaks directly to the circumstances of our lives, even the ones that we are unaware of, that had gone under the radar. Then the scriptures light it and it says something to me about that unseen part of life. This is illuminating to me and it gives me a different sense of where I need to go or what I should do. Not as a command but as a gaining of perspective. You do that long enough in your life and you look at your life through the illuminating word and you gain wisdom.[37]

This statement of how the message of the Bible (its "*logos*") becomes a reality in the believer's experience (and thus a *rhema*—an active word) is echoed in the words of a female elder from House of Restoration Church who also makes this distinction between the two Greek words, *logos* and *rhema*: "The combination of the words in the Bible get[s] you closer to God. There's a point in your life that the word becomes from a *logos*— a written word—to a *rhema*, a word that gets you that experience."[38] Moreover, to be able to experience the message of the Bible oneself and to believe on one's own terms is what makes "that word become real in my life." The elder went on to affirm that such was the teaching reflected in her pastor's preaching in House of Restoration (later confirmed in a personal interview with Bishop Torres). The elder described the teaching this way, "We are to seek that unique [personal] experience; the pastor says. 'It doesn't matter what I preach, from here you should go home and check what I say from the pulpit.' We are trying to define a verse or explain a verse to for our own understanding or our own benefit." Thus each listener is charged, in this understanding of scriptural authority, to seek their own signification of scriptures, not just something that is spoon-fed in some kind of hierarchical approach to reading scriptures.

Sara, another participant from the women's group on the West Coast, resonated with this claim from Yvette on the East Coast, and expanded it:

> Taking that living path makes it shine upon your life and the lives of your children and this is what is meant by a biblical legacy. That legacy is how

others in the family lived according to their faith in the Bible—your mother, your grandmother. They pass it on to you through how they teach it and how they live it in their lives and you see it and it makes sense because you see their lives being blessed, you see that they have wisdom that the other people around them don't have so you figure that you better live this too and it keeps on getting passed on. The truth that it blesses you keeps each generation coming back to it and obeying it...now this is what gives the Bible authority.[39]

Thus, according to Sara, a legacy of experience of the scriptures from one generation to the next is what bears witness to scriptural authority. Nonetheless, she also affirms that each generation must have its own experience of their authorized writings.

Latino and Latina Muslims also described experiential affirmation of the Qur'an as well as the Hadith and other Islamic teachings. The five daily prayers require that the surah al-Fatihah from the Qur'an be recited every day. Over half of the LALMA members interviewed described the importance of having this daily Qur'anic prayer woven into their lives. For most LALMA members the proof of scriptural authority resided in the daily experience of reading the Qur'an and practicing Islam. One member described the Qur'an as her "daily bread."[40] Though many interviewees noted turning to other Muslims, whether fellow LALMA or mosque members; friends; and family, for guidance in interpreting the texts, they still fundamentally trusted their own feelings about and experience of the Qur'an. While describing both her reversion experience as well as her now regular reading of the Qur'an as a Muslim, Ana said that she knew the Qur'an was true because she felt it in her heart. Upon her first reading the Qur'an she felt a great relief, and she still feels it in her heart; reading the Qur'an "feels good."[41] Ana's experience of reading the Qur'an confirmed its authority.

Moreover, Ana makes a point similar to Sara's. Ana noted the importance of the generational experience of the Qur'an, especially focusing on the experience of having the Qur'an in the heart that she could see and hoped to continue seeing in her children. Others discussed the increased self-awareness and awareness of God's work in their lives that reading the Qur'an brought them. One interviewee described reading the Qur'an to be challenging at first, but then "I discovered that I had a better life or a better spirituality or quality of life in general by following this."[42] Her general experience of everyday life affirmed the truth of the Qur'an.

Although the Bible remained "inspired scripture" for many of the Christians interviewed in this research study, the content of that inspiration often took the form of the life circumstances of the individual believer.

As discussed by Latina theologian Ada Maria Isasi-Diaz in her work on *mujerista* theology (womanist theology from a Latina perspective), the everyday circumstances of daily life, *lo cotidiano*, often drives scriptural interpretation that is authentic for those who study the scriptures of their tradition.[43] How each person gives meaning to their scriptures in their lives transforms such meaning into a faith story that becomes authoritative for how others live their lives of faith subsequently. The interpretation becomes autobiographical and experiential because those are the lenses through which persons read their scriptures.

The question remains whether this personal interpretation has authority over the lives of others besides the person and his or her family. In some Latino/a communities, the answer to such a question depends on the position of power and authority of the interpreter. If the interpreter is an authority figure like a pastor, his or her preaching and teaching, which invariably entails autobiographical interpretation, could be turned into a communal norm. At House of Restoration, one female elder claimed that the approach to reading scriptures there included "declare and believe it because if the word says that 'by his stripes we are healed' and we know this and we believe this, we are bringing [that word] into action. By declaring it to be so it activates that word and it becomes life. That's what it means to me." The elder affirmed this to be the teaching at House of Restoration, allowing for a multiplicity of voices to be heard.[44] However, one sermon cast doubt on this "declare it and it shall be true for you" approach to scriptural authority. Bishop Torres was preaching on leadership and came down from the pulpit and asked another elder—a man—to join him in front of the congregation to illustrate a point. Then the bishop picked up the man, who was bigger than he was, and carried him on his shoulder for a few steps, indicating how difficult it was to move the church forward if he has to carry his leaders on his back. Then he asked the elder to run parallel to the bishop or behind him, but not ahead of him, to illustrate how much easier it was to run together or, at the very least, just behind the bishop. This claim for leaders to run with or behind, but not ahead of, the titular head of the church seems to indicate where the ultimate authority for congregational decisions and reading scriptures lies. It did not seem to be in the heart and experience of an individual believer, but in the directions and instructions given by the church's bishop.

Yet, many interlocutors in the Latino/a scriptures research project expressed an individualized, experiential understanding of reading scriptures and thus inverted the order of interpretation found in the more hierarchical, authoritarian perspectives illustrated by the bishop's sermon at the House of Restoration Church. Moreover, the importance of the individual Latino/a believer's experience of faith as a resource in response to their scriptures more often than not transcends Pentecostal, mainline Protestant, and Roman Catholic expressions of the Latino/a Christian contexts we explored and also the Islamic contexts. In some cases, persons began with the focus on the words of their scriptures and then addressed their life questions to those words. However, another starting place could be the spiritual and socioeconomic experiences that came before the readings. The readings may then affirm experience, explain experiences or even enhance them. Thus a variety of elements are brought to bear on the interpretation of scriptures. Previous interpretations by authority figures, especially those readings that are presented as singular and final, are not necessarily enthroned.

For example, in the case of the Latina/o community at St. Mary's Roman Catholic Church, its leader, Father Carlos Zapata, asserted that the Bible study programs he conducts along with lay people from the congregation equip his parishioners such that they "feel empowered for witness to others." According to Father Zapata, the people who take part in this church would not really understand the questions about "authority" and what constitutes authority. In fact, for many of these Latino/a immigrants to invoke the term "authority" is to remind them of the police or immigration agents. However, Zapata asserts, if the church parishioners were asked about biblical authority another way, such as "when you see something in the Bible that confuses you or surprises you, what do you do? To whom do you turn for clarification?" He says that priests have a key role in interpreting scripture and guiding sacramental practice. However, he says that in the spiritual renewal efforts that his congregation is undergoing, the goal is getting everyone to share the mysteries of faith, to be able to give witness to their spiritual experience. All are to feel welcome, to know that God is at work in their lives, and that they are of importance to the church. Hopefully, the Father affirmed, they will be able to express these feelings and affirmations to others, who will in turn join the church.[45] Moreover, the "feelings" are not just internal to church and spiritual life, but intimately related to their lives outside the church, including their lives as poor, working class and in many cases at St. Mary's, more recent immigrant communities, including some without legal status in the country. Father Zapata and other lay leaders indicated that such lack of status does not stop this church community from engaging the lives of their parishioners in engaging the scriptures, in song, prayer, and the preached word.

Thus, many of the Latinos and Latinas in this study do not think of scriptural authority in the abstract, but have a sense of personal faith and experience, have assurance that the Bible or the Qur'an is the word of God, and work closely with their priest or minister, or local Islamic scholar or imam, all of whom help them feel as though they have ample authority with which to operate. A Pentecostal pastor from the West Coast affirms this tendency when he says, "God reveals himself to us in deep spiritual experiences that people have. The experience can come without the word. The experience with God then opens up the power that the word could have in our lives—the Bible for us and the Qur'an for the Muslim."[46] It is interesting to note that for this pastor the Qur'an is also the word of God. This is not a frequent understanding within his Pentecostal religious body. For this pastor, God is seeking a relationship with humanity. God may begin this encounter with humanity through experience and later the text may verify the experience. The uniqueness of the experience already signifies God differently. The space in which a person finds this God is outside of the traditional religious institution. This person claims that God in one's spiritual experiences can go beyond the text as well as the tradition. Spiritual experiences become places of signification on scriptures as well.

Latino and Latina Muslims would describe and inflect daily spiritual experiences differently than the Christians in this study, however. Yet their description of how they turn to the Qur'an, and other texts and people, in their daily life reveals the importance of Islamic spiritual experience as a site of signification and transformation. While all of the interviewees listed reading the Qur'an as informing their reversion, they also all described moments of experience outside of texts, experiences with Muslims and in the practice of their religion, which drew them to the texts. Latino and Latina Muslims are known for describing their experience of becoming Muslim as "reversion" precisely because the term signals self-recognition, a realization that being Muslim was somehow who they had always been at their core. One interviewee described her reversion experience in this way: "And a lot of things made sense to me. I used to think, I always thought that I always thought in the past in an Islamic way...Islam made sense to me."[47] These Latinos and Latinas came from other religious backgrounds in which they had a sense of what Hjamil A. Martínez-Vázquez terms "spiritual anomie."[48] Many of the interviewees stressed that they had reverted to Islam, that Islam spoke to the person they had always been:

If this book didn't exist I would always strive to make sense of everything. I think that's what a lot of generations have tried to do and I think in our heart we know what it is good and what is bad. And what do we get if we do bad and what do we get when we do wrong and I think I would've come to that. I wouldn't have let's say for example maybe some of the traditions or ways to pray, maybe I wouldn't. But of course if I were in this world and would see that I had this beautiful sky, fruits, vegetables, whatever, trees. I would've asked myself who created all this for me and my family. And I would have to, I would try to figure out the systems of Allah.[49]

Before finding Islam, these reverts looked for answers, but they did not find them in their home traditions. Their turn to Islam was marked by active searching and intellectual reflection, and it has been contrasted with the more emotional "conversion" experience ascribed to Christianity.[50]

Resonance and "Making Sense": Meaning-Making through an Encounter with Scriptures

Thus a third area of commonality in the research sites studied was this experience of the scriptures making sense in their lives. There was a resonance with what they heard, what they experienced, and what they read. Some of the Latino/a Muslim reverts, for example, were seekers who had looked into other religions, whether alternate forms of Christianity or Hinduism, before becoming Muslim. Yet all of them noted a unique experience of resonance with the practices and beliefs found in Muslim communities, a resonance that was affirmed in the experience of reading the Qur'an. One interviewee described that after befriending a Muslim, he began reading about Islam and coming to LALMA meetings before becoming a Muslim himself. Then "everything started making sense." This experience of "making sense" led to his reversion when he

> picked up the Qur'an and it also explained to me something about the Bible and the Torah that kind of gave me inspiration and it gave me security.... It speaks about my past as far as like the Bible and I feel that all the teachings that it says, because to us as Muslims, it comes directly from God, it kind of clears the way to where you know what you're supposed to do. And I think that's more than enough for you to know what to do and how to follow. I mean it's self-explanatory to me.[51]

First, this individual studied about Islam with Muslims, and finding it made sense, he turned to the Qur'an and found it made sense of his own past religious experience, it made sense of the Bible, and it made sense for his daily life.

Thus from both Christian and Islamic contexts we learned that when experience is brought to bear on their scriptures it has the potential of signifying on that scripture, giving meaning both to the scripture and to the experience. If a traditional interpreter is looking at the experience in light of the scriptural text then the text may be used to superimpose meaning upon the experience that may not have been the original understanding of the person who had the experience. One Latino pastor put it this way:

> God reveals himself in whatever place a person is seeking for him. That was my experience and I have seen it take place in the lives of others. People can have very deep spiritual experiences with God. The scripture itself says that God is seeking those who are looking for him. I believe that in whatever place, whatever religion, whatever scripture, as long as the person is seeking with all of their heart, then God will reveal himself to that person using whatever way the person has used to seek him.[52]

This openness to finding meaning for their lives by means of experience with the divine, over and against a particular denominational affiliation or approach to scriptures is not usually stated so explicitly by the participants of this study, but it reflects the implicit theology of many who focus on personal spiritual experience as an ultimate authority more so than a written text.

Nonetheless, some of the participants, especially those who teach at Bible institutes or bear some other positions of authority in church, school or mosque, acknowledge limits to how we can make sense of life with an appropriate, community-wide approach to scriptural interpretation. These limits are shaped by

> the parameters that the international family or the church where one grew up places limitations on us...because for me the reach of how I use the Bible or the way that we live it out is defined by the tradition we grew up in or became a Christian in. I mean, it can take us so far or it can keep us limited, right? For example, so many Pentecostal churches don't have the classical spiritual traditions that put us in a place of permanence instead of exploration or experimentation.[53]

Such a view demonstrates an openness to consider that a belief in the inspiration of scriptures can be liberating as well as limiting. For this interlocutor, understanding of scriptures is constructed by the different traditions and those traditions are constructed by their cultural, social and political situations or locations, that is, "the international family." Traditional or fundamentalist claims often limit the inclusion of any social-political analysis in reading scriptures and thus limits making meaning of life and faith in the larger context beyond our religious traditions.

Guidance

"Guidance" represents a fourth theme that was echoed many times by interviewees in both the Christian and Muslim sites explored by the Latino/a research team. Interlocutors claimed that reading their sacred texts gave them guidance. What is meant by guidance? This theme emerged when participants discussed their conversion, reversion, and faith stories. Their stories were places where scriptures and daily life intersected and created meaning in light of faith. Sacred texts provided symbols and narratives that helped explain life circumstances. As they told their stories, both Christians and Muslims spoke of how guidance from scriptures had to do with finding one's way in a chaotic world.

For example, one Latino Muslim said, "I always do [things] in the context of what it says in the Qu'ran. So it does guide my life on a daily basis."[54] A Christian Latino studying at the LABI said, "I could be back where I was when I took an overdose. By way of the Bible I was able to understand that God had a plan for my life and I am here with a sense of God's calling in my life, a sense of purpose that comes from God who helps me know who I really am and not from the people who made me feel like I was nobody, you know."[55] His classroom colleague added,

> Yeah, that happened to me too but it was different. The Word has turned us around from tragedy and self-destruction to life. I did not have other options except what my friends and people around me were doing—drugs, prostitution. The Word gave me like another answer, another way to see my life, to find solutions; it gave me another way out. Because when youth pass through the problems of depression because of what is happening in your house or school or your friends or you know people close to you, you feel like this life has nothing for you and the Bible has a different answer. You do have life. You have to look for it first in God then inside of yourself but God helps you find it inside through the way the word guides you.[56]

Thus, in times of trouble and upheaval, scriptures become a source of guidance and a way out of the trouble, according to these testimonies.

Latina/o Muslims engage the Qur'an, as well as traditions about Muhammad's life, for daily ethical guidance. Most reverts interviewed were attracted to Islam, in large part, because of what they observed in the daily ethical behavior of their Muslim friends. Practitioners expect Islam to pervade daily life, influencing details like the food they eat. Most interviewees welcomed such influence and suggested that it served as a reminder of the presence of God in daily life. As one interviewee affirmed, "I feel that the Qur'an, number one, is...a book for guidance. Without direction, you wouldn't know how to build something....I give God the authority to...he has authority over me to, without question, follow his word."[57] Muslim interlocutors hope that in following the Qur'an, they too will exhibit the same ethical behavior that drew them to the religion. When asked about the role of sacred texts in her daily life, one interviewee responded, "You know my daily life I'm like, I'm not like, I'm not tolerant. And now here I learn to be tolerant....When I get, one day I get mad, I remember that God said don't get angry. Don't get angry because getting angry, you lose your mind, you lose your control."[58] She was not alone in describing how sacred texts impacted her daily life by helping her to be more tolerant, more loving toward others, more helpful toward others, or helping her to gossip less. Sonia, who described the Qur'an as her "daily bread," elaborated on that statement, asserting that God provides, through the Qur'an, "a special guide for everyday life."[59]

Related to this notion of guidance, the role of the Qur'an as a source of transformation and solace in daily life was also referenced by our Muslim interlocutors: "The Qur'an makes sense to me...I don't feel empty...like life has no reason."[60] When asked, as part of the interview survey in the Latino/a research study, "What if the Qur'an were not in my life?" one interviewee answered, "Basically the Qur'an saved me because I was so depressed and I was so big. I was 450 pounds because I was eating my sorrows away....When I found the Qur'an I felt relief...I felt that something lifted from my chest. I felt a relief. I felt happy."[61] Ana had earlier defined her reversion to Islam as an experience of finding refuge from an otherwise difficult life:

> I was very happy, and it just felt like every time I went there [LALMA meetings] I felt like my whole world, all my problems that I had at home, or everything, had just totally disappeared, it seemed like for that moment, from the time I was there, and it felt so good being there, it was right for me.[62]

The sentiment that scriptures provide a lifeline out of moments of desperation appeared across several religious contexts. A Christian interviewee, for example, explained the reasons scriptures had this effect on his life: "In the Bible I find a God who loves me. As I read the Bible I find myself, where I'm at, where I'm confused; not only the fact that I'm confused but the reasons why I'm confused and I can untwist myself." Thus he found a measure of self-identity in the encounter with scriptures, accompanied with a sense of rescue from a personal world of disorder: "The Bible is the book that took me out of chaos and the destiny of destruction it leads to and now it guides me."[63] Thus guidance from scriptures continues as an ongoing experience beyond initial encounters.

Further, several interlocutors described how their lives had taken destructive turns and the reasons for such. External social and economic forces threatened body and soul, they said, in very real and personalized ways. The difficult socioeconomic contexts in which many Latinos and Latinas, especially the young, find themselves, including poverty, racism and gender discrimination were described earlier in this essay. Many Latinos and Latinas, including some interviewed for the research report, find it hard to see options for themselves outside of these circumstances. For some, there were few sources of relief in their environment. Encountering religious communities and the sacred text of those communities in the midst of their suffering presented them with a different option to consider, an option of hope. This is why many cite the guidance afforded by reading scriptures as critical for their lives. One young LABI student put it this way: "The Bible gives you wisdom for everything you need to move forward in life whether in the secular or spiritual realm of your life. Without the word there is no guidance for anything."[64] This rather strong and positive sentiment about the meaning of scriptures for guidance in life was echoed by many of those interviewed in for the research project, whether Christian or Muslim, male or female, young or older.

A ritual experienced by one of our researchers vividly exemplified this dependence on scriptures for guidance. During a worship service of a national meeting of the Association for Hispanic Theological Education, a mostly Protestant organization of Latino/a Bible institute and seminary educators, the congregation sang the following *corito* (short song chorus) just before the reading of the scriptures:

> God's Holy Word has provided light for the way we are going;
> Along our pathway we're guided; destiny's seed it is sowing.
> We have in the Bible springs of living waters, of illumination,
> Food that will sustain us. Your word summons all to deeper understanding;
> When it is proclaimed, it never returns empty.[65]

While the congregation sang, liturgical dancers processed with the Bible in hand. The dancers paraded the Bible throughout the sanctuary among the people and over their heads almost as a gesture of blessing and power moving among them. This built an anticipation of what the Bible would bring to the worshippers when it was opened and read. Some in the gathering were moved to tears by the experience. Toward the end the main dancer placed the Bible into the hands of the designated reader who was waiting at the pulpit in the front of the room. The passage for the evening was read aloud and immediately the preacher stepped into the pulpit repeating a phrase from the passage, and thus began the exposition of the scriptures that had been read.

This ritual dance with scriptures in hand as a prelude to the evening preaching at this Latino Protestant religious gathering exemplified belief in the role of the Bible to give guidance to the gathered people of God. The community expected their sacred scriptures to be opened up to them with a fresh word of guidance for their daily lives. For many in the room, no matter how many times a particular passage has been read and explained before, each time it is read anew it is expected that a new and different understanding will be brought to them to help meet their needs as Latino and Latina people of faith. Thus they signify on their scriptures in new and fresh ways each time it is re-presented. The ritual helped the community see that a special moment for such signification was about to be taking place. Moreover, the authority of these scriptures is verified not by whether or not somebody told them they were authoritative, but by whether or not they bring meaning to the lives of the hearers, whether they answers the critical questions being asked in that moment as individuals or as a community. In other words, do these scriptures give guidance?

Resistance to Scriptural Traditions and Authority

However, not all participants in the Latino/a research study on scriptural practices received traditions and teachings about the role of the scriptures in their lives so positively. In what follows, we will read some dissenting or at least alternative and more critical views of reading scriptures in Latino/a America. This will include some particularities of the groups explored in the research study.

A women's Bible study group explores the role of scripture in their lives as leaders

Researcher Elizabeth Conde-Frazier conducted group interviews with fourteen Latinas from a variety of Christian denominations, including the

Pentecostal, Mainline Protestant, and Roman Catholic traditions. Several of these women had legitimate calls to pastoral ministry or to other types of official religious leadership. Yet many of their religious communities adhered to interpretations of their scriptures that disallowed official recognition of female leadership. During these interviews, the women expressed hopes of finding some new insights about the approval and authority of their calling to ordained or recognized ministry as they reread their scriptures.[66]

Thus they discussed the issue of the authority of scriptures, to which many of their traditions held dearly. One woman stated the dilemma thusly: "The Bible as revelation has been turned into an interpretation that has become creed and doctrines that have excluded and oppressed us as women." Another agreed, however, affirming that "the Bible does have authority, but the authority is in its ability to transform our lives." Moreover, "its authority is not in that we must follow all of the interpretations that others have made without allowing others into the conversation." Thus, "the scriptural authority that is claimed today is not about the scripture itself." Rather, this woman claimed, authority is given to an interpretation of scriptures "as if there was only one way to see that passage."

Others argued that many of their traditions claim these interpretations as valid and authorized because of the test of time. Over time, "the witness of the church" validated various readings of scriptures, including those that limit the roles of women in ministry. Bad interpretation, over time, has become "good" and therefore "authoritative" readings of the scriptures. Some of the women in the group presented as a response to this dilemma the need to read scriptures in ways that affirm justice rather than tear it down. For some, this lies in offering an "experiential hermeneutic" in the reading of their scriptures. One of the interlocutors of this group put it this way: "We need to test what is happening in the lives of people who seek to live under that interpretation. If there is suffering then the interpretation needs to be reformed." Suffering and injustice, all agreed, is the situation of many Latinas in the church. Reformation is needed, they argued, because the "authorized" reading of scriptures does not allow for women to be called to officially recognized leadership roles in the church, namely, in this conversation, ordination.

Yet another part of the dilemma for many of these women, as they themselves stated, is they are not willing to give up adherence to theologies of authority and inspiration of their sacred texts. They simply find error in certain interpretations of the text. For example, not all feminist critiques of the authority of scriptures are acceptable to them because the critiques often do not give the same level of authority to their scriptures. Some of the women try to find alternative interpretations of biblical texts on women's roles based on the study of Greek and Hebrew words and historical-critical methods. Yet this is not always satisfying to them.

While many of the women in this group have been taught that one never should question the way the authority of the scriptures has been defined, others wondered if scriptural traditions themselves have circumscribed a boundary of authority around themselves such that the sources for seeking understanding has been limited. Yet, because the women are seeking their place in the authority structures of the church, they want to make their voices heard. Generally, they say, they want to do so, while maintaining the authority of their scriptures in place.

However, one joint experience of Bible study during this series of group interviews demonstrated that the women could push the boundaries of their own approaches to scriptural authority. The women chose to study together the gospel passage in which a Canaanite woman confronted a reluctant Jesus about healing her daughter, which seemed to go against traditions of Jewish-Gentile contact. One women in the group expressed discomfort with the passage because it did not represent "the Jesus I know." The Jesus she knew, who had been preached and taught in her churches, would never had acted so harshly or so weakly with this Canaanite woman. Nonetheless, the women in the group came to agree that this Jesus just "did not get it." They agreed that the "human side" of Jesus was on display. However, they also wondered why this "human side" was not explored more fully by the church. After all, the historic Christian creeds affirmed the dual nature of Jesus in its Christological statements. Yet, if "Jesus had to grow into this understanding, just as we have to grow into certain understandings that go beyond our prejudices," as one woman suggested, then Jesus is not "perfect." Perfection has to be redefined as a process, not an absolute state.

Thus, the women discussed how age-old christologies about the perfect, sinless Jesus had to be reconsidered. Further, they wondered, if their christologies had to be reconsidered, what about their views on the authority of their scriptures? As one woman said, "We wanted to change only one thing [i.e., the scriptural interpretation of the role of women in the church] because we were uncomfortable, but not the whole thing." Yet, many of the women concluded that to arrive at truth, one could not depend on how the scriptures have been used to maintain a particular religious system. As one woman put it, "Oh, my God, we have a religion, not a truth. Even the Bible is in service of that religion and we can't hear the truth in it."

For these Latinas, the Bible maintained a measure of authority, but they wanted to uncover truths in it that bring liberation and not assume that theological and ecclesial traditions, mostly created by men, are the end-all of how they should read their scriptures. While such approaches that could challenge "business-as-usual" in the reading of scriptures in Latino/a America might bring dislocation to some, many felt they needed to engage such risks.

Students at the Latin American Bible Institute reflect on "authority"

The research report on Latino/a scriptural practices indicated that students at the Latin American Bible Institute seemed to accept language about the authority of the Bible without too much questioning or reflection on what that really meant. Yet, one classroom experience observed by our researchers yielded some striking results. Students had been asked to produce sermons that exemplified their beliefs about the authority of scriptures in their lives. One young woman, Esperanza, a twenty-two-year-old Latin American immigrant with Native American roots, offered the following sermon based on the gospel story in which Jesus heals a blind beggar:

> Others sermons put the spotlight on Jesus and his power to heal/save others. However, I as a Hispanic, I see the social status of the blind man. I think Luke wants to show the social apathy toward the poor on the part of Jesus and the crowd. I think the blind beggar represents those people sitting at the margin with no name, no identity, no legal papers, IDs, depersonalized, in hospitals, emergency rooms, streets waiting for a job, homeless, etc. They are begging for a little bit of the abundance of others. They are begging not asking begging for mercy. They are begging for compassion, help, love, etc. They can't see their oppressors but can feel the oppression. They don't exist to society. Society passes by them, even those that are going to celebrate the Passover. They are part of society but are ignored and rejected. Society deliberately chooses to overshadow them with their laws and regulations....
>
> [D]eep inside, the blind man wants to see; more than seeing, he wants to change his social status. He wants to have access to the temple. He wants security. He wants to be "somebody" in society. Even though, immigrants do not have an identity in America, they have a voice. The blind man cried out twice in order to be heard and immigrants need to keep crying out for help. Some of course have lost hope in the government or even God and

therefore choose to ignore the injustices around them. However, the blind man was one man and he was able to get Jesus' attention and eventually all people's. He made himself known in the environment. He was heard. Latinos have a voice. They can be heard. We cry out for mercy and Jesus does not always hear us like the blind man whom he did not listen to immediately. We must stand up not begging but knowing that we cry out for what is ours, human dignity until God listens to us.

Esperanza boldly challenges that notion that God or Jesus always hears and that the Bible is always helpful, and suggests that the miracle of this story lies not in the healing of the blind beggar but in that the marginalized blind man spoke out, like the Latino or Latina immigrant should speak out today.

> The miracle in itself is not that Jesus healed but that the blind man dared to be known in the multitude of people. He took a step further into a world where he did not belong. He took a step to go into the center to speak to those who were there. Eventually after two times of screaming like crazy, he was heard. But he changed his status from beggar to believing that he was a person. The undocumented today need that miracle too."[67]

In the ensuing discussion of the sermon in class, fellow students challenged Esperanza's seeming lack of faith in Jesus and the Bible to be always available to those in need. However, she stuck to her convictions: "Yes, God does not always hear and God does not always look upon the poor." She spoke from her own experience and, like other interlocutors in the Latino/a research study, suggested that it is the experience of the reader that lends authority to an encounter with scriptures, not some absolute state of the scriptures themselves. In fact, she practically paraphrased a Jesus gospel saying ("You have heard it said, but I say . . . ") when she argued, "This is what they told you [that when you pray Jesus always answers prayer] but you need to test what they have said to you with what is the reality that you are living. The Bible has authority, not by itself but along with the reality of our lives. It is in dialogue with our lives and together they are authority. The Bible alone is not the authority but the experience of our lives." While this was not an acceptable "doctrine of scripture" in her school, Esperanza kept her often difficult circumstances as a Latina immigrant at the forefront of her thinking, and eloquently espoused "a hermeneutic of experience" in her reading of scriptures.

A Bishop's Sermon: The "Blessing of the Fourth Generation" at House of Restoration

Across the country, in another Latino/a religious setting, also Pentecostal and historically tied to evangelical traditions on the authority of scriptures, a worship service at House of Restoration Church in Hartford culminated in a sermon by the church's pastor, Bishop Jeremiah Torres. In this sermon, the fourth in a series on the book of Genesis in which Bishop Torres took the congregation through the various generational shifts in Israel's early history from Abraham to Isaac to Jacob, the fourth and final generation, that of Joseph, is made parallel, in Torres's scriptural analysis, to the life of Latino/a people of faith in urban Hartford at this point in their history. Bishop Torres sees his congregation and its fifty-year history, since its founding in 1957, as entering its fourth generation—four pastors, four buildings, four generations of parents and children who have been with the church, along with newcomers. This new stage, or generation, includes a new building, a name change from its classical Pentecostal roots to more charismatic independent mode, and now, reaching out not just to Spanish-speaking immigrants from Puerto Rico or elsewhere in Latin America but new generations of English-dominant Hispanics, as well as African Americans and others in its surrounding urban context in Hartford. This "fourth generation," Torres insists in his sermon, like the generation that Joseph spawned in Egypt, has risen from poverty to working- and middle-class status. Many have bought homes, whether in Hartford or just outside it in the immediate suburban rim communities. Many are holding down good jobs, better than their parents and grandparents did and holding down debt. In other words, like Joseph, according to Torres's exegesis, who overcame his marginalized status in Egypt to rise to the height of power and thus be able to help his family and people in hard economic times, Latina and Latino adherents to the faith of House of Restoration have high hopes in terms of spiritual and socioeconomic advancement. The stories of the people Israel, like that of Joseph and his antecedents, have become analogs for these expectations of modern-day people of faith like the Latinos and Latinas in this church.

Thus it seems that Bishop Torres and his church continue to have a more positive attitude about the authority of their scriptures than some of the young people in LABI and some of the women in the Los Angeles Women's Bible Study Group. Yet, part of this may be a particular male orientation toward the reading of scriptures in this community, although there are plenty of women who exercise leadership and reflected positively with our researchers on the role of scriptures in their lives. In fact, as noted earlier, since our initial research in the church, Bishop Torres has stepped aside officially as senior pastor of House of Restoration. His wife, Rev. Miriam Torres has taken over. Moreover, the movement over which Bishop Torres presides ordains women and appoints them to pastoral roles. Nonetheless, a moment of ritual blessing that Bishop Torres undertook after his sermon on Joseph and the fourth generation indicates certain expectations about the male role in the families of House of Restoration. After the sermon, the Bishop called forth, first, the married men of the congregation to the altar so they might receive "the blessing of the fourth generation" by a handshake with Bishop Torres. Upon receiving this blessing the men returned to their seats and passed on the blessing through prayer to their families. Afterwards, single mothers in the church were called forward to get their blessing directly from the Bishop, since they have no men as heads of household. They must pass on the blessing to their children. Single men and women followed the single mothers to altar. In this way, posited Bishop Torres, this entire congregation will move forward into the new existence that God has prepared for them, just like Jacob and his sons and families will join Joseph in Egypt to reap the benefits of the fourth generation spiritually, physically and economically, even in a strange land. Bishop Torres claimed the land of Hartford not only for Latino/a, men and women of faith, but those of other racial and ethnic communities in the city as well. Scriptures play a key role in forging these new horizons.[68]

Scriptural Rituals and Icons in a Latino/a Roman Catholic Parish in New Britain, Connecticut

When we turn to significantly different traditions of Latino/a religiosity—a Roman Catholic parish and a Latino/a Muslim association—some additional distinctions are to be noted. First, in New Britain, Connecticut, a smaller but also diverse urban setting near Hartford, a group of Latino/a Catholic worshipers, mostly poor and newly immigrated, exhibited strong support for the role of scriptures in their life through song and study, but especially through ritual and iconic representations.

Researcher Brian Clark noted how Latino/a parishioners at St. Mary's church brought their Bibles to Wednesday-evening Mass and the prayer/Bible study that followed it. In his Wednesday-evening homilies, Father Zapata emphasized the role of the believers in evangelizing others as "apostles sent by God." Bible study that included personal ownership of well-worn Bibles, copious note-taking and regular highlighting of favorite texts was an important preparation for those roles. However, most important for this parish, which belongs to nation-wide movement Catholic Charismatic Renewal groups, was the creation of a distinctively ritual space. Thus the chapel where they met on Wednesday evenings included a "tabernacle" front and center to the pews where they sat. This "tabernacle" consisted of a small silver cabinet on top of an altar, which holds the host that had been consecrated during the mass that preceded the prayer service. The chapel seating and placement of podiums for readers and speakers, as well as musicians all secures that the tabernacle is the focal point of worship and study.

Thus when they discussed the role and authority of scriptures in their lives, these Latino/a Roman Catholics of New Britain, did so with a keen sense of "the presence of Jesus" in their midst. They study scriptures best, they said, in community, with everyone contributing a little ("*un granito*"—a small piece) and the scriptures must serve a purpose. One does not just read scriptures; one "does" them; as some of the interlocutors asked each other, "How do you practice what the text says in your daily life?" Thus favorite scriptures for many in this community were those to resonate with personal piety and sense of calling out in the community.

While many of the songs this community sings in worship can be found in Latino/a charismatic worship across the country, whether Catholic or Protestant, there was also a strand of the singing that distinctively represents Catholic sacramental piety and Marian devotion. One song talks about the closeness of Jesus to the community, but it was made especially real for these parishioners because of the physical presence of the consecrated host in their worship space. Similarly, songs, prayers and scriptures that invoke the devotion to the Virgin Mary were concretized by an altar at the entrance to the chapel devoted to *La Virgin de Guadalupe*, the iconic figure of Mexican Catholicism and piety.

All in all, the study of Latino/a Catholics in St. Mary's Church of New Britain showed patterns similar to their Pentecostal, Protestant, and Muslim peers who are also Latino or Latina. They valued the communal aspect of studying scriptures, the role of God's presence as they study and practice the scriptures, and the importance of the personal experience of the believer as they encounter various aspects of their scriptures. However, these Roman Catholic Hispanics also value the ritual presence of Jesus through the mass and ongoing physical presence of the consecrated host from that mass, and they, like good Latin American Catholics in particular, venerate their connection to their own version of the Virgin Mary, the Virgin of Guadalupe.

Reversion and Reading the Qur'an with "Spanish Eyes" in LALMA

Three specific aspects resonated between Christian and Qur'anic scriptures according to research with participants in the Los Angeles Latino Muslim Association. First, several Latino/a Muslim interlocutors emphasized that once they saw "familiar faces" in the Qur'an—Jesus and Mary, for example, these Muslim scriptures resonated with them. As one Latino Muslim pointed out, "I knew they believed in Jesus as a prophet, but I read more into it and I saw how they respected Jesus and they had a chapter on Mary…I read that and I read about Jesus and I go you know what this is, this is the right religion."[69] In fact, some Latinos/as would not have become Muslim if this respect or veneration for Jesus and Mary did not exist in Muslim scriptures.

Second, Latinas associated with LALMA appreciated the respect and honor afforded women both in the Qur'an and in Muslim practice. As seen among several Christian groups in the research study, Muslim Latinas felt free to actively engage scriptures with regard to the dynamics of gender and appreciated that surah 4 in the Qur'an was dedicated to the role of women in Islam. In Islam, broad ethical behavior included respectful ways in the treatment of women and that the role of God in daily life clear and honoring roles for women. As one Latina Muslim put it, "I met Muslim students that I didn't know they were Muslims actually. I just knew they were different, different in character and different in the way that they treat me as a woman. And that really got my attention."[70] Most of the interviewees felt it was important that this treatment not be confused with patriarchy, and one interviewee's interests in the work of Asma Barlas suggested that at least some of the Latina Muslims were attentive to a gendered lens in interpreting the Qur'an.

A more difficult matter, apparent in the research, was how families reacted to their young adult children, whether women or men, turning toward Islam. One Latina spoke poignantly about not being able to talk to her father for a decade, since her "reversion" to Islam. While LALMA does have programs to help family members learn about their children's new religion, without imposing the change upon them, this remained a sensitive area for newer members of the LALMA community.

What has drawn these mostly younger Latinas and Latinos to Islam in the first place? What is this phenomenon called "reversion," perhaps the most distinctive term in all of this research with Latino/a religionists and their scriptures? It has to do with the discovery that so much of Islam has historical roots in Spanish culture and so much of Latina/o culture, even today, is rooted in Islam. First, as noted by researcher Jacqueline Hidalgo, most of the Latino/a Muslim interlocutors, even those struggling with family rejection of their acceptance of Islam, were also absolutely convinced that they continued to be rooted in their home Latina/o culture, whether they describe it as Hispanic, Latino/a, or, more specifically, Mexican American, Mexican, or Peruvian, and so on. As Elena explains,

> You know my food is Mexican, my friends are all Mexicans. The only thing I added is that I pray more and I fast and I come to the mosque. But otherwise I'm the same person. In the sense that not because I'm a Muslim now I have to adopt a different culture because many people think that, okay, you're a Muslim now you have to become Pakistani or Arab or any other Middle Eastern determination and you know that's a misconception.[71]

These Latina and Latino Muslims made it clear that they did not have to become from another culture to become Muslim, even if they married a Muslim from another culture. They are still Latina or Latino.

In fact, many argued that they are better or more complete Latinos or Latinas because they have rediscovered the Hispanic roots of Islam. Thus they have "reverted" to a more original state of what it means to be Latino/a. One of the main themes discussed in Sunday meetings and public programming, for example, was the history of al-Andalus and the Islamic heritage of Spain and Latin America. Marta Khadija, one of the founders of LALMA, makes regular presentations that explore the history of Muslim Spain and reveals patterns of Islamic art and architecture that can still be found in Latin America. Some Latino/a Muslims viewed learning about al-Andalus and Islamic influences in Latin America, not just as part of their cultural heritage, but also as part of the spiritual heritage that lay behind their reversion, proving the compatibility of Islam and being Latino or Latina. Many Latino/a Muslims described the study of this Spanish-Islamic history an act of recovery, of retrieval of a cultural memory that had been denied them. Thus, in effect, these histories, artwork, architecture and literature, whether from Spain or Latin America, became part of the scripturalizing practices of these US Latina and Latino Muslims. The legacies became re-inscribed as part of their life and faith in North America.

Conclusion

A Culture of Reverence and Critique

This chapter has presented both similarities and differences regarding the role of scriptures among diverse Latino/a communities of faith in the United States. First, whether Catholic or Protestant, Muslim or Pentecostal, there is great reverence for the Bible or the Qur'an among these various Latino/a religious communities. Sometimes this reverence is expressed as a doctrinal statement that parallels fundamentalist theologies in the United States, such as "the Bible is the inerrant word of God;" "the scriptures have authority over my life," and so on. However, as one explores actual community practice, there are various understandings of what this reverence means. For some, the authority of the scriptures lies in its power to transform lives. Many participants in the research study on Latino/a scriptural practices made claims about changed lives as a result of their encounter with scriptures, whether it was the Christian Bible or the Qur'an. Moreover, for some among these it was not just that reading scriptures changed their lives, but also that changed lives helped interpret or signify the meaning of those scriptures. The clash of cultures between ancient biblical culture and modern Latino/a culture impacted the process of scriptural reading and interpretation. Many Latino/a interlocutors believed that God-inspired scriptural texts are not static doctrine. They believed instead in letting these texts take hold in people's "hearts" by personal appropriation of them, including interpretations of them based on an individual's experience in everyday life. Pentecostal participants in particular exhibited this approach to their scriptures, especially those that spoke of the "*logos*" and "*rhema*" understanding of the words of scripture (*logos*) and the actual word of God to be "acted on" for the reader of said scripture (*rhema*). Latino/a Muslims did not express that kind of hermeneutic in their reading of the Qur'an, although they certainly affirmed the transformation that the words of the Qur'an had brought to their lives.

Reverence for scriptures was also exhibited in the various rituals around the Bible and Qur'an that various Latino/a communities practiced. From liturgical dances where the Bible was featured in Latina/o Christian worship to ritualization of ancient biblical blessings in the House of Restoration Church to the recovery of Muslim and Qur'anic images and architecture in Spanish and Latin American history, these communities may have different expressions for the nature and extent of biblical authority, but they show great respect for their scriptures in a variety of visible incarnations and symbols.

However, such reverence did not preclude critique. The women's Bible study group, most of whose members were nurtured in faith circles that did not officially affirm their leadership (e.g., ordination), shared strong reservations about long-held, official interpretations of scriptures. They opted for more liberative and experiential practices of scriptural interpretation, which affirmed their roles as longtime (unofficial) leaders of their churches. However, most of these women did not decry the scriptures themselves for negative views of women's roles in leadership but, rather, bad interpretations of those scriptures. They problematized interpretation rather than scriptures. For them, bad interpretation had been "scripturalized," but they did not believe that oppressive texts had been scripturalized and authorized as normative.

The young people of LABI seemed less concerned with adhering to historical critical methodologies preoccupied with what their scriptures had to say in its ancient setting and protecting authorized denominational interpretations. Rather, many among these young Latino and Latina interpreters advocated for a liberating text that had something to say about their status, or lack thereof, as immigrants and the poorest members of society. For them, authority ultimately lay in liberation.

Whether problematizing interpretation or the scriptures themselves, all the groups we studied sought guidance from scriptures, both for daily living and for long-term plans. They therefore had "canons within canons." While some Muslims advocated reading the Qur'an in conjunction with authorized commentaries on the Qur'an—the Hadith or the *tafsir*—others insisted on reading just the Qur'an because therein one could truly encounter Allah for guidance for life. Latino/a Christians saw in various parts of their scriptures the kinds of words they needed for spiritual solace. In the Latino/a Roman Catholic parish in working-class New Britain, Connecticut, texts were read and songs were sung that showed God's concern for "the least of these." Some in that community believed that suffering today draws the faithful closer to God as it did for Christ. Yet, the worship experience in this Latino/a Catholic parish, as in other Latino/a expressions, did not labor too long on the negative aspects of life's journey, but quickly moved to spirited singing and praying that lifted them beyond suffering to hope and expectation in a liberating God. Traditional Latina/o instruments, such as guitars, maracas, and tambourines accompanied many of the worship services observed in LABI, House of Restoration, and St. Mary's of New Britain.

These too signified the joyful aspects of their scriptures, their faith and their Latino/a culture.

What Their Scriptures Signify about Latino/a Status in America

In this chapter, we have seen how Latino/a peoples use their scriptures with a measure of authority for their lives. Researchers explored how different communities defined such authority. However, perhaps the most important issue explored was the purpose and determination with which Latino/a persons approached their scriptures. They shared dreams and aspirations, carried on spirited conversations and sharp critiques, and grappled with issues of power, poverty, *mestizaje*, marginalization, gender inequality, depression, nihilism, and hope. In the hearts and minds of the persons explored in the research project and discussed in this chapter, their scriptures, whatever their power or shortcomings, provide a higher authority than that of the various oppressors of their situation in America. New interpretations of scriptures arise that are used for building not only personal identities but also an oppositional worldview that reconstructs a different orientation and a communal consciousness as they confront the state of being Latino or Latina in North American society.

Thus, as we consider the social, economic, immigrant and educational status of many Latinos and Latinas in the United States, which was described at the beginning of this chapter, we must also consider that many, though by no means all, Latinos and Latinas turn toward religion and the scriptures of those religions, to help them navigate the often rough waters of their status in America. Sometimes in history, those scriptures have been used against them, to oppress and marginalize. However, as we learn from the history of African Americans and their use of the Bible, in which at every turn, from slavery to emancipation to civil rights, they took "the book of the white man" and turned it against him,[72] Latinos and Latinas, whether Pentecostal, Protestant, Catholic, or Muslim, have taken back the text. In their scriptures, even as some among them, perhaps too few, acknowledge its oppressive features, they have found its liberating aspects and employed those to foster justice in their midst and recovery for their culture.

Notes

1. I am grateful to my colleagues Elizabeth Conde-Frazier, Jacqueline Hidalgo, and Brian Clark for their collaborative efforts in the research project "Seeking Guidance from the Word: U.S. Latino/a Religious Communities and Their Scriptures," part of the

Reading Scriptures, Reading America project of the Institute for Signifying Scriptures of Claremont Graduate University, under the direction of Professor Vincent Wimbush. This research report, including artifacts from each of the communities studied, was presented at a national conference on October 16, 2009 in Claremont.

2. The interview guide included the following questions: Describe/discuss your spiritual journey; How did you find out what it means to be a [Christian/Muslim]? What did you read? What did you watch? What was the role of the scriptures in your journey? What gives the scriptures authority for you? What is the history of that authority in your life? How do you define authority when it comes to the scriptures? Who or what are authorized interpreters of scripture? Who or what do you turn to in order to give authority to scripture or an interpretation of scripture? Are there any specific texts that you turn to more or that are particularly important in your daily life? How does this text (as a whole or in parts) define your religious practices/expectations? How do your practices—what the text says you should do—relate to your daily life? How do God, daily life and text go together? Do you have a story about this? What would happen if the scripture was not a part of your life?

3. Conde-Frazier, *Hispanic Bible Institutes*, xii–xiii. For more specifics on this approach, see Charmaz, "Ground Theory Methods: An Explication and Interpretation," 109–126; and Strauss and Corbin, *Basics of Qualitative Research*.

4. See the highly nuanced, thoughtful, and helpful discussion of this complex "question of nomenclature" by Segovia, "Toward Latino/a American Biblical Criticism: Latin(o/a)ness as Problematic," 209–214.

5. "The Hispanic Population: 2010," U.S. Census brief, available online at http://www.census.gov/prod/cen2010/briefs/c2010br-04.pdf, p. 2.

6. Ibid., 6–7, including the data in table 2, p. 6.

7. Ibid., table 1, p. 3.

8. Ibid., 2–3.

9. Davis, *Magical Urbanism*, 21. The population of Dominicans in the United States did grow some 85 percent from 2000 to 2010, mostly in New York State. However, Dominicans still do not outnumber Puerto Ricans in New York City. See "Hispanic Population 2010," 2–5, 7–8.

10. "Hispanic Population 2010," 4–5, 8.

11. Ibid., 3.

12. US Census Bureau, "State and County Quickfacts: Hartford City, Connecticut," accessed online at http://quickfacts.census.gov/qfd/states/09/0937000.html.

13. Davis, *Magical Urbanism*, 2.

14. Ibid.

15. "Hispanic Population 2010," 13.

16. Ibid.

17. Davis, *Magical Urbanism*, 3.

18. Ibid., 7.

19. "Hispanic Population," 5–8, including data in tables 2 and 3 and figure 3.

20. Proctor and Dalaker. "Poverty in the United States: 2002."

21. School Enrollment in the United States: 2006, available online http://www.census.gov/prod/2008pubs/p20-559.pdf (accessed February 10, 2010

22. Ibid.

23. Davis, *Magical Urbanism*, 8–9.

24. The Pew Forum on Religion and Public Life and the Pew Hispanic Center, *Changing Faiths: Latinos and the Transformation of American Religion* (Washington, DC, 2007).

25. Ibid., 16.

26. See Martínez-Vázquez, *Latina/o y Musulmán*, 2.

27. Since this research study was conducted, Bishop Torres stepped down as senior pastor of House of Restoration Church so he could concentrate his efforts on the bishopric of his denomination, which has churches all over the United States, Puerto Rico, and Latin America. Interestingly, his wife, the Rev. Miriam Torres, became Senior Pastor. At a recent New Year's service, which I attended, Rev. Torres was the lead preacher, but since it was a bilingual service, Bishop Torres was the translator for his wife (from Spanish to English), which presented an interesting dynamic between current pastor and former pastor, local pastor and bishop, and wife and husband!

28. Gonzalez, *Theological Education of Hispanics*.

29. Some of these books are being published and/or distributed by the Association for Hispanic Theological Education (AETH, based on its Spanish name), an association of Latino/a seminary and Bible institute instructors in the United States and Puerto Rico. One of the series produced by this organization, in conjunction with Augsburg Fortress Press, is a Spanish-language commentary series, *Conozca su Biblia* (*Know Your Bible*).

30. For a careful and helpful study of the role of Bible institutes in the development of Latino/a religious leaders, see Conde-Frazier, *Hispanic Bible Institutes*.

31. LALMA website, "Nosotros: Mision," http://lalma.org (originally accessed February 10, 2010). "LALMA" now stands for La Asociación Latino Musulmana de America, but it is still based in the Los Angeles area.

32. Latino/a Muslims generally (though not universally) refer to the choice to become Muslim as "reversion." While "conversion," still used by a few of the LALMA members interviewed, signals a change from something to something else, Latino/a Muslims often believe they were always somehow Muslim, that they are "putting members back together (re-membering and dis-membering) and 're-collecting' things that have been dispersed." See Martínez-Vázquez, *Latina/o y Musulmán*, 87.

33. José, interview by Jacqueline Hidalgo, Islamic Center of Southern California, Los Angeles, CA, August 12, 2007.

34. Pastor Jose, interview by Efrain Agosto and Elizabeth Conde-Frazier, Hartford, CT, January 11, 2007.

35. Ibid.

36. Juan, interview by Jacqueline Hidalgo, Islamic Center of Southern California, Los Angeles, CA, August 5, 2007.

37. Interviews conducted by Elizabeth Conde-Frazier with Rosa and Eva from the women's Bible study group in Los Angeles, April 2007. These and other interviewees in the research study were referencing, whether they knew it or not, the hermeneutical perspectives of Pastor Paul Yong Gi Cho of one of the largest churches in the world, a Pentecostal church in South Korea. His popularization of the difference between the Greek word *rhema*—the spoken word—and its counterpart *logos*—the written word—and how the former supersedes the latter in Christian practice of faith has had far-reaching impact around the world (but not without controversy), including in

Latino/a Pentecostalism in the U.S. His many works on this and related topics, including *The Fourth Dimension: The Key to Putting Your Faith to Work for a Successful Life* (Plainfield, NJ: Logos International, 1979) have been translated not just into English, but also Spanish, among many other languages worldwide.

38. Yvette (elder, House of Restoration Church), interview by Efrain Agosto, Hartford, CT, June 2007.

39. Sara (women's group, Los Angeles), interview by Elizabeth Conde-Frazier, April 2007.

40. Sonia, interview by Jacqueline Hidalgo, Islamic Center of Southern California, Los Angeles, CA, August 12, 2007.

41. Ana, interview by Jacqueline Hidalgo, Rancho Cucamonga, CA, May 17, 2007. In describing her reversion experience, Ana also mentioned that she felt "chills all over her body," that it felt "good," and that she knew "this one is for" her. She also felt like a weight had "lifted off [her] chest."

42. Elise, interview by Jacqueline Hidalgo, Masjid Omar Ibn Al-Khattab, Los Angeles, CA, July 15, 2007.

43. Isasi-Diaz, *En La Lucha*.

44. Interview with Rosa, House of Restoration Church, Hartford, CT, May 2007.

45. Father Carlos Zapata, interview with Brian Clark, St. Mary's Church, July 2008. More on the Roman Catholic setting will be shared in a separate section below.

46. Pastor Ray, interview by Elizabeth Conde-Frazier, La Puente Bible Institute, La Puente, CA, February 13, 2007.

47. Interview with Elise.

48. Mártinez-Vázquez, *Latina/o y Musulmán,* 49–51.

49. Gloria, interview by Jacqueline Hidalgo, Islamic Center of Southern California, Los Angeles, CA, August 5, 2007.

50. Mártinez-Vázquez, *Latina/o y Musulmán,* 47. In the interviews conducted with Muslim interlocutors by Jacqueline Hidalgo, all of her interviewees told a reversion narrative that revealed a mixture of gut feeling combined with slow, reasoned thinking. Most of them described part of their attraction to Islam in terms of it making sense, seeming like common sense, being reasonable, appearing ethical and right, as well as feeling good or giving them chills.

51. Interview with José.

52. Interview with Pastor Ray.

53. Carlos (Bible Institute teacher), interview by Efrain Agosto, La Puente, CA, February 13, 2007.

54. Interview with Juan.

55. Pedro (student), interview by Conde-Frazier, La Puente Bible Institute, April 2007.

56. Francisco (student), interview by Conde-Frazier, La Puente Bible Institute, April 2007.

57. Interview with José. This sentiment came up frequently in the interviews when interlocutors were asked about sacred texts in daily life: that the Quran serves as guidance because it is the word of God, and they granted God authority over their life.

58. Interview with Sonia.

59. Interview with Sonia.

60. Interview with Elise.

61. Interview with Ana.

62. Interview with Ana.

63. Interview with Rafael at the Latin American Bible Institute, April 2007.

64. Interview with Pedro.

65. "En la escritura encontramos luz para nuestro camino, nos guía por donde anda-
mos para marcar el destino. En la Biblia hallamos manantial de vida, fuente que ilumina,
que da alimento. Tu palabra llama al que está en tinieblas y al ser predicada no vuelve
vacía." Eleazar Torreglosa, *En la Escritura* (NY: GBG Musik, 2004), translation by S. T.
Kimbrough Jr.

66. Since, as detailed in the research report, these were freewheeling conversations
recorded over several weeks, no ascription of names is given to the transcribed quotes of
the participants.

67. Sermon by LABI student Esperanza, cited with her permission.

68. The series of sermons that Bishop Jeremiah Torres preached on Genesis and
Israel's history as a model of Latino/a church and community life and growth in the
twenty-first century have been collected into a book that he has recently published in
Spanish under the title, *La Bendición de la Cuarta Generación* (*The Blessing of the
Fourth Generation*). A DVD of the sermon series is also available in the archives of this
research project at the Institute for Signifying Scriptures.

69. Interview with Edward. Belief in the Qur'an because it spoke of familiar Christian
themes, though with somewhat different understandings, appeared in over half the interviews in the research study. Another example comes from Juan: "my interest in Islam grew
after I had found out about the belief in Jesus, which is kind of really weird...I would
read parts of the Qur'an that would confirm what I knew and Christianity to, kind of, like
as fuel for more motivation to read more...I would never be able to convert to religion
or a belief to a religion where belief in Jesus didn't exist, you know...even though now
I don't believe in Jesus like that like I know I'm familiar with it you know and like and
that like makes it okay."

70. Elena, interview by Jacqueline Hidalgo, Masjid Omar Ibn Al-Khattab, Los
Angeles, CA, May 20, 2007.

71. Ibid.

72. For an outline of this history, see, for example, Wimbush, "Bible and African
Americans?", 81–97.

CHAPTER 4 | Asian Americans, Bible
Believers

An Ethnological Study

TAT-SIONG BENNY LIEW

THIS CHAPTER LOOKS AT how Asian Americans who profess biblical inerrancy and/or authority read the Bible, as well as the relations
between their readings of the Bible and their lives and identities as
Asian Americans, particularly their sociopolitical inclinations, decisions, and choices.[1] It is based on face-to-face and telephone interviews
conducted within two broad regions of California: one in the northern
part, and the other the southern part of the state. A stratified sampling
method enabled us to ensure that the largest Asian subgroups had some
representation, while the social networks of our research team gave us
obtained convenience samples. Our interview questionnaire (see appendix 2.1) focuses on three issues that have particular relevance to Asian
American Bible believers: homosexuality, charity, and evangelism. The
question of homosexuality has, of course, been known to be an anathema
in conservative churches because of their reading of the Bible, but—as
many have pointed out—the Bible actually contains many more references to the question of poverty and charity than so-called homosexuality. Both questions are important for Asian Americans, since, on the
one hand, there is a tendency for the dominant culture—because of the
specifics of racialization—to see all Asian American male as gay but all
Asian American women as straight (Eng and Hom 1998: 1); on the other
hand, conservative Christianity has had the reputation of "privatizing"

faith and morality to help fashion and reinforce Asian Americans as an economically successful but sociopolitically innocuous "model minority." We also choose the topic of evangelism because, as we will see in greater detail below, Asian Americans have generally been racialized in this country as not only "foreign" but also "heathen" in need of the Christian gospel.

History and Identity

The Asian American population has been growing rapidly in the last fifty years. From 1990 to 2006, the number of Asians in the United States more than doubled (from 6.9 to 14.9 million). Between 2005 and 2006, Asian Americans, with a growth rate of 3.2 percent, registered the highest growth rate of any racial group in the United States.

Asian Americans include twenty-five different ethnic/nationality groups. In addition, a sizable number of Asian Americans are of mixed racial heritage (1.6 million in 2000). Heritage for Asian Americans often involves a vital linguistic dimension: Chinese, Tagalog, Vietnamese, and Korean are each spoken in more than a million homes (US Census Bureau, "Asian/Pacific American Heritage Month, May 2008," press release, April 24, 2008).

Along with ethnic and linguistic diversity, educational and economic disparity characterizes Asian America. While almost 50 percent of Asian Americans have college degrees (compared to 27 percent of all Americans), 50 percent of Southeast Asians in the United States do not have a high school diploma. Similarly, while 45 percent of Asian Americans are employed in management or professional occupations, less than 20 percent of Southeast Asian Americans are in these occupations. Despite all the rhetoric about Asian Americans being an economically successful "model minority," the median family income of Southeast Asian Americans (including Cambodian, Hmong, Laotian, and Vietnamese) is substantially lower than that of the entire United States (US Census Bureau, *We the People: Asians in the United States,* Census 2000 Special Report, December 2004).

Despite these many differences, Asian Americans have become a collective or a community. This formation has much to do with the racism and imperialism—what Daryl J. Maeda calls "the twin 'Chains of Babylon'" (2009: ix)—of the larger US society. While one might debate when and which group of Asians came to the United States "first,"[2] one needs to acknowledge that when sizable groups of Asians began to come and seek entry into the United States in the mid- to late nineteenth century (e.g., over 50,000 Chinese arriving in 1852 for the Gold Rush), the United States was just becoming a world power (mainly through its expansion into Asia). This change in the global positioning of the United States turned the relatively young nation not only imperialistic but also sinophobic and racist. It is equally important to acknowledge that these "first arrivals," regardless of when and from where in Asia, actually did not tend to identify themselves as "Asians," not to mention "Asian Americans." Instead, they generally thought of themselves as "Chinese," "Filipinos," "Indians," or "Japanese." These largely ethnic-specific self-identifications, though they never completely disappear, gradually, since the 1960s, turned into an Asian American racial identity and political movement that includes all these ethnicities.

Many have documented what people of Asian ancestry in the United States have experienced in terms of racial discrimination and exclusion. Again, Maeda provides a convenient mental mapping—what he calls "cycles of migration, exploitation, and exclusion" (2009: 20)—with his twofold point that: (1) these shared experiences of racialization by Asian groups of different ethnicity are tied to US imperialism; and (2) the formation of Asian American as a multiethnic collective since the 1960s has been a result of the intertwined dynamics between racism and imperialism (2009: 19–39). By "migration," Maeda refers to the early imperialist—and capitalist—desire of the United States to incorporate Asia into its political and commercial orbit that led to trafficking of goods and humans as goods. Rather than understanding "immigration" through the conventional "push-and-pull" emphasis—with "push" representing undesirable conditions in Asia and "pull" favorable ones across the Pacific—Maeda's view is, if we might use the words of Lisa Lowe, that "[t]he material legacy of the repressed history of U.S. imperialism in Asia is borne out in the 'return' of Asian immigrants to the imperial center" (1996: 16). With "exploitation," Maeda refers to how the United States simultaneously recruits cheap Asian labor for work in the United States and restricts those Asian laborers' eligibility for immigration into and citizenship in the United States. While the 1882 Chinese Exclusion Act is arguably the best known piece of racist legislation in US history, the so-called Asiatic Barred Zone being created by the Immigration Acts of 1917 and 1924 as well as the Tydings-McDuffie Act of 1934 made it clear that Asians of various ethnicities and nations were a "distinctly non-white racial bloc of undesirables" in the eyes of the US state (Maeda 2009: 22).

It is little wonder that while the United States was willing to expand its "for-whites-only" Naturalization Act of 1790 to include blacks in 1870 and Native Americans in 1890, Asians were once again deemed an alien bloc ineligible for naturalization.

Finally, Maeda uses the term "exclusion" to summarize setups that make Asians both legally inadmissible and socially inassimilable to mainstream US society. Antimiscegenation laws in California, for instance, were amended not only to aggregate different East Asian ethnicities into a single category of forbidden "Mongolians" but also to add the "Malays" as another forbidden "race" in order to ban Filipinos from marrying whites. Functioning to both regulate desires and normalize a racial hierarchy, these antimiscegenation laws helped establish and reinforce Asians as a race of unwanted—indeed unsafe—pollutants.

In addition to categories like "Mongolians" and "Malays" or derogatory terms that are somewhat ethnic-specific (like "Chinks," "Japs," and "Gooks"), labels like "Yellow," "Yellow Peril," and "Orientals" had, since the mid-nineteenth century, been functioning as effective and damaging weapons to call Asians out as one unwelcome and unpropitious group. In fact, "Orientals" had become more or less the "standard" way to refer to people of Asian heritage until "Asian Americans" became their own chosen self-designation. While it is difficult to pinpoint when the Asian American movement came into existence, many have pointed to the Third World Liberation Front strike at San Francisco State University in 1968 as a convenient marker to signify the movement's struggle against not only white supremacy within the United States but also US imperialism abroad (Maeda 2009: x). The connections between the 1968 Strike and the Black Power and anti–Vietnam War movements also helpfully point to the interracial and transnational dimensions of the Asian America movement even at its beginning stage.

As we discuss Asian America in relation to US racism and imperialism, we must not lose sight of how those racist and imperialist policies and practices against persons of Asian heritage are partly—perhaps even largely—played out on religious grounds. Since the mid-nineteenth century, when "Orientals" became a way to call Asians out, this targeted group was also often described as "heathens" because of their other-than-Christian religious traditions (Liew 2008: 26–27). In fact, when Greenberry G. Rupert helped popularize the threat of a "Yellow Peril" with his book of the same title, he subtitled the book tellingly with the words, *Or, The Orient Vs. the Occident as Viewed by Modern Statesmen and Ancient Prophets* (1911; originally published in 1848). Rupert's "ancient prophets" was a reference to the Christian Bible. Understanding people from "China, India, Japan, and Korea" through the phrase "the kings of the east" in Revelations 16:12 (King James Version), Rupert himself made a religious *and* political prophecy that Jesus Christ would stop these "kings" and their menace against the Western world (1911: 9–22). Even more telling is Rupert's "introduction" to the third edition of his book, where he outlined the three main questions "the world" needed to settle, because they would determine the ultimate question of "who shall rule the world" (1911: 6). Rupert's three questions are: (1) "the race question...between the colored races of the world and the white race"; (2) "the religious question...between the eastern nations, who are not professed Christians, and the western nations, who profess to be Christians"; and (3) "the financial question involv[ing] the wealth of the world" (1911: 6). In one short page and three succinct questions, Rupert demonstrated the intricate intersections between religion and racism and capitalism/imperialism against Asians.

Because of these intersections, it should be no surprise that Sui Sin Far, the "first Chinese American fictionist" (Solberg 1981), not only wrote about "Chinese-American Sunday Schools" and "The Bible Teacher" but also made a link between "Americanizing" and "Christianizing" in "The Chinese in America" series she did for the journal, *Westerner*, in 1909 (Ling and White-Parks 1995: 254–55, 257–58). As Mary Ting Yi Lui points out, Christian mission—particularly Sunday schools and Bible classes—"performed an important function as a major Christianizing and Americanizing influence on the Chinese population, acclimatizing them to life in American society" (2005: 112). Even the teaching and learning of the English language in those early decades were often carried out through the reading and reciting of Christian scriptures. For the same reason, when the Japanese immigrant Takao Ozawa petitioned for naturalization in 1922, one of the arguments he made for his eligibility or qualification was that "he spoke English at home and sent his children to Sunday school" (Maeda 2009: 24). If, as we have seen from Rupert, Christianity is closely connected in the popular cultural imagery with what it means to be Western in general and American in particular, then becoming a Christian might be one way for Asians to achieve Americanization.

Asian American Christianity has, therefore, a long and complicated history since the Presbyterian Board of Foreign Missions helped establish the first Asian Christian church in the United States for the Chinese in San Francisco in 1853 (Yang 1999: 5). According to the most recent and

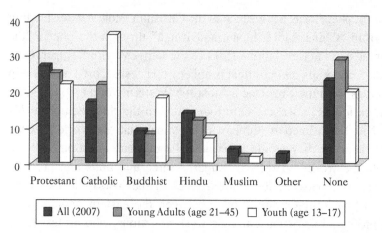

FIGURE 4.1 Asian American religious affiliation. Data from Pew Forum U.S. Religious Afiliation Survey 2007 (N ~ 700); Social Capital Community Benchmark Survey 2000 ages 21–45 (N = 460); and National Study of Religion and Youth 2000 (N = 45).

largest survey of Asian Americans, 27 percent of Asian Americans were Protestant Christians (17 percent Evangelical; 9 percent Mainline); 17 percent were Catholic; 9 percent were Buddhist; 14 percent were Hindu; and 4 percent were Muslim in terms of religious affiliation (Figure 4.1; Pew Forum on Religion and Public Life, "U.S. Religious Landscape Survey," February 2008). In fact, the numbers of Asian Americans professing non-Christian religions have almost tripled with the influx of new immigrants in the last two decades.

If one takes into consideration that another 20 percent to 30 percent of Asian Americans stated that they had no religious affiliation in that same survey, one might say that religious pluralism is also a distinguishing mark of Asian America. This is especially so since the higher percentage of "no-religion" status reported by Asian Americans—compared to the national average at 16 percent (Pew Forum on Religion and Public Life, "U.S. Religious Landscape Survey," February 2008)—might have more to do with their tendency to interpret "religion" for that survey in terms of exclusive doctrinal tenets and weekly congregation-based activities (like they know "Westerners" tend to do). In other words, "no religion" for many Asian American might only mean that they are practicing multiple spiritual traditions (including folk religion) and home rituals, and they do so in a nonexclusive and pluralistic way.

While Asian America's religious pluralism often reinforces for many the stereotype of Asians in America as "pagan" or "heathen" (though more in terms of non-Christian than no religious affiliation), Asian

Americans actually affiliate most as Christians (see also Lien and Carnes 2004: 44–50). Recent studies have suggested that religious affiliation facilitates and supports Asian Americans, especially but by no means exclusively first-generation immigrants, in their adaptation to and acculturation into US society as well as in the maintenance and transmission of their own racial/ethnic heritage (Chen and Jeung 2000; Suh 2004; Jeung 2005; Chen 2008). How then does Christianity function in the identity development of this sizable Asian American population who affiliate with the very religion that has long been used to racialize them? This chapter, as we indicated in the beginning, aims to look at a more specific question within that larger question by sampling a smaller subgroup (also in terms of age and geography) within that larger population. While our interviewees—primarily young professionals in California, including both those who have had significant involvement with parachurch organizations and first-generation immigrants who are non–English speaking—might not be representative of Asian America in general, it is actually quite representative of a "Bible-believing" Asian America in particular. For example, in recent years the percentage of Asian Americans in parachurch organizations like Asian Baptist Student Koinonia, Campus Crusade for Christ, and InterVarsity Christian Fellowship (ICVF) have increased exponentially. A multicultural organization like IVCF saw its Asian American population grow by 267 percent nationwide over the last fifteen years, from 992 to 3640 (Kim 2006). Parachurches have become a distinctive subculture in Asian America that has caught the eye of many scholars (Busto 1999; Jeung 2005; Kim 2006).

Interpretation and Institution

With what he calls "interpretive community," Stanley Fish suggests that meaning resides in neither the individual reader nor a particular text but in or through an institutionalized set of reading assumptions and practices (1980). While we pursue this study by way of individual interviews, we have learned from these individual interviews that their Bible-reading practices are, as Fish suggested, always already effects of institutions that are social as well as historical. However, we have also learned from these interviews something that Fish does not emphasize: institutions are not only established realities but also ongoing processes (see Weber 2001: xv, 7–13, 19–21, 155–56). In other words, when it comes to reading practices, we must attend to both an institution's power to impose limits on its membership and membership's potentiality to improvise, negotiate, challenge, subvert, and even transform an institution.[3] In fact, our interviews show that understanding institution as both an enforcing power and a negotiable process is essential to an adequate understanding of Asian American Bible believers.

An interpretive community's instituting or enforcing power *on* Bible believers can be clearly seen from Janet, a fourth-generation Japanese American who works for the national office of a major parachurch organization that is known for its work on college and university campuses in general and with Asian American students in particular.[4] Like the vast majority of Asian American Bible believers we interviewed (93 percent), Janet has been part of many group Bible studies. More importantly, as a "campus minister" of the national office, she has been trained to lead group Bible studies "throughout the country" (interview, September 1, 2007). In fact, Janet was "convicted" to move away from a "cultural Christianity" when she "met the person Jesus [in her] freshman year of college" in a small group Bible study organized by the same parachurch organization that she now serves.

Talking about one of these "very formalized [training] programs" she went through to become a Bible study leader in a major convention, Janet mentions that "they would train about seventy-five of us for about 18 months" (including about eight days of "on-site" training). What she calls the "inductive manuscript study" involves "a lot of rules to really keep people engaged and on track." First of all, biblical passages are printed out doubled-spaced on regular letter-size paper with "huge" margins. Then participants are asked to do "an observation exercise" with pencils and color markers to come up with a list of observations and questions about the text. These observations and questions will, according to Janet, help one "understand an author's intent" and "the cultural nuances" so that one will know how to separate the "[biblical] principles" from the "colorful cultural artifacts." The final step of this Bible study method will center on interpreting the "application" of a biblical passage "for today."

While Janet talks about "an author's intent" and "the need to enter the story in their cultural context, in their time and place," she also mentions that part of the method involves spending a lengthy time "just reading the passage." Janet continues, "Hopefully, it is too much time and people get bored, because I find that once you start getting bored, then you start getting very creative." Janet does not explicitly explain the relationship between a writer's "intent" and a reader's "creativity," but her following comments may help to shed some light:

> You will have read it and read it, and think this is boring and I understand it. Then start coloring the letters. I used to do this in church. I colored in all of the Os and put them in pink. Count how many Ls there are. You know just stupid stuff, but then...I began to notice there were these patterns of where the Os were showing up. And then I noticed that the word "look" is repeated over and over and over again....So I try to give them way more time than they would need, and then we share questions...and I just sort of try to listen to what God is bringing up with the group, which may or may not be the same thing in my lesson plan. (Interview, September 1, 2007)

Though Janet seems to assume a hierarchical order from the reader at the bottom to biblical text to biblical author to God at the top, her narrative also seems to move almost seamlessly along an author's intent, a reader's creativity as well as questions, and God's nudging, making a person's involvement in reading the Bible indistinguishable from not only his or her projection onto the Bible but also the author's or even God's own voice. We will need to revisit this friction and/or fluidity, but let us focus in the meantime on a contradiction in Janet's comments between emphasizing her brand of group Bible study as both an unmediated experience and an evidently mediated one. On the one hand, Janet and her fellow Bible study leaders are required to go through eighteen months of "very formalized" training. On the other hand, Janet repeats several times that these Bible studies would not use commentaries ("We would go with no commentaries. I might use another translation, but generally no commentaries...I won't go to a commentary just to figure out what it means" [interview, September 1, 2007]). While reading practices—as Fish points out—are always already being institutionalized, and perhaps no institution is ready to be absolutely upfront about its own historical contingency and thus social relativity, Bible readers who embrace biblical inerrancy and/or authority often do assume or hypostasize its practice of Bible reading as "natural." Janet's emphasis on "inductive" observations and her willingness to jettison her lesson plan imply an unmediated encounter with the Bible, although such an encounter is always led by a leader who has been trained for eighteen months and is thus armed with leading questions. This is especially significant given Janet's emphasis on not using commentaries in her group Bible study, but she admits, in response to a question about how she learns about and/or from the Bible, that she does so through her own teaching and training; through commentaries, "other people's sermons"; and from conference speakers (see also Ammerman 1987: 56). The language that Janet uses to refer to her own formation as an inductive Bible study leader is that of apprentice and mentor. "I would say that everything that I teach now," she continues, "every method I teach now, I was apprenticed into it by someone else" (interview, September 1, 2007).

Janet also makes a quick reference to seminary when she talks about her own learning of the Bible, although she does not tell us if she has a seminary degree or which seminary she has in mind. Yuk Yee, an Asian American female who teaches the Bible in a seminary that teaches the Bible as God's "inspired and infallible Word," shares that she "usually downplays" academic methods of biblical criticism in her courses; instead, she "just explain[s] that they are human reconstructions or human constructions to understand the Bible, the message, and God, and that human constructions can be limited in the way how we express or make sense of this God or the Bible" (interview, January 18, 2008).[5] Yuk Yee's response shows not only that seminary professors, like staff members of parachurch organizations, may play the role of institutional brokers or agents but also that institutionalization process works through an antagonistic process (see also Ammerman 1987: 8). Just as Janet's comment about "no longer hav[ing] the same DNA as my old church group" and leaving "cultural Christianity" and its Jesus who "had no opinion on anything" but finding in those "inductive manuscript" studies of the Bible a Jesus she "had never seen before" (interview, September 1, 2007), Yuk Yee and perhaps her students contrast the Bible—like God and unlike any methods of biblical criticism—and human construction. To Yuk Yee, the Bible is natural or, more accurately, supernatural. When asked if her students may end up feeling that their own reading of the Bible is also a human construction, Yuk Yee responds by returning to the difference of the Bible, or the difference that the Bible makes:

> I think application is very important. We don't just talk about the academic stuff but how does all this stuff mean to us now. What does this mean to the church, or to our personal life? So I think, ah, at the end of any academic discussion or class, I would spend some time making applications to our present context...I guess sharing our own personal testimonies of how the Bible has influenced my own life, so that they can see a real person with real experience. (Interview, January 18, 2008)

In other words, the difference that the Bible makes in the lives of Bible believers is invoked as the basis of an authority that transcends "human constructions" and hence is an affirmation of the difference of the Bible.

Alison, an Asian American professor of the Bible in another seminary that embraces biblical inerrancy, actually would like to discuss these critical methods with her students even if she is not in complete agreement with the methods. However, she finds herself constrained by her institutional context. "You know," Alison comments, "teaching is very limited in terms of what we can do, but I do try to incorporate" these academic criticisms (interview, January 10, 2008). Alison does not elaborate on the specifics of her institutional constraint, but her following remark—"I also feel like it is part of my responsibility if I am going to introduce something that is really going to bother [my students] and I don't have an opportunity to help them. I feel like it is my responsibility to really only introduce as much as I can give them time and space to process" (interview, January 10, 2008)—indicates that her constraint is at least partly related to the theological background of her students.

This kind of communal or institutional constraint is nothing new for Alison. When she was considering where to pursue her PhD degree in biblical studies, "a few people in [her] tradition expressed concern;" although Alison was also quick to point out that "the vast majority of people...were very supportive and enthusiastic." Here we see that (biblical) interpretation not only results from but also breaks and makes communities. This concern over a different other is, of course, related to the institutional practice of constructing identity over an antagonistic other (a practice that is by no means limited to Asian American Bible believers). Given this concern, it should not be surprising that institutional power might also incline toward isolation and control. Being "institutionalized" often involves being anxious about what an-other community may do as well as what one's own community may think. These anxieties help present and preserve various limits and limitations on one's social network, and hence one's interpretive community. If the "concern" over Alison's entry into a major university of a different tradition came from only "a few," Sharon's entry into the Bible-believing circle is surrounded by a lot more—and greater—social "pressure." Recalling those college days, this second-generation Filipina American not only refers repeatedly to the "pressure" to conform by renouncing her Catholic upbringing but also relates that "pressure" to an almost exclusive social circle on the part of most Bible believers:

> I think I felt that pressure because I wanted to be like other people...I was part of this core group...something called *kapwa*; and *kapwa* is a Tagalog word meaning, for me, "shared identity"...the tension was more trying, to be more like how the majority was out of my fellowship...who they

associated with were all Christians, their whole family went to this church, which is super different from my upbringing. I mean, I went to church with other church families; we went on Sundays. Maybe that's a criticism: that maybe Catholics only go to church on Sundays...I think a lot of churches I see are very insular...you hang out with each other; it's kind of exclusive. (Interview, August 9, 2007)

One can see in Sharon's words the mutually reinforcing dynamics of an isolated group and an isolating process. Interestingly, while Sharon goes on to emphasize that her current local church is different and that it is very "outwardly focused," she proceeds to define that "outward focused" merely as "neighborhood focused" with these words:

So I would say 75% of people that go to our church live in a five-by-five block area. So it is very community oriented. We are neighbors with each other. We see each other a lot. We are really in each other's lives almost daily. So Susie that you met at the front step [just before the interview], she is my neighbor; she goes to my church. I used to live with her. So we really try and strive for a whole community. So we are living together, being together, eating together, working together, going to church together. (Interview, August 9, 2007)

An exclusive social network is a convenient institutional means to not only naturalize authority and autonomy, but also to cultivate and exploit a member's anxiety over her or his own loyalty to the community. This is particularly important for Asian American Bible believers, as many of our interviewees belong to Christian communities that are primarily made up of fellow Asian Americans. If their participation in these racial and ethnic minority churches indicates certain awareness of their own minoritized social status, the pressure to remain loyal in order to remain in the communities may be felt even more acutely. This may partly explain why interviewees are reluctant to share their own personal position on a divisive topic like ordination of homosexuals.

While 81 percent of our interviewees have problems with ordaining homosexuals and 74 percent of our interviewees state in some way that the Bible is against homosexuality, 14 percent respond that they are "neutral," meaning that interviewees are conflicted or have not thought about the issue. Regardless of their stance on ordaining homosexuals, many—even among those who believe that the Bible condemns homosexuality—do *not* feel that it is a major issue that deserves attention.

A few of our interviewees do express sympathy and even support for ordaining homosexuals. For example, Maria (interview, September 19, 2007), a second-generation Chinese American graduate student, uses "scientific studies"—thus an extrabiblical language and argument—to talk about homosexuality: "If you do the research, you look at the studies, there really seems to be some fundamental brain differences, physically and chemically, between gay and straight people. How do you question that? How do you deal with that and bring it to theology?" These studies—despite their tendency, we must add, to simplify human sexuality, for example, by not taking into account a spectrum of sexualities, genders, and gender identities—suggest to Maria that homosexuality is inherited, genetic, and not a (sinful) choice.

A couple of our interviewees even support ordaining homosexuals with their own Bible- or Christian-based language. For Laurel, a 1.5-generation interviewee of both Chinese and Filipino descent, the scientific studies serve only to supplement her experience of knowing her best friend, who is a lesbian, and confirm her position that homosexuality is natural and hence God-given. She explains, "So my argument really is, like, if I don't think God would make something that is inherently sinful in you—that's just not the way He [*sic*] works" (interview, September 2, 2007). Since she believes that homosexuality is God-given, she feels that she cannot judge it as a sin. Consequently, she unwaveringly supports ordination of homosexuals.

Janet, who supports ordination if the homosexual is nonpracticing, states that the way to judge a church leader is by the leader's success in ministry:

We shouldn't stand in the way of the ordination of someone who is fruitful, and who[m]... it's pretty obvious that the Lord is with. The reason that I point that out to you, is that that is a similar argument for me about women in ministry. (Interview, September 1, 2007)

For Janet, when a minister is fruitful—though she never specifies her definition of fruitfulness—God is clearly with him or her, and so one should support that minister, whether that minister is a woman or a (nonpracticing) homosexual.

Notice how both Laurel's and Janet's comments point to personal relationships. Laurel's case is clear, as her best friend is a lesbian. Janet's comment is relational in the sense that this criterion or quality of "fruitfulness" does not refer to a minister's ministry but a minister's person. It implies therefore a personal familiarity or relationship with a minister. These comments seem to confirm the "Aunt Susan" and "My Friend Al" principle that personally knowing or loving someone of a different religion, ideology, or religious ideology might change one's attitude—including hostility—against that religion, ideology, or religious ideology (Putnam and Campbell 2010: 526–32). If so, an Asian American Bible believer's social network makes a difference. The intersection between Asian Americans and Bible believers signals overlapping communities, and thus speaks against the autonomy and authority of any single interpretive community (Liew and Wimbush 2002: 34–35). It explains the insulating emphasis that was felt and articulated by some of our interviewees. In fact, a few interviewees express fear of ostracism for holding positive views of homosexuals. Maria explains:

> The Christian community can be very, very strong in ostracizing people, and just pressuring people without meaning to. I know that there are a lot of Christians who agree with me, or have the same issues that I have struggling with this issue, but would probably not say it, or would know too many people who would question them. And just not be that vocal about it. (Interview, September 19, 2007)

If some Asian American Bible believers might not share what they really think of homosexuality among fellow Bible believers, would they do so with those who are not Bible believers? Would they, at least, in non-Christian circles, embrace neutrality? As it turns out, all but one of the interviewees who claim to be neutral or in support of ordaining homosexuals were interviewed by the only non-Christian interviewer in our research. This means that if this interviewer's interviews were discounted from the study, there would be an almost unanimous agreement against homosexual ordination; the lone exception here is Archie, a second-generation Chinese American, who says that he is neutral. Nancy Ammerman has suggested that Bible believers speak a "proper language" to go along with their ideas and practices (1987: 87–88). In other words, fellow Bible believers can recognize one another as well as spot an outsider by the way people speak, act, and speak. If so, it is likely that our interviewees may well know when they are being interviewed by a non-Christian and tailor their responses accordingly. If so, do the neutral or supportive responses regarding the ordination of homosexuals represent these interviewees' "authentic" positions about the issue, or are these responses themselves attempts to avoid conflict with a non-Christian whose own view on homosexuality is not known to the interviewees? Or are they a mixture of both?

In ways that are at least partly related to our discussion about how institutional power cultivates and exploits an anxiety among its members over losing their social network, Asian American Bible believers seem to actively avoid conflict both within and beyond their Bible-believing circles. Forty-four percent of our interviewees, like Maria, claim that they actively choose not to engage in action for or against the issue of ordaining homosexuals. Winnie, a second-generation Filipina American, claims that Jesus is the only judge and adds that withholding judgment expresses Christian humility and allows you to become friends with and evangelize homosexuals (interview, May 12, 2008). There are also first- and 1.5-generation interviewees who express that they are apolitical. Others say that they are not interested in an unimportant subject like ordaining homosexuals.

Fifteen percent of our interviewees state that they are nonconfrontational. In fact, 37 percent of our interviewees say that they would actively avoid the issue of homosexuality if a fellow Christian disagreed with them. Phuong-Anh, a first-generation Vietnamese American in her fifties, states that the most important thing for Christians is to remain faithful and together in their faith, so one should not bring up a contentious issue:

> Generally speaking, we need to understand one another, and the bottom line is faith. I base my faith on the Bible and I won't compare the Bible law with eloquent arguments and social reasons.... Therefore, the best way to be able to stay together is not to talk about the issue. (Interview, April 14, 2007)

Similarly, Danh, a 1.5-generation Vietnamese American in his thirties, remarks:

> The [important] matter is that those who do not have the same ideas with ours also have the same belief. They also believe in Jesus Christ and are also saved. So, it is not necessary to argue to cause problems. No need. (Interview, April 15, 2007)

Some interviewees express relief that the issue has not arisen in their own local church. These expressions are important to note, given the ideals attached to church leaders as models of morality by some of the same interviewees. If a minister were to announce his or her homosexuality, the issue would be unavoidable for the church community, and there would probably be conflict and possibly even divisions and separations.

Conversations about such issues would cause some people to be upset, some to feel ostracized, and would possibly lead some not to be saved. Instead of discussing it, many would avoid the issue for the sake of the cohesion of the larger community and the souls of a few.

Intertextual Negotiation and Fusion of Horizons

Having discussed the reality of institutional power over the reading practice of Asian American Bible believers, let us turn and look at what these institutionalized practice of reading the Bible actually looks like.

An overwhelming 81.4 percent of our entire sample prize the Bible for the guidance it provides for personal directions and decisions. Many value the Bible for the relationship with God it mediates, some even referring to the Bible as a divine "love letter." This reverential regard for the Bible motivates our interviewees to read more than just words and sentences in the Bible.

For instance, most of our interviewees are aware that a text like the so-called Great Commission found in Matthew 28:19 has a historical location quite different from contemporary America. As Kenneth, a second-generation Chinese American undergraduate student, puts it:

> Christ is talking with his disciples, "Alright, you've been hanging out with me for three years now and you have seen the things that I have done. You understand who I am. Now go and tell people about it." (Interview, October 22, 2007)

Despite recognizing the passage's particular time frame as one far removed from the present, Kenneth continues:

> I've heard some folks say that we do not have to do that because it applied to the disciples at the time, only to those eleven guys. It's not our job. It was their thing. Only problem with this is later in Acts, it talks about spreading the Word in Judea, Samaria, and to the ends of the earth. And so I do think we do have not an obligation, but if you do get the opportunity, we should do it. (Interview, October 22, 2007)

In such readings, as we saw earlier in Janet's blurring the differences between a reader's creativity and a biblical author's or even God's "intent," the Bible straddles the line between carrying "fixed" messages for particular recipients and disseminating fluid effects that go beyond temporal, geographical, or cultural specificities. Kenneth's reference to John's Gospel (Jesus as having three years of earthly ministry) and to Acts in his reading of Matthew 28 also shows a reading practice that transcends the limits of any particular biblical book. Reading a biblical passage alongside other biblical passages may neutralize "problematic" dimensions to preserve the cogency of a "larger" meaning. Hence, Jesus's injunction to his immediate disciples ("those eleven guys," as Kenneth calls them) in Matthew's Great Commission becomes, when read with the book of Acts, a commission for all who currently respond to Jesus's message. Additionally, Matthew's Great Commission is mixed and merged with other social texts that emerge from various situations in life. Kathy, a second-generation Vietnamese American undergraduate, does this mixing and merging rather effortlessly:

> There is a lesson for each [of Jesus' interactions with his disciples]. Even after Jesus goes to heaven, the book that the other apostles wrote to the church…the care and the problems within the church are really relevant because the problems that the church experiences today are still relevant. (Interview, May 31, 2007)

In one interpretive sweep, the textual particularities of a biblical text mix and merge with the contemporary particularities of a twenty-first century reader. With this reading practice, the Bible becomes a timeless center along a somewhat linear history. Despite the awareness of the Bible's location in a specific time, place, and culture, Asian American Bible believers render the Bible a referential template that is broad enough to address issues emerging from their own immediate context. This reading practice reinforces, then, a view of the Bible as something more than just a collection of diverse literary texts—each with its own integrity from beginning to end, and each located within a specific time and space. The Bible, read as a whole rather than in terms of its separate books, provides life-defining meanings and applications. Reading in this way facilitates, in a Gadamerian sense, a "fusion" of the horizon of a text and that of its contemporary reader, despite temporal, spatial, cultural, and racial/ethnic differences. The most common and basic outcome of this so-called fusion is, however, the church-based teachings that Asian American Bible believers learn through weekly sermons and small group Bible study. As we mentioned before, an overwhelming majority of our interviewees (93 percent) are involved in some form of small group study of the Bible with particular formats and approaches, whether the study is organized by para-church organizations for younger, college-going interviewees or by local churches. Alfred, a third-generation Chinese American graduate student, speaks of how the Bible figures as a kind of dated but never outdated center through such studies:

> In our Bible study right now, we're looking at the topic of social justice and what does the Bible have to say about that...the Bible doesn't use the term, "social justice." So it's been a challenge for us to go backward and say, "Well, we have this idea of what social justice is, but where do we really find that in scripture? And does scripture really support our ideas of what social justice should be?" (Interview, March 31, 2008)

The horizon that an Asian American Bible believer brings to a biblical text is multilayered. At a personal level, it ranges from profound emotional engagements to life-wrenching crises, but they all heighten a reader's perception of the Bible as something more than just a literary text. Bao, a first-generation Vietnamese American male pharmacist, avows, "I love to read the Gospels because they are easy and they are about Jesus's life. He is the one I worship and idolize. Therefore I read them passionately" (interview, April 22, 2007). On the other end of the spectrum, Kathy regains her grounding amid a debilitating bout of depression:

> That was when I was lying on my bed crying. I felt the Bible right underneath my head. I just picked it up and opened it up to a random verse in Timothy. It said, "If we endure, we will reign in him." I think that was powerful for me....The Bible was the only thing that was there for me when I really needed someone. (Interview, May 31, 2007)

The Bible, with these readings, is appropriated and further enlivened by its readers to transgress its textual constrictions and perform the role of an active agent. Our data shows that the Bible animates these readers' life decisions and attitudes on issues including tithing, choice of friends, and, as we have seen, ideological positions on human sexuality.

Beyond the personal level, there is a broader horizon that influences a Bible believer's reading of the Bible, and it includes the reality of racial dynamics in the United States. Rather than push our interviewees to make categorical statements on what make their readings of the Bible typically Asian American, we let them consider how reading a passage like the Great Commission would be important for Asian Americans. While a significant

79.1 percent interpret the Great Commission as an injunction for evangelism, many also make conscious interventions through or intersections with one's particular location as Asian American. According to Alfred, "There is a tension [for Asian Americans] between wanting to reach out and be inclusive of all peoples and, at the same time, of wanting to preserve the ethnic heritage of whatever group we come from" (interview, March 31, 2008). This practice of reading with a heritage displaced in time and space is extremely nuanced and complicated. For example, Chien, another first-generation Vietnamese American who is also retired, reads the conquest and settlement narratives in the Hebrew Bible as betraying the Jewish bias of its authors and thus compromising the Bible's infallibility (interview, April 20, 2007). He comes to this conclusion by referring to his home country's jingoistic history, which has silenced its own systematic campaign of destruction and its occupation of minority communities to become the country it is now. One observes in Chien's comments that the racial/ethnic heritage that informs his reading of the Bible is one he both remembers and from which he keeps a critical distance.

This broader horizon of an Asian American Bible believer should not, however, be limited to a narrow sense of "heritage," in which certain attitudes and practices become a kind of "deposit" that is traceable to many cultural complexes known to be—perhaps stereotypically—"Asian." As we have seen from Alfred and Chien, cultural practices and remembrances of a time and place that are, in some sense, quite removed from one's location as an "American" do exist, and they do impact how an Asian American Bible believer might read the Bible. Reading with this narrow sense of "heritage" incorporates a loss and an attempt to overcome the displacement. Yet, the horizon of Asian American Bible believers is not only broader but also more fluid, since "Asian America" is a much more complex site of negotiation. Their broader horizon is therefore not just a throwback to something like "once upon a time and somewhere in Asia," but a dynamic and ongoing process of self-definition and cultural invention. Their readings of the Bible then become both a result of and a resource for this negotiating process.

We can see this, for instance, in how some of our interviewees read Matthew 28:19. Maria reads Matthew's Great Commission as a grammar of evangelism to parse and override what she observes as her church's tendency toward self-isolation (interview, September 19. 2007)—or, as Jack, a 22-year-old second-generation Chinese American, puts it, the tendency to "cluster together" (interview, June 1, 2007). Maxine, another second-generation Chinese American undergraduate, concurs, "I think it's because we are Asian Americans. Even though we have the American culture, for the most part the Asian side is more dominant. As a group, we really just focus on our own communities" (interview, October 25, 2007). Statements such as these reflect an underlying awareness of one's minoritized status in the United States and a need for incorporation with the mainstream, so the Great Commission becomes a biblical injunction for pursuing and performing such incorporation.

While an overwhelming percentage of our interviewees, as we have seen, read the Great Commission as a command to evangelize, and a significant percentage (53.5 percent) also avow that they have incorporated its implied command, actual exposure to and interaction with religious difference seem to elicit the most cautious interpretations of this biblical command. Of our interviewees, 48.8 percent express deference on the possibility of an actual confrontation with and conversion of people who profess another religion. In fact, most see living and sharing a biblically informed model life—that is, a life that is visibly noticeable and exemplary in demonstrating success and personal well-being (see also Busto 1999)—as the best strategy for building relationships across religious differences. When interpreted in terms of this model life, Matthew's Great Commission is read and negotiated as a nonaggressive and amenable bridge across racial/ethnic and religious boundaries.

What about the Great Commission's emphasis on "making disciples" (or discipleship) and Asian cultural practices that carry non-Christian religious implications? For instance, while "ancestor worship" is generally considered an indelible part of one's Asian heritage, it is often seen as a practice that contests what the Bible says about Christ's centrality. This example was actually brought up by some of the interviewees themselves. Three interviewees suggest that they would read the Great Commission as cultural and religious imperialism if it were to imply or demand denial of one's racial/ethnic heritage. JoAnne, a fourth-generation Japanese American, calls such readings "bad cultural biases" (interview, July 24, 2007). While most may refrain from the practice of "ancestor worship," some of our interviewees claim that such practices can be compatible with their reading of the Bible in general and Matthew's Great Commission in particular when these practices are understood as ritual acts of respect rather than acts of worship. These comments show Asian American Bible believers actively at work to negotiate a perceived dissonance between their horizon as Asian Americans—which often includes a sense of cultural loss and mourning—and their horizon as Bible believers. In these negotiations, the Bible is secured and assured as the center, but the concentric cultural zones around that center are also not neglected or abandoned.

The racial dynamics involved in the interpretive negotiations of our interviewees become even more complex in light of another set of cross-textual references that they use in reading the Bible. Through the course of our interviews, many brought up texts like Josh McDowell's *More Than a Carpenter* (1977), Oswald Chambers's *My Utmost for His Highest* (1937), Bruce Wilkinson's *Secrets of the Vine* (2001), and Rick Warren's *The Purpose Driven Life* (2002). These texts, though authored by white males and emerging from a particular form of religious configuration and cultural complex in the United States, seem to have become transferrable to the communities and lives of contemporary Asian American Bible believers. These book titles suggest, again, biblical parameters that speak to the model life our interviewees often invoked. Are these texts, then, betraying again the felt need of our interviewees to be incorporated into the larger US cultural complex, even or especially because of their awareness of racial/ethnic difference? Their reading of Matthew's Great Commission underscores a tension as well as an intention to negotiate between isolation and assimilation.

The way Asian American Bible believers read the Bible with their experience and use the Bible to negotiate their experience can also be seen in how Vietnamese Americans relate the Bible to their practice of charity. Vietnamese American Bible believers we interviewed not only strongly support but also equate missions in Vietnam—which includes both actual going back for charitable activities in Vietnam and imagined return through sending aid to Vietnam—to Christian charity. Their concept of charity is largely informed by their view and their reading of the Bible, since most of them view the Bible as the Word of God and thus a most authoritative guide for their lives (81 percent of the first- and 1.5-generation we interviewed accepts no authority outside of the Bible). What Jimmy, a 47-year-old accountant, says is rather representative of this group:

> The Bible is the Word of God, being inspired and blessed by God for teaching and guiding our life....I think that the Bible has an absolute authority higher than all the leaders of the church....I respect the pastor's personal experiences, but I won't do what he says if his words do not contain [*sic*.] the Bible or they are opposite to the Bible or opposed to the Bible. It doesn't matter whatever position he holds, I will not listen. (Interview, April 7, 2007)

The Bible passage that is cited most to interpret charity is the parable of the sheep and the goats in Matthew 25:31–46. Here are the verses that were frequently quoted by our Vietnamese American interviewees:

> "For I was hungry and you gave me food, I was thirsty and you gave me something to drink, I was a stranger and you welcomed me, I was naked and you gave me clothing, I was sick and you took care of me, I was in prison and you visited me." ... And the king will answer them, "Truly I tell you, just as you did it to one of the least of these who are members of my family, you did it to me." (Matthew 25:35–36, 40, New Revised Standard Version).

In their reading of this text, they emphasize an ethics of love as the heart of Christian discipleship. Being Christian is inherently characterized by love and hence a commitment to do good works as Jesus commands. It is not the reward or the punishment in the last judgment that motivates them to practice charity; rather it is God's love in them. According to Eva (interview, April 6, 2007), a second-generation college student who cites this passage, "God's love can be demonstrated because we give. How will people know God unless God lives in us and then we show people through our charitable deeds that God exists and that He [sic] cares for them?" Chien also comments, "When we do charity, we reflect the love that God teaches us. Christianity is [a] religion of love. If we claim that we belong to Christianity, we must love others, and that love must be shown by doing charity" (interview, April 20, 2007). The Bible parable provides them with a rhetoric and an ethics of love; it is this core Christian value that motivates charity. It is a universal love for everyone, including Christians and non-Christians, Asians and non-Asians.

We see in these comments by our Vietnamese American interviewees their experience of hostility and alienation. They were marginalized in their home country, and, as immigrants in the United States, they have faced considerable antagonism from the dominant society. In response, this group of Bible believers differentiate themselves from others by identifying themselves as a loving people. This rhetoric is especially significant to their view of missions in Vietnam as charity. Those who left Vietnam, particularly those called "boat people" and former political prisoners, were often regarded as "traitors" of the country. Now they return to their homeland where they were cast out, not to seek justice, but to bring healing to Vietnam for the sake of love.

The appropriation and interpretation of this parable are also significant to this particular group due to their experience as immigrants. Since most of the Vietnamese Americans in this group were boat people or families of former political prisoners, they had struggled to survive the sea, refugee camps, and prisons before they came to the United States. In this foreign land, they also experienced or continue to experience a period of uncertainty and difficulty. Their lives in this transition reflect the image of Kari Lydersen's book title about Latin American immigrants in the United States: *Out of the Sea and into the Fire* (2005). Through this parable in Matthew 25, they see their own stories with the suffering of the needy and how love transforms their plight. To borrow the words of R. S. Sugirtharajah, this Bible passage is where "text and life coalesce" (2001: 216). Listen to Hoang, a 62-year-old retiree, as she tells her own story of Matthew 25:

> In 1975, the Vietnamese came here from refugee camps; they were so needy. There were not as many Vietnamese as today. The Vietnamese population was very small. Therefore, when we sponsored five or seven families to come here, we and even the American congregation took all the care for them. We bought them even chopsticks, spoons, cups, beds, pillows, and whatever they needed. I myself experienced receiving these things....We also told them that we did so because of God's love. (Interview, April 16, 2007)

While Vietnamese American Bible believers construct a rhetoric of universal love through this chosen text regarding charity, their practice of charity is aimed primarily at their own racial/ethnic group. Their specific practices of charity place an emphasis on the Vietnamese people back home and those newly emigrated to the United States. More than 56 percent of the Vietnamese American interviewees say that they support missions in Vietnam. This paradox suggests—as we have seen of Asian American Bible believers in general through their reading of Matthew's Great Commission—that while the Bible is for this group of interviewees the central or centering text on and around which they construct their lives, there are also other subtexts that "scripturalize" their practices. The subtexts they bring into their practices are, once again, their experiences of diaspora and of being a religious minority in Vietnam. Their racial- and ethnic-specific practice of charity is affected by their diaspora experience. As immigrants, Vietnamese Americans, though they might have settled well in the United States, are never completely at home. In a *Los Angeles Times* article entitled "Vietnamese Refugees Finally Find Home," Scott Tran quotes a refugee to illustrate the need for the Vietnamese community to be and to remain together: "We are like birds in the sky: We flap together. We would be lost if we did not live together" (2000). It is because of homelessness that Vietnamese people stay together to feel home and to build a community to carry on the cultural traditions of Vietnam. This sense of homelessness has also been well articulated in diaspora discourse. Yen Le Espiritu, in her book about how Filipino/a American lives are shaped through their memory of and ties to the homeland with their transnational connections, states, "The process of immigration is not only about arrival and settlement but, crucially, also about home orientation and return" (2003: 2). Desire for home is an inevitable part of experiencing and living in diaspora. It resonates with Vietnamese Americans who are still home bound and seeking to reconnect with the Vietnamese homeland. In the words of Duong, a 61-year-old man who manages an auto shop:

> I know that our Vietnamese people here have relationships with those in Vietnam. It is the same as a saying goes: "When the blood sheds, the heart aches." Though we are here, but [sic] our homeland is Vietnam. Therefore, Vietnamese people here are very interested in practicing charity to the people back home. Not only Christian mission associations but other organizations make mission trips to Vietnam. There are medical trips to Vietnam every year. (Interview, April 20, 2007)

Vietnamese Americans' attachments to Vietnam reveal that it is precisely their experience of homelessness in diaspora that forges their sentimental ties to the homeland. Charity becomes a means of maintaining this linkage, a means of connecting to the homeland, and a way of coping with the alienation in the country of their settlement.

In addition, their experience as a religious minority in Vietnam plays a significant role in their practice of charity. Most of our Vietnamese American interviewees came from the Evangelical Church of Vietnam, which was introduced to Vietnam by the Christian and Missionary Alliance in 1911, and they were seen as following an "American religion." This group is still marginalized by their religious affiliation and deemed a minority in the sociocultural context of contemporary Vietnam. According to the 2007 International Religious Freedom Report released by the US Department of State, the number of evangelical Christians in Vietnam—including the Evangelical Church of Vietnam—is approximately 1.6 million, thus making up just about 1.9 percent of the country's population ("Vietnam: International Religious Freedom Report 2007": www.state. gov/g/drl/rls/irf/2007/90159.htm). Their experience of being not only a minority but also followers of a foreign religion is passed on to the younger generation who grew up in the United States, as we can see from the comment of Cindy, a 19-year-old college student:

> My mom always tells me that Asian people that are nonbelievers think that Christianity is a white people's religion and so I think it is really important for us to share our faith with our own people and tell them, "Asians, we are Christians too but we're not white." (Interview, April 9, 2007)

This minority experience continues to impact Vietnamese Christians living outside the homeland. For our Vietnamese American interviewees, charity as a Christian practice is racialized as a means to vindicate disadvantaged peoples in the world where Christianity is a minority religion as well as a means to evangelize. Cindy continues:

> Just because you're an Asian American doesn't mean you have to donate to your home country or your mother country. But I guess by Asian American being charitable to their own people—especially Christians, because a lot of Asians aren't Christians but Buddhists and other religions—I guess it would be an example but also inspire more people, especially those who are more disadvantaged... and that would be a great opportunity to share your faith also. (Interview, April 9, 2007)

The awareness of their "religious minority" status demands Vietnamese American Bible believers to improve their public image and popularize their faith. Charity is important to this group because it is seen as an effective way to win converts among those in need, especially those they sponsor from Vietnam or from refugee camps in Asian countries. Perhaps this is where their more ethnic-specific reading of Matthew 25 and the Asian American reading of Matthew 28 meet. Vietnamese American Bible believers consider sponsoring Vietnamese refugees as their mission, hoping that their deeds, as Bao said quoting another verse from Matthew's Jesus, will "shine before men, that they may see your good deeds and praise your Father in heaven" (Matt. 5:16; interview, April 22, 2007). Part of their goal in doing charity is the conversion of Vietnamese to Christianity. Charity in this sense is one way for Vietnamese American Bible believers to return to their own ethnic group for evangelistic missions and deal with their long-standing experience as a religious minority in Vietnam.

For this reason, some of the interviewees feel that charity is ineffective if people leave the church after receiving help. Danh, a 34-year-old engineer whose church has worked to help some people emigrate to the United States, opines, "Sometimes charity is not effective. For example, at my church, we have tried our best to help them, but just several months later, they left us" (interview, April 15, 2007). Hoang also articulates her disappointment: "Now there is only one family among those thirty families we sponsored standing firm in faith until today.... Therefore I realize that if we make good works [a] priority, it is not surely fruitful" (interview, April 16, 2007). Yet, charity, despite being deemed ineffective because of its failure to accomplish the mission, is still being supported. In fact, many Vietnamese American churches still reach out to help bring their own people to the United States when opportunity arises. Their experience as a religious minority in Vietnam and hence their desire to increase the number of Christian converts seem to prevail despite the tension or uncertainty involved in using charity for evangelism.

Living in diaspora, Vietnamese American Bible believers construct charity as a way of return to their homeland, in both literal and symbolic ways. While the Bible offers them stories, language, or rhetoric about a universal love for God and neighbors, their practice of charity is racial and ethnic specific and brings them back home through mission trips, remittances, tithing, and services. Being Vietnamese Americans and Bible believers affect their choice in what biblical texts to appropriate and how to interpret and practice those texts. Their engagement with the Bible is inseparable from their racial/ethnic and religious difference as well as their diasporic nostalgia for their homeland.

While 53 percent of the Asian American Bible believers we interviewed assert that the Bible is literally true, and 44 percent say that the Bible is inerrant, 51.2 percent also characterize their own interpretive predisposition as "contextual." This predisposition underscores the negotiations necessitated by the complexity and occasionally self-conflicting contours of this interpretive community of Asian American Bible believers. Does the complexity end up exerting enough pressure for our interviewees to complicate their view of the Bible itself? We see a hint of this in Chien's earlier comment about the "Jewish bias" in the conquest and settlement narratives of the Hebrew Bible. Given the negotiations and fusions performed in their practice of reading, why do our interviewees insist on and persist in professing biblical authority and/or inerrancy? Do they lack self-awareness, or does this profession about the Bible do something for them? What are the specific needs and benefits—whether psychological, social, and/or cultural—at work and at play in connection with an uncompromising profession? Why do many of them say that the Bible is "a grounding thing," "God's very words," and "completely without fault"? We will turn to these questions in our next section.

Improvisation and the Practice of Freedom

Infallibility implies, of course, without fault. In light of one's belief in a sacred text that knows no error, how does one make decisions, especially given the claim by many of our interviewees that the Bible governs their life decisions (ranging from worldviews to choices of behaviors, relationship, and careers)? Do they get "perfect" results as long as they make decisions on the basis of their Bible reading? What happens if the decision yields "poor" results? Does this cause doubt, regret, or a change in one's view of the Bible as a reliable or infallible source? In this section, we analyze responses to these questions to understand our interviewees' decision-making process, and how they maintain their belief and negotiate their doubt regarding their "biblically informed" decisions. We find that all our interviewees maintain their belief that the Bible is an authoritative and/or inerrant text regardless of their doubt, but the way they handle and negotiate doubt varies. While some express that they have never doubted their "biblically-informed" decisions and therefore maintain confidence in their decisions, others express deep ambivalence, decide to correct their decisions, and sometimes even dispute if those "biblically-informed" decisions are "good" or "sound."

Maggie, a second-generation Chinese American graduate student, articulates the need for Christians to make decisions based on the Bible: "I think the big thing with the Bible is that if you're saying it's the authority in your life and then you don't use it to make your decisions, then you're saying…that it's not that important to you" (interview, November 4, 2007). Many of our interviewees agree with Maggie; in fact, among our interviewees who have significant parachurch experience and are between eighteen and twenty-four years of age, biblical authority is mentioned in almost every interview, and every interviewee has had an experience of making a life decision based on their reading and understanding of the Bible.

Jack, another second-generation Chinese American, adds:

Absolutely without qualification, yes. It [the Bible] ought to [guide your decisions]. It should be the first and foremost source. It makes broad claims about itself with regard to decision making, that it's sufficient for all things because it's God's very words and it's not like God hadn't foreseen every eventuality. (Interview, June 1, 2007)

Jack suggests prioritizing the Bible as the first source to consult on any decision because, with foresight, it can provide everything; it is like speaking to God's self. Furthermore, many of the young adult interviewees with parachurch experience say that the Bible influenced their vocational choices and decisions to take religious leadership positions. They are able to become, somewhat like Janet, Bible study leaders and take on full-time ministry positions as a result of reading the Bible. While most college students are looking for activities that will boost their resume and for lucrative jobs in, say, consulting and investment banking, some of our interviewees are able to choose alternative paths in their extracurricular activities and vocational choices because of their confidence in the Bible.

Both Cherry, a second-generation Korean American undergraduate student, and Donna, a second-generation Chinese American graduate student, found confidence in their decision to lead Bible studies through reading the Bible. When Cherry was presented with the opportunity to lead a Bible study at her campus fellowship, she was initially hesitant because it would require more work and create more stress than she thought she could manage. She then read "John 15" and found her "reassurance" that "Jesus was the one who's doing all the work" and that his "yoke is easy and his burden is light" (interview, December 7, 2007).[6] Cherry gained emotional and psychological encouragement from the Bible, which helped her ease into her decision to lead the Bible study for her fellowship. The comfort that she received from the passage allayed her initial fears and gave her the confidence that she would be able to handle the workload. It helped that she also read some unspecified Bible verses—Matthew 11:12; Luke 16:16?—that, in her words, called her to "pursue the kingdom of God with violence and force, basically everything you have" (interview, December 7, 2007). So she not only gained encouragement but was also affirmed by this charge to give as much as she could to the kingdom of God by leading a Bible study. Through reading these biblical passages, Cherry says, she confidently accepted this leadership position.

Similarly, Donna was initially hesitant about leading a Bible study because it was outside her comfort zone. She had never done anything like it before and was not sure if teaching high school youth was a good fit for her. She "struggled" with the decision and found it was a "harder thing" than she had expected (interview, November 27, 2007). She then consulted her pastor and read several Bible passages: "I remember making a list of all the Bible passages that related to it... definitely 1 Timothy, 2 Timothy... [the passages said to] teach the word always, reach out and care for those people in need. So the passages all generally pointed toward teaching" (interview, November 27, 2007). As a result of reading these passages, Donna felt affirmed in her decision to be a teacher to these high school students despite her initial feeling that it was a poor fit for her. The Bible changed the choices and decisions of both Cherry and Donna. Neither would have chosen to be Bible study leaders if it had not been for those Bible passages.

Additionally, three individuals based their decisions to enter full-time ministry as a career option because of their encounters with the Bible. Archie decided to go to seminary because reading about the "Apostle Paul's ministry really inspired me" (interview, December 17, 2007). After a year of working in the corporate world, he decided that business is not a good fit for him; instead, he is finding that he can better tap into his potential through full-time ministry. Archie takes Paul's ministry as an inspiration to go to seminary. Jack vacillated in his decision to go to seminary because his parents did not want him to do so right away. Feeling compelled or convicted by passages in the Bible on the importance of obeying parents, he decided to delay applying to seminary. Finally, William, another second-generation Chinese American like Archie and Jack, decided to become a campus minister after going through a three- to four-week discernment process that "employed a number of tactics to speak into every crack of [his] context" (interview, November 13, 2007). He balanced his time to "reflect personally . . . and join with others praying for [him]." Several biblical passages stood out for William during that time: Exodus 3:10 (Moses and the burning bush), Genesis 12 ("Go forth into the land and I will show you"), 2 Chronicles 32 (God is with King Hezekiah despite the battles). With these passages to back his decision, William gained a stronger sense of direction and peace that going into full-time ministry was the right decision for his life. He says, "[T]here was an idea or concept around being sent. I felt that should I go, God would be with me and that I wouldn't be alone. . . . [The Bible] spoke to moments of fearing to go alone." William also received emotional encouragement through reading the Bible and a strong sense of calling through the process.

It is important to note that at the same time that Donna articulated confidence in her decision to teach high school students, she also experienced strong doubt. She quickly found that sometimes the youth were not as pleasant as she had hoped, and she even found them occasionally to be "unlovable." As a result, she felt like quitting a few times, but she couldn't "back out of it because I basically committed to a one year thing. . . . [It] would be messed up. So I was stuck with it" (interview, November 27, 2007). Even after reading some biblical passages in Timothy and gaining the belief that this was the right decision, she still wavered and, to a certain extent, might have regretted her decision. Similarly, while Archie was moved by Paul's ministry to enter seminary, he also articulated a constant hesitation about his decision: "I doubt it every day. When you go to seminary, I think you still doubt. It's really hard sometimes because you don't know" (interview, December 17, 2007). From Donna's and Archie's responses, one can see the ambiguity and ambivalence that exist for them even or especially when they believe that the Bible is a flawless text. Our interviewees have a range of attitudes toward doubt and a range of ways to negotiate doubt. As mentioned previously, some say they have never doubted; others say that their doubt was a part of their growth process; still others say that they not only doubt but also disagree with some of their own "biblically informed" decisions.

Many of our interviewees—33 percent to be exact—say that they have never doubted their "biblically based" decisions. Regardless of the outcome, these interviewees feel that because they have honestly made their decision based on this authoritative text called the Bible, they are able to sustain their confidence in the text's ability to correctly guide their decisions. Robert and Kathy—a second-generation Korean American and a second-generation Vietnamese American, respectively—claim to have never doubted a decision that they made on the basis of the Bible. We will illustrate later their thinking process and how it leads to sustaining not only their belief in the inerrancy of the Bible but also the inerrancy of their decisions. Let us note here, however, that there is a stigma attached to doubt for many of our interviewees. Some admit that they had doubted their "biblically based" decisions, but that it was because they were "in sin" or "separated from God" (21 percent). Their doubt was, in other words, a result of a shortcoming in their faith or spirituality. Some of our interviewees, therefore, might have doubted their decisions but feel uncomfortable to admit it. At the same time, some interviewees openly articulate that they had doubted decisions that they made on the basis of the Bible, but they interpreted their doubt as being part of their spiritual development (21 percent) or as a lack of understanding of the Bible (38 percent).[7]

Two of our interviewees with parachurch experience say that they have never doubted or could not recall such a moment. For Robert, the very fact that he made a "decision...in faith even if it seems bad, or bad to the world, because you've obeyed God, it's good" (interview, December 15, 2007). Robert prioritizes the grounds on which he has made his decision (the Bible) over the outcome or the perception of the outcome. He gives an example to further illustrate: "If I spent a lot of time at church at the expense of my academics, but it's truly for God then I wouldn't regret it." It is as if the virtue of obeying God cancels out any negative consequences of that decision; a dip in his academics would be forgivable if it is for the sake of obedience to God. Poor grades might have been enough of a negative consequence for other individuals to doubt or regret their decision, feeling that they should have studied harder rather than spent time at church. Robert separates himself from the paradigm of "the world" and holds a different set of values; while "the world" would negatively view poor grades, Robert values grades differently so that they hold neutral weight. Robert goes on to say, "God did say through Paul that He [*sic*] does everything for the good of those who love Him [*sic*]" (Romans 8:28). Robert finds further textual evidence in the Bible that supports his understanding that all things will work toward good, even if there are some disadvantages to his academics. Robert's belief in the inerrancy and authority of the Bible actually helps him maintain his convictions and overcome potentially negative consequences.

Kathy also cannot think of a concrete time when she doubted a decision she had made on the basis of the Bible. She comments, "I would never doubt that the Bible isn't the way and the truth" (interview, May 31, 2007). When she has questions or doubts, she would "pray about it and trust that God is going to answer it in the future." It is easy for her to let go of the doubt because she uses prayer and has the patience to await a future explanation. Since she knows that "the time will come," she has little need for doubt. Kathy uses prayer as her means to maintain her confidence in the Bible's inerrancy and authority and resolve any uncertainty that she may have.

Both Robert and Kathy maintain not only the inerrancy of the Bible but also their confidence that the actual decisions or outcomes will be favorable. Even though there are not immediate positive results, both believe there will be good results in the future. They do acknowledge that there are moments of doubt, but these moments are short-lived because there will eventually be an answer to every confusion. Their resolution or dissolution of doubt relies heavily on the fundamental belief in an inerrant and authoritative text that knows no wrong. The circumstances or outcomes that are born out of their own decisions are deprioritized in favor of obedience and trust in the Bible's infallibility.

In many ways, this psychology to resolve doubt is expected of Bible believers. According to Ammerman, Bible believers "have to learn to accommodate doubt" (1987: 211). Those who acknowledge doubt have various ways to think about it. Some hold onto the view that the Bible is infallible and inerrant by dealing with doubt in a more circular, embodied, and experimental manner. There is a sense of reading, interpreting, living, and then going back again to do another round of reading, interpreting, and living. There is room for many readings and changes between first and later readings. Doing so does not change their basic conception of or belief in the inerrancy and authority of the Bible; their more circular readings do allow for questioning.

Maggie and Jack, for instance, recognize that reading the Bible is a learning process. When Maggie first became a Christian, she encountered many hardships so she had doubts about the claims that some made about the Bible and the Christian life. Then she reread the Bible and found that it actually called her to a life of suffering (interview, November 4, 2007). Jack was convinced that the Bible did not forbid playing online poker; after hearing another person's interpretation of the Bible, however, Jack changed his mind and began to see poker as not being in line with teachings of the Bible, so he stopped playing (interview, June 1, 2007). Both of them are flexible in changing their interpretations of the Bible.

Cherry shares a critical story about a life event that caused her to doubt a decision she had made based on reading the Bible. The following is an excerpt of Cherry's story about a time in high school when she was evangelizing to her classmates:

> There was one point in high school when I was really fired up about the idea of evangelizing...in a very explicit way, the same way that Jesus' disciples did....Jesus went around the county and was basically preaching and teaching and that's what the disciples did too in Acts after Jesus went back to join God...so our high school Christian club president decided to mobilize a small team who would go out during lunch wearing signs that said "Ask me about Jesus."...We'd get into conversations with people as we went through hallways. It was hard for me because I'm very shy.
>
> There was this one time where this girl who was in my math class, and I thought that God wanted me to tell her that He [*sic*] loved her. So I called her up at home and told her that..."God wants me to tell you that He [*sic*] loves you." She was so weirded out by that. Our relationship was awkward after that. That was definitely a point where I thought I should have used a lot more wisdom and common sense, but I was pretty much in the mode of not considering it from an outsider's perspective. (Interview, December 7, 2007)

Cherry and her high school Christian club members applied their reading of Acts and the Gospels to their high school context, essentially mimicking the actions of Jesus and the disciples in the Bible. They walked around the hallways to talk about their faith, much as Jesus might have walked around neighborhoods to share the good news. Since they believed in an inerrant biblical text, they made the decision to mimic the stories directly. The same actions would likely lead to the same results, they thought, because the Bible was never wrong. So in a high school where gossip and ridicule were rampant, they fearlessly walked around with signs because they felt validated by an authoritative and infallible text. Cherry even took the step of calling her friend to tell her that Jesus loved her. For Cherry, this was a deeply sincere act, but it had unexpected results. She believed in an infallible text, but her actions turned out to be, in her view, utterly fallible.

We see with Robert that even though his actions may have led to negative results, he is able to explain away his doubt through his interpretation of the differences that exist between "the world" and his belief system. With Kathy, she is able to pray and wait it out in order to understand why things seem doubtful to her. For Cherry, however, her response is "I don't know if I'd do it again." Unlike Kathy and Robert, who resign their doubt, Cherry acknowledges that she did not get the results she was expecting (conversion). The fact that her friend was "weirded out" and their relationship turned "awkward" led her to believe that this might not have been the wisest decision for her. She experienced the ambivalence as she stood between acting on the basis of an inerrant text on the one hand and finding that her actions did not yield positive results on the other hand. Looking back, Cherry reflects that she should have "used a lot more wisdom and common sense." In other words, through the ambivalence that she experienced between the text, her reading of the text, and the results of her action, she is able to come back to the same commitment to evangelism but with a more complex understanding of it: namely, something akin to the model-life emphasis expressed by many in their reading of Matthew's Great Commission. Even after this experience, she says that she still reads the Bible as if God were "trying to tell me things through it, which I know He [sic] is" (interview, December 7, 2007), but she has become more sharply aware of the importance of looking at the cultural context of biblical passages. Cherry took the doubt, reflected on it, corrected her behavior, and gained a new way of reading the Bible using a more "contextual" lens. She still maintains her belief in the timelessness of the Bible and that it is God's very word, but she learns from her experience and recognizes her flawed reading and interpretation of the Bible for her high school context.

If we take this principle of reading and rereading the Bible in order to ascertain its full meaning and apply it to an issue like homosexuality, a more controversial topic among this population, it gets even more complicated. Changing one's perspective on whether online poker is or is not against the Bible arguably does not carry the same stakes as discerning whether the Bible is or is not against homosexuality. For Laurel, a student of Chinese and Filipino descent whom we have referred to before, her main doubt about the Bible centers on this very issue:

> Catholic beliefs…they are very anti-homosexual. And that's something I struggle with a lot because I have friends who are gay. My best friend is actually gay and it just drives me nuts how she is not allowed to marry, how she cannot have a good life.… She's really religious, probably more religious than I am. The Catholic Church rejects her [even though] she definitely has a strong personal relationship with God. So that's like one thing that…that's one thing I struggle with and still have no resolution at this point. (Interview, September 2, 2007)

Since there are well-formed perspectives against homosexuality from those who have more literal readings of the Bible, it is challenging for Laurel to reconcile these readings with the friendships she has with people who are homosexual. Could Laurel also use a more circular reading of the Bible, like Cherry's? Cherry read the text, lived it out, experienced an error or setback, then reread the text with a different lens to give herself a different outcome. For Laurel, alternative readings of the Bible and different results seem to be unavailable or inaccessible with a weightier issue like homosexuality. It starts with a reading of the text, and that is where things seem to end. The cycle of living out, experiencing setback, and rereading the text is largely unexplored. The extent to which doubt and error are acknowledged and explored seems to depend largely on the explosiveness of the issue in question. Saying that the Bible is infallible seems to suggest that it is also possible for people to make infallible decisions based on their reading of the text. Yet, through these stories, one can see that the actions that are born out of the text can be full of "errors"; there is room for correction and room to be wrong. While our interviewees may not go so far as to say that the Bible is a fallible text, some of them are able to acknowledge that their actions, though thought to be based on the Bible, are fallible and flawed. To say that one believes in an infallible text is not to say that one is an infallible reader of the text.

What if the Bible is actually infallible but the way that people interpret it and live it out is flawed and open to error? It seems that for Asian American Bible believers like Jack and Cherry, what is actually infallible is the concept of infallibility itself. Infallibility is an ideal that people claim the Bible holds, but it remains an abstract concept as long as readers are not able to live it out. To say that these people are inerrant readers of the Bible suggests not only a conservative tendency but also a static quality to their reading of the Bible. For some of our interviewees, this is true. Being an infallible reader sometimes means that they directly mimic the actions in the Bible, and sometimes they make "poor" decisions just because the Bible says so. Some of them maintain these conceptions of the Bible by maintaining and resolving their doubt by prioritizing obedience and faithfulness over the actual results of their "Bible-based" decisions. For others, their reading of the Bible is more interactive and flexible. The attitude that they take to the Bible is actually more circular and more open to correction and disagreement, and they change their reading of the text and the practice of their obedience. They evolve in their readings and do not necessarily read the same texts in always the same way. These interviewees capitalize on an ideology of infallibility to perform fallible reading freely and liberally. If institutional power operates in such a way that Bible readers in general and Bible believers in particular have been reading the Bible not being fully cognizant of the institutional rules that govern this interpretive game, then Asian American Bible believers may just as well make up the rules even as they read and reread the Bible. Professing biblical authority and/or inerrancy does not, in these cases, impose a straight jacket that is rigid and restrictive; in contrast, it allows one the space and freedom to read and reread—and hence to decide and re-decide—again and again.

Reading Back

Figure 4.2 is a graphic representation of the major arguments we have presented thus far on how the Bible functions in the reading and the lives of Asian American Bible believers. The history and identity of Asian Americans in general and Asian American Bible believers in particular aside, we began with the interpretive community and its institutional power on Asian American Bible believers, particularly how authority can become even more pronounced if members are insulated from other communities, and how this kind of insulation, isolation—and hence autonomy of a reading community—creates anxiety for its members and prevents them from articulating any differences of opinion.

When Asian Americans in our sample read the Bible, they read it in ways so that the Bible functions and signifies unlike other literary texts. Such

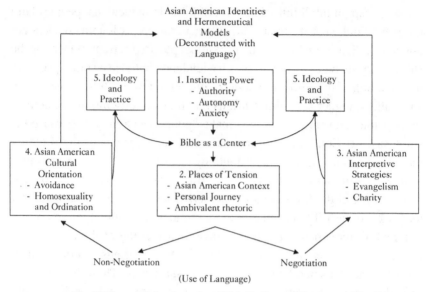

FIGURE 4.2 The Bible and Asian American Bible Believers. Courtesy of Tat-siong Benny Liew.

readings secure the Bible as a centering object. Reading Asian Americans read the Bible involves, therefore, not only reading Asian Americans extracting the Bible's textual content or Asian Americans reading their subjectivities and heritages into that extraction, but also reading the forms in and techniques by which the Bible is activated as a centering device that they call scripture. To read the Bible as scripture seems to involve two important dynamics for this community of readers. First, it offsets the need to reconsider or question the Bible's authority because of its internal differences and even contradictions; coherence is achieved, as we have seen earlier, through readings across different books within the Bible. Second, it overcomes the limits of the Bible's textual content through readings that facilitate crossings over or intersections across multiple and conflicting layers of personal and larger sociocultural presuppositions to bring together the disparate worlds of the Bible, Asia, and America. These readings incorporate and are further informed by extrabiblical texts, such as *The Purpose Driven Life,* to arrive at something believed to be a biblical grammar. An example of this is a model (Asian) American life—which includes and, in fact, features, a practice of charity through missions for Vietnamese Americans—that facilitates the performance of reading and living as a minoritized community.

The Bible as scripture helps Asian American Bible believers pry through the layers of personal and larger racial dynamics. In doing so,

Asian American Bible believers experience and express ambivalence as both Asian Americans and Bible believers. Out of that double ambivalence, they develop an ambivalent rhetoric around the Bible, adopt particular interpretive strategies to negotiate what the Bible says about evangelism (through their reading of the Great Commission in Matthew 28) and charity (through, say, their reading of Matthew 25), and resort to a particular cultural orientation to avoid negotiating what the Bible may or may not say about homosexuality. Both of these paths of negotiation and nonnegotiation show that while the practice of Asian American Bible believers may differ from the ideology of biblical inerrancy and authority, the ideology of biblical inerrancy and authority may also—in an ironically delightful way—provide the very space that is needed for a different practice or to practice difference. Their profession of belief in something like biblical infallibility allows them to perform fallible readings and alter decisions. These paths of negotiation and nonnegotiation—in addition to demonstrating improvisation and hence transformation on the part of the Asian American Bible believers—make up what may be understood as an Asian American identity and hermeneutical model. Just as language has been shown and used to deconstruct identity in the larger world of literary/cultural studies, the narratives provided by our Asian American Bible-believing interviewees can be used to show that Asian American identity and hermeneutics are also fluid processes. Identity, interpretation, and institution are not static or stable, and hence will continue to be sites of struggle. To put it positively, the future does remain open, and readings of the Bible, particularly those that have not been institutionally sanctioned, may yet function dangerously to exert pressure and open up new possibilities for not only Asian Americans but also other minoritized populations.

Reading Badly?

Confronted by the question of ordaining homosexuals, most of our interviewees tend to avoid the issue. Jimmy, the 47-year-old accountant says, "The community in Vietnam is so conservative that homosexuality seems not to be an issue. If so, it happens somewhere else such as in the bar or on the beach, but not in the church at all" (interview, April 7, 2007). In other words, Jimmy claims that the issue of homosexuality—let alone ordination of homosexuals—has not been an issue for Vietnamese Christians. Some interviewees, in like manner, may not have used the Bible to address directly the issue of ordination, because homosexuality itself seems to them to be an issue only for non-Asian and/or non-Bible-believing Christians.

On the other hand, 43 percent of our interviewees do cite passages—like Genesis (including references to Sodom and Gomorrah, as well as the creation of Adam and Eve), Leviticus, Romans, 1 Corinthians, and 1 Timothy—to show the Bible's disapproval of homosexuality. Another third of our interviewees do not cite any particular passage, but make a general reference to the Bible and assume that the Bible is against homosexuality. Of course, the stunning contradiction is that while almost three out of every four of our interviewees (74 percent to be exact) express the opinion or belief that the Bible condemns homosexuality, as we have mentioned, 44 percent of our interviewees would actively choose not to engage in action for or against the issue of ordaining homosexuals, and 37 percent would actively avoid the issue of homosexuality if a fellow Christian disagreed with them.

This nonnegotiation, while perhaps partly derives from Asian American cultural reticence to discuss questions of sexuality in general, also results from a failure on the part of the interviewees to find appropriate language to bridge what they think the Bible teaches and what they face in life both within and beyond the church.

The Rev. Dr. Ken Fong, senior pastor of Evergreen Baptist Church (a large, multigenerational and "pan-Asian" church based in Rosemead, California), hosted an evening forum in 2008 on the very topic of homosexuality and the church. To a standing-room-only audience, the three openly gay Asian Americans Fong had invited spoke of their struggles regarding their sexuality, their faith, and their community's response to the seeming incongruities between the two. Fong had designed the event to open up a "conversation," and explicitly proscribed any attempts at determining theological conclusions about human sexuality. Still, as Fong recounts in a blog posting two days after the event, some listeners could not hold back their stridency. Fong recalls:

> I know for a fact that there were some in attendance who came with these convictions [of biblical certainty] and left with these concerns because I observed [two] of them near the end of the evening... *well-worn Study Bibles firmly in hand*—spent about 10 minutes spelling out the above concerns (and more!) before I told them that their time with me was up. ("Some of My Thoughts about the Conversation about Homosexuality Event," *Sedaqah* (blog), May 12, 2008, http://sedaqah.xanga.com/weblog/?uni-22-direction=n&uni-22-nextdate=5%2F12%2F2008+23%3A46%3A46.267; emphasis added)

Even though Evergreen's vision statement includes a commitment to "biblical reconciliation," the church's overall mission could not contain the zeal with which its presumed members brought their Bibles as a kind of shibboleth or symbol to protest Fong's prescribed rules of engagement during that evening's proceedings.

Most of us are perhaps familiar with this image of Bible believers, whose firm conviction of how they should live and how the world ought to be is authorized by the object they hold in their hands, well-worn Bibles at the ready, wielding them like the "two-edged sword" that a biblical writer calls the word of God (Hebrews 4:12). It is perhaps for this reason that Fong's recollection of this encounter is full of a resigned fatigue. The *well-worn Study Bible firmly in hand* makes the power of biblical authority and/or inerrancy one that even ordained members of the church must wrestle with, a double-edgedness that can be as threatening to institutional order as much as it grants legitimacy. As we read from the words of Jimmy, established and expected lines of authority in the institutional church can easily, even if simply rhetorically, be overturned: "I respect the pastor's personal experiences but I won't do what he says if his words...are opposed to the Bible. It doesn't matter whatever position he holds, I will not listen" (interview, April 7, 2007). There is certainly a danger in such individual dissidence, as Protestant churches since the Reformation have learned all too well: competing readings and divergent interpretations lead to splintering institutional formations, and can indeed risk a kind of hermeneutic solipsism that threatens to undermine the tradition of scriptural reading as a communal practice. Thus, even as 93 percent of the respondents claim that they are engaged in some sort of small-group Bible study, there remains what Ivy, a Chinese American who immigrated to the United States with her parents from Taiwan at the age of seven, calls "places of tension" (interview, March 4, 2008), when everyone interviewed also testifies to the importance of their *individual* study of the Bible. While this phrase is used by Ivy to talk about her struggle to come to terms with biblical paradoxes (such as being last to be first and gaining life by losing life), it might also describe the frictions that can result whenever communal and individual readings of the Bible turn out to be in conflict with each other rather than mutually constitutive. However seldom these two modes of reading the Bible might happen to be in conflict, at the margins of each Bible believer's interpretative horizon resides a potential for friction that must be disconcerting to Bible study leaders, not to mention clergy or institutional officers like Fong.

Yet the assertion of biblical inerrancy and authority is, once again, not only an epistemological boundary but also a space in which to maneuver as much as it may be a place of tension. If what is actually infallible is the concept of infallibility, we might wonder what possibilities emerge when such passionate commitment to the ideal of infallibility compels a reader to read and read again. Such reading and rereading might lead to a reading that is outside the bounds of what is often called "tradition," which is nothing more than experience given the armature of ecclesial power and law. What does that reader feel when she opens her Bible, finds a verse that resonates deeply with the exile of her longing, a feeling that she knows is out of bounds from what her pastor or study leader has established? Does she feel crazy, as Laurel does with regard to her best friend? "It just drives me nuts how she is not allowed to marry, how she cannot have a good life" (interview, September 2, 2007). Laurel would be considered a "bad" reader of the Bible, differently "bad" than the "bad" subjects who confronted Fong; but in both cases the determination of proper and improper reading is premised on contextual circumscription, what is outside the bounds of "good" reading *at a given moment*.

And herein lies the potential power of claiming biblical infallibility for Asian Americans: attachment or allegiance to biblical authority and/or inerrancy might yield a haunting emotion that might feel like you are going crazy, but can also compel you to imagine that feeling as something akin to revelation. And while this is not exclusively theirs, we would suggest that this feeling is distinctively Asian American. For the last half century, Asian Americans have been the "model minorities" of the US racial landscape, the emblem of how to be the "good" racial subject out of which social rewards are bestowed in the form of material mobility and mainstream appreciation. This well-established trope, of course, emerged most prominently in the mid-1960s to truncate the legitimacy of racial injury claims on the part of black, brown, and red social formations; since then, Asian Americans have reentered the national vocabulary during moments of social crisis, such as the conflict over affirmative action in the 1980s, the urban unrest in Los Angeles in the early 1990s, and the spy scandal surrounding Weng Ho Lee at the turn of the century. Asian Americans, in these moments, tended to mitigate the crises by shoring up the social order at the expense of those most targeted by the violence wrought by unequal public policies and their effects.

This model minority status granted to Asian Americans is no less compelling with regard to Christianity. As we have already alluded, Busto has argued, Asian Americans, especially those who populated US colleges and universities, constitute a kind of moral model minority: colored Christians who hew so closely to institutional and authoritative formations of evangelical Christianity that in many ways they now assume positions of leadership and power that make them discursively almost indistinguishable from the so-called dominant (1999). It is therefore not a surprise that when our interviewees face the question on whether charity and evangelism are important for Asian Americans, a significant plurality chooses not to speak of Asian American specificities toward these practices. (Of those who do, the majority either talk about Asian American deficiencies to ideal practices or to develop specific acts of charity or evangelism to Asian countries *outside* the United States, but not to people *within* the United States). It is not so much that Asian American expressions of culture and religion have become deracialized but rather that Asian American racial formation follows, with a kind of deliberation, what author Chang-rae Lee calls the "textbook examples" of "how it ought to be done" (1995: 170).

But *at that moment* when an Asian American knows how she *ought to* read the Bible through the lens of infallibility, outside the panopticon of authority, institution, and community pressure, something happens that makes the reader feel crazy because she has experienced an emotion that does not feel right or good. More often than not, this feeling is one of fury, inchoate anger that barely finds legible expression because she does not quite know whom the target of this fury might or should be. Asian American literature is full of examples of a rage that so haunts characters that it is utterly transformative: author Hisaye Yamamoto called this conversion a process of being "burnt black" (2001: 150). The process of reproducing one's model minority identity, like the process of reproducing one's faith in the Bible's infallibility, *momentarily* breaks down in the inability to account for the friction and failure of the textbook example. And when this happens, all the trauma of Asian American history—of war, of displacement, of exile, of difference—that she has submerged or sublated to being the "good" subject of the United States and the "good" reader of the Bible comes rushing back in an emotional, even spiritual, tempest whose melancholy cannot be reconciled or contained, ghostly memories that gesture to a potentially different time. "Following the ghosts," Avery Gordon writes, "is about making a contact that changes you and refashions the social relations in which you are located. It is about putting life back in where only a vague memory or a bare trace was visible to those who bothered to look. It is sometimes about writing ghost stories, stories that not only repair representational mistakes, but also strive to understand that conditions under which a memory was produced in the first place, toward a countermemory, for the future" (1997: 22). While such countermemory is best produced as a community, sometimes that countermemory must begin with that sole person who looks crazy for pursuing her ghosts.

Laurel's craziness is surely dangerous, which is why such "bad" reading might be recognized but cannot be fully acknowledged, at least not yet. For Asian Americans, "bad" reading is necessarily provisional and momentary, because to extend that feeling of haunting fury would be to begin to dismantle the very structures that make such haunting possible. The provisionality of reading "badly" is what compelled some of our interviewees to cite Leviticus' and Romans' supposed injunction against homosexuality *and then do nothing about it*. It is what we notice as the general acclamation by Asian Americans to practice charity and evangelism, but also to hold something back as an autonomously Asian American, even if this autonomy is coded as deficiency or responsibility to Asia. It is the doubt of some of our interviewees, an ambivalence that is enabled precisely because of their claim to unwavering allegiance to infallibility's infallibility. *With well-worn Study Bibles in hand*, Asian Americans demonstrate their community's "deserved" status as model minorities and model readers. But even amid this very public display of "good" reading, some—maybe just one—may be feeling crazy as she reads alone, confronts that which erupts as a haunting fury, a fury that makes her a "bad" reader from the perspective of some institutionally sanctioned reading. "Bad" readers risk alienation, risk being called aliens, which is exactly what Asian Americans are most fearful of being called. To read "badly" then is a lonely endeavor. To read "badly" is to read in exile. But as Edward Said reminds us (2000: 173–86), it is this very practice of alienated reading, reading as an alien, that might be the conditions through which something contrapuntal might emerge, the conditions of possibility out of place, a space of maneuverable tension from which a community might someday gather to turn "bad" readers into prophetic ones—or even ethnography from collecting and interpreting data to making culture (Lam 1999: 392).

Notes

This chapter is, in many ways, the collaborative product of my entire research team. While individual team members wrote initial drafts of different sections of this chapter (Brett Esaki on responses to the question about ordaining homosexuals; Russell Jeung on Asian American demographics; Helen Jin Kim on the issue of doubt; Lalruatkima on readings of Matthew's Great Commission; James Kyung Jin Lee on "reading badly"; and Quynhhoa Nguyen on Vietnamese Americans and charity), we as a team had spent a whole weekend reading and discussing all the interview transcripts before any of the drafts was written. We also spent time responding and giving feedback to the drafts. The drafts were then rewritten, rearranged, and woven together into one single chapter by me, though I must admit that the changes I made on most of the provided drafts are minimal.

1. We refrain from using the conventional theological or denominational categories like "fundamentalists," "evangelicals," or "mainline" because research seems to suggest that Asian American Christianity defies these "straight-jacket" categorization (Liew 2002: 11).

2. Suggestions regarding "earliest arrival" include (1) Buddhist missionaries arriving in the West coast of North America in the fifth century; (2) Chinese shipbuilders being brought to California by Spain in the sixteen century; and (3) Filipino settling in Louisiana by way of Spanish galleons in the eighteenth century. See T. P. Fong 2000: 13.

3. Pierre Boudieu falls into a very similar trap in his theorization of practice (1984). Emphasizing only how practice is conditioned by a kind of cultural repertoire (what Boudieu calls *habitus*), Bourdieu makes not even a single mention of how practice might also change or transform *habitus*.

4. Following the protocol of ethnographical research, the names of the interviewees have all been changed to protect their anonymity. However, related information about the interviewees, like ethnicity, gender, age, and occupation are, all accurate and factual.

5. Because of the limited number of female Asian American professors of biblical studies in this country, we need to do more to ensure the interviewee's anonymity. In addition to name change, we are also providing less rather than more biographical description (like nativity or ethnic specificity).

6. Note that the verse being quoted by Cherry is actually from Matthew 11:30 instead of John 15.

7. For the particular interview subset of young parachurch organization participants (twelve interviewees), 16 percent say they never doubted; 50 percent, that doubt was part of their growth process; 42 percent, that it was because of a lack of understanding; and 25 percent, that it was because of sin or separation.

| # Maronite Catholics, Orthodox Christians, and Sunni Muslims from the Arab Region

Between Empire, Racialization, and Assimilation

NADINE NABER AND MATTHEW STIFFLER
WITH THE ASSISTANCE OF ATEF SAID AND SANA TAYYEN

THIS CHAPTER IS BASED upon ethnographic research among Sunni Muslims in California and Maronite and Orthodox Christians in Michigan. All our interlocutors are from Arabic-speaking countries.[1] Their articulations of Christianity and Islam entail notions of religious identity that primarily refer to the domain of the divine or a sense of spirituality that transcends the boundaries of historical and political realities. At the same time, they articulate religious identity and their relationship to scriptures in ways that are entangled in a range of historical realities including: (a) the transnational social and cultural fields, or the networks of social relationships that link Arab immigrant communities in the United States to their homeland;[2] (b) US-led wars and other projects in the Arab region; (c) the related internal histories and politics of their nations of origin; and (d) the pressures of anti-Arab racism, immigration, and assimilation in the United States. Our report illustrates how, for the diaspora communities from the Arab region that are the focus of our study, religious and scriptural concepts and practices are entangled in historical and material realities that are transnational in scope.

Our research shows that our interlocutors articulate religious identity and practices through multiple attachments that both accommodate and transgress the geographic boundaries of the United States. The concept of diaspora helps explain connections to a prior home that are so strong that they inspire a resistance to erasure or assimilation that are stronger than the sort of difference implied by the term "ethnic" (Clifford 1996). Our research is guided by theorizations that explain diaspora in terms of an "entanglement" or "intertwining of the genealogies of dispersion with those of 'staying put' " or the sense that "diasporic communities are organized around different modalities of power that are inserted into prevailing modalities of power" (Brah 1996). Diaspora connotes a sense of being a people "with historical roots and destinies outside the time/space of the host nation." It implies a constant mediation, lived tensions, and the experience of living separately from the homeland while remaining entangled with it "over here." It entails living "over here" while remembering or desiring another place (Clifford 1996).[3]

Here, our interlocutors' entanglement in US modalities of power entails engaging with US discourses and practices related to the war on terror, which lumps a diverse spectrum of people from a range of nations and religious groups into the category "Middle Eastern, Arab, Muslim" enemy. Many interlocutors contend with these discourses and practices as they articulate their religious beliefs and practices and engage with scriptures. Yet we are cautious not to reduce our interlocutors' engagements with religion and scriptures to an engagement with geopolitics related to the particular relationship between Arab nations; US economic, military, and political projects in the Arab region; and the racialization of Arabs and Muslims in the United States. For some interlocutors, their articulations of religion and their relationship to scriptures hailed them into communities they perceived to be global—that transcend the boundaries of nation or racial/ethnic categories. More importantly, as practicing Christians and Muslims, our interlocutors are deeply rooted in spirituality and a relationship to the divine in ways that cannot be explained or rationalized through socio-historical or worldly analytical frameworks. This is why our project highlights the significance of nation-states, cultural identity and geo-politics to scriptural engagements among our interlocutors while it also shows how religious and scriptural practices and beliefs extend beyond a historical, cultural, or political domain.

How does the community name itself and how has it been named by others? How has this naming and self-naming changed over time? What are its origins in the United States?

Since 1945, nations for which the primary language is Arabic have combined to form the Arab league and the members of the Arab league are considered the Arab nations, including Algeria, Bahrain, Djibouti, Egypt, Iraq, Jordan, Kuwait, Lebanon, Libya, Morocco, Oman, Palestine, Qatar,

Saudi Arabia, Somalia, Sudan, Syria, Tunisia, the United Arab Emirates, and Yemen. Although US popular cultural representations often conflate the categories "Arab" and "Muslim," not all Arabs are Muslim and not all Muslims are Arabs. The top six countries with the largest Muslim population are Indonesia (202.9 million), Pakistan (174 million), India (160 million), Bangladesh (145 million), Egypt (78.5 million), and Nigeria (78 million).[4] Only one of these countries is Arab. Arab countries include a diversity of linguistic, ethnic, and religious groups. Religious groups include, but are not limited to Christians, Jews, and Druze. Non-Arab ethnic minorities include, but are not limited to, Kurds, Amazighs, and Armenians.

Ever since the late 1880s when the first significant group of Arab immigrants came to the United States, the terms of Arab identity among government officials and among Arab immigrant communities have been contested and shifting.[5] The first significant group of immigrants was from the Ottoman provinces of Syria, Mount Lebanon, and Palestine. Scholars have tended to study Arab immigration to the United States in two periods, pre- and post-World War II (WWII), and have argued that the first large influx of Arab immigrants was predominantly Christians from Mount Lebanon and came from Greater Syria at the turn of the twentieth century (Naff 1985; Suleiman 1999; Shakir 1997; Aswad 1974; Elkholy 1969). In this literature, a general consensus is that early migrants came to the United States out of economic necessity and for personal advancement. Post-WWII immigration and displacement to the United States was more diverse than in the early years. Immigrants came from nearly every Arabic-speaking country and included nearly equal numbers of Christians and Muslims (Suleiman 1999, 9). While early Arab immigrants were primarily Christian and from Greater Syria, post-WWII immigrants have included Arabs from Gulf States and from North Africa as well as a greater number of Muslim immigrants, adding a greater variation in appearance and skin color, cultural patterns, and religious groupings, including a greater number of Muslims than had previously come to the United States from the Arab region. Post-WWII immigrants and refugees have also been more diverse in terms of socio-economic class. Moreover, post-WWII immigration has included more individuals and communities who have come to the United States due to displacement by war, colonialism, neocolonialism and imperialism than before.[6] Increasing US economic and military intervention in the Arab region since World War II has underscored a deepening continuity between US-led war in the Arab region, processes of immigration and displacement from the Arab region to the United States, and the escalating targeting of Arab immigrants and Arab Americans.

Several scholars have explored representations of "the Arab" in terms of what Edward Said referred to as "Orientalism," or the colonialist academic, political, and literary discourses on Arabs, Islam, and the Middle East originating in England and France and later in the United States (1978).[7] An analysis of the historical fascination with the Holy Land in US popular discourses is critical to understanding representations of the "Arab" in US popular culture (Little 2002; McAlister 2005). The Puritan fascination with the Holy Land entailed a profound ambivalence about what dominant US discourses referred to as " 'infidels'—mostly Muslims but some Jews" (Little 2002, 9). This fascination has permeated US popular imagination ever since the early days of European colonization in the United States four centuries ago in which representations of Native Americans paralleled representations of Muslims and Jews (Little 2002, 9; Rana, forthcoming). Between the eighteenth and nineteenth centuries repeated imagery portraying Islam as a wicked and barbarous religion permeated US popular culture (Little 2002; McAlister 2005; Edwards 2000, 16). In the early twentieth century, the "Orient" was increasingly represented in terms of sexualized imagery in US popular culture (Shohat and Stam 1994; Steet 2000; Little 2002).

Racialized US government practices have also shaped the ways Arabs have named themselves in the United States. Most early Arab immigrants were Christian. Overall, "while the credibility of whiteness was periodically called into question by government authorities and public opinion," on the other hand, Arab American proximity to whiteness facilitated efforts to qualify for citizenship (Gualtieri 2009). The post–World War II period in which the meaning of "race" shifted in the United States was also a period of growing anti-Arab sentiment coupled with an escalation in pan-ethnic Arab American political activism. Anti-Arab racism can be explained in the context of US histories of immigrant exclusion (i.e., the history of Asian exclusion, anti-Mexican racism, and Japanese internment) in which the racialization of particular immigrants as different and inferior to whites has relied upon the notion that "they" are intrinsically inassimilable and potentially threatening to national security (Naber 2006). Since World War II, the proliferation of anti-Arab government policies and perceptions of "the Arab" as Other within US popular culture has coincided with the increasing significance of oil as a commodity to the global economy and the United States' expanding interest in military and economic intervention in the Middle East. US geopolitical interests in the

Arab region set the stage for the 1970s US-Arab oil wars that contributed to the production of the image of the "greedy Arab oil sheiks" within the United States and the strengthening of the United States' alliance with Israel in geopolitics. At the same time, the United States was embroiled in a conflict with Arab nationalists over its growing support for the state of Israel. The 1967 Arab-Israeli war signified a turning point in the impact of US involvement in the Arab region on Arab diasporas in the United States. The 1967 war marked the United States' confirmed alliance with Israel as well as an intensification of US military, political, and economic intervention in the Arab region, anti-Arab media representations, and anti-Arab discrimination and harassment within the United States. It also marked the intensification of representations of Islam as a signifier of evilness and Otherness, which was exacerbated in the aftermath of the Iranian Revolution, when hegemonic discourses on the "Arab Other" in the United States increasingly deployed the assumption that all Arabs are Muslim and that Islam is an inherently backward and uncivilized religion.[8] As "Islam" gained an increasingly global appeal as a framework for expressing political sentiments, US government policies increasingly targeted individuals who were associated with a constructed "Arab Muslim" enemy.

As Naber (2008) has argued elsewhere, the 1960s and 1970s (particularly the aftermath of the 1967 Arab-Israeli war) inspired among Arabs and Arab Americans the sense that the state and media had waged a war against them. Arab American activists and scholars responded by establishing several Arab American organizations, many that were pan-ethnic in character, such as: the Organization of Arab Students in 1967, the Arab American University Graduates (1968), and the National Association of Arab Americans.[9] This pan-Arab American activism emerged within a broader context of the civil rights movement and third-world liberation movements (Naber 2008). Between the 1970s and 1990s, coupled with an increasing convergence between US and Israeli policy, several events facilitated the expansion of US control in the Arab region, including the 1970s US-Arab oil wars, the 1980s Iranian Revolution, US intervention in Lebanon in 1982, the US bombing of Libya in 1986, the 1990s Gulf War, the US bombing of Sudan and Afghanistan in 1998, and the United States' continued support of Israel and bombing of Iraq.[10] US political, military, and economic expansion in the region paralleled a rise in the institutionalization of government policies and law enforcement that specifically targeted Arabs and Arab Americans.[11] Since the 1970s, the corporate media has increasingly portrayed persons associated with the category "Arab/Middle Eastern/Muslim" as not only culturally backward, uncivilized, exotic, or potentially dangerous, but also as potential enemies of the United States. The 1980s and 1990s brought an intensification of images of Arab terrorists.[12]

The aftermath of the 9/11 attacks on the Pentagon and the World Trade Center consolidated the conflation of the categories Arab, Middle Eastern, and Muslim and the notion of an Arab/Middle Eastern/Muslim enemy of the nation (Volpp 2003). According to Louise Cainkar, "the U.S. government's domestic legislative, administrative, and judicial measures implemented after 9/11 have included mass arrests, secret and indefinite detentions, prolonged detention of "material witnesses," closed hearings and use of secret evidence, government eavesdropping on attorney-client conversations, FBI home and work visits, wiretapping, seizures of property, removals of aliens with technical visa violations, and mandatory special registration" (2003). Cainkar adds that "at least 100,000 Arabs and Muslims living in the United States have personally experienced one of these measures" and that "[of] thirty-seven known US government security initiatives... twenty-five either explicitly or implicitly target Arabs and Muslims in the United States" (Cainkar 2003). Federal government discourses have rendered men perceived to be Arab/Middle Eastern/Muslim (and/or South Asian) as "potential terrorists" and justified US-led war on Afghanistan and Iraq by purporting that Arab/Middle Eastern/Muslim women need to be saved from a backward and uncivilized culture and/or religion.

Immigration policies related to 9/11 targeted not only Muslims but also a range of people who fit the amorphous characterizations of a "terrorist profile" through FBI investigations and spying, and Immigration and Naturalization Services (INS) raids, detentions, deportations, and interrogations of community organizations and activists. The INS, for example, targeted noncitizens from Muslim majority countries as well as some individuals from Muslim majority countries who were naturalized. Paralleling federal government policies, day-to-day forms of harassment, violence, and intimidation in the public sphere also targeted a range of people who were hailed into dominant US concepts of "Islamic fundamentalism" and "terrorism."

Nadine Naber has shown that post-9/11, anti-Arab government policies and everyday forms of harassment in the public sphere have produced disciplinary effects in the everyday lives of Arab and Muslim immigrant communities (Naber 2006). Naber's extensive fieldwork with Arab Muslim and Christian immigrants in the San Francisco Bay Area in the two-year period following the attacks has shown that Muslims and

Christians alike tended to renegotiate the extent to which they displayed emblems of Arab or Muslim identity in the public sphere. These negotiations ranged from decisions over changing one's name to altering one's form of dress as a strategy for avoiding the potential of harassment, surveillance, or violence.

More than years have passed since September 11, 2001. The Bush administration has lost much of its credibility. While in the Obama era there has been a shift beyond the discourses of the war on terror, there have been limited shifts in Obama's policies in Muslim majority countries (e.g., Palestine, Iraq, and Afghanistan). Our Muslim interlocutors disproportionately feel the impact of post-9/11 US-government discourses and policies in their daily lives, although they impacted Muslims and Christians alike.

Christians from the Arab Region: Methods and Demographics

We interviewed a representative number of Maronite Catholic and Antiochian Orthodox parishioners in the Metro Detroit area, including clergy, male and female lay leaders, recent immigrants, American born, and non-Arab converts. We conducted twenty in-depth interviews over a period of a little more than a year, from summer 2007 to fall 2008. The questions that elicited the most response or discussion were the ones pertaining to the role of faith in the everyday lives of the parishioners; the role of the priest; and the intersection of faith and heritage, including discussions of liturgical language. In addition to conducting interviews, we engaged in participant observation by attending masses, social events, and festivals.

The Metro Detroit area is home to one of the largest Arab and Middle Eastern populations in the United States, as well as to some of the largest and oldest Christian communities from the Arab region. The continual immigration from the Middle East since the late 1800s has created a diverse population of more than a dozen nationalities and every religious denomination found in the Arab region. The diversity of Christians from the Arab region is also reflected in the Metro Detroit population, as there are over twenty churches in the region, such as Antiochian Orthodox, Maronite Catholic, Chaldean, and Coptic. The Antiochian Orthodox and the Maronite Catholic congregations, on whom we focused our study, are two of the largest denominations in the area and were among the first to establish churches.

Our ethnography reveals that the term Arab Christian or Arab American Christian does not adequately capture the range of ways that Christian groups from the Middle East self-identify. The term "Arab Christian" has been used to refer to Christian groups historically and ancestrally tied to the Middle East. These religious groups and their homeland countries include the Antiochian Orthodox (Lebanon, Syria, Palestine, and Jordan), the Coptic Orthodox and Coptic Catholic (Egypt), the Chaldeans (Iraq), the Maronite Catholics (Lebanon), and the Melkites (Lebanon). But not all these Christian communities agree with being grouped together under the identifier Arab. They would rather self-identify as Phoenician, in the Maronite case, or Chaldean, or by nationality, such as Lebanese or Palestinian. Our project uses the inclusive terminology "Christians from the Arab region." Our interlocutors would not argue that they or their families come from what is generally understood as the Arab region. Because they speak Arabic, and because many interlocutors who do not self-identity as Arab admit that they do come from "the Arab world," they are comfortable with this terminology. Of course, for the most part, we identify individuals by their religious identity as either Maronite Catholic or Antiochian Orthodox. The nuances of the terminology and the identity categories will be discussed further in the section "Cultural Identity."

Both the Maronites and the Antiochian Orthodox in the Detroit area are largely suburban, professional, and middle class, and almost all speak English, even many of the recent immigrants from the Middle East. Because of these attributes, their experiences in America are similar. Both church communities celebrate their Middle Eastern heritage through food, music, and language; but the hierarchs of both churches have recognized the importance of balancing tradition with becoming an "American" church by adapting to the needs of the community. Much of this balancing act has pivoted on the liturgical uses of their ancestral languages.

For example, the Antiochian Orthodox Church made English the official liturgical language in the 1960s, though Arabic is still used for many prayers and hymns. Father David of the Maronite Church explicated an example of the language issue, in which the patriarch in Lebanon asked priests to "fully retain certain prayers in Syriac...so that the commonality of the Maronite Church will be maintained no matter what language you're using as the main language." Father David continues, "So we still maintain three or four prayers always in Syriac no matter what we're using as the main language. That displays the unity of the Maronite Church worldwide." These examples reflect the constant tension in both communities concerning the maintenance of tradition, mostly through ecclesiastical use of Arabic and/or

Syriac, and a desire to minister to newer American-born congregants as well as non-Arab converts. We discuss these ideas more fully in the section "Authenticity: Language and Leadership from the Holy Land."

Both faith traditions maintain ties to their homelands through the transnational social spaces of religion, culture, and politicized action. A pertinent example of their transnational religious ties is the pride both communities take in the fact that their religions originated in the Holy Land in the Middle East. On the front of their weekly church bulletin, *Al-Nour* (*The Light*), the Antiochian Orthodox Basilica of Saint Mary has the verse from Acts 11:26, printed in both English and Arabic script, which gives credence to their ancient religious identity: "And the disciples were first called Christians in Antioch." Similarly, the Maronite parishes use a Syriac symbol on the front of their bulletin that reads *bet maroon* (house of Maron) and refers to the priests, monks, nuns, and the faithful that make up the Maronite religion worldwide. These are only small examples of the ways that these communities mark themselves within their transnational social spaces. This report will explore not only the scriptural engagement of the Maronite and Antiochian Orthodox communities of greater Detroit, but will highlight their cultural and sometimes political connections to their Middle Eastern homeland and how those connections function within an American religious and sociocultural context.

The Maronite Catholics of Detroit: Two Parishes, One Mission

The Maronite Catholics are the largest Christian community in Lebanon. They trace their origins to St. Maron, a monk who lived in the mountains of Syria in the fifth century. As one of the Eastern-rite Catholic Churches, the Maronites have never cut their ties with Rome, but they have resisted Latinization. The services in the United States are in Arabic, English, and Syriac, which is a spoken form of the ancient Aramaic language. Maronite Catholics made up a large portion of the first wave of immigrants from the Mt. Lebanon area of Syria and settled mostly on the east coast of the United States and in industrial centers. The Lebanese Maronite Catholics have been a continual presence in southeastern Michigan since the first decade of the twentieth century and built the first of two churches in the 1920s. Members of the Maronite churches are also leaders in the Lebanese-American community, holding prominent positions in organizations such as the Lebanese American Chamber of Commerce. They are also known for their entrepreneurship and have opened some of the Detroit area's first Middle Eastern restaurants.

Detroit served as the hub of Maronite Catholicism for the entire country during the 1960s and 1970s. Because of Detroit's large number of Maronites, the Vatican appointed Bishop Francis Zayek to lead the nation's first diocese of the Maronite Church, with its See in Detroit, in the late 1960s and early 1970s. But at the onset of the tragic civil war in Lebanon, the diocese was eventually moved to New York to be closer to the United Nations and Washington, DC (Beggiani n.d.). There are currently two eparchies, or dioceses, of the Maronite Catholic Church in the United States, one in Brooklyn and one in Los Angeles, both of which must answer to the patriarchs in Lebanon.

We conducted fieldwork at two Maronite churches in the Detroit area. St. Maron, the first Maronite church in the region, is an old, brick building with wooden pews and tile flooring. It is jammed between a rough neighborhood in the city of Detroit and an ever-sprawling Chrysler automotive plant. "Chrysler's all around us," laments Father David. The parishioners are typically older, less wealthy, and less "Americanized" than the congregants at the suburban St. Sharbel, a new church with cushioned pews and a carpeted sanctuary. There is certainly enough membership to sustain both churches, considering there are over 4,000 families on the membership rolls, even though a much smaller number actually attends regular masses, according to Father David.

St. Sharbel was birthed in the 1980s from the "mother church," St. Maron, as the members will tell you, a result of the continual movement of parishioners to the suburbs of Detroit. St. Sharbel is an expansive church complex, complete with a bingo and banquet hall, and was built with the intention of replacing St. Maron, though the older generations of parishioners have always resisted closing St. Maron. There is recognition that because of their locations and the different populations they serve, it is important to maintain both. When we conducted our fieldwork with the two parishes, St. Maron was temporarily without a priest, so Father David was administrator of both parishes, a daunting task indeed. But he is committed to maintaining the integrity of both churches. He assured his congregation at St. Sharbel, following a mass, that "St. Maron will close over my dead body."

The Antiochian Orthodox: A Basilica for the Future

The Antiochian Orthodox Church is best described as being the Arab branch of Orthodox Christianity. It shares the exact same doctrinal and liturgical aspects as the Greek Orthodox Church, but because it developed in the Middle East and historically had its religious See or Patriarch in the city of Antioch (it is now in Damascus, Syria), it is linguistically and culturally distinct from the Greek, Russian, Serbian, Romanian, and other nationalist Orthodox Churches. Father John, a long-serving immigrant priest educated at the Orthodox seminary in Lebanon, describes the church thusly: "Really the original name of the Church should be the Greek Orthodox Church of Antioch but I think for some reason, the founding fathers of this Church...I think we chose to take the Antiochian name to refer that we are from the Middle East and Arab American."

The Antiochian Orthodox began arriving in the United States with the first wave of immigrants from the Middle East in the late nineteenth century, along with Maronite and Melkite Catholics, from Lebanon and Syria. Many Antiochian Orthodox communities were established in the early 1900s, mostly in industrial centers in Massachusetts, New York City, Pittsburgh, Detroit, and Toledo. The first Antiochian Orthodox Church in the United States began as the Syro-Arab Mission of Brooklyn, a part of the larger Russian Orthodox Church in 1904. The Church in the United States was referred to as the Syrian Antiochian Orthodox Archdiocese until the 1960s, when it dropped "Syrian" and adopted the title "Antiochian" to recognize the Church's roots in the city of Antioch, where followers of Jesus were first called Christians. There are now nearly 250 parishes in North America, broken up into seven dioceses, all under the jurisdiction of Metropolitan Philip Saliba, who has served as primate of the Archdiocese for over forty years. Unlike the Maronites, the Orthodox have gained a more autonomous relationship with respect to their patriarch in Syria, and are thus able to make some organizational decisions without approval from Damascus, but all theological issues are still conducted through the hierarchy in Syria.

Like the Maronite community of greater Detroit, the Antiochian Orthodox churches in the area serve as an important hub for the religion in the United States and as an important part of the Arab American community of Metro Detroit. Our fieldwork was conducted at one of the large, suburban parishes in southeastern Michigan. Similar to the history of the Detroit Maronites, St. Mary's is an offshoot of an original Antiochian Church, one of the older Orthodox parishes in the Midwest that was originally founded in the city of Detroit in the 1910s. St. Mary's is firmly implanted as one of the largest and continuously growing Antiochian parishes in the country, and has hosted regional and national archdiocesan conventions.

In the 1970s, Father John, the current priest, was sent from Syria to Michigan to help develop the parish. What started with "4–5 women and 2 men," according to Father John, kept growing through the 1970s because "the war kept going in Lebanon and Palestine," so there was continual immigration to the area. What started with a few first-generation Lebanese and Palestinians has now grown to an immense parish, including nearly 400 church school children. Deacon Mark describes the church building as the central meeting space for all life's events, for the young and the old:

> There are all the sacramental services of the church; baptism, weddings and all these things. This happens a lot here. It's a big community and in fact a week ago, we had a day that was so draining because we started with funeral of a very young woman who lost her life to cancer and left a very young family. An hour later, we jumped right into a baptism of a brand new Christian. An hour later we had a wedding, a very large family. So we had that element and mostly this happens during the weekends but that was an unbelievable day. But all week long we have opportunities for infants all the way to seniors to gather here at this church.

Between Homeland Politics and Americanization: The Transnational Christian Communities of Greater Detroit

Even though we conducted research with two different Christian faith traditions, the members of both communities share similar histories and both function as transnational religious communities, constantly engaged in the tasks of building their churches and developing their communities in the United States, with a constant eye on their homeland, and always within the context of US politics and interventions in the Arab region. This section will elaborate on the shared histories and dynamics of the Antiochian and Maronite Churches in the United States, focusing on the church as a space of worship as well as a cultural center and its role in the transnational activities of these ancient faith communities. But we recognize that this space is spiritual and divine. As much as we can evaluate and present the Maronites and Orthodox as simply an ethnic or cultural affiliation, their transnational communities are still formed around and based on the church building, the priest, and their scriptures. You will find in this chapter that in each section we move closer to the scriptural engagement of the Christian communities under study, even as all the sections are premised on the fact that these are transnational religious communities shaped by the Arab/American divide in various ways.

Regarding the role of the space of the church among Christians from the Arab region, we found the following: first, it was the stage upon which an ethno-religious community was made and remade in America. Church leaders explained that the church is not a building at all, but constituted the body of their religion. Second, it is the place where the liturgy works through the worship of people. It is also the place of communion, where people encounter Christ in the Eucharist, one of the central pillars of their faith. Many explained that it is the people that make the church and that their faith is based upon worshiping together. Third, several interlocutors stressed that the church is a place made up of people with a shared culture and therefore is much more than a religious venue. They feel at home at church. Others value it as a place to pass on their culture to their children and to participate in keeping their cultures and histories alive. Especially for those who live in predominantly white neighborhoods, the church provides them with a space of belonging in the face of cultural difference and isolation. At the same time, this produces the challenge that for some people the church becomes a space for building an ethnic or cultural community more than a religious place. Church leaders shared concern about this. From our fieldwork it is apparent that the church space serves numerous roles.

Although many of our interlocutors discussed their cultural identity in relation to the church, none of these concerns is new for either the Maronites or the Orthodox. Since their arrival in the United States in the late 1800s and early 1900s, these mostly Lebanese and Palestinian immigrants have struggled to balance their faith, their cultural identity, and the processes of Americanization. Scholars of Arab American history and scholars of the history of religion and immigration in general have always seen the church or other places of worship as a site which can act not only as a place of socialization into the American way of life, but can simultaneously have an insular effect in which the community can maintain its cultural traditions.[13]

Arab American scholars who focus on religion have always written about religious identity as a first-order loyalty among the transnational Maronites and Orthodox.[14] It was through their religious affiliations that most Maronites and Antiochian Orthodox responded to events in the homeland. Even the secular social and cultural clubs were closely affiliated with the churches in that the leaders of these clubs also tended to be active members of their respective churches.[15]

Historians of these early mostly Syrian and Lebanese communities write that groups of immigrants from the Arab region living together did not feel like a community until they had established a church, or at least had their own priest.[16] The church was a space for families, for education, to receive news from the homeland and to hold fundraisers to build up their communities here and back home, celebrate, eat Middle Eastern dishes, and speak Arabic. All of this was, of course, in addition to the church serving as a space for connection to the spiritual and the divine. From the responses of our interlocutors, it is clear that the church is not just a place, but an ideal. Deacon Mark, who is Antiochian Orthodox, says it best:

> To me, the church is not a building at all. It's everybody, and not just the priest. If we put our hope in the priest, God help us. In the bishops, God help us. But together, it's the body of Christ on earth. [...] Christ talked about, and the Christians in the early church talked about, liturgy. *Leiturgia* in work means work of the people. Our life is to work to worship.

The Maronite and Antiochian parishioners see church as a joyful place where they come to see family and friends and worship together, regardless of the language spoken or the types of food served at luncheons and dinners after services. Hoda, an active parishioner says, "I don't come to church because it's an obligation. I come because I love to come to church. The celebration of our Maronite mass, I feel like I'm going to a party. It gives me such a joy; I don't know how to explain it to you. It's so beautiful to me." Barbara, a fellow Maronite woman explains that "I've come to love all the Maronite people, it's like family here. I just feel at home here. I feel it's my second home. When I was going to Roman Catholic churches, we had a business, we'd leave, we never really got involved so since I've been at St. Maron, I've really gotten involved, and it's why I said, it feels like family now." A long-serving Orthodox deacon recognizes that "you can't go just only to go to church... but many people say, 'I want to go see my cousin or friend or this and that.'" Later, this deacon elaborates on the purpose of the church: "The purpose for the church—it is just like the hand, the chicken—when they hold her babies under her wings, that is what the church does. It protects us under her wings."

But in an immigrant and transnational community, feeling like church is a space for sharing your life with family and friends is only a short distance away from seeing it as a space for cultural preservation. Being protected like a chick by its mother may also mean the insulation from the processes of Americanization that immigrant communities often lament. Consider two Orthodox women who locate themselves within the space of St. Mary's in very similar ways.

Rita says, "People I hang out with everyday are from the church community. A community with a shared culture. It's important to be with each other because we understand the rules... raise kids together. My kids go to Arabic school, Sunday school, and I take them to as many events as I can." She says her children are what "brought her back to church" as well as being around "other Arabs and Palestinians." She continues, "We live in a white area... we are the minority... me and my friend are only Arabs in [our town]... I take her to church to socialize with other Arabs."

Another Orthodox woman who recently moved to the area says her fellow parishioners are her close friends now. "Plus," she says, "the culture is that we all pretty much grew up the same and have the same rules so it's easier to relate to them. We all go to church together. I fit in within the first week. I had invitations to go to people's houses for dinner and I speak Arabic fluently so I fit in great with the people. I just felt welcomed right away."

In the Maronite and Antiochian Orthodox communities of greater Detroit, faith and culture are always joined, especially in the context of the homeland/hostland divide. To be Maronite is to be Lebanese. To be Antiochian Orthodox is to support the Palestinian cause. The connection between a religious and political/national identity is one way these transnational communities engage with their homelands within the US context.[17]

We do not use the term "transnational" lightly or only because it is a contemporary buzzword across many disciplines. The communities we work with are truly transnational in that there is a constant engagement with the homeland through political, cultural, and religious social spaces, and much of it occurs through the space of the church. Politically, the members of both congregations are highly aware of issues in their homelands of Lebanon and Palestine. The priests will give updates about casualties or even on the political situation in the homeland during announcements before or after service or during their homilies. The archdiocese for both faith traditions sponsors charities that give money directly to humanitarian causes in Lebanon and Palestine, whether for seminaries, hospitals, or the refugees of recent conflicts. Also, the members may show support for political figures in the homeland.

At one Sunday Maronite mass, many men wore buttons depicting former general and political leader in Lebanon Beshir Gemayal, a Maronite. The mass had been offered, in part, for the twenty-fifth anniversary of his assassination during the Lebanese Civil War.[18] During a break in the mass, a Maronite deacon read a letter to the congregation in Arabic, invoking the memory of Beshir Gemayel and discussing his importance to Lebanon. After the mass Elie, a young immigrant parishioner, said that the

Gemayel family was like the Kennedys because of all they had sacrificed for Lebanon.[19] The incident is one that you would only find at a Maronite church, because of the political affiliations. Even though Gemayel was a Lebanese political and military figure, Lebanese Shi'a or Sunni Muslims as well as most Orthodox Christians would not see him as a figure worth honoring. Only a deep transnational connection to the homeland would make it possible for a Sunday mass at a parish in greater Detroit to be sponsored in part by a Lebanese political party. An episode like this is important to this project because it vividly demonstrates how the space of church becomes a major site through which to express a shared religious, political, and cultural identity.

Similar connections to political developments in the Middle East occur frequently in the Antiochian Orthodox Church as well. During the Israeli siege on Gaza in the winter of 2008/09, Father John read updates from the pulpit that had been written and distributed by the archdiocese, and many of his sermons offered hope for peace. The congregants also took up special collections to send to the victims of the fighting in Palestine. Although this can be seen as a political action in the context of US involvement with Israeli interests, the Orthodox parishioners, many of whom are Palestinian, see it mostly as a Christian, humanitarian act. The archdiocese has large charities in place that support the refugees of the Palestinian conflicts, showing not only where their interests lie but also their continued transnational connections with their collective homelands. Many interlocutors, mostly Maronite, discussed the idea that their religio-cultural identity came with an a priori political identity. Hoda, a devout Maronite and Lebanese-born immigrants quips, "Once you're Lebanese it runs in your blood, the politics."[20]

Culturally, both congregations highlight their Middle Eastern heritage through church sponsored *haflat* (parties), dinners, and *mahrajanat* (festivals). Food and music is a major identity marker for the congregants of both traditions. Father David drummed up support for an upcoming banquet celebrating the arrival of the bishop by announcing from the pulpit, "We can *debkeh* until our Lebanese feet fall off." The *debkeh* is a popular Middle Eastern folk dance. When asked about their cultural identity, most of the second- and third-generation parishioners discussed the foods they grew up eating, such as kibbee, hummus, and rolled grape leaves, as evidence of their cultural heritage. Food is also celebrated by these Christian communities at annual festivals. Each summer the churches hold large-scale cultural festivals as fundraisers, complete with Arabic music, dancing, and traditional food. These festivals are meant to attract outsiders in order to make money. During the festivals, the parishioners play up their Lebanese of Arab heritage, again making the church the main site for cultural identification.[21]

In the religious context, the hierarchies of both faith traditions continually travel between Lebanon and Syria to attend synods and weigh in on decisions that affect the religions worldwide. Priests from the Balamand Orthodox Seminary in Lebanon continue to arrive in the United States to serve as clergy. Many parishioners watch services from Lebanon via Arabic satellite channels. The religious dimension of the transnationality of the Maronites and the Orthodox is perhaps the strongest and most vivid dimension for the parishioners, especially concerning the liturgical use of Arabic and Syriac. As we explore in the next sections, one's religious identity as either Orthodox or Maronite typically structures, or at least influences, the cultural expressions of the congregants in the United States. Parishioners came to the church not just to pray and worship but also to explore and express their identities as Maronites, Antiochian Orthodox, Lebanese, Palestinian, Arab, or Phoenician.

Cultural Identity

Though both communities are positioned similarly vis-à-vis US media depictions of Arabs and the Middle East, US imperial and military ventures in the Arab region, and the discourses of terrorism and homeland security, they express themselves differently, mostly through their religious identities, as a result. Below is a lengthy exploration of the intersections of political, cultural, and religious identity among the Maronite and Antiochian Orthodox of the greater Detroit area. We thought it was important for this section to reflect the discussion among our interlocutors *in their own words*. What this section demonstrates is that the term "Arab Christian" is too broad and is not applicable or relevant to many of our respondents, especially the Maronites. It is our explicit intention to complicate the term "Arab Christian" by showing that many Christians from the Arab region reject the term "Arab" as a marker of self-identity. As mentioned in the introduction, US government and corporate media discourses have constructed an Arab Muslim enemy. People perceived to be in this category have been targeted, especially after 9/11, regardless of the fact that many of those perceived to be Arab Muslim include non-Arab Muslims as well as non-Muslims. Our interlocutors, even though they are Christian, have been forced to contend with these discourses, and this has helped to shape the way they identify themselves in the American context.

For some of our interlocutors, it resulted in a deemphasizing of their Arab background and an enhancement of their Christian identity. Others emphasize their experiences as Arab Christians as distinct from the problems that their Muslim counterparts have faced.

Maronite Catholics' Cultural Identity

Concerning the cultural identity of Maronite Catholics, our research illustrated the following: First, most Maronites felt strongly that they were Lebanese or Phoenician, not Arab. Many had a disdain for the label "Arab." Disassociating from that label was, in part, a strategy for disassociating from the negative imagery associated with Arabs and Muslims in the United States. Second, there is a strong association between being Maronite and being Lebanese. Consider, for example, that one of the churches uses the national symbol of Lebanon, a cedar tree—which sits at the center of the Lebanese flag—to represent their church.[22] Third, liturgical language, whether Arabic or Syriac, plays a major role in defining a Maronite religio-cultural identity.

A large percentage of our interviews began with a discussion of the terms "Arab" or "Arab Christian," since we introduced the project to our interlocutors as one that would explore the scriptural engagements of Arab American Christians. This often prompted lengthy responses about respondents' uneasiness with being included in a study about Arabs or Arab Americans. Offered here is a sampling of how the parishioners of the Maronite churches envision themselves in relation to the term "Arab" or the national identity of "Lebanese":

> Fouad, a middle-aged Maronite immigrant: I would say I'm Lebanese. Until I'm proven that I'm Arab, which I don't think I'm proven that I'm Arab because I want to go back to the old, old times. The Arab country was not where Lebanon was, so that came around after and then they announced it as an Arab country after so many years. So I want to be distinguished then [from] Arab because when you say Arabs then they associate you right away with terrorism.

Notice that Fouad connects being labeled Arab with being considered an enemy Other in the America context. He continues:

> To us, now more than ever there is terrorism involved and when you say Arab right away they associate with them; I do want to make a distinction.

That's why I go back to the old times way back in the biblical times and Lebanon was not an Arab land. But it's hard; this is where it becomes hard for people to distinguish between terrorist and not terrorist. That's very important to us and I'm glad you're doing this interview because we can share our side of the story.

Another male parishioner says simply, "Actually, I like to be Lebanese American. I speak Arabic. I mean we speak the Arabic language, but I'm Lebanese-American." Hoda, an active Maronite parishioner, says she considers herself Lebanese because she was born in Lebanon, and Maronite Catholic, but also American because she has lived in the United States longer than in Lebanon.

An immigrant physician and long-serving member of the Maronite community in greater Detroit offers this explanation:

I have a lot of friends in the Arabic community. But there's a misconception in this country. They lump us all together. We are descendants of the Phoenicians. The Phoenicians are not Arabs....

The Maronite Christian people are descendants of the Phoenicians. These are our grand grand grand grand grand fathers. But in this country, sorry to say, they don't understand the difference between Maronite, Melkite, Orthodox, first of all, the Christian element of the community, and they don't understand who's an Arab and who's not an Arab. Now, the Arabs have their own glorious history, glorious tradition. We had to study all their traditions. And they had fantastic people who were very, very smart, who contributed a lot to the history of the Arab region, but to say that we are Arab Christians, it is wrong because it is not so.

Finally, Maronite priest Father David furthers the distinction between Muslims as Arabs and Maronites as Lebanese and Christian:

Because for us Lebanese, Arab means, usually means, Muslim, it means non-Christian, it means invaders, in some ways. And so, they never identify themselves as Arabs. They were always Lebanese: Lebanese American, Lebanese period. And always from Mount Lebanon, that area of Lebanon which is the Maronite stronghold of today. The lines have been blurred, and clearly today many Lebanese have no problems being called Arab American. But to those of us who are second, third generation, we do. Because we grew up having hammered into us: you are *not* Arab, you are *not* Muslim.

Based on this discussion we took seriously the charge of recognizing the importance of how the Maronites identify themselves. As researchers, it is easy to label them Arab Americans or Arab Christians, but it is clear that they see themselves as something more nuanced and distinct. And especially because this identity is tied up with spiritual belief (i.e., the Maronite faith), we honor their self-identification.[23]

The connection between being Maronite and being Lebanese is also heightened when these parishioners discuss the role of the church in their lives, especially the liturgical use of Arabic or Syriac, which is discussed again in later sections because it is a major theme of the project. Regardless of the language of the mass or the country in which it is performed, the parishioners are adamant that the essence of the faith is preserved:

> Obviously, you don't go to Lebanon and hear a mass in English. But, everything else is the same. The mass is the same in Lebanon, the same in Argentina, same in Brazil, same in Lebanon, with the exception of the language in Lebanon, they don't say it in English. Other countries, they say it in their language partly and then in the language of Arabic.

In this section on cultural identity, we want to highlight how the use of non-English languages in the mass can actually create tensions between the generations of parishioners. One parishioner explains, "Now you can see that the gospel was read in both languages, the epistle was read in both languages [today]. The reason for that is for the younger generation to understand what it means because they come in and they sit and they are bewildered as to what's going on. They don't know what's going on. They don't have the background like we did. They were born in this county, never exposed to it. Consequently, that was limited to what we teach them." As Father David explains, the fact that the church is in America and not Lebanon makes the language/culture discussion more pertinent:

> Younger people want to come here because we use English. And they're beginning to identify more spiritually with us than ethnically. So even though we're Lebanese, they begin to see themselves more as Maronites. And Maronites are more than just Lebanese. But Maronites are far more than just Lebanese, that's the point. [...] We have been using English as our main language for the last forty years. Now, in many of our churches, Arabic's becoming the main language. And we've had many of our American-born Maronites drifting away because they will not go back to a foreign language.

Sam, an older immigrant parishioner, breaks down the divide between the generations by highlighting the different masses:

> You have one mass in English and one mass half of it English, and unfortunately we lose a lot of the younger generations who are born in the States because they speak only English and there's a big competition between the Latin Church where families will migrate, especially because of the school, to send their kids to the Latin Church.

This leads to the final point, that beyond all the discussions about culture, language, or politics, the parishioners are still members of a faith community. When they were asked, "What does it mean to be a Maronite Catholic?" many of their responses took on a cultural or historical element, as well as a spiritual one. One parishioner spoke of the "tradition" of the faith: "Well, we are born with this tradition, as you know. We don't choose our religion. It is chosen for us. We grew up with it. We learned all about it. We practiced it. And we love its history."

The idea of the Maronite faith being a "tradition" came up numerous times. For example, "It's a glorified tradition, it's an excellent tradition and we practice it daily and weekly. And we baptize our children in the same rite. We confirm them in the same rite. We teach them all about the rites before we eat, before we gather together. We say certain prayers that are appropriate to our rite and we maintain religion in all aspects of our life." Every one of the Maronite Catholics we talked to said that they were Maronite because their parents were Maronite.[24] There are very few converts in the churches where we conducted our fieldwork. We believe this has to do with the nature of the Maronite religion being so intertwined with a specific national or cultural identity. We found more converts in the Antiochian Orthodox faith. Even though the Antiochian Archdiocese is affiliated with the Arab region and many parishioners are from there or have at least part of their ancestry there, there is a concerted effort to not be merely an ethnic church, but an Orthodox church. Of course, there are tensions around this, especially in a large parish where over 95 percent of the congregants are of Arab heritage.

Antiochian Orthodox Cultural Identity

In discussions on cultural identity, the following themes emerged: first, Antiochian research participants shared a close connection to an Arab or Arab American cultural identity that was directly connected to their Antiochian identity. Consider that Antiochians nationwide as well as at

St. Mary use many "Arab" cultural symbols in their church and church literature, including self-Orientalizing images of camels and sheikhs, as well as historical imagery such as Arabic calligraphy and tapestries. Second, a commitment to being part of one "family" and "community" was central to their Arab cultural identity. Third, the different generations (immigrants and second-generation members) created a chance for cultural continuity but were also a site of tension and difference. For instance, our interlocutors frequently brought up the issue of language, and whether or not using Arabic in liturgical services was a hindrance to the nonimmigrants or even the non-Arab congregants. Finally, we found the biggest difference between the Maronites and the Orthodox to be that the Orthodox envision themselves as a church that welcomes non-Arab converts. Whereas the Maronites are always also Lebanese, the Orthodox more often put faith before cultural identity, even though the majority of the interlocutors closely identified as both Arab and some other nationality, such as Lebanese or Palestinian, in addition to Antiochian Orthodox.

Father John helped to explain the balance that the Antiochian Archdiocese has tried to maintain in the United States. He spoke of the leadership of Metropolitan Philip Saliba, who has headed the archdiocese for over forty years. Within the first few years of Saliba's enthronement, he pushed to change the name of the archdiocese from the Syrian Antiochian Orthodox Church to its more simplified Antiochian title, which refers more to the birthplace of the theology than the birthplace of the parishioners. Even though Metropolitan Philip was instrumental in keeping English as the official language of the archdiocese and has pushed for and accepted converts of all faiths and nationalities, Saliba continues to use both Arabic and English in speeches, letters, and services. As Father John says, "Matter of fact, Metropolitan Philip never attended a church service or presided over a liturgy but used one-third of his service in the Arabic. I think he encouraged it. He is the man who believed that Orthodoxy can be of help and can be of light to America but never to give up truth."

Father John is hinting here at the fact that many Antiochian Orthodox churches, especially those in areas that do not continually receive large groups of new immigrants from the Middle East, such as Kansas, Oklahoma, and Pennsylvania, are now a majority non-Arab converts. Although some people embrace this fact as a sign that the archdiocese is growing and has shed its national or cultural identity, others worry that the Church may lose its roots as the Arab branch of Orthodox Christianity. This tension is not only generational, as you will see, but also exists between converts and "cradle" parishioners, as they are called.

The parishioners and clergy feel deeply connected with a mother church that is "still alive in Antioch today in Damascus headed by the patriarch and the holy senate," as Father John elaborates. "We are a living member of that church. Everyone needs to have roots." In the Antiochian Orthodox Church, those roots are firmly planted in Lebanon and Syria, where the religious See is currently located. Although many agreed that first and foremost, they are committed to "seeking the Kingdom of God," in the words of a convert deacon, at the same time "being Arab is crucial." Deacon Mark, a white American deacon illustrated this sentiment when he said that it is a compliment when people at church assume he is Arab.

As Arab culture is typically seen as being very family oriented, it is not surprising that the parishioners of St. Mary connect "family" with "church." Comments such as those from Fadi are not the exception: "This church, I think it's a family here. I like coming to a family. Father makes them feel at home so much that they worship the ground that he walks on. They love him and his family." Deacon Mark picks up on this love of "church family" and connects it to what he sees as an element of "Middle Eastern culture":

There is another verse I learned that I live my life by...."a new commandment I give unto you that you love one another even as Christ has loved you"...that's the new commandment, that's the 11th commandment. It doesn't overwrite anything but...I think that it cancels the rest of them. This is the message and this is what [Fr. John] has taken very seriously in the ministry he has been entrusted with. [...] I'm thankful that it has that culture because there is something about the Middle Eastern culture that I love. There is an ethos that is very family based and love based and this is where Christ is from, this is where Christianity was established and I think that in America, we have a lot to learn about love. I think it is self love, *eros* or erotic love of yourself, when we need to be looking for *agape* love, it's Godly love.

Deacon Elias echoes Deacon Mark:

Our people are very peaceful people, very generous people and they love each other, especially when somebody dies....They stand together, they unite together, they love each other, they like to help each other. This is very important between the families because we came from one country, a small country like Ramallah [in Palestine], so we know each other and we came here. Just a few families migrated and came to the United States in 1932. Our people are very nice people.

Cultural Identity through Language and Generation

One of the questions we asked of every interlocutor that always elicited a quick and emotional response was about the use of Arabic during church services. Some parishioners and clergy liked the "flavor" the Arabic language gave to the liturgy, while others saw it as a hindrance to their ability to worship. While it would be less messy to say that the differences in reactions broke down along generational lines, or between the Arab and non-Arab members, that is not necessarily the case. Deacon Mark, for example, is trying to learn certain prayers in Arabic so he can be more active during liturgical services. Father John says young parishioners always ask him to perform their wedding services in Arabic, even if the bride or groom does not speak the language. "It's a way to connect," he says. "I find out even when young people want to get married, want baptism, they say, Father, please use Arabic." Sara, a young second-generation Palestinian American and active youth-group member says, "I really don't understand Arabic too much. I can read and write but I don't really speak it that much. So if I were to just stay in church and they just did it in Arabic, I probably wouldn't go." What we found, then, is that everyone had an opinion about the use of Arabic in church and that it was not possible to predict who would feel which way about it. Everyone tended to agree, though, that the use of Arabic as a liturgical language was connected to a sense of cultural identity.

A young Arab American subdeacon lays out the range of issues that we encountered in our ethnographic work:

> There's always a constant struggle over which language to use in church.
> People get offended over this. People want what they are comfortable with.
> I speak fluent Arabic, but the Arabic we use in church is more classical
> Arabic and I don't understand all of it. I studied a good amount before I was
> able to understand and I still don't understand everything but it enhances it.
> I think the culture in general, because in the Middle East and Greece, they
> understand what Orthodoxy is.

As we will explore in the section "Authenticity: Language and Leadership from the Holy Land," the faith's historical and cultural linkages to the Middle East are what the members take the most pride in. The Maronite Catholics and the Antiochian Orthodox have to navigate this balance of being a church in America that needs to minister to a growing American flock, while simultaneously maintaining their ancient connections to the Holy Land, which is what truly sets these faith traditions apart from other Christian denominations in the United States.

Afterword: The Relevance of September 11, 2001

Much of the discussion about the post-9/11 experience among the Maronite and Orthodox parishioners and clergy focused on the need for the American public to understand that not everyone from the Middle East is Muslim, and that there are indeed large groups of Christians in the Arab region. The interlocutors were not being malicious in separating themselves out from Muslims; instead, they were merely trying to differentiate themselves. Numerous respondents praised the project because it would help show the American public that there are many types of faith communities from the Middle East, and Arabs in the United States are not the way they appear on TV and in movies. Hoda wants people to have an accurate picture of Christians from the Arab region and to not be lumped in with Muslims, though she assured me that she was not prejudiced. She wanted people to be educated about the differences among peoples from the Middle East.

Our interlocutors also felt the need to differentiate themselves from Arab Muslims, because the Christians, for the most part, did not see themselves as victims of any post-9/11 backlash, but felt thankful that they did not experience the same dilemma as the Muslim communities.[25] They were also sympathetic to the Muslim plight. Father John spoke of this following 9/11: "I was asked this question by many senators and congressmen and FBI. But we [the people of St. Mary] have never once had any problem. Don't forget at least in general public you do not distinguish an Orthodox from an Italian, but you can distinguish a Muslim by his habit." Another interlocutor spoke about experiencing the aftermath of 9/11 in ways that were different from Arab American Muslims. A congress person who met with them after 9/11 reinforced the difference by privileging them over the Muslims in the area and telling them they had nothing to worry about. Following 9/11, parishioners turned to prayer with feelings of fear and gave special prayers for peace, and said that more and more people prayed and came together. The church was a comforting space during this time. The aftermath of 9/11 also brought Muslims and Christians together and created unity since Arabs and Muslims were facing similar problems. Father John was involved in numerous interfaith programs. The role of prayer following 9/11 is discussed again later in the section "Scriptural Reading."

Authenticity: Language and Leadership from the Holy Land

The spiritual fathers. The desert fathers. These are phrases we heard often when talking with Orthodox and Maronite Catholics. They refer to the early Christian theologians and religious leaders from the Middle East. For Arab and Maronite Christians, the Middle East is not only the birthplace of Jesus but also the birthplace of their Orthodox and Catholic churches, as well as the birthplace of their ancestors; and for many members of the Maronite and Antiochian Churches, the land of their own birth. Both churches are tied to the Holy Land by both language and history. This engagement with the ancient Christianity of the Middle East is most evident in the ways in which the congregants frame their ecclesiastical use of Syriac and Arabic as languages which can bring them closer to the historical and spiritual Jesus. Also, the leadership, as in patriarchs, bishops, priests, and deacons, are seen as both literal and figurative descendants of Christ's apostles and living connections to the homeland/ Holy Land. Whereas US popular and political discourses figure Arabs and peoples from the Middle East as Muslims and therefore threats, these Arab and Maronite Christians have continually played up their identity as descendants of the first Christians from the Holy Land. Perhaps Rita, an Antiochian Orthodox parishioner stated it most succinctly: "As far as 'Holy Land' ... people use it as bragging rights. We come from the holiest place in the world, where Jesus was born."

In the sections that follow, we discuss the claims to this religious authenticity that the Antiochians and Maronites have: those of ancient languages and ecclesiastic authority, both of which stem from their connection to the Holy Land. As we did in the previous section on cultural identity, in this section we will show, on the local level, how these communities have negotiated the ways that United States and European imperialism have given value to certain identity categories. We have shown how the claims to and avoidance of the label of "Arab" in the cultural context was borne out in the comments and stories of our interlocutors. Here, as well, the Maronites and Orthodox stake their claims to a specific ancient Arab or Middle Eastern identity, but within a religious context.

The Orthodox believe that they hold the key to the unchanging Church of Christ, spiritually descendant from St. Peter of the city of Antioch, where followers of Jesus were first called Christians. Further, they believe their Church is physically linked with the Middle East, the Holy Land, because their membership is overwhelmingly Lebanese and Palestinian. Theirs is a critical two-part claim to authenticity. First, they are doctrinally orthodox and the physical descendants of the spiritual, desert fathers of the Holy Land. The Church maintains that the ordination of their bishops and priests can be traced back to the laying on of hands by St. Peter who ordained Christianity's first hierarchs in the city of Antioch. This sort of authenticity of the priesthood plays out in the ways in which the priest is imbued with much of the authority of the Church. In both the Orthodox and Maronite denominations, in the absence of a priest there are very limited prayer services that can be done. A liturgy cannot be performed without a priest, as he is learned and the only one who can bring it to life.

Second, the Arab members of the Antiochian Orthodox Church are culturally linked to the Middle East because it is their homeland. There is a reason that much of the music is sung or canted in Arabic, even in the congregations where only a small percentage of parishioners actually speak Arabic: it is their tie to the authentic Christianity of the Middle East. This sort of historical, cultural, and hierarchical provenance is unique to Christian churches originating in what is now known as the Arab region and often referred to as the Holy Land. At St. Mary's, the vast majority of the liturgy is conducted in English. There are hymns that the choir sings in Arabic. The Epistle, the Gospel, the Nicene Creed, and the Lord's Prayer are read or recited in both English and Arabic.

Authenticity in the Maronite Church in America functions in similar ways to the Orthodox. The members still speak of the spiritual fathers, but they are also more likely to mention the continual use of Syriac in their services as proof of their authenticity. Syriac, the members will tell you, is the language of Jesus, or similar to the language of Jesus, or dates from the time of Jesus, depending on whom you talk to. All Maronite priests learn Syriac, and many of the crucial prayers during the mass are in Syriac. The members are adamant that Syriac must be kept alive as an authentic aspect of Maronite Christianity. St. Maron in Detroit has been holding basic Syriac language classes for its members, but they still rely on the priests and the hierarchs to sustain the language. The Maronites also maintain a sense of connection to the landscape of the Holy Land through references to the "desert fathers" and examples like the "Faith of the Mountain" religious-education series, which is a coloring book series for Maronite children. The "mountain" refers to the mountain in Syria where St. Maron lived. Finally, as discussed in other sections in this chapter, the American Maronites' ongoing historical, political, cultural, and family ties to Lebanon maintain the idea of being a part of the ancient church of the Holy Land.

As far as priestly authority and authenticity go, the priest seems to be charged not only with maintaining the Syriac language tradition, and thus a sense of ancient Christian authenticity, but also with continuing the tradition started by a fifth-century monk from the mountains of Syria; this means that the priest's authority is partly a result of the continued embodiment of this ancient desert father from which the Maronite Church sprang. Much like the Orthodox Church, there are very limited services that can be done in the absence of clergy. A service conducted without a priest would not be unauthentic, but it would be unauthorized by the patriarchs in Lebanon and the hierarchy in the United States.

Language and Authenticity

A physician and a prominent member of Detroit's Maronite community offered an examination of the role of Syriac: "What most Christians don't realize, and I didn't realize until a few years back, that really Jesus, when he spoke, he didn't speak Hebrew. Hebrew was the language of the rich and around Jerusalem. And the common people, the poor people…were speaking Aramaic. And Jesus's language, as far as we know, was Aramaic. That's why the Maronite Church prides itself in having the Aramaic, the western Aramaic." Syriac was a spoken dialect of Aramaic. "And I think it's a lovely language, which some of us are pursuing here and we're going back to our roots." Nabil is referring to the Syriac classes that his parish offers. They are only basic courses, but the point is that the churches in the United States are playing an active role in keeping the ancient liturgical language alive. He says that since the Arabs have dominated Syria and the surrounding areas for over 1500 years, "You have to learn Arabic, you know." But speaking Arabic, for him, doesn't make him Arab. "I've been in this country 33, 34 years, obviously I speak English. Does it make me English?" Syriac signals not only his identity as a Maronite Catholic, but his identity as a Lebanese Christian and a non-Arab, exemplifying the complex ways that religious and cultural identity are interwoven in the Maronite and Antiochian Churches.

St. Mary's, like many Antiochian parishes across the country, especially those with immigrant populations, also offers classes in its ancient liturgical language. Although the official ecclesiastical language of the ancient Orthodox Church was Greek, the Antiochians have celebrated their liturgies in Arabic for centuries, and much like the Maronites, tend to see their cultural and religious identities through language.[26]

But there is a slight disconnect between the clergy and parishioners on this matter. An Orthodox subdeacon connects the liturgical language debate to more important aspects of the faith: "When you stick to Arabic, it's because that's what we did before. It has no theology. It's a tradition with a little 't.' One of our modern theologians, he's a metropolitan in

England, he says a tradition with a big 'T' is something like a dogma of the church; the trinity, the virgin…things like that. Traditions with a little 't' are things like dyeing [Easter] eggs red, speaking a language in church and such things. So it's o.k. to lose the little 't's, although I think they are nice sometimes, we can never lose the big 'T's."

Father John and Father David, though they both love the tradition of keeping Arabic or Syriac in the liturgy, understand that this is only a tradition with a small "t." Father David seems to downplay the role of Syriac in "captur[ing] a sense of scripture and a sense of spirituality," because he says "that can be communicated in any language."

> Syriac is our official language, but we've used Arabic, we've used Greek in Cyprus. So we do have different languages that have been part of our tradition, even though Syriac has always been our main liturgical language. So linguistically it doesn't make a whole lot of difference because the prayers are relevant in any language.

But that ever-present tradition with a small 't,' is significant to the life of church, especially concerning language, even though it may not affect doctrine or big 'T' tradition. Father David says that since Maronites "are now to be found on every single country in the world," keeping the main prayers in Syriac will maintain the "commonality of the Maronite Church…no matter what language you're using as the main language."

Father John sees Greek as the true language of Church scripture, but makes certain to tie Arabic closely to it. It is also an argument that is more about culture and style than scripture: "Don't forget when you read scripture in its original language Greek, and translated to Arabic, there is this ethos of chanting. And when you chant in Arabic or Greek, it sounds more alive than chanting in English, because English is not really a prayerful language. It is a business language. But we have beautiful choirs that sing in English. We're learning. We're adapting to write music, hymns that are in Byzantine tunes instead of western notation or western style."

Even though the clergy recognize that the church is the church no matter the language, the parishioners continually view the use of Arabic or Syriac as important to both their cultural and religious identity. "You have to look at the liturgy as part of tradition. You cannot look at it any other way," explains a Maronite lay leader. He continues:

> There's lots of words in the Maronite mass which are Syriac, but they are [kept] to a minimum especially after Vatican II when they changed a lot of

how the mass is said. [...] The flavor, if you want, of the Maronite masses has kept some Syriac in. It's to go back to our roots. And the liturgy itself, I think it's a wonderful liturgy. It's a fulfilling liturgy. I am very happy the way it's conducted. I attend the 11:30 mass which is English, Arabic and Syriac. So, it has all three flavors and I don't mind it. It's a little bit longer. It takes time to repeat things sometimes because if you say the gospel in two languages, obviously if the priest is going to say his sermon in two languages, it takes more time than one language. If you want a short mass, an English mass, come to the 9:30 mass. If you want a mass with flavor, come to the 11:30 mass.

Another parishioner is more adamant and wants Syriac to be more than just a "flavor." "I wish, actually, as a matter of fact I wish that they [...] can go back to the whole thing in Syriac. [...] I think we'll benefit a lot more if we go back to the language that spiritually, you know, to the language that Christ was speaking." "It's not easy language. But I'll be willing to [learn it] if they go back to the whole thing." A Lebanese Maronite man sees the loss of Syriac as part of the Church's movement through time and space: "We have now only a few paragraphs that are said in the Syriac language that was spoken by Jesus Christ in the past. Our mass used to be almost 100 percent said in Syriac, and now as time has passed, most of the mass is now said in Arabic. And then after that, now that we are in the States, it's said in English."

In the Antiochian parish, Father John says that when he does weddings, the bride and groom always ask, "*Abouna* [Father], please do the service in Arabic," even though neither speaks Arabic. The use of Arabic in the Church is also a link to the homeland for both recent immigrants and second- and third-generation Arab Americans who may have never been to the Middle East.[27]

But it is also more than part of an ancestral or homeland identity: it is what sets them apart from other Christian denominations. The Maronites and the Antiochians have a valid claim to the Holy Land through language, culture, and history. Consider the words of two non-Arab members of St. Mary's, one clergy and the other a lay leader. Even for a non-Arab member, the claim to an authentic ancient Christianity is salient:

What I love about the Antiochian churches, and I'm so thankful that this is the church that my [dad] was ordained in, is because again it's scriptural [...] where were people first called Christians? In Antioch. I love this. This connection to Christianity, and there was a church established there at that time and now we have a patriarchate there. So I love that.

Another non-Arab member also sees a potent relation between the Arab Christian tradition here and the more ancient version: "Well, I think to me that it plays out at Easter time, for Orthodox people because [...] during those services during [Holy Week] there is a service everyday leading up to the resurrection. There are some awfully emotional services and I think people really empathize with being there, with really being there with the string of people that were there. So I think there's a lot of emotion in this church and faith unlike some of the more western, distant traditions from the Holy land." "I think they view themselves as being relatives of the apostles [laughs], literally." He laughs, "[Father John] probably thinks he is closer to Christ than I am because of where he came from."

Leadership and Authority

The authority of the priest in the Maronite and Orthodox faiths is threefold. In the Orthodox Church he is canonically the only person who can preside over a Divine Liturgy, other than a bishop. Without the priest, the types of worship services that can be conducted are severely limited. A deacon can lead some services when the priest is absent but cannot preside over the consecration of the Eucharist, the most important element of the liturgy or mass. Second, the priest in the Orthodox Church is charged with maintaining the succession of ordination handed down from St. Peter. In the Maronite Church, as we have seen, the priest is expected to uphold the use of Syriac and also carry on the foundations of the faith laid down by St. Maron in fifth-century Lebanon. Finally, as we explore more fully in the following section on scriptures, since the liturgy is inherently scriptural, the priest is seen as the bearer of the Word of God to the people.

The role of the priest and the deacons is much more than just orchestrating the Sunday services, according to Father David. "So each of us has a role to play....And they're living liturgical roles." Father David goes on to say that everybody is involved in bringing the liturgy to life:

> If you look at the Antiochian tradition, the Maronite tradition, you would see that the priest has a role to play, but so does the deacon and the subdeacon. [...] And the laity plays a unique role. The congregation is much more responsive, they have much more of a prayer life than just sitting there. They're not an audience in a theater. They are active participants.

But the priest is, above all other roles, the one who makes the liturgy work; in fact, the only one who can. "He is a leader of the community, but he's also the one who is chosen by the bishop to represent him and also to transform, as it were, the bread and the wine into the body and blood of Christ, and that can only be done by him." Father David adds that the Eastern-rite churches, "unlike the Roman Church, do not have a priest-less liturgy." Even a lay leader in the Maronite Church who has been an active member for over a half a century knows how limiting the absence of a priest can be: "Everything we do, we have that done by a member of the clergy." As a young Orthodox congregant, Sara, quipped, "Like having church on Sunday without Father John, that would never happen."

The priest is an important role model for parishioners especially because he is human and fallible. It is also easier to accept him as a person. Hoda says, "A lot of people, they see the priest as God. And that's something very wrong because the priest is, while the priest is a holy person, he's a regular man just like you and me and he has [his] own mistakes. So once you look at the priest as holy and [as] God, when he makes a mistake that makes you resent him." But if you see the priest more as a "disciple on earth, the sooner you will realize that they're human, the better you understand them."

Many interlocutors in both faith traditions used the language of familial ties to discuss their view of the role of the priest, or their relationship with him. One Maronite woman says, "[F]or us the patriarch is not simply the head of the Maronite Church, he's the spiritual father. And you don't refuse your father's requests. And it's very much thought of in that light." An Orthodox parishioner sees Father John not only as a connection to the word of God, but to his homeland and the ancient Christianity. "Oh yes," he says of Father John's role, "it has more importance here because we are far away from the Holy Land and the greatest thing that we have with us is Father John."

The Orthodox priest envisions his role in much the same way the Maronite priest does. Father John, for example, uses the same idea about "living the liturgical role" that Father David espouses. Father John says of priests, "we live the scripture, because when I stand up on Sunday and I will preach my homily, I base it on the scripture. So it is a living dynamic within the model of the church."

So far we have explored the space of the church and the cultural and religious identities of the Lebanese Maronite Catholics and the predominantly Lebanese, Palestinian, and Jordanian Antiochian Orthodox communities of greater Detroit. Each of these subcategories has been explored with an eye to the transnational nature of these religious communities. This was not our forcing a theoretical framework on the words and ideas of our many interlocutors. Instead, we simply recognized, through our ethnographic work within these faiths, that the geographical and cultural divide between America and the Arab region played a real role in how they located themselves religiously and culturally. Now, we focus on the practice of reading and engaging with scriptures among the Maronite Catholics and Antiochian Orthodox. Even here, we found that the transnational positions of these communities was borne out of their engagement with scriptures, whether in liturgy or mass or during their own personal readings of the Bible.

Scriptural Readings

In drawing the distinction between Catholic and Protestant churches, it is almost a truism that the members of Catholic churches do not know their scripture and are not well versed in the Bible or do not have a personal relationship with it because they rely instead on a highly structured, ritualized mass or liturgy led by an ordained priest. Many of our respondents, especially the clergy or lay leaders, elaborated on this perceived lack of scriptural connection in the Orthodox and Catholic faiths. They recognized the anxiety among the congregants within their own parishes, many of whom do not believe that they know the Bible well enough. What we eventually found is that the members of both faith traditions are not only exposed to scriptures at every church service but that scriptures play an active role in both their liturgical experience, as they recite and memorize scriptures, and in their personal lives. As Father David, Father John, and Subdeacon Michael pointed out, "[T]he people just don't know that they know it."

Both the Orthodox Divine Liturgy and the Maronite mass consist almost wholly of biblical references.[28] St. Mary's offered an eight-week class called Understanding the Divine Liturgy in which parishioners explored the scriptural underpinnings of the major parts of the liturgy. For example, the faithful learned that the prayers of the Anaphora and the Consecration, which are the prayers during the preparation of the Eucharist, are taken word for word from Bible passages. "Take, eat, this is my body which is broken for you for the forgiveness of sins," which the priest chants as he lifts up the bread, is taken from 1 Corinthians 11:24. Father John and Deacon Mark led the weekly class, which averaged about ten adult attendees. A mixed crowd of Arab immigrants, non-Arab converts, and second- and third-generation Lebanese American parishioners explored just how scriptural their faith really was. The few who attended this class found out what Orthodox and Maronite clergy already know: that the Church is scriptural and not some kind of polar opposite of the Protestant tradition when it comes to scriptural engagement. An Orthodox subdeacon stated it most effectively:

> In comparison to the Protestant churches, we don't memorize the Bible as much, word for word, know which verse says what. But if you look at our liturgy and I think that [it] is the ultimate expression of Christian worship. Why is that? Because it combines church history and scripture and dogma and spirituality and every aspect of being a Christian; it combines in our divine liturgy. In the liturgy, you find a lot of scripture but I don't think our people know that. I don't think they know where a lot of our lines come from.

Part of the goal of an educational opportunity such as the Understanding the Divine Liturgy class, is to change that perception.

The Orthodox view of the relationship of scripture to church is actually not relational at all. Both Father John and Deacon Elias, a long-serving immigrant deacon known in the church for his personal connections to the scriptures, are emphatic that you cannot discuss "scriptures" as if they are separate from "the Church." Deacon Elias explains extemporaneously, but in a manner showing the amount of time he has spent ruminating on these ideas:

> In one way, I think scripture can only be understood in the confinement of the church. So when we talk about church, we talk about scripture, we talk about worship, spirituality and the church in a way. It is called a holy tradition. So they are inseparable, but the church in our view have [separated them]—the scriptures was produced in the church and by the church and in the early days, it was for the church. [...] An Orthodox cannot be defined only in relationship with the Bible or the scripture. You have to have that membership in the totality of the body of the church. We see the Divine Liturgy as scripture, it's mostly taken from the book of Revelation, the worship...our church is designed as a temple. It is the Holy of Holies but we don't offer a blood sacrifice; we offer bread and wine which is a bloodless sacrifice. But the danger when you say it's only scripture, you've taken away the other...the body from it.

At our first meeting with Father John, when we were explaining the nature of the project and the types of questions we would be asking, he interrupted and interjected his own analysis of the our questions, and in doing so uncovered a new manner of approaching the topic. He said that he was concerned that the questions did not apply to the Orthodox context because "there is no such thing as religious scripture." Elaborating on such a seemingly odd declaration, he explained that Orthodoxy is about "living scripture" and living the scripture. Scripture is not separate from the church. We must not look at it in a Protestant manner, he said.

Remember the earlier discussion in the "Authenticity" section on the role of the priest as an authority and a direct connection to Jesus and the Apostles. It is the liturgical basis on scripture and the priest's solitary authority to enact that liturgy or mass, which further solidifies his place as the light and life of each parish. As one Orthodox parishioner stated, "For me, [scriptures] come through the priest. We have a lot of trust in him and we just try and he passes down the Bible to us when he tries to connect to people's lives. We don't really [need] to read bible—I wouldn't understand it." Unlike most Protestant sects, the laity have a much more passive role in the service, but their presence is utterly important, as each congregant is "living their liturgical role," as Father David stated so eloquently. The members are usually unaware of how scriptural they are being just by going to liturgy and reciting the Nicene Creed, every line of which is a direct reference to scripture.

So, even though the stereotype of Orthodox and Catholic parishioners is that they are unversed in the Bible and lack a personal relationship with the scriptures, our research shows that this is an unfair and untrue depiction. This chapter will show that the scriptures are the foundation of the liturgy, which is the heart of the faith. It is at the liturgy where all congregants gather to hear the Word and reflect on current events, including homeland crises, through the homily. The liturgy is also an important space through which to experience their cultural identity through the use of native and ancient languages, such as Arabic and Syriac. This is especially significant for parishioners who do not speak these languages but still love hearing scripture recited in them. Further, the parishioners take scriptural passages and messages, either from their own personal Bible reading or from the liturgy, Gospel readings, or the homily, and use it as guidance for their lives.

Personal Application of Scriptures

Most of the parishioners tended to define scriptures as "God's word" or the words of Christ as written in the Bible. The clergy, though, understand the deeper connection between "the church" and "scriptures." But the clergy and parishioners are on the same page in that most of the respondents said that they tended to experience scriptures primarily through the liturgy in church each Sunday. For many, this was more important in their lives than reading the Bible—although church leaders and some members said they do read the Bible or attend some sort of Bible study. The interlocutors say that the Orthodox and Maronite faiths are very oral, and that they most often encounter scriptures through the priest as he conducts the liturgy. Regardless of how they encountered them, whether through church services or private Bible reading, scriptures were critical to people's everyday lives because they provided them with moral guidelines about how to be a good person and how to live like Jesus on earth. The scriptures were critical to people's engagements with everyday life—whether in terms of raising kids or living a healthy life in fast-paced America. Because they are members of transnational religio-cultural groups, the scriptures also played a role in their engagements with structural issues, such as racism, the targeting of Arab Americans after 9/11, as well as the forces of war and US imperial projects in their homelands (particularly in Lebanon, Palestine, and Iraq). The scriptures were highly significant sites through which people sought comfort in relationship to war in Lebanon. It helped them forgive others when loved ones were killed, and to be compassionate during times of intense hatred and war.

Both the Maronites of greater Detroit, as a congregation of Lebanese immigrants and Lebanese Americans, and the Orthodox, as predominately of Palestinian and Lebanese heritage, have learned to deal with crisis and tragedy both in the United States after 9/11 and in the homeland during decades of civil war in Lebanon and war and occupation in Palestine. The duration of our research within these communities also brought us into contact with them following the Israeli war with Lebanon in summer 2006, and encompassed the siege on Gaza in winter 2008/09. We were able to see first-hand how these communities mobilized support for their families and church families here and abroad though prayer and the collection of donations at church. Further, as we will explore below, the liturgy on Sunday became a space where everyone would gather to hear the latest news and to hear a homily that typically connected that day's Gospel reading to the crisis. It was through scripture and the church's teachings that most of interlocutors searched for comfort during times of homeland and hostland crisis. A pertinent example of this comes from the Maronite Catholic tradition, as told by Father David:

> One of the stories that is very big in the Syriac world is the five wise men and
> five foolish virgins. That story's always been a very big one in the Middle

East, not just with Maronites, but with many in the Syriac world because constant vigilance meant something to them. Because living in terror, living in fear for their lives made them very conscious of being constantly ready and being prepared. So many of those parables having to do with the end times, having to do with preparedness, have taken on a central meaning in their lives. Among many of the things they quote is "keep your lamp ready."

Well, that's scripture. They may not identify with it directly, but that is sacred scripture.

Following 9/11, a number of the parishioners looked to their Christian faith for guidance. Though they may not have been the victims of any sort of overt discrimination—in fact none of our interlocutors said that they were—they dealt with a sense of loss. Hoda, for example, said that the Church

> helps you be compassionate about others and I think that's after, where the 9/11 happened, you feel the pain of other people. When you're so religious and so into God and the love of God, I think you see through the eyes of God. So you pray more for the people. [. . .] I came from a war [in Lebanon]. Yeah, I lived in the war for a while and I am so thankful that I am here.

Barbara looked to her faith to try to find the kind of compassion and understanding that Hoda described:

> Well, being an Arab American, and not being from there originally, being born here, I love America, but I do feel a connection because that's where my grandparents and great-grandparents were from. I did lose a cousin in the World Trade Center, so it hit home for us. But you can't hold all Arabs responsible for the acts of a few. They say it was in the name of God, but it's not really in the name of God. So, I have difficulty with not understanding what the Muslim religion is. But then, Father had some Bible studies. He brings things more clearly and we were going to do something on the various religions so that we have a better understanding of it. I guess it hurt that people looked at Arab Americans in that way. But, we are Americans, we are Arabs and we are Americans and we need to unite.

The idea of peace above all else was frequently cited by our interlocutors. Even during times of extreme violence, such as the Israeli siege on Gaza in December 2008 and January 2009, the priest of the mostly Palestinian and Lebanese St. Mary's preached peace and understanding during his sermons:

> We gather on the first Sunday of the New Year to pray as a community. We gather with a heaviness of heart and mind and soul that the world once again is at war. And this war is back home. Those who are powerful claim self-defense and those that are occupied claim a sense of humiliation. I do not know if the gun can solve this conflict. It is when the world will stand up to defend what is right. A child is a child...whether Jew or Palestinian.

Remembering the recent violence in Lebanon, Fouad, a young immigrant Maronite, credits the church for trying to "keep everything in perspective." "You have people that want peace and you have people that don't want peace. You have people who wanted to be without war and people that want war...So basically the church's position is pray for peace and pray that people have the common sense and hopefully they do and not start wars for stupid reasons or whatever reasons you know."

"I don't know if you know a lot about Lebanon," begins Adele, a Maronite immigrant and active choir member:

> We had a war and a lot of Christians were hurt by others. Somehow we had the war of others on our country. So, we were divided; Muslim against Christian—for a while, not for too long. Some people killed my uncle in the village. So when we came back, we left the village for about three years. When we came back, everybody [was] carrying bitterness and hatred toward each other from my dad's family and for the other's family inside our village. But, I've only always felt I'm not supposed to offend anybody. I want to forgive everybody around me.

What is interesting about Adele's story is that it was most likely sparked by that day's liturgy in which Father David spoke about forgiveness within the "Middle Eastern culture." He quipped that "we of the Middle East" will recall who wronged our great-grandfather, and carry a grudge about it. Adele's internalization of this message shows how the delivery of scripture through liturgy, in the form of recited prayers or homilies, can and does have a very personal effect on the parishioners. As Rita, an Orthodox woman says, "The liturgy helps me to live healthy, make the right choices, and learn through the sermon. It's important to me to pray with the community."

Another aspect of the personal connection to scripture is that many of the parishioners did not separate scriptures, church, and their own lives, but instead spoke of these elements as being interwoven. Nabil, a prominent physician and active member of the Maronite community relays his view of the interconnectedness of church, scripture, and life: "Scriptures are a part of the church. Without scriptures you have no church. The church bases its beliefs and its sermons and its homilies and everything else on the scriptures. It plays a role in my life every day. I do not go to sleep once without saying my prayers. I teach that to my children."

Speaking from a priest's position, Father John similarly views the church, scripture, and the parishioner as one, interconnected system:

> We live the scripture because when I stand up on Sunday and I preach my homily, I base it on the scripture. So it is a living dynamic within the model of the church. So when I would say that the Holy Church for example on Sunday, I remind the people that our Holy Church assigned readings from scripture after Easter to explain about the awesomeness of God, of renewal of man, the healing, the removal of doubt, the power that comes with the risen Lord. That's the way it fuels one's own faith. So it is not a detached relationship...it is like your body...Scripture can be one of the organisms.

Liturgy as Scripture

For both the Maronites and the Orthodox, the liturgy is the center of their faith. Deacon Mark insists that "nothing could happen unless there was liturgy. Everything we do, and it's on a daily basis, is all in relation to our communing with God, to our liturgy, to our worship of God and to our encounter with Christ. That happens on Sunday." The liturgy is not only the one time when everyone convenes together; it also holds all the key prayers, such as the Creed and the Lord's Prayer, and is the only context in which communion or the Eucharist can be celebrated. The liturgy in both traditions is also essentially scriptural. As Father David articulates, "Our Maronite Liturgy is like most Eastern Catholic and Orthodox Liturgies, [and] is based very heavily upon the Sacred Scriptures. Many prayers can be traced back directly to either the Old or New Testament Scriptures. The Anaphora of St. James Brother of the Lord goes so far as to cite scriptural references in its margins. Forming liturgical prayers around the Scriptures is pretty much a standard practice throughout the Eastern Church traditions." Though many parishioners do not realize it, the words and rituals of the liturgy are either based on biblical passages or reference biblical events. While many outsiders tend to peg Antiochian Orthodox and Catholics as being less knowledgeable about the Bible or scriptures because it seems there is less emphasis on individual reading and understanding of scripture, the Maronite and Antiochian Orthodox clergy know that this charge is misleading. The liturgy is also the site of the weekly homily or sermon. It is in this expository opening in the very structured and ritualized liturgical service that the priest is given a chance to connect that day's epistle or gospel reading to current events or contemporary trends. In the Maronite and Antiochian Orthodox churches of greater Detroit, these sermons typically become a space in which to discuss crises in the homeland.

So what we see, as we have explored in the previous sections of this chapter, is that Maronite and Arab Christians do use scripture, whether from personal Bible reading or attendance at liturgy and other church services, to negotiate their faith and its relation to their own lives. Their faith is especially important when homeland crises, past or present, are involved. As members of transnational religions, they have the double duty of applying their faith to their lives in America, as well as taking into consideration their ongoing connection to crises in the homeland, which is also the Holy Land.

The liturgy, as scripture and as a time for parishioners to convene, is a uniting factor in the American context. When asked whether there would be anything left for congregants if you removed the liturgy, Father David responds:

We would say in this country, no, because for many of us, our experience, the whole experience of the Maronite tradition is based on liturgy. So our bishop would say our liturgy has become our life, our life has become a liturgy. So for us the liturgy becomes—is central importance. And while in Lebanon they had the *ethnic* to hold them together, here we don't, because our church is made up of Irish, Italians, we have blacks, African Americans [...] they're all Americans. And so for them, liturgy becomes a central uniting factor. And for most of us American-born, it is also.

Muslims from the Arab Region

We conducted research at the Islamic Center of Claremont (ICC), one of the most active Muslim communities in Southern California. Our research entailed in-depth interviews with six men and six women, including three teachers of Arabic and Islamic studies and four community leaders. College students from the Arabian Gulf who were looking for a place of worship in 1984 founded this mosque. It currently serves nearly ten thousand Muslims, approximately 75 percent of whom are Arab immigrants. Twenty-five percent are non-Arab. The mosque is geared primarily toward immigrants, and specifically those of Arab descent. One interlocutor stated, "This is probably the most Arab mosque around here." It is a mixed-generation group. Approximately 90 percent of the adults are immigrants. During Friday prayers, the mosque receives between 500 and 600 worshippers, a number far beyond what this small mosque originally planned to accommodate.

The Islamic gatherings, lectures and services are conducted at the ICC in English and Arabic depending on the targeted audience. The ICC Imam is from Egypt. He studied the Islamic sciences and came to the United States specifically to take the position of Imam at the ICC. However, because he does not have a high command of English, the ICC receives visiting Imams to deliver the Friday prayer *Khutbah,* or "lecture," instead. In many cases the visiting Imam is not a trained Islamic scholar but a lay Muslim who has acquired some knowledge of the Islamic sciences. Divine grace and mercy emanates from the remembrance of God and the scriptural readings themselves, not from the Imam.

The ICC offers a full-time school for Muslim children. It conducts academic instruction in accordance with the standards set forth by the Western Association of Schools and Colleges. Along with the core subjects, which are taught in English, students also receive instruction in Arabic, Qur'an, and Islamic Studies. One interlocutor stated that many children in the community maintain the ability to speak in Arabic and in English. A wall at the school is painted with images of Muslim children and words that read: "I am proud to be an American Muslim."

First and foremost, our interlocutors spoke about the mosque as the most crucial place in their lives for practicing spirituality and achieving religious education. It is a place where people can go to conduct their five daily prayers (one of the five pillars of Islam). It is a place where people come together in weekly group gatherings for the pursuit of Islamic knowledge, or *Halaqas. Halaqas* are conducted in Arabic and English for different age groups. There are youth groups, women's groups, and groups for adult men and women. People also come to the mosque to memorize the Qur'an together.

The mosque also works as what Arjun Appadurai theorizes as a diasporic public sphere with its own specific articulations of collective consciousness and transnational connection (Appadurai 1996). It is the space where interlocutors make and remake community in the diaspora. Interlocutors tend to attend this particular mosque because most people there speak Arabic and support Arab cultural norms with which they are familiar. In their countries of origin, people do not tend to celebrate *Eid al-Fitr*, an important Islamic holiday, at their mosque. In Claremont, California, however, people do tend to celebrate Eid at their local mosque. Similarly, they attend a communal observances of breaking of fast during Ramadan and participate in a range of social activities, such as skit performances. Overall, people view the mosque as a safe place for kids to socialize and a crucial site of community building in the United States. Some interlocutors' families lived in neighborhoods with few Arabs and/ or Muslims nearby. They felt strongly that the mosque was where they came for community. As Aisha, one interlocutor put it,

> We were always at the *masjid* for *salah,* for Ramadan, *iftars, Eid* prayers, carnivals, weddings, you name it. That was where we had most of our festivals. We had some non-Muslim friends as children, but most of them were people we met at the *masjid*. It was the most important aspect of my life. It was the community I grew up in.

Another interlocutor expressed the fluidity of the boundaries between spirituality and religion and community life when she said: "Actually, we live in Islam. It's not like there is regular life and then there is Islam."

Building community with and through the mosque in ways that appeal to second-generation youth requires community leaders to incorporate what they perceive to be American forms of sociability into their events. Leaders teach Islam through play and activities such as basketball on Saturdays.

What scripturalizing practices/rituals are in evidence in this community? Who are the principal actors and authority figures in relationship to scripturalizing practices in this community?

The most crucial scripturalizing practice in this community relates to the Qur'an. Muslim scholars are the principal actors and authority figures in relationship to the Qur'an. Our interlocutors commit to learning and engaging with the Qur'an as they simultaneously negotiate racist/ Islamophobic perceptions of the Qur'an and Islamic fundamentalism in US society. Interlocutors view the Qur'an as the most critical source of knowledge about Islam. The Qur'an, they explain, transcends any geographic or cultural location. They add that knowledge about the Qur'an and the Hadith is the most essential aspect of Islam and that these are the most crucial scriptural sources. Every interlocutor engages with the Qur'an in everyday life and seeks personal guidance and insights from the Qur'an. They quote the Qur'an to represent their worldviews and life decisions. Yet they refrain from making exegetical interpretations, *fatwas* (decrees) on their own. They agree that this requires the training of a Muslim scholar, or *Alim*. Scholars' lineage or place of origin, they explain, did not determine whether or not they were qualified to interpret Islamic scriptures. Interlocutors explain that Muslims recognize scholars for their dedication to and knowledge of the scriptures, and they encourage and support legitimate objection to a scholars' opinions on *fatwas* and exegetical interpretations. They explain that some issues are open to interpretation while others are not. For example, monotheism is nonnegotiable. The Qur'an and Hadith are very clear on the oneness, the Divine Unity of God. However, issues of *fiqh* (Islamic jurisprudence) may have a variety of interpretations. At the same time, there are limits on what scholars can change. Several interlocutors explain that Islam does not support scholars to establish new *fatwas* if the situation does not call for it.

FAYZA: I think it's really important for someone to have extensive Islamic education and knowledge of Arabic to interpret the Qur'an. The Qur'an is not just an independent entity. It comes with the Hadith, the Tradition of the Prophet. Sometimes we superimpose our ideas on it.

ASHRAF: I definitely think that regular people and lay people should be able to interpret the scriptures. It's part of our religious duty to understand what God wants us to do. At the same time, I don't think it should be our religious duty to say that this is the correct answer or this is what God meant by this verse.

Overall, interlocutors explain that Islam supports the idea of lay Muslims seeking their own guidance from scriptures. This explains why some interlocutors read and study on their own without forming their own exegetical interpretations, but study the variety of interpretations and choose their own path. Some choose to go directly to specific sheikhs, scholars, or knowledgeable people with whom they feel comfortable.

While the scholars' place of origin did not determine their knowledge of Islam, it determined another crucial aspect of their credibility. Every interlocutor agreed that Islam places significant value on scholars' ability to interpret Islamic scriptures in light of cultural problems and historical situations and contexts. Scholars, many explained, must be able to connect with their audiences. For example, a scholar from the Middle East cannot give religious advice or *fatwas* to Muslims living in the West without knowledge and understanding of Western culture and life.

> MARWAN: I think there are different pressures facing each community and that obviously affects how they look at scriptures.
>
> FAYZA: Now that there's more interaction with Western society, there's a different way of reading into the Qur'an. We notice different things in the Qur'an that perhaps we didn't notice before.
>
> SALMA: Islam has always provided answers to the Muslims of India, Egypt, Mecca, and China. Everybody has their own problems that they used to bring back to the Qur'an. The Muslim scholars have always found answers to their questions. You could visit the Muslims in China and learn about their ways of life and you would find that they took the Islamic teachings and adapted them to their own needs.
>
> MAZEN: I'm not going to listen to a person that lives in Egypt on whether we should vote in the United States or not. There are different understandings in terms of how scholars come up with these decisions.

Interlocutors agree that scholars are required to uphold excellent training in the Arabic language. They explained that this was because the Qur'an emerged within a context and knowledge of the Arabic language is crucial for grasping its Arab context and meanings. The general sentiment was that meaning is lost in translation. Classical Arabic is ever more very important to Islamic scholarship. This did not mean that any native speaker of Arabic qualified as a Muslim scholar. A Muslim scholar must study classical Arabic as a science.

> TAHA: Speaking the language is something, and being proficient at the language is something else. I believe it's very hard if you don't speak the *language to understand what the prophet is* talking about. It has to do a lot with whether we speak Arabic well enough to understand what it really says. Sometimes I do the translation into English, and I find it very hard to get to the right meaning of what the sheikh is saying. It depends on the translator and how he translates it.
>
> ASHRAF: Even memorizing the Qur'an doesn't really mean anything if you don't understand what you're reading.

MARWAN: Speaking Arabic is central to understanding the Qur'an. Every single bit of Arabic that I learn, I feel like I like the Qur'an more. It makes a huge difference in being able to have a relationship with the Qur'an. Progressive Muslims and these terrorists, a lot of them don't speak Arabic and say, "Oh, it says in the translation da da da da da da da," and then they'll say this obviously means this and that's one of the big problems that people have; they're trying to do things on their own.

ASHRAF: I get really concerned when I see people who don't know Arabic, don't know the context of verse, and they'll come in and interpret the Qur'an in this way. This happens all of the time when it comes to issues of the *hijab* and issues of the Islamic covering. We have to talk about context, purpose and revelation. We have to talk about when it was revealed. We have to talk about what...the word meant at that time and how it was applied at that time.

Critiques of Orientalist scholars were woven throughout interlocutors' discussions about authenticity. Interlocutors question the sincerity and intention of Orientalists in their interpretation of Qur'an, Hadith, and Islam in general. Interlocutors are particularly suspicious of their motives as well as the accuracy of their scholarship and their credibility.

RAYAN: I think that the Western media is a big problem. Some people are sincere and some have this superior/inferior attitude when they go into it.

Engagements with Orientalism inspire many interlocutors to learn more about what they perceive to be true Islam. This allows them to respond to charges of Muslim backwardness or stereotypes about Muslim women's oppression.

FAYZA: Because there is so much negativity about how Islam treats women, lots of girls in America need to know what Islam really says about women. It was important for me to be reminded of how Islam deals with women. I wanted to know....What are all of the sources, not just the ones that are always highlighted for us? What does Islam say, how are the women of the Prophet treated and what we can learn from them because the prophet says, "My companions are like stars, if you follow any one of them, you will be guided." So let's look at the women who lived at the time of the prophet. Read about them.

They were in the army, fighting in the army, one was pregnant and she was fighting alongside the Prophet. He looks to his right and she's defending him, alongside her husband and sons. When is it that women in America started joining the army?

ASHRAF: A lot of time their [Orientalists'] intentions are not genuine and you could definitely point that out through their writing Orientalists don't have the standards that Muslims are bounded by in terms of their interpretation of the Qur'an. We have to be ethical.

Many interlocutors are similarly critical of what they refer to as people who used scripture without correct guidance from scholars. These discussions ranged from critiques of what some referred to as liberals who attempt to instill new, Western, liberal ideals about homosexuality and mixed-gender prayers into Islam to critiques of the Bin Ladens and militant Muslim extremists. Interlocutors tend to paint either group as upholding a nonauthentic approach to Islamic thought and a lack of knowledge in the Arabic and Islamic sciences. Some interlocutors also critiqued Muslims who interpret Islam through cultural ideals. They explain that blurring the lines between religion and culture meant that they were not following God's words. They add that these Muslims were projecting untrue images of Islam to the outsider. Overall, the targets of their criticism are what they referred to as "unqualified" people who were scripturalizing through their words or actions in ways that do not reflect a true Islam.

AMAL: If scripture is misinterpreted it can give a whole different meaning. For example, when you have people reading that Muslims are told to kill the enemy wherever you find them. You have to be at least a sheikh or something. At least be fluent in Arabic or scholar, and not anti-Islam.

MARWAN: The problem with terrorists is that they are trying to interpret stuff on their own. They come up with these ideas; you've heard all the stupid things that they say. On the other side—you have progressive Muslims. They're looking at these books on their own and coming up with these crazy ideas. They're making the religion go to that way. But it should be the other way around. They have to conform to the religion.

Interlocutors spoke extensively about the term fundamentalism. They critiqued the way dominant US discourses attach it to Muslims as a way to legitimize the idea that all Muslims are terrorists. They articulated the relationship between Islam and fundamentalism on their own terms. This entailed distinguishing the aspects of Islam are open to change and those that are not. Everyone agreed that the five pillars of Islam cannot be changed.

TAHA: Fundamentalism. Whenever I hear it on the radio and on the TV, it's attached to Islam. *They're* trying *to put a negative mark on Islam* as if Muslims stick to a rigid opinion and will not change their opini*on—that they are close[d]-minded*—I don't believe Islam is that way.

IMANI: Yes, Islam is fundamentalist on certain things. There are things in Islam that can't be changed like the five pillars of Islam—like there is no god except Allah and Muhammad is his final messenger or establishing the prayer, to establish the care, *and to establish your fasting* for Ramadan and do your *hajj*, if you can afford it, to Mecca.

ASHRAF: There's general knowledge in Islam that anyone can give you an answer for. Should we pray with our hands on top or hands on the bottom? Should we do this with our finger, point it up and down or should we do nothing with our finger? I think things of that matter are generally enough for any scholar can give you their opinion, their interpretation.

MAZEN: Islam gives you many ways to choose. You have the option to enter Islam or not to enter. After you become a Muslim and you want to pray, it is preferable to pray on time and as early of the time of the prayer, but there is an open arena for you to pray at your convenience. The *hijab* of the woman is fundamental because you have to wear a *hijab*, but the question could be, 'What color?', 'What kind of *hijab*?' It is up to you.

ASHRAF: I'm not going to listen to someone who is in Zimbabwe or Malaysia about whether we are allowed to buy homes in the United States based on interest or not. I would like that interpretation to come from over here. Certain rulings are going to change because of minority verses majority but there are those rulings in Islam that do not change no matter where you are. For example, the pillars of faith. Those things are essential beliefs of a Muslim that can never change and that can never be compromised.

FAYZA: Now that we have working women, does the woman have to contribute certain parts of her salary or does she have to give her husband all of her salary? Or, because Islam says, the woman can just keep her money to herself. This is just one example of where I see people wanting to look back to the scriptures. This is a new situation. I know we have this idea that there is the right of the man to be obedient to his wife, but it's given to him only if he can provide for the family.... Muslims need to go back to the scriptures to see how we can interpret certain verses in the right way to have the right answers to upcoming situations. I feel our Muslim scholars today do not see exactly how certain answers in *fiqh* or jurisprudence do not take into consideration the side of the woman or what's good for her. They see it from the man's point of view and what's good for him.... Nowadays women are expected to work as both man and woman at the same time and they are not given the inner support by their husbands.... The Muslim scholars should state clearly that because of the changing times, women, if they are forced to work outside the home or [to] spend her money on the household then we should, by the same token, address the man, the husband, and it is your duty to help your wife at home.... I feel that these certain areas in the Islamic *fiqh* are still lacking.

What are the forms of expressiveness in relationship to which scripturalizing practices are carried out?

Interlocutors carry out their scripturalizing practices with and against their engagements with concepts of culture. They share in a commitment to create new forms of Muslim identity that differ from concepts and practices of Islam in their countries of origin—concepts that are wrapped up in ideals and practices of "Arab culture." Yet while they strive to practice an "Islam" devoid of "Arab culture," their religious community and life world are shaped very much by concepts and practices of Arab ethnicity and the distinct historical circumstances facing Arab immigrant communities. At the same time, while my interlocutors are working on disaggregating religion from culture, they maintain a commitment to understanding and interpreting Islam in a way that must be relevant to the cultural and historical context in which they live (the United States).

Interlocutors generally privilege a religious (Islamic) identity over a cultural (Arab) identity. Over and over, interviews critiqued nationalist identity. This critique is reflected in comments such as these:

AYMAN: If all people are from God and identity is based in religion then there is a sense of equality among humanity, as opposed to nationalism which remains the divisive element within humanity.

ASHRAF: I'm a Muslim if I'm in Lebanon, if I'm in America, if I'm in Egypt, if I'm in Africa.

MARWAN: The idea is that you're not part of a nationality—that all people are equal and from God, so you shouldn't really care about this whole Arab thing.

Interlocutors tend to share a critique of the way Arabs living in Arab countries practice Islam. They contend that they practice Islam in a cultural way rather than an Islamic way. They agree that the conditions of life in the United States—where Muslims are positioned as different and inferior—inspired them to value Islam more than it is valued in their countries of origin. They privilege what they perceive as the disaggregation of Islam from Arab culture.

MARWAN: In a lot of the Arab countries that are supposedly Muslim countries, the religion is actually less practiced than in a country like the United States where you're a minority. In the United States, you have an extra duty to represent your religion. A lot of Americans look to you to be a representative of Islam or a representative of the Muslims in general, so we end up with a deeper tie to our religion.

BASIL: Back home in Egypt, the people are raised as Muslims but they don't value what they have. When I came here I valued it more and more.

AMAL: Culture gets on my last nerves. When I went to Jordan last summer for my cousin's wedding and all the girls were saying to me, 'Why are you wearing *hijab*?' I said, 'I wear it all the time.' They said 'It's your cousin's wedding. You're going to wear it?' I realized that every time I go to a wedding of someone really closely related, a lot of people don't take the *hijab* seriously.

AMAL: Religion is important, but the problem with Arab Palestinians, Jordanians, is that culture plays too big of a role. Even I would think something is a religion thing and now that I'm growing up I realize that I don't really have to do that because it is not religious.

Second-generation young adults were more inclined toward disaggregating the categories Arab and Muslim than their immigrant counterparts. Their second-generation social location provides them with access to resources that were often unavailable to immigrants, including Islamic educational networks through their college campuses. Through these networks, they enter into approaches to Islam that are different from their parents' generation. This led most young adults to identify less with Arab culture than their parents. Some are more rigid in their Islamic practice and develop closer relationships to scriptures than their immigrant parents' generation.

Most interlocutors explain that their location in the United States is crucial to the way they understand the Qur'an and *Shariah* (body of Islamic religious law). They explain that issues that Muslims in the United States face are substantially different than those faced by Muslims living elsewhere. They overwhelmingly agree that Muslims should take into consideration the cultural context in which they live when determining how to approach and interpret scriptural authority. This is why they feel strongly that it is crucial that the scholars to whom they turn are knowledgeable about the United States and its cultural context.

> ASHRAF: I definitely think that we need scholars that are American born. We can't fully rely on scholars that got the knowledge from back home then come back here and try to apply it. Hassan: It's different because the issues here are different than there. Daily life is totally different.

Interlocutors explain that in the United States, Islam provides a viable framework for negotiating the pressures of Americanization and assimilation. Many rely on Islam for guidance in grappling with aspects of US society that they do not support, including teen dating, alcohol, and stereotypical "American" norms related to the lives of adolescents and young adults. Many also explain that many families face deep challenges related to raising their children in the United States according to Qur'anic principles and norms. This leads some parents to become more religious in an effort to protect their children from the pressures of Americanization. Community leaders spend a great deal of time trying to make Islam appealing to young adults who "want to have their American identity and do the American thing." They promote what they perceive to be American activities in teaching Islam to younger generations.

> TAHA, A COMMUNITY LEADER: The majority of our students know the Arabic language, but we live in America. Their school teaches regular American classes—English, science, and math. If you talk to the child in Arabic, 90% of the time the answer comes back in English.
> AISHA, ALSO A COMMUNITY LEADER: A lot of the parents face difficulties with raising their children. They become naughty at a certain age and it's hard to control them. When they become teenagers, they're exposed to a lot of influences like drugs. Some Muslim kids actually got influenced by their peers outside the *Masjid* [mosque] and a lot of the parents have turned back and said, 'I want my kid to come

back to the Masjid, I want to start praying, I want my child to actually learn Qur'an.' A lot of parents become more religious as a result of that because they feel that this is the way they could maintain a healthy family life and society.

AMAL: My mom was just saying the other day that the problems you find here [in the United States], you will never find there because of scriptures. Like teen pregnancy and homosexuality... because religion is so big. If someone does something, the smallest thing, it's a bigger deal because of scripture, because of Hadith, because of religion.

ASHRAF: We moved here from Lebanon when I was a child. I started to get a little more Americanized and I started to fall into some of the mistakes of the American culture—the smoking weed, dressing bad fad and all of that garbage. After that, around junior and senior year in high school and beginning years in college, that's when I started to change my life a bit more. I went from not being religious at all to being too religious for my family. My mom, she just wanted to listen to KBIG in the car and I'd say, "That's *haraam* [forbidden], turn it off." I went from those two extremes.

MARWAN: When I was growing up in high school, there was this constant pressure from your peers to go with the crowd, but Islam was a counterweight. It said, "Be different from them!" It was encouraging me to be different, not to be Americanized. If they shave, you grow your beard. If they wear such and such clothes, you wear something else. That definitely contributed to the whole not-being-American. I really saw things in black and white and thought," That's American; that's non-Islamic."

TAHA: There are a lot of things in American society that are not acceptable from an Islamic perspective. It's just totally forbidden. When you come there, you find it is so easy to do the forbidden thing in our religion. You can go in any gas station and they sell alcohol. Our kids are growing up in that. We get engaged and married; we don't have girlfriends and boyfriends. This is a big challenge for our kids when they go to school and get called names if they don't have a girlfriend.

Interlocutors also share a critique about US policies related to Muslim people and Muslim majority countries. They share a sense that the United States upholds anti-Muslim policies and that there is a great deal of anti-Muslim racism or Islamophobia in the United States. They also speak about what they perceive to be their duty in responding to the forces of racism and war. Many were forced to respond to Islamophobia in their everyday lives, especially in the aftermath of 9/11.

ASHRAF: When I first went to college, I thought I'd take a couple of classes, learn political science and that was about it. Then I learned that Islam and Muslims in this country are definitely not only a minority, but are at a weak point. We're looked upon in very negative ways. There's a lot of Islamophobia around. As a Muslim community that's standing up for social justice issues, we need a deeper level of how to convey the message to the general population other than just books. The general masses aren't into reading. We have to come up with new innovative ways, commercials, advertisements, things of that nature to convince people to take different stances. My understanding of the religious scriptures has pushed me into business and marketing so I can try to effect change in these ways.

MARWAN: I definitely don't think that they [Muslims] were just upset about people drawing cartoons. People are angry about Western domination. I actually had a big argument with a professor on almost the first day of a political science class about this and it was really funny because he just said, "Oh, that's just how Muslim people are, they're just, you know, 9/11, they don't have our values." A political science professor! I raised my hand and I tried to explain that it's not just about cartoons or a religious attitude; it's about all the stuff that's happening in the Muslim world. The U.S. supports dictatorships—Iraq, Palestine—there's no support for real democracy.

AISHA: I was about seven or eight years old when the Oklahoma bombings happened, and immediately Muslims were blamed for a terrorist act. Most of my mom's friends were afraid to go shopping, especially if they were wearing the *hijab*. Even if they weren't, they were still afraid because they're Muslim and they were afraid of being targeted. My mom was the only one to say, "I need to go shopping right now and get groceries so we're going." It was the second day after the Oklahoma bombings. I like to wear the scarf and I was wearing a t-shirt and jeans and totally childish clothing, but I had the scarf on my head. This one lady in the deli said, "Oh, look at those terrorists." She was sneering at us, so I ran to my mom. My mom wasn't scared and she said, "Excuse me ma'am, what are you talking about? My daughter heard you." My mom was not afraid. "We're not terrorists!" she said. "You've seen me bombing the place? I'm Muslim, but that's nothing to be made fun of."

MAYSA: The first time I went to public school was high school. It was the second week of school when 9/11 happened. I got a lot stares from my class on the day of 9/11 or 9/12. I wore the *hijab* and everything and so I was obviously Muslim but I remember people were going out and donating blood. We were discussing this in class and I said that my mom and her friend were going to donate blood. Some girls were staring at me like, "Are you serious? Your mom went to donate blood?" If there are victims out there, people who need blood, we'll donate blood. It's your duty because you need to save a life. It's as if you saved all humanity. I was making a speech in a debate and this one kid said, "When I grow up, I'm going to start a terrorist group. Won't you join me?" said, "I'm sorry. I'm Muslim, but I don't do that. You could start your own but I don't do that."

FAYZA: I have repeated debates with people about my *hijab*. It's like African Americans and racism. The American public doesn't like their black skin, so should they take it off? No, there's nothing they can do about it. It's the [US] culture that is not accepting, uneducated and has to change. I deliberately try to wear things that get them to think and to stop stereotyping, it is part of my obligation to continue in this vein and just change the way people think. If we change, and melt into society we are losing something not just for us, but to mankind—something that would have enriched them, and enriched their society, and even fixed it up and treated some of its social ills.

Despite the tendency toward disaggregating the categories Arab and Muslim, cultural identity persisted as an important signifier of identity for many interlocutors. That the mosque is predominantly Arab exemplifies the significance of Arab identity to our interlocutors. Many explained that they build community with other Arabs because they share the same language, and language is a source of unification. Yet over and over, they added that the Qur'an overpowers Arabic language or culture as a force of unification. Most interviewees revisit their countries of origin. Some return to their countries of origin to strengthen their Muslim identity.

ASHRAF: I understand I am an Arab American, it's not necessarily debatable. I identify myself as Muslim and if people ask me where I'm from, I say Lebanon.

TAHA: We have a scholar here whose main language is Arabic. It's the common nature of everybody to feel comfortable with him because he speaks Arabic.

Why do some in this community persist in relating to scriptures? What work do they make scriptures do for them?

Our interlocutors turn to the Qur'an for guidance related to every aspect of their everyday lives—from concepts of who they are to their worldview to matters of family, gender, and community development. This community has faced Islamophobia and racism more than ever before after the events of 9/11. Interlocutors turned to the Qur'an to challenge Islamophobic interpretations and understandings of Islam and the Qur'an.

Our interlocutors explained that the Qur'an and Hadith (or *sunnah*, "words of the prophet") are their primary modes of guidance on everyday life issues, ranging from theological to personal issues. People relied on their personal knowledge of God to craft their world views and perspectives on family life, community, politics, peace, and justice. Every interlocutor expressed their world views and perspectives through scriptures and every interlocutor quoted Qur'anic verses in Arabic or in the English meaning form that they had memorized. Interlocutors have generally been in awe of the Qur'an. For them, the Qur'an scripturalizes the Greatness of God. It entails scientific depictions, practical and political applications, and interpersonal or personal implications. Over and over, interlocutors used phrases such as, "Knowing the Qur'an is the happiest thing in my life." Interlocutors said that they conform their lives to scripture. One person stated, "The Qur'an is a goal I want to conform my life to." They read the Qur'an, memorize it, and strive to live directly by the Qur'an and its teachings. They interpret the Qur'an according to authoritative exegetical interpretations. Nearly every interlocutor had favorite Qur'anic passage or Hadith traditions that they recite by heart and tie into their worldview. Interlocutors shared the sense that the Qur'an always brings something new, even in cases where people have read the same chapter or passage many times. They tend to be inspired by the ways that new understandings repeatedly appear to the reader, listener, or devotee. In their view, the Qur'an is a living, dialectical form of scripture.

TAHA: The prophet Muhammad's mannerisms and behavior were the Qur'an itself. The life of the prophet, peace be upon him, it's a role model, even for the other prophets. We as Muslims in this community are doing our best to live the life of the prophet.

SALMA: I would try to live an Islamic way of life as God wanted us to live, based on the Qur'an and the *sunnah* of the prophet. Muhammad's our *sunnah*. It's everything in my life. I can't be who I am or think that I am the person that I would like to be if I didn't have the spirituality that is based on the Qur'an and the *sunnah*—the Prophet, Peace Be Upon Him.

ASHRAF: I love it. Every time I open the Qur'an I find something completely new, completely different, even if I read the same verse over. That's one of the miracles of the Qur'an. There are so many lessons that you could derive from one story. I don't think I ever made the distinction between the word of God and what the scripture was. Hadith would be considered scripture since it's a bit more practical in the sense that it's more relative in terms of how we're supposed to be doing things and it's more applicable in terms of how you do things and the Qur'an, the word of god, is more like the general rules and regulations or the general structure of humanity. Everything that we do in the youth group was based on two things. Number one, the Qur'an; number two the *sunnah*, being basically the Hadith, the prophet or the sayings.

Our interlocutors related their identities or concepts of who they are directly to the Qur'an and Hadith. They similarly spoke about finding themselves in the scriptures and relating themselves to people mentioned in scripture. They shared a sense that even though the events they refer to took place at the time of the prophet and emerged out of a different historical context, they are similar to their own and can act as a means of direct guidance.

TAHA: I've been here since 1990 and the *masjid* (mosque) since the early 80s. I believe what gathers us all here together is the Qur'an. The sheikh is always busy with people's problems. If there are two people fighting over business, they come to the sheikh to solve the problem before the final option of going to the court. If there is divorce happening, it goes through the Islamic way before it reaches the court outside. I see a lot of marriages saved because of following the Qur'an. I see a lot of children protected because of following the Qur'an and the *sunnah* in daily life.

SALMA: The Qur'an and Hadith are a guide to us. If you buy a new car, you have to buy its manual that tells you how to fix it if something happens. Basically, we're human beings and we know exactly what's right and what's wrong. We may come up with some ideas on our own, but then we are fallible. So God sent us prophets and sent down scriptures to guide us and to tell us the dos and don'ts, and to tell us everything that he created in this world is for us to enjoy and everything has been dedicated to our service as human beings. We are the masters of this world, but we should not forget that God is our master and worshiping him is our main goal.

AMAL: You always need a guide. And the Qur'an and the Hadith is a guide.

FAYZA: We were poor and he's the one that gives us our food and our nourishment. We were orphans and we couldn't even have existed. The Prophet turned to Allah, because he was his only means of support. All of us are like that. Our parents can help us in this world and the next, but ultimately we turn to Allah for help and guidance. When Allah wouldn't leave the Prophet—it feels like Allah is speaking to us.

ASHRAF: We'd also try to apply it in terms of where we're living, because in our understanding the Qur'an is the manual for life. It's the to-do guide for life. So we don't necessarily take it as just beautiful words that are said; it's more applicable, it's a lot more relevant.

AISHA: When I am really stressed or I feel depressed or overwhelmed, I tend to really want to read the Qur'an. I just want to set everything aside and read ten pages or more from the Qur'an and contemplate it. It really consoles me. As a child I had two favorite prophets: Yusuf and Suleiman. It's always consoling to read about the prophets' lives and see all the hardships they faced and how they trusted Allah. They still did their best and upheld their moral standards and maintained their ethical actions even though it might only bring more peer pressure or obstacles to them, but they're going to do what's right, no matter what. After every hardship, there is peace and so it's repeated. It reminds me that no matter what obstacles you're facing, they'll never persist forever.

SALMA: I want to say Qur'an is not only a book to read to worship Allah (SWT). This is a part of it, but Qur'an is also a guide to every single step in our life from when we wake up in the morning until we sleep at night. It has everything that we are supposed to do. Some people don't follow everything and I don't follow every single thing, but I still I know what I'm doing wrong.

AISHA: It is a part of our life. We can't separate between Qur'an and how we act every single moment in our life because it comes from the Qur'an. Qur'an is not just a word on book; it has a guide, like the law.

ASHRAF: In any class that I took in college, I always tried to relate it somehow to the Qur'an and the Hadith. In Biology class you learn amazing things and I'd always relate it. How do the sciences in the Qur'an relate to the Biology class that I'm taking right now? We learned this new leadership tactic in business, so where do I see that throughout the prophet's life? How can I relate these things to the time of the prophet or how it is stated in the Qur'an? Is it different than how it is stated in the Qur'an or is it the same? It helps me understand where the Qur'an is coming from and where Allah is coming from. It helps me understand the topic at hand, 'cause I understood a lot more.

AMAL: I'm shocked sometimes how the answer to everything is always in the Qur'an and the Hadith. One Hadith that I really like is the one that says "Treat your brother how you would like to be treated," because if everyone followed that rule, our world would be perfect. There're other ones about oppression. If you're quiet about oppression then it will come back to you on the day of resurrection.

Interlocutors repeatedly referenced particular passages from the Qur'an. They were familiar with the name of the passage, its content, and its meaning.

ASHRAF: I'm remembering one verse in the Qur'an and Allah (SWT) says at the end when all creation will die. Islamically, we believe that, near the end of times, all creation will be dead and then resurrected to be judged. So at that time Allah (SWT), God says to the rest of everyone, "And to who is the kingdom, or who is the kinship or to whose the strength or the power today when all of you are deceased and pretty much dead at this point," just to emphasize the power of Allah SWT and that life is not yours for you to screw around in. The purpose of life is not to have fun. There is a deeper purpose in life and that Allah (SWT) establishes very clearly, *liman al-mulk al-yawm*. All of those people who are arrogant, for all of those people who thought they were something in this life. It's a very powerful statement to me and I love that very much.

AISHA: I like the verse, *Rijaloon Sadaq Allah Ma'Ahadoo Alai*. It refers to people who have been truthful to what they promised Allah in terms of supporting the *deen* [religion]. There's another verse Jesus says, "And who are my victorious ones?" His disciples tell him "We are your group, oh prophet." Basically they're saying to the Prophet Jesus that we are going to be your group of victorious ones. We're going to make you victorious in the long term. I try to make myself part of those people.

TAHA: The last verse in the third surah in the Qur'an, *surah ali Imran*, "Oh you who believe *isbiru* have patience as a group, *wasabiru* and have patience individually *warabitu* and whole fast together, so that you may be from the righteous ones." That verse always sticks in my mind because any time there is a calamity that happens, any time there is a situation that happens, that always brings things back into perspective and gives me that motivation, that optimism, that things are going to get better.

The Qur'an was particularly relevant to interlocutors' concepts and practices of family. Interlocutors' parents encouraged them to grant special value to the Qur'an regarding parent-child relationships and communication. Some parents encouraged daily Qur'an family reading time. Parents also stressed forms of behavior they stated were upheld in the Qur'an. Within many families, childhood and adolescent years include typical scenes of Qur'an reading and memorization. Some interlocutors also spoke about women's issues in light of the Qur'an. Many male scholars came across as gender-biased, and women interlocutors tended to take special interest in interpretations and reinterpretations of Qur'anic verses related to gender and women.

ASHRAF: Gender issues in the Qur'an have been one of those things that's been really pivotal point in my life. The basis of my whole relationship is religious scriptures: the Qur'an and the *sunnah*. Even when I'm talking to the sister, our whole conversation is about how we are going to implement the Qur'an and the *sunnah* in our lives. It's really so awesome because our connection, our relationship is not based on infatuation, it's not based on love, it's not based on how she dresses, things of that nature. It's based on Allah (SWT) and we came to the conclusion that a successful relationship should be based on something that's eternal and something that's perfect. What a better way to base a relationship other than God, Himself.

AMAL: I had this far cousin that died from the usage of drugs. He was afar. I didn't know him. You would never find these kinds of things there because religion means so much. If someone does even the smallest thing, it's a bigger deal, because of scripture, because of Hadith, because of religion.

AISHA: A lot of the parents are turning back and saying, 'I want my kid to come back to the masjid, I want to start praying, I want my child to actually learn Qur'an.' A lot of the parents become more religious because they feel that this is how they could maintain a healthy family life and society. Religious scriptures…are a source of guidance to help you maintain a certain standard of healthy interaction with other people, keeping your family ties strong and not allowing the family to break up and just being productive members of society rather than just being a drug addict.

Interlocutors perceived the Qur'an as a unifier of community and essential to community formation. Community members settled disputes based on the authority and word of the Qur'an. In addition, normative ideals that structured the community were based upon the word of God. In this sense, the Qur'an was a living reality in the lives of our interlocutors.

> TAHA: What gathers Muslims, whether they are Arab or non-Arab, is the Qur'an. It relates us all together. When I go to any other mosque around the area that doesn't speak Arabic, I feel very comfortable because we could disagree about a lot of things but when it comes to Qur'an, we all sit down and share the same *khutbah*. That's what unites us. I believe that the Qur'an and the Hadith are the leaders. Regardless of your culture, your original ethnicity, it's the Qur'an that makes us. It doesn't matter where you were born or live. The Qur'an is our master, our leader, what we all follow.
>
> TAHA: Islam calls for unity. On many occasions, you find Islam talks about unity and being united, and I believe if we apply that rule unto ourselves we should be able to move forward, to be united, to be heard, instead of being counted as numbers.

Interlocutors shared a sense that dominant US discourses often misrepresent the Qur'an and Hadith. They also turned to the Qur'an and Hadith as crucial sites for coping with the aftermath of 9/11. Many shared stories of feeling recharged or revived when they turn to the Qur'an after reading Islamophobic news reports. Several also contended that tragedies such as the 9/11 attacks can inspire non-Muslims to become interested in reading the Qur'an or becoming Muslim. The Qur'an also provides guidance in evaluating life priorities and whether and to what extent persons should invest in particular issues over others.

> ASHRAF: Nowadays, people can just jump online and easily find a misinterpretation of the Qur'an. They can find part of a random verse

like "Kill them where ever you find them," and then they'll start saying, "Oh, look at what this means: blah, blah, blah, blah…"

MAZEN: From October to next October after 9/11, 34,000 Americans
accepted Islam. The Qur'an was the number one most read book in
the United States and number one best seller for at least seven months
after 9/11. One verse in the Qur'an that stuck in my mind was *ija ja'a
nasr ullahi wal fath, wa ra'ayta al nassa yadkhulunah fi deenallahi
afwaja….* It's about the *nasr*, the victory of Allah, the opening—we
saw people coming into the religion or coming in the *afwaja*, coming
to the group in large numbers. Although what happened was a huge
tragedy and mistake and whoever did it needed to be repaired in terms
of justice and Muslims in the United States were hit hard because of
it, we saw the exact opposite also happen. People started wanting to
understand Islam and people started embracing Islam.

FAYZA: After reading a lot of newspapers and criticisms of Islam and
Muslims, it made me want to know more. Sometimes when everything out there is negative, it makes you doubtful in a way. Whenever
I'm at an all-time low, I have to go and read some Qur'an. Simply
reading it gets me to a completely new place. It recharges me. When
I go back and listen to what he says, I'm like, wow, this man wasn't
even ordinary, like how wise the Hadith are, how soaked they are
with meaning. When I share them with my non-Muslim friends,
they're all blown away.

AISHA: The Qur'an is the most feminist book, especially considering
its age, but also specifically looking into it, it causes us to probe
certain questions that maybe in the United States aren't asked. Most
American women have been intent on knowing what this is all about
and I think that's important because the Orientalist perspective aims
at weakening our belief in the Qur'an.

Conclusion

Interlocutors conceptualized their relationship to religion and scriptures
with and through varied relationships to the concept of "Arab cultural
identity" in ways that were very much entangled in the historical realities
of anti-Arab racism, particularly in the aftermath of 9/11. Some Christians
de-emphasized their relationship to Arab histories and cultures and
overemphasized their Christian identity. This strategy provided a shield
from anti-Arab racism, particularly in the aftermath of 9/11. Muslim

interlocutors did not have access to this privilege, as they could not escape the racialized connotations associated with Islam. Muslims tended to disaggregate the categories "Arab" from "Muslim" (ethnicity/nationality and religion) for different reasons. They tended to privilege the ideal of true Islam and the idea that cultural norms taint or cover up true Islam. At the same time, they agreed that the Muslim scholars to whom they turn should be knowledgeable about the particular cultural contexts in which they are practicing Islam. Different cultural contexts raise new issues and challenges for Muslims. For example, living in the United States raises the challenge of assimilation, racism, and Islamophobia.

Our research only scratches the surface of the multiple religious affiliations and practices and varying kinds of relationships to scriptures among Arab Americans. Yet our ethnographic focus on three specific religious communities provides a rich entry point into the urgent need to avoid simplistic generalizations about Arab Americans, religion, and scriptures. This is why we center our interlocutors' voices and privilege the ways that they speak about their faith and their relationship to scriptures. This approach helps us illustrate the complex, multidimensional, and historically contingent ways that Arab Americans relate to faith and scriptures. We caution our readers away from the one-dimensional conceptualizations of "Arabs" and "religion" that proliferate US government and media discourses. More provocatively, we highlight the need for specific understandings of the various religious sects within "Muslim" and "Christian" groupings from the Arab region. At the same time, we point to the need for historically situated research that takes seriously how diasporas from the Arab region relate to faith and scriptures with and through their engagements with the pressures of immigration, assimilation, racism, Orientalism, and US empire-building projects in the Arab region. Our research thus shows that on the one hand, there is a pressing need to take the internal diversity of Arab American religious practices and scriptural readings seriously. On the other hand, despite this diversity, Christians and Muslims from the Arab region have a shared history of engagement with US popular media and political discourses that lump all Arab Christians and Muslims together within a racialized, Orientalist discourse about terrorism and Islamic fundamentalism. While specific Muslim and Christian individuals and communities relate to dominant US discourses differently, religious practices, understandings, and spaces of worship continue to serve as key sites through which they negotiate cultural identity and their relationship to the US discourses and practices of race, assimilation, and war.

Notes

1. All interlocutors' names are replaced with pseudonyms, though we do identify which place of worship they represent. A complete list of interviews is included in the appendix.

2. See Schiller and Fouron (2001), for their definition of transnational social fields.

3. Their concepts of religious practice and scriptural engagements reflect what Gilroy (1993) refers to as maintaining identifications outside the US nation in order to live inside, with a difference.

4. For the full list of Muslim country population statistics, see the Pew Research Center's report *Mapping the Global Muslim Population* (2009).

5. Although Arab immigration to the United State predates the nineteenth century, the first significant group came to the United States in the 1880s. See Kayyali (2006) for a description of Arab immigration to the United States before 1880.

6. McAlister (2005) offers an overview of these post–World War II population movements, referring to Lebanese immigration in the context of the Lebanese civil war, Palestinian displacement to the United States in the context of Israeli occupation, the displacement of Iraqi refugees in the context of US-led war on Iraq, Yemeni immigration in the context of civil war in Yemen, and general worsening of economic conditions in the region during this period and beyond.

7. Said argues that Orientalism constructs a binary opposition between East and West that assumes that the two categories are mutually exclusive and that the "East" is different than and inferior to the "West." Orientalism, according to Said, has operated as a discursive, ideological justification for Western colonialism and imperialism in the Middle East (Said 1978).

8. The portrayal of Islam as an inherently violent religion has a long history. Said argues that throughout the Middle Ages and in the early part of the Renaissance in Europe, "Islam was believed to be a demonic religion of apostasy, blasphemy, and obscurity" and Mohammed was believed to be a false prophet and an agent of the devil (1981, 5).

9. Other organizations included Nadja: Women Concerned About the Middle East (1960); Pal-Aid International (1967); U.S. Organization for Medical and Educational Needs (1961); and the American Arab Association (1961).

10. See Rashid Khalidi (2004) for a more detailed analysis of growing US involvement in the Arab region.

11. Nixon's Operation Boulder in 1972 was the first in a string of FBI policies that entailed the harassment of Arabs and Arab Americans, particularly students, who were targeted by the state, and denied their constitutional rights, specifically those related to free speech. Based on presidential directives, it authorized the FBI to harass individuals of "Arabic speaking descent" with phone calls and visits without evidence of criminal activity based on the assumption that they may have a relationship with "terrorist activities" in Palestine and Israel (Akram 2002, 5). Also during the 1970s, several government agencies, including the Federal Bureau of Investigation, the Justice Department, and the Immigration Department carried out a wide-ranging campaign of investigation and surveillance of Arab Americans through tactics such as spying and wiretapping that were ordered from the White House under the guise of uncovering the activities of persons potentially involved in sabotage (Hussaini 1974). Also see the L.A. 8 case as an example

of US government harassment of Arab Americans activists. See Hasso (1987) for more information on the implications of this case for Arab Americans.

12. See, for example, the films *True Lies* (1994), *The Siege* (1998), *Back to the Future* II (1985), and *GI Jane* (1988).

13. In particular, see the essays in Min and Kim (2002), for examples of this among the different religions in Asian America. For Arab American accounts, see Philip M. Kayal (1975) and the essays in Hourani and Shehadi (1992).

14. See Naff (1985) and Orfalea (2006).

15. See Bawardi (2009) for an in-depth discussion of the political and cultural intersections early of Orthodox and Maronite communities in the United States.

16. See Ham (1997) and McGuire (1974) as two examples.

17. For a full discussion of the politicized engagement of these transnational religious communities see Stiffler (2010).

18. The mass was sponsored in part by "The Lebanese Forces and the Kataeb," a Maronite-led political party in Lebanon.

19. Beshir Gemayel's son had also just recently been assassinated.

20. This is especially apt in the religious context. Because Lebanon's government is built on a confessional system, religious leaders often take on politicized roles in Lebanon, and affiliation with one religious group tends to equate to support of a particular political viewpoint. Nubar Hovsepian (2007) writes in his entry to his edited volume, "The Lebanese were recognized not as citizens or members of civil society, but as members of the officially recognized confessions" (35).

21. See Stiffler (2010) for a lengthy theoretical and historical discussion about the role of food festivals in Arab Christian communities, specifically the Antiochian Orthodox.

22. The front of St. Sharbel is adorned with a gold cross with three bars, shaped like a cedar tree. This is sometimes referred to as "the Maronite cross," and its three horizontal bars are supposed to refer to the unity of the trinity, but it is also deliberately shaped like a cedar tree, which is a national symbol of Lebanon.

23. There is a slight difference in generations, though, where younger and more recent immigrants have less problem identifying as Arab or Arab American. A Maronite priest explains: "For most of us, we come from—we're second-, third-, fourth-generation American. We see ourselves very clearly as Lebanese Americans. And really are affected by the term Arab American. But newcomers have no problem with it, and we look at them and say, 'How could you accept that title?' Because if I said I was an Arab growing up, my grandfather would knock me across the room." Elie, a Lebanese immigrant in his twenties says, "I'm Arabic basically. I was raised in Lebanon. What defines the Arab world is [...] traditions and cultures. I was raised among those customs and traditions. I was raised, in Tripoli, around a lot of Muslim people, so we all share the same traditions and customs. So, I consider myself Arabic and a Christian."

24. One scholar of Arab American religions speaks of the religious identity of Arab Americans as being "primordial" (Kayal 2002). Though this may be a bit of a reduction, there is a sense that among the Christians we interviewed, religious faith does seem to be something that is seen as "inherited" from parents or ancestors. Also, within the Arab American community at large, people are often identified by their religion.

25. For more context about the role of religious identity in post-9/11 "Arab Detroit," see Howell and Jamal (2009).

26. Scholars are uncertain exactly when Christians would have had Arabic Bibles and Arabic liturgies, but it is widely believed that it could have been as early as the seventh century. See Thomas (2007).

27. We observed a potent example of the Arabic language's power as a liturgical language in the Antiochian Orthodox Church in America. There was an older Arab gentleman with a cane seated in the pew in front of us. Mostly everyone in the church was standing, as is customary, during Deacon Mark's reading of the Gospel in English, except for the elderly man in front of me, obviously not physically comfortable standing for long periods of time. As soon as Deacon Mark finished reading, Father John entered through the Great Doors and announced the Gospel reading in Arabic. The elderly gentleman stood right up, as if the sound of the scriptures in Arabic snapped him to attention. He stood for almost the entire reading.

28. See Constantine Nasr's *The Bible in the Liturgy* (1988) or his *Journey Through the Divine Liturgy* (1991), which trace the biblical underpinnings of every line of the Divine Liturgy. A letter in the preface of *The Bible in the Liturgy* from Metropolitan Philip Saliba, the leader of the Antiochian archdiocese of North American, reads, "Thus we Orthodox Christians chant the verses of the Bible each time we celebrate the Holy Liturgy and all divine services."

APPENDIX 1 | Chapter 1 Research Information

Research Team

Coordinator:	Andrea Smith, University of California, Riverside
Interviewers:	Chris Finley, University of Oregon
	Angela Parker, Dartmouth College
	Marcus Briggs-Cloud, Independent scholar
Consultant:	Justine Smith, Harvard University
Transcriber:	Lee Ann Wang, University of Michigan

Contextual information provided by interviewees (in response to the question, what would you like readers of this report to know about you?)

People Interviewed at Living Waters Gathering (August, 2007)

CASEY CHURCH: I am Potawotami from Michigan. My father is the Crane clan, and my mother is the Bear clan, my Native name means "Hole in the clouds."

DELFINA JOHNSON: I am Navajo My parents are full Navajo, both of them. My dad is 68 [years old] and my mom is 65.

GLEN PEDRO: I'm from Cancho, OK. I was raised in a Native American church, real traditional family, went to Sundance every year. [Went to] Native American church meetings every weekend from when I was a child to when I left the household

RICHARD TWISS: My name is Richard Twiss. My Lakota Name is Taoyate Obnajin: He Stands for This People. I am 52 years of age, I was born among my mother's people on the Rosebud Sioux reservation in South Dakota; my father is Oglala Lakota from Pine Ridge and my mother is Sicangu from the Rosebud Reservation in South Dakota.

EDITH WOODLEY: My father is Shoshone and my mother is Choctaw. My husband is Randy Woodley, and he just turned 51. He is United Keetoowah Cherokee from Tahlequah.

RANDY WOODLEY: My name is Randy Woodley and I'm a legal descendent of the United Ketoowah Band of Cherokee Indians of Oklahoma, and I guess you would say, the reason you guys are doing this is because I've been influential in this Native American Contextual Movement people would call it. I'm happy to be here.

NICOLE YELLOW OLD WOMAN: Siksika nation, part of Blackfoot Confederacy about 60 miles east of Calgary, Alberta, Canada. I was born Oct. 9th 1977. My Indian name, I have two, one when I was a little girl, which is "Mexican Woman." And then when I become Tribal Princess, "Silent Raider Woman." I was pretty much born in church, knowing Jesus Christ as my personal savior. I knew him when I was born through the example of my parents. And I accepted him as my personal savior when I was 7. So the spirituality of being a born-again Christian has always been in my life and I grew up to that. My parents have been married for 33 years. I have an older brother, who has his masters. We've both gone to Bible college and graduated. So that's us.

VINCENT YELLOW OLD WOMAN: Vincent Yellow Old Woman, from the Siksika, Blackfoot Confederacy. Both of my parent have deceased, gone to their place, looking forward to meeting them again. My father's name is Edward, my mom's name is Betsy, both full-blooded Blackfoot which makes me a full blood.

People Interviewed at 2007 NAIITS Conference

CHERYL BEAR: My name is Cheryl Bear, I'm—First Nation, Northern British Columbia Canada. We're part of the—nation, and I'm from the Bear clan.

DAVID BIRD: I am David Bird. I am of Cree Soto descent, father of one ten-year-old boy. I was pastor for about fifteen years, just recently stepped down in September. So now I'm just doing a lot of writing

ROGER BOYER: My name is Roger A. Boyer II. My Ojibwe name translates in English into "a bear who goes around and helps other bears get out of traps."

ANITA KEITH: My spirit name is She Who War Dances, it's a Mohawk name given to me by a Mohawk elder. And my Canadian name is Anita and my last name is Keith. What would I want people to know about me? Well I am a mom, with three wonderful children and four grandchildren, I'm raising one of my grandchildren. She is 20 and she is a joy, they all are in my life. I'm an instructor in an Aboriginal educational program at a local college, called Red River College in Winnipeg, Manitoba. Our students are all aboriginal, most of them are funded by their bands or reserves and they come into the program, there are a few programs. One is computer applications and business so it's business and computer focused, but in there we also teach a course called Exploring Aboriginal Cultures and Issues. I developed it; it's four courses, 1, 2, 3, 4, and it's module base and what we're trying to do is indoctrinate or teach our students about our cultures, and many of them know absolutely nothing because they went through the mainstream and there's nada. One woman said to me, what is colonization? Not even knowing we are oppressed or that this has happened to us. We go through, who am I as an Aboriginal person, our health, who am I in my community and family, and then we move the modules out into larger issues like treaties, land claims, and how we fit into those structures and the issues that flow out of that. So, I teach those courses and also I teach an aboriginal self-governance program, and this year I teach research and ethics and next term I teach aboriginal law and aboriginal world issues, which is exciting because it's international based and the students love it. I love what I do with the students but of course we're always in crisis with them. Joe won't be here today because he was stabbed last night and we won't be expecting him for three [weeks] or a month, or so and so is not coming because grandma died and they will be gone for a week, and so I tailor my course for students and I teach from an aboriginal perspective and I allow for all of these crisis that flow through their lives and I allow them to get caught up, and so there is no rigid deadlines in my courses, except they get the final mark....So if students know if crisis hits they can keep breathing and get the work done in a certain amount of time, and it works for them. And so I think it's important for people to know that about me, and my perspective and worldview about education our dropout rate in Canada is like 75–85 percent of aboriginal students in our school. So the students that we get in our program can be like grade 10, 11, maybe grade 12 and so they've fallen out of that system, but they are trying to get their life back on track and so this is where we pick up on them. So we try to help them along their journey and get them through. The other thing I'd like people to know is that I've written four books, two on aboriginal education helping people to understand educators to understand that we learn differently, and [using] the mainstream template on us just doesn't work. The teaching model has to be geared for the aboriginal person, so I'm very much in favor of aboriginal teachers teaching aboriginal students in an aboriginal community context. So I've written two books on aboriginal education, one on authentic partnerships with aboriginal people, because partnerships have not always been authentic, they've been the power over—we're gonna come into your community and show you how's it done. And that just doesn't work, so what does equality or equal partnership look like? And I speak about that in my book. The fourth book is the most painful but my best the so far, it's called "For Our Children Our Sacred Beings: Understanding the Impact of Generational Trauma in Our Aboriginal Youth," and it talks about how the plagues were systematically placed into our communities ripped across the land and taking out millions of our people, just died within weeks and days. And how that trauma has been passed down from one generation to the next and we are still feeling the reverberations of that today. And what are the symptoms of that and what does that look like, and so when people read the book they begin to understand, ok I am not crazy and this is actually a normal response and then a direction on how to get past that.

JANINE LeBLANC: I'm Janine LeBlanc from Edmonton, Alberta Canada. I am a Micmac woman from the east coast of Canada and I'm studying at Asbury Theological Seminary and will be done in May

JENNIFER LeBLANC: I am Jennifer LeBlanc, Janine's twin sister. I am studying at Sioux Falls Seminary. I am Micmac by heritage and French as well, so Metis, and I am enjoying working at the intercultural center at my school.

TERRY LeBLANC: My name is Terry LeBlanc I am a Micmac from the Bouctouche First Nation, I am also of Acadian extraction from my other side, just across the river from Bouctouche in New Brunswick, married with wife of 35 years, three children, twin girls and my son Matt. I've been making my home in the western part of Canada for about 37 years now; I am originally from Eastern Canada.

DOUGLAS MACDONALD: My name is Douglass Spencer McDonald, my family comes from Manitoba. My mom is from north side of Lake Winnipeg, my dad is from the southern part of Lake Winnipeg. I don't know my background too much on my dad's side—both my parents actually as far as my native side. I'm half Scottish half Cree, third generation half Scottish half Cree. In that area it's really hard to get away from that because the Hudson Bay Company hired these guys from Scotland and brought them over to Canada. And they, according to my great grandfather's journal, when he came over when he was 17, the non-Native people only lasted two winters, and then they died, they only lasted two years, they just did not know how to survive in this country. So, they had to marry native women, to show them how to live and in the wilderness and also it was good for them business-wise, to make those connections into the family so they could have good business with the native people. So anyways, that's background from my family, I was born in British Columbia and grew up out there with the hippies.

People Interviewed at Envision 2008 Conference

RAY ALDRED: I thought that the gospel story was big enough for Aboriginal people too, and that, somehow that it was possible to believe and not know that actually being in a relationship in Christ would actually make a person a better, or, help them. They would be becoming who they were meant to be, and that Christian maturity wouldn't suddenly say oh I am different than I ever thought, but rather would say, we are exactly who we are meant to be. So then, spirituality was about being truly human.

People Interviewed in Oklahoma (2007)

DICEY BARNETT: My name is Dicey Barnett, I was born and raised in Henrietta OK, I graduated from high school in Bristol, OK, I have twenty grandchildren, and four great-grandchildren, and my clan is Kono and my tribal town is Kvlice. I worked part time at Muskogee sovereignty initiative, I have been there since December, I'm fairly new to the organization.

MARCUS BRIGGS-CLOUD: My name is Marcus, son of the Wind Clan people, Grandson of the Bird Clan people, from the Miccosukee village from the Great Muscogee nation. I am from Florida originally, the Big Cypress reservation, but been here four year at University of Oklahoma. I teach Muscogee language at the University. I belong to the Christian tradition and the Muscogee ways.

LINCOLN HARJO: I'm a member of the Creek and Seminole nations of OK. There is also a Seminole nation of Florida, really one in the same blood, but just one of us was brought to OK at one time, one branch, and some stayed and never surrendered to the government which was probably a good thing in some ways. I think they are the only tribe that I know of that never actually signed, but if they did sign anything they put a knife through it and said it was all a lie so why bother.

I'm a believer of Jesus Chris that's who I am essentially, spiritually. God is not a religion or a denomination, some people are going be surprised to find out he's not a Baptist, Methodist, Catholic, Pentecostal, Assembly of God or any denomination. He is God; He is a spirit, all powerful, all supreme, and you can't lock him into a box. Unfortunately, that is what denominations have sought to do throughout the world, or any religion for that matter, try to capture God in a box and say this is how He is, but that's not how He is. He is exactly how he says he is in the Bible and that's limitless. Pure energy you might say, nothing can hold pure energy. That's what God holds in spirit, that's what God tries to show us, not to lock ourselves and to find real identity. That in a nutshell is the world's whole problem—a lack of identity—which God can give you if you let him. He's not going to force it on you, not gonna, just like a magician pulls a rabbit out of a hand, or bam, hit something with a magic wand and presto all of a sudden you are something different. He's going to wait for you to develop a relationship; that's how God will unfold yourself to you when you understand who you are you will understand Him. That's how he operates. That's what I would like people to know about me, my whole journey from point A to point B in my life, and I'm still learning and there are still things that I have to conquer in my life, my outward appearance, being overweight, it's an identity issue. I have to find out what God says about me rather than what I believe about me, what others believe about me, what others may think of me, what I may think of myself, and if I get that issue settled, I know this will go away. Now that does not mean I will exclude exercise; it's just that until I get my mind right, until I get the discipline in here right, of what to do with my body, that's when the change will come, then I will know God in that area of my life. That's what God is, He takes every area of your life, no matter if it's alcohol, sexual impurity, God can change it, if you're willing to listen. If you're willing to find out, what your real roots are, everything goes back to him, Adam and Eve, our true mother and father of all people, across the whole world. They know God from the beginning because he breathed his life into them, but when they gave themselves to sin that's when they lost a lot of knowledge; man didn't become dumb over night, it's become a gradual process. There are some astounding human beings that are far more astounding then we are, we see that in a lot of our Native history, and our archeological findings, so man didn't become dumb over night, it's been a slow gradual process. Man didn't just die at 70 years, at one time either, he lived for thousands of years, he didn't' know how to die because he was once walking with God in the garden, he knew what life was, man has forgotten that and has just filled himself with earthly knowledge, but spiritual knowledge is way above that. That's the person I am in a nutshell, if you really want to know me, I'm sure some people don't want to know this, they're like you're loony pretty strange you know, but so what that's what I know.

LUCY ANN WILLAMS HARJO: I am Lucy Ann Williams Harjo, I am Navajo. My husband and I have been married 27 years and we have four children, they range [from] sophomore in college to a third grader. I have a son in high school and a son in middle school. My faith is why I am still here. It makes up who I am and what

I do. I am the coordinator of Indian education for Norman public schools. I love my job because it's surveying Native American families and students.

CHEBON KERNELL: My name is Reverend Chebon Kernell. I am a member of the Seminole Nation of Oklahoma, born and raised here in Oklahoma City, here in the state of Oklahoma, a lifelong member of the United Methodist Church, probably since I was about 8 years old, came into full membership when I was about 12.

SHAUNDAY LITTLE: My name is Shaunday Little. I'm a Creek Seminole, enrolled in Muskogee Creek Nation, I have two beautiful girls, I work full time with the Muskogee Creek nation, great benefits by the way, I'm in the process of kind of learning my language, not really on top of it but I work with ladies that do speak it so they teach me words now and then. My name is a Kiowa Indian name, it means little girl or little one.

MARGARET MCKANE MAULDIN: I was born in 1940. I was raised right here on the land where I am now sitting. I was very close to my grandmother I had no grandfathers. I am full blood Creek. I say that even though my mother is half Seminole, that would make me ¼ Seminole, but I've always been told that we're one tribe, so that's what I believe. So I don't think that I'm different in any way than the Seminole. The language is the same, and I know we may say things slightly different but all in all it's the same language.

MARGIE YAZZIE: My name is Margie Yazzie, I'm a Muscogee Creek Seminole. I'm a grandmother, I'm a homemaker, raised three children, learning Creek language, something I used to know when I was little but then I grew up and I lost it, now trying to get back into it, exciting makes you feel warm inside, what you learn, that's me.

Interviewed in Washington (2007)

Virginia Mason

I am 79 years old, I'll be 80 in February of next year, I belong to the Colville Confederated Tribes, which is made up of 12 bands, and I am an Arrow Lakes Band.

Interview Questionnaire

A. Religious Background

1. How did you become a Christian? Briefly tell me your story.

B. Context: You and the Bible

1. Our research is focused on the Bible. How do you learn about the Bible?
2. Have you ever attended or do you currently attend a group Bible study/class? If so, describe a typical scene.

C. Anecdotal: The Bible and Your Life Decisions

1. Do you think that the Bible should play a role in the way people make life decisions? If so, why? If not, why not?
2. Has reading the Bible ever influenced an important life decision you've made?
   A. If so, what? What significance did this decision have on your life?
   B. If not, has the Bible ever influenced any kind of action you've taken in life?
3. Have you ever doubted a decision you made based on the Bible? What did you do in that situation?

D. Current Issue: Charity

1. What do you believe the Bible says about charity?
2. How often do you practice charity?
   >>Very frequently, Frequently, Not Often, Rarely, Never <<
   Follow up: How have you given? (If "Never," why?)
3. Do you think that practicing charity is important for Asian Americans?
4. Have you ever felt that charity was ineffective?

E. Current Issue: Homosexual Ordination

1. In many Christian churches, openly homosexual people are allowed to be ordained as clergy. What is your stance on this issue?
   >>Strongly Against, Against, Neutral, Support, Strongly Support<<
2. What are your reasons for this stance?
3. Given your stance on the ordination of homosexual people, have you ever become actively engaged in this issue? Why or why not?
4. Do you know any other Christians who would disagree with your stance on the issue? If so, how would you respond to them?

F. Scripture Interpretation

Here's a passage in Matthew, often called the Great Commission, that says:

> Therefore go and make disciples of all nations, baptizing them in the name of the Father and of the Son and of the Holy Spirit, and teaching them to obey everything I have commanded you. (Matthew 28:19)

1. What do you think this passage means?
2. Have you incorporated the message of this passage into your life? If so, how?
3. Is this an important message for Asian Americans? If so, why?
4. How might this passage influence the way you approach people of other religions?
5. Have you ever disagreed with the way that this passage teaches you to live your life?

G. Conclusion

1. Do you have anything else that you would like to add?
2. Do you have any questions for me?
3. Can you provide any feedback or suggestions for me?

B rett Esaki received a PhD in religious studies from the University of California, Santa Barbara, in 2012 and an MA in African American religions from the University of South Carolina in 2006. His research areas include the arts and popular culture, the intersection of race and sexuality, and American history. His dissertation explores strategies of silence by Japanese American artists to resist oppression and to preserve religious ideas.

Russell Jeung is Associate Professor of Asian American Studies at San Francisco State University. He is the author of *Faithful Generations: Race and New Asian American Churches* (2004) and co-editor of *Sustaining Faith Traditions: Race, Ethnicity, and Religion among the Latino and Asian American Second Generation* (2012). He also coproduced the documentary *The Oak Park Story* (2010).

Helen Jin Kim is a doctoral student at Harvard University in the Committee on Religion where she is focusing on the history of American religion. She is interested in religion, race, and gender, with a concentration in transnational evangelical movements and Asian/Asian American Christianities.

Lalruatkima is a doctoral candidate in religion at Claremont Graduate University. His dissertation focuses on the dynamics of imperial conscription of wild races in colonial India.

James Kyung-Jin Lee is Associate Professor and Department Chair of Asian American Studies at the University of California, Irvine. He is the author of *Urban Triage: Race and the Fictions of Multiculturalism* (2004). Lee also serves as the director of UCI's PhD program in culture and theory.

Quynh-Hoa Nguyen is a PhD candidate in New Testament at Claremont Graduate University. Her dissertation focuses on biblical engagement as it is appropriated by evangelical Christians in Vietnam to construct an "otherworldly" identity that negotiates a distinctive mode of being in response to domination and marginalization by the state and by mainstream culture. She is interested in scriptures and peoples, Christian identities, Vietnamese/Americans and the Bible, as well as ethnography.

Sharon A. Suh is Associate Professor and Department Chair of Theology and Religious Studies at Seattle University. Her research examines the intersection of Buddhism, gender, race, ethnicity, religion, and immigration in the United States. She is the author of *Being Buddhist in a Christian World: Gender and Community in a Korean American Temple* (2004) and several articles on Buddhism, gender, race, and ethnicity. Suh is currently also Co-chair of the Asian Pacific Americans and Religion Research Initiative.

APPENDIX 2.3 | Chapter 4 Interviewee List (with Pseudonyms)

1. Alfred, a 36-year-old third-generation Chinese American graduate student, interviewed on March 31, 2008.
2. Alison, an Asian American professor of the Bible, interviewed on January 18, 2008.
3. Andrew, a 51-year-old first-generation Vietnamese American contractor, interviewed on April 15, 2007.
4. Archie, a 24-year-old second-generation Chinese American, interviewed on December 17, 2007.
5. Bao, a 59-year-old first-generation Vietnamese American male pharmacist, interviewed on April 22, 2007.
6. Cherry, a 22-year-old second-generation Korean American undergraduate student, interviewed on December 7, 2007.
7. Chien, a 72-year-old first-generation Vietnamese American male retiree, interviewed on April 20, 2007.
8. Cindy, a 19-year-old 1.5-generation Vietnamese American college student, interviewed on April 9, 2007.
9. Danh, a 34-year-old 1.5-generation Vietnamese American engineer (male), interviewed on April 15, 2007.
10. Dena, a 42-year-old 1.5-generation Vietnamese American homemaker and part-time student, interviewed on April 17, 2007.
11. Donna, a 23-year-old second-generation Chinese American graduate student, interviewed on November 27, 2007.
12. Duong, a 61-year-old Vietnamese American auto-shop manager (male), interviewed on April 20, 2007.
13. Eva, a 23-year-old second-generation Vietnamese American college student, interviewed on April 6, 2007.
14. Hoang, a 62-year-old first-generation Vietnamese American female retiree, interviewed on April 16, 2007.
15. Ivy, a 1.5-generation Chinese American graduate student, interviewed on March 4, 2008.

16. Jack, a 22-year-old second-generation Chinese American, interviewed on June 1, 2007.
17. Janet, a 32-year-old fourth-generation Japanese American parachurch organizer, interviewed on September 1, 2007.
18. Jimmy, a 47-year-old first-generation Vietnamese American accountant, interviewed on April 7, 2007.
19. JoAnne, a 21-year-old fourth-generation Japanese American private-school teacher, interviewed on July 24, 2007.
20. Julia, a 65-year-old second-generation Korean-Caucasian American realtor and homemaker, interviewed on June 30, 2007.
21. Kathy, a 22-year-old second-generation Vietnamese American undergraduate student, interviewed on May 31, 2007.
22. Kenneth, a 20-year-old second-generation Chinese American undergraduate student, interviewed on October 22, 2007.
23. Laurel, a 21-year-old 1.5-generation undergraduate student of Chinese and Filipino descent, interviewed on September 2, 2007.
24. Louise, a 28-year-old second-generation Chinese American, interviewed on April 9, 2008.
25. Lynn, a 26-year-old second-generation Korean-Caucasian American professional concert violinist and wellness consultant, interviewed on April 18, 2007.
26. Maggie, a 25-year-old second-generation Chinese American graduate student, interviewed on November 4, 2007.
27. Maria, a 23-year-old second-generation Chinese American graduate student, interviewed on September 19, 2007.
28. Mariah, a 49-year-old first-generation Filipino American public high school teacher who also serves as the director at her local church's children ministry, interviewed on September 10, 2007.
29. Maxine, a 20-year-old second-generation Chinese American undergraduate, interviewed on October 25, 2007.
30. Paul, a 35-year-old 1.5-generation assistant manager, interviewed on April 20, 2007.
31. Phuong-Anh, a 57-year-old first-generation Vietnamese American tailor (female), interviewed on April 14, 2007.
32. Robert, a 24-year-old second-generation Korean American, interviewed on December 15, 2007.
33. Sara, a 45-year-old first-generation Filipino American realtor, interviewed on April 29, 2007.
34. Sharon, a 30-year-old second-generation Filipina American family therapist, interviewed on August 9, 2007.
35. Sue, a 60-year-old first-generation Vietnamese American homemaker, interviewed on April 9, 2007.
36. Susan, a 23-year-old 1.5-generation Chinese American graduate student, interviewed on October 17, 2007.
37. Sylvia, a 20-year-old 1.5-generation Vietnamese American student, interviewed on April 6, 2007.

38. Ted, a 25-year-old second-generation Chinese American computer systems analyst, interviewed on July 28, 2007.
39. Thomas, a 44-year-old 1.5-generation Vietnamese American salesperson, interviewed on April 17, 2007.
40. Tina, a 24-year-old second-generation Korean American student, interviewed on May 29, 2007.
41. William, a 25-year-old second-generation Chinese American graduate student, interviewed on November 13, 2007.
42. Winnie, a 30-year-old second-generation Filipino American, interviewed on May 12, 2008.
43. Yuk Yee, an Asian American professor of the Bible in a seminary, interviewed on January 10, 2008.

APPENDIX 3 | Chapter 5 Interviewee List (with Pseudonyms)

Interviews with Christian participants were conducted between summer 2007 and fall 2008 at two churches in Michigan.
  Name, interviewer, affiliation.

1. Abraham, interviewed by Atef Said, St. Maron Maronite Catholic Church
2. Adele, interviewed by Matthew Stiffler, St. Sharbel Maronite Catholic Church
3. Barbara, interviewed by Atef Said, St. Maron Maronite Catholic Church
4. Charles, interviewed by Atef Said, St. Maron Maronite Catholic Church
5. Deacon Elias, interviewed by Nadine Naber, St. Mary Antiochian Orthodox Church
6. Deacon Mark, interviewed by Matthew Stiffler, St. Mary Antiochian Orthodox Church
7. Edward, interviewed by Matthew Stiffler, St. Maron Maronite Catholic Church
8. Elie, interviewed by Matthew Stiffler, St. Sharbel Maronite Catholic Church
9. Fadi, interviewed by Nadine Naber, St. Mary Antiochian Orthodox Church
10. Fouad, interviewed by Matthew Stiffler, St. Sharbel Maronite Catholic Church
11. Father David, interviewed by Matthew Stiffler, St. Sharbel Maronite Catholic Church
12. Father John, interviewed by Matthew Stiffler, St. Mary Antiochian Orthodox Church
13. Hoda, interviewed by Matthew Stiffler, St. Sharbel Maronite Catholic Church
14. Kathy, interviewed by Matthew Stiffler, St. Mary Antiochian Orthodox Church
15. Nabil, interviewed by Matthew Stiffler, St. Maron Maronite Catholic Church
16. Richard, interviewed by Nadine Naber, St. Mary Antiochian Orthodox Church
17. Rita, interviewed by Nadine Naber, St. Mary Antiochian Orthodox Church
18. Sam, interviewed by Atef Said, St. Maron Maronite Catholic Church
19. Sara, interviewed by Matthew Stiffler, St. Mary Antiochian Orthodox Church
20. Subdeacon Michael, interviewed by Matthew Stiffler, St. Mary Antiochian Orthodox Church

Interviews with Muslim participants were conducted at The Islamic Center of Claremont in California from June 2007 to July 2007. All the interviews were conducted by Sana Tayyen. The following are pseudonyms:

1. Aisha
2. Fayza
3. Salma
4. Amal
5. Imani
6. Maysa
7. Ashraf
8. Marwan
9. Taha
10. Rayan
11. Ayman
12. Basil

BIBLIOGRAPHY

Akram, Susan. "The Aftermath of September 11, 2001: The Targeting of Arabs and Muslims in America." *Arab Studies Quarterly* 61 (Spring 2002): 61–118.

Alfred, Taiaiake. *Peace, Power, Righteousness*. Oxford: Oxford University Press, 1999.

Ahlstrom, Sydney. *Religious History of the American People*. New Haven, CT: Yale University Press, 1972.

Ammerman, Nancy Tatom. *Bible Believers: Fundamentalists in the Modern World*. New Brunswick, NJ: Rutgers University Press, 1987.

Ammi, Ben. *Platform of Righteousness: The Platform for the 21st Century; The Millenial Sanctification and Separation*. Washington, DC: Communicators Press, [1999?]. Adobe e-book.

Andrews, William L., ed. *The Oxford Frederick Douglass Reader*. New York: Oxford University Press, 1996.

Angelou, Maya. *I Know Why the Caged Bird Sings*. New York: Random House, 1969.

Appadurai, Arjun. *Modernity at Large: Cultural Dimensions of Globalization*. Minneapolis: University of Minnesota Press, 1996.

Arnheim, Rudolf. *The Power of the Center: A Study of Composition in the Visual Arts*. Berkeley: University of California Press, 1988.

Asante, MolefiKete. *The Egyptian Philosophers: Ancient African Voices from Imhotep to Akhenaten*. Chicago: African American Images, 2000.

Aswad, Barbara, ed. *Arabic Speaking Communities in American Cities*. New York: Center for Migration Studies of New York and Association of Arab-American University Graduates, 1974.

Atkinson, Robert. *The Life Story Interview: Qualitative Research Methods*. Thousand Oaks, CA: SAGE Publications, 1998.

Baker, Houston A. *Afro-American Poetics: Revisions of Harlem and the Black Aesthetic* (Madison: University of Wisconsin Press, 1988)

Barber, Karin. *The Anthropology of Texts, Persons and Publics: Oral and Written Culture in Africa and Beyond*. New York: Cambridge University Press, 2007.

Barnes, Esther. "Native People Need Native Missionaries." *Faith Today* 7 (May–June, 1989): 58–59.

Bawardi, Hani. "Arab American Political Organizations from 1915 to 1951: Assessing Transnational Political Consciousness and the Development of Arab American Identity." PhD diss., Wayne State University, Detroit, 2009.

Beegle, Dewey. *Scripture, Tradition and Infallibility*. Grand Rapids, MI: Eerdmans, 1973.

Beggiani, Chorbishop Seely. *Aspects of Maronite History: The Maronites in the United States,* n.d., http://stmaron.org/marinusa.html.

Benston, Kimberly W. *Enactments of African-American Modernism*. New York: Routledge, 2000.

Bloesch, Donald. *Essentials of Evangelical Theology*. San Francisco: Harper & Row, 1978.

Bloom, Harold. *Anxiety of Influence: A Theory of Poetry.* New York: Oxford University Press, 1997 (1973).

Bloom, Harold. *A Map of Misreading*. New York: Oxford University Press, 2003 (1975).

Bomer, Norm. "The Anthropologists' 'Paradise.'" *World* 11 (November 23, 1996): 20–21.

Bourdieu, Pierre. *Distinction: A Social Critique of the Judgment of Taste*. Translated by Richard Nice. Cambridge, MA: Harvard University Press, 1984.

Brah, Avtar. *Cartographies of Diaspora: Contesting Identities*. London; New York: Routledge, 1996.

Brown, John. *The Self-Interpreting Bible: Containing the Sacred Text of the Old and New Testaments*. New York: Hodge and Campbell, 1792 (1778).

Busto, Rudy V. "The Gospel According to the Model Minority? Hazarding an Interpretation of Asian American Evangelical College Students." In *New Spiritual Homes: Religion and Asian Americans*, edited by David K. Yoo, 169–87. Honolulu: University of Hawai'i Press, 1999.

Cainkar, Louise. "Targeting Muslims, at Ashcroft's Discretion." *Middle East Reports Online*. March 14, 2003. http://www.merip.org/mero/mero031403.

Caruth, Cathy. *Unclaimed Experience: Trauma, Narrative, and History*. Baltimore, MD: John Hopkins University Press, 1996.

Cave, Albert. "Canaanites in a Promised Land." *American Indian Quarterly* 12, no. 4 (Autumn, 1988): 277–97.

Chambers, Oswald. *My Utmost for His Highest: Selections for the Year*. New York: Dodd, Mead, 1937.

Charmaz, Kathy. "Ground Theory Methods: An Explication and Interpretation." In *Contemporary Field Research: A Collection of Readings*, edited by Robert M. Emerson, 109–26. Prospect Heights, IL: Waveland Press, 1983.

Chen, Carolyn, and Russell Jeung. "Creating and Sustaining Our Communities: Asian American Religious Institutions." In *Asian American Studies: Identity, Images, and Issues Past and Present*, edited by Esther Mikyung Ghymn, 231–54. New York: Peter Lang, 2000.

Chen, Carolyn. *Getting Saved in America: Taiwanese Immigration and Religious Experience*. Princeton, NJ: Princeton University Press, 2008.

Cho, Paul Yong Gi. *The Fourth Dimension: The Key to Putting Your Faith to Work for a Successful Life*. Plainfield, NJ: Logos International, 1979.

Claus, Tom. *On Eagles' Wings*. Unknown location: Thunderbird Indian Company Incorporated, 1976.

Clifford, James. *Routes: Travel and Translation in the Late 20th Century.* Cambridge, MA: Harvard University Press, 1996.

Cole, Alan. *Text as Father: Paternal Seductions in Early Mahayana Buddhist Literature.* Berkeley and Los Angeles: University of California Press, 2005.

Conde-Frazier, Elizabeth. *Hispanic Bible Institutes: A Community of Theological Construction.* Scranton, PA: University of Scranton Press, 2004.

Davis, Jessica W., and Kurt J. Bauman. "School Enrollment in the United States: 2006." http://www.census.gov/prod/2008pubs/p20-559.pdf.

Davis, Mike. *Magical Urbanism: Latinos Reinvent the U.S. City.* London and New York: Verso, 2001.

Deloria Jr., Vine. *For This Land.* New York: Routledge, 1999.

Deloria Jr., Vine. *God Is Red.* Golden: North American Press, 1992.

Dixon, Herti. "Indigenous Christians Embrace Tradition." *Charisma* 31 (April, 2006): 32–33.

Du Bois, W. E. B. *Souls of Black Folk.* New York: Bantam, 1989 (1903).

Edwards, Holly. "The Garments of Instruction from the Wardrobe of Pleasure: American Orientalist Painting in the 1870s and 1880s." In *Noble Dreams, Wicked Pleasures: Orientalism in America, 1870–1930,* edited by Holly Edwards and Brian T. Allen, 11–58. Princeton, NJ: Princeton University Press, 2000.

Edwards, Jonathan. *The Works of Jonathan Edwards.* 2 vols. Peabody, MA: Hendrickson Publishers, 1998.

Eisenstadt, S. N., L. Roniger, and A. Seligman, eds. *Centre-Formation, Protests Movements, and Class Struggles in Europe and the United States.* New York: New York University Press, 1987.

Eliade, Mircea. *Images and Symbols: Studies in Religious Symbolism.* Translated by Philip Mairet. Princeton, NJ: Princeton University Press, 1991 (1952).

Elkholy, Abdo A. "The Arab Americans: Nationalism and Traditional Preservations." In *The Arab Americans: Studies in Assimilation.* AAUG Monograph Series 1, edited by Elaine C. Hagopian and Ann Paden, 3–17. Wilmette, IL: Medina University Press International, 1969.

Eng, David L., and Alice Y. Hom. "Q & A: Notes on a Queer Asian America." In *Q & A: Queer in Asian America,* edited by David L. Eng and Alice Y. Hom, 1–22. Philadelphia, PA: Temple University Press, 1998.

Ennis, Sharon R., Merarys Ríos-Vargas, and Nora G. Albert. "The Hispanic Population: 2010." http://www.census.gov/prod/cen2010/briefs/c2010br-04.pdf.

Espiritu, Yen Le. *Home Bound: Filipino American Lives across Cultures, Communities, and Countries.* Berkeley: University of California Press, 2003.

Fish, Stanley E. *Is There a Text in This Class? The Authority of Interpretive Communities.* Cambridge, MA: Harvard University Press, 1980.

Fong, Ken. "Some of My Thoughts about the Conversation about Homosexuality Event." http://sedaqah.xanga.com/weblog/?uni-22-direction=n&uni-22-nextdate=5%2F12%2F2008+23%3A46%3A46.267.

Fong, Timothy P. "The History of Asians in America." In *Asian Americans: Experiences and Perspectives,* edited by Timothy P. Fong and Larry H. Shinagawa, 13–30. Upper Saddle River, NJ: Prentice Hall, 2000.

Francis, Robert. "Colonization: Weapons, Gifts, Diseases and Medicine." http://www.midamericanindianfellowships.org/PDF/DCRS%201%20Colonization%20Weapons%20Gifts%20Diseases%20Medicine.pdf.

Francis, Vic. "Christians from 32 Countries Reclaim Native Customs." *Charisma* 22 (April, 1997): 47–48.

Frankenberg, Ruth. "The Miracle of an Unmarked Whiteness." In *The Making and Unmaking of Whiteness*, edited by Birgit Brander Rasmussen, Irene J. Nexica, Eric Klinenberg, and Matt Wray, 72–96. Durham, NC: Duke University Press, 2001.

Fuller, Daniel. "On Revelation and Biblical Authority." *Journal of the Evangelical Theological Society* 2 (1973): 67–72.

Furstenberg, François. *In the Name of the Father: Washington's Legacy, Slavery, and the Making of a Nation*. New York: Penguin Press, 2006.

Gilroy, Paul. *The Black Atlantic: Modernity and Double Consciousness*. Cambridge, MA: Harvard University Press, 1993.

Gonzalez, Justo. *The Theological Education of Hispanics: A Study*. New York: The Fund for Theological Education, 1988.

Gordon, Avery F. *Ghostly Matters: Haunting and the Sociological Imagination*. Minneapolis: University of Minnesota Press, 1997.

Grady, J. Lee. "Native Americans Use Culture for Christ." *Charisma* 28 (July, 2000): 22–23.

Grady, J. Lee. "Former Rock Musician Now Brings 'Native Praise' to Indian Communities." *Charisma* 30 (November, 2004): 35.

Gruszka, Dennis. "God's Holy Fire." *Native Reflections* 10 (Winter, 1997): 2–5.

Gualtieri, Sarah. *Between Arab and White: Race and Ethnicity in the Early Syrian American Diaspora*. Berkeley: University of California Press, 2009.

Gundaker, Grey. *Signs of Diaspora, Diaspora of Signs: Literacies, Creolization and Vernacular Practice in African America*. New York: Oxford University Press, 1999.

Ham, Herb. *Worshipping the Undivided Trinity: A Cultural History of St. Elijah Orthodox Church* [in Oklahoma City, OK]. Guthrie, OK: St. James Orthodox Press, 1997.

Hammon, Jupiter. "Address to the Negroes in the State of New York." In *Afro-American Religious History: A Documentary Witness*, edited by Milton C. Sernett, 34–43. Durham, NC: Duke University Press, 1985.

Hasso, Francis. "Conspiracy of Silence against Arab Americans." *News Circle* 26 (Feb–Mar 1987): 26.

Henry, Debra, and Elizabeth Levesque. "The Lost Generation of Manitoba." *NAIITS Journal* 2 (2004): 39–50.

Holmes, Barbara A. *Joy Unspeakable: Contemplative Practices of the Black Church*. Minneapolis, MN: Fortress Press, 2004.

Hood, Ralph W. Jr, Peter C. Hill, and W. Paul Williamson. *The Psychology of Religious Fundamentalism*. New York: Guilford Press, 2005.

hooks, bell. *Rock My Soul: Black People and Self-Esteem*. New York: Atria Books, 2003.

Hourani, Albert, and Nadim Shehadi, eds. *The Lebanese in the World: A Century of Immigration*. London: I. B. Tauris, 1992.

Hovsepian, Nubar. "State-Society Relations and the Reproduction of the Lebanese Confessional System." In *The War on Lebanon: A Reader*, edited by Nubar Hovsepian, 28–49. Northampton, MA: Olive Branch Press, 2007.

Howell, Sally, and Amaney Jamal. "Belief and Belonging." In *Citizenship and Crisis: Arab Detroit after 9/11*, Detroit Arab American Study Team, 103–34. New York: Russell Sage Foundation, 2009.

Hubbard, David Allen. *What We Evangelicals Believe*. Pasadena, CA: Fuller Theological Seminary, 1991.

Huckins, Kyle. "Potlatch Gospel." *Christianity Today* 44 (June 12, 2000): 66–69.

Huggins, Nathan. "Deforming Mirror of Truth: Slavery and the Master Narrative of American History." *Radical History Review* 49 (1991): 44.

Hurston, Zora Neale. *Mules and Men*. New York: Perennial Library, 1990 (1935).

Hussaini, Hatem. "The Impact of the Arab-Israeli Conflict on Arab American Communities in the United States." In *Settler Regimes in Africa and the Arab World: The Illusion of Endurance*. AAUG Monograph Series 4, edited by Ibrahim Abu-Lughod and Baha Abu-Laban, 201–20. Wilmette, IL: Medina University Press International, 1974.

Hyatt, Susan. *Essential Elements of a Pentecostal/Charismatic Theology of Womanhood*. Dallas, TX: Hyatt Press, 2000.

Indian Life Ministries. *The Council Speaks*. Winnipeg: Indian Life Books, 1999.

Isasi-Diaz, Ada Maria. *En La Lucha: Introduction to Mujerista Theology*. Maryknoll, NY: Orbis, 1997.

Jacobs, Adrian. *Aboriginal Christianity: The Way It Was Meant to Be*. Rapid City: Self-published, 1998.

Jacobs, Adrian. *Pagan Prophets and Heathen Believers*. Rapid City, SD: Self-published, 1999.

Jeung, Russell. *Faithful Generations: Race and New Asian American Churches*. New Brunswick, NJ: Rutgers University Press, 2005.

Jeffers, Lance. *My Blackness Is the Beauty of This Land*. Detroit MI: Broadside Press, 1970.

Kadir, Djelai. *Columbus and the Ends of the Earth*. Berkeley: University of California Press, 1992.

Kayal, Philip M. "So, Who Are We? Who Am I?" In *Community of Many Worlds: Arab Americans in New York City,* edited by Kathleen Benson and Philip Kayal, 90–106. New York: Museum of City of New York/Syracuse University Press, 2002.

Kayal, Philip M., and Joseph M. Kayal. *The Syrian-Lebanese in America: A Study in Religion and Assimilation*. New York: Twayne, 1975.

Kayyali, Randa A. *The Arab Americans*. New Americans series, edited by Ronald H. Bayor. Westport, CT: Greenwood Press, 2006.

Khalidi, Rashid. *Resurrecting Empire: Western Footprints and America's Perilous Path in the Middle East*. Boston, MA: Beacon Press, 2004.

Kim, Rebecca Y. *God's New Whiz Kids? Korean American Evangelicals on Campus*. New York: New York University Press, 2006.

Kort, Wesley. *"Take, Read": Scripture, Textuality, and Cultural Practice*. University Park: Pennsylvania State University Press, 1996.

LALMA. "La Misión de lalma." http://lalma.org/nosotros.html.

Lam, Wan Shun Eva. "The Question of Culture in Global English-Language Teaching: A Postcolonial Perspective." In *Tokens of Exchange: The Problem of Translation in Global Circulations*, edited by Lydia H. Liu, 375–97. Durham, NC: Duke University Press, 1999.

Law, John. *Aircraft Stories: Decentering the Object in Technoscience*. Durham, NC, and London: Duke University Press, 2002.

LeBlanc, Terry. "Compassionate Community, or Unchecked Greed?" *Mission Frontiers* 22 (September, 2000): 21.

Lee, Chang-rae. *Native Speaker*. New York: Penguin, 1995.

Levering, Miriam, ed. *Rethinking Scripture: Essays from a Comparative Perspective*, Albany: State University of New York Press, 1989.

Lien, Pie-te, and Tony Carnes. "The Religious Demography of Asian American Boundary Crossing." In *Asian American Religions: The Making and Remaking of Borders and Boundaries*, edited by Tony Carnes and Fenggang Yang, 38–51. New York: New York University Press, 2004.

Liew, Tat-siong Benny, and Vincent L. Wimbush, "Contact Zones and Zoning Contexts: From the Los Angeles 'Riot' to a New York Symposium." *Union Seminary Quarterly Review* 56 (2002): 21–40.

Liew, Tat-siong Benny. "Introduction: Whose Bible? Which (Asian) America?" *Semeia* 90-91 (2002): 1–26.

Liew, Tat-siong Benny. *What Is Asian American Biblical Hermeneutics? Reading the New Testament*. Honolulu: University of Hawaii Press, 2008.

Lindsell, Harold. *Battle of the Bible*. Grand Rapids, MI: Zondervan, 1976.

Ling, Amy, and Annette White Parks, eds. *Mrs. Spring Fragrance and Other Writings*. Urbana: University of Illinois Press, 1995.

Little, Douglas. *American Orientalism: The United States and the Middle East since 1945*. Chapel Hill: University of North Carolina Press, 2002.

Long, Charles H. "Perspectives for the Study of African American Religion." In *Down by the Riverside: Readings in African American Religion*, edited by Larry G. Murphy, 9–19. New York: New York University Press, 2000.

Lowe, Lisa. *Immigrant Acts: On Asian American Cultural Politics*. Durham, NC: Duke University Press, 1996.

Lui, Mary Ting Yi. *The Chinatown Trunk Mystery: Murder, Miscegnation, and Other Dangerous Encounters in Turn-of-the-Century New York City*. Princeton, NJ: Princeton University Press, 2005.

Luis Rivera Pagan, *Evangelización y violencia: La conquista de America*. San Juan, P.R.: Editorial CEMI, 1992. Translated as *A Violent Evangelism: The Political and Religious Conquest of the Americas*. Louisville, KY: Westminster/John Knox Press, 1992.

Lydersen, Kari. *Out of the Sea and into the Fire: Immigration from Latin America to the U.S. in the Global Age*. Monroe, ME: Common Courage, 2005.

Machado, Daisy L. "El gran avivamiento del '33." In *Futuring our Past: Explorations in the Theology of Tradition*, edited by Orlando O. Espín and Gary Macy, 249–76. Maryknoll, NY: Orbis Books, 2006.

Maeda, Daryl J. *Chains of Babylon: The Rise of Asian America*. Minneapolis: University of Minnesota Press, 2009.

Malone, Henry Thompson. *Cherokees of the Old South*. Athens: University of Georgia, 1956.

Martey, Emmanuel. *African Theology*. Maryknoll, NY: Orbis, 1994.

Martin, Marty. *Religion and Republic: the American Circumstance.* Boston: Beacon Press, 1987.

Martin, Marty. *Righteous Empire: Protestant Experience in America.* New York: Scribners, 1986.

Martínez-Vázquez, Hjamil A. *Latina/o y Musulmán: The Construction of Latina/o Identity among Latina/o Muslims in the United States.* Eugene, OR: Pickwick Publications, 2010.

Mbiti, John S. *Introduction to African Religion.* 2nd ed. Oxford, UK: Heinemann International Literature and Textbooks, 1975.

McAdams, Dan P. *The Redemptive Self: Stories Americans Live By.* New York: Oxford University Press, 2006.

McAlister, Melani. *Epic Encounters: Culture, Media, and U.S. Interests in the Middle East since 1945.* Updated edition. Berkeley: University of California Press, 2005.

McClain, William B. "African American Preaching and the Bible: Biblical Authority or Biblical Liberalism." *Journal of Religious Thought* 49 (Winter 92/Spring 93): 72–80. Also posted on the African American Lectionary website, 2008, http://www.theafricanamericanlectionary.org/pdf/preaching/AfricanAmericanPreachingandtheBible_WilliamMcClain.pdf.

McClintock, Anne. *Imperial Leather.* New York: Routledge, 1995.

McDowell, Josh. *More Than a Carpenter.* Wheaton, IL: Tyndale, 1977.

McGuire, James P. *The Syrian and Lebanese Texans.* The Texians and Texans. San Antonio: University of Texas at San Antonio and the Institute of Texan Cultures, 1974.

McLoughlin, William. *Cherokees and Missionaries, 1789–1839.* Norman: University of Oklahoma Press, 1995.

Mihesuah, Devon, and Angela Cavendar Wilson, eds. *Indigenizing the Academy.* Lincoln: University of Nebraska Press, 2004.

Miller, Donald E. *Reinventing American Protestantism: Christianity in the New Millennium.* Berkeley: University of California Press, 1997.

Min, Pyong Gap, and Jung Ha Kim, eds. *Religions in Asian America: Building Faith Communities.* Walnut Creek, CA: AltaMira Press, 2002.

Morrison, Toni. *Playing in the Dark: Whiteness and the Literary Imagination.* New York: Vintage Books, 1993.

Mosala, Itumeleng. *Biblical Hermeneutics and Black Theology in South Africa.* Grand Rapids, MI: Eerdmans Publishing, 1989.

My People International. *Vacation Bible School Curriculum,* Year 1, Book 1. Evansburg, Alberta: My People International, 2000.

Naber, Nadine. "The Rules of Forced Engagement." *Cultural Dynamics* 18, no. 3 (2006): 235–68.

Naber, Nadine. "Introduction: Arab Americans and U.S. Racial Formations." In *Race and Arab Americans Before and After 9/11: From Invisible Citizens to Visible Subjects,* edited by Amaney Jamal and Nadine Naber, 1–45. Syracuse, NY: Syracuse University, 2008.

Naff, Alixa. *Becoming American: The Early Arab Immigrant Experience.* Carbondale: Southern Illinois University, 1985.

Nasr, Constantine. *Journey through the Divine Liturgy*. Oklahoma City, OK: Theosis Publishing, 1991.

Nasr, Constantine. *The Bible in the Liturgy*. Oklahoma City, OK: Theosis Publishing, 1988.

Nelson, Bryce. "Mideast War Spurs Unprecedented Formation of Arab Groups in U.S." *Los Angeles Times*, Oct. 25, 1973, sec. A12.

Noley, Homer. *First White Frost*. Nashville, TN: United Methodist Publishing House, 2000.

Nottage, Lynn. *Crumbs from the Table of Joy*. New York: Dramatists Play Service, 1998.

Orfalea, Gregory. *The Arab Americans: A History*. Northampton, MA: Olive Branch Press, 2006.

Payne, Daniel Alexander. "Education in the AME Church." In *Afro-American Religious History*, edited by Milton C. Sernett, 243–51. Durham, NC: Duke University Press, 1985.

The Pew Forum on Religion and Public Life and the Pew Hispanic Center. *Changing Faiths: Latinos and the Transformation of American Religion*. Washington, DC, 2007.

Pew Research Center's Forum on Religion and Public Life. *Mapping the Global Muslim Population: A Report on the Size and Distribution of the World's Muslim Population*. Pew Forum website, October 2009. http://pewforum.org/Mapping-the-Global-Muslim-Population.aspx

Price, Robert. "Neo-Evangelicals and Scripture: A Forgotten Period of Ferment." *Christian Scholars Review* 15, no. 4 (1986): 315–30.

Proctor, Bernadette D., and Joseph Dalaker. "Poverty in the United States: 2002." http://www2.census.gov/prod2/popscan/p60-222.pdf.

Putnam, Robert D., and David E. Campbell. *American Grace: How Religion Divides and Unites Us*. New York: Simon and Schuster, 2010.

Preus, Robert, and Earl Radmacher, eds. *Hermeneutics, Inerrancy and the Bible*. Grand Rapids, MI: Zondervan, 1984.

Qaumaniq, and Suuqiina. *Warfare by Honor: The Restoration of Honor, a Protocol Handbook*. Portland, TN: Indigenous Messengers International, 2007.

Reed, Ishmael. *Mumbo Jumbo*. New York: Scribner Paperback Fiction, 1996 (1972).

Rupert, Greenberry G. *The Yellow Peril: Or, The Orient Vs. the Occident as Viewed by Modern Statesmen and Ancient Prophets*. Britton: Union Publishing, 1911.

Said, Edward W. *Covering Islam: How the Media and the Experts Determine How We See the Rest of the World*. New York: Pantheon, 1981.

Said, Edward W. *Orientalism*. New York: Vintage, 1978.

Said, Edward W. *Reflections on Exile and Other Essays*. Cambridge, MA: Harvard University Press, 2000.

Sanders, Ronald. *Lost Tribes and Promised Lands*. Boston: Little, Brown and Company, 1978.

Scott, James C. *Domination and the Arts of Resistance: Hidden Transcripts*. New Haven, CT: Yale University Press, 1990.

Schiller, Nina Glick, and Georges Eugene Fouron. *Georges Woke up Laughing: Long-Distance Nationalism and the Search for Home*. Durham, NC: Duke University Press, 2001.

Segovia, Fernando. "Toward Latino/a American Biblical Criticism: Latin(o/a)ness as Problematic." In *They Were All in One Place? Toward Minority Biblical Criticism*, edited by Randall C. Bailey, Tat-siong Benny Liew, and Fernando F. Segovia, 193–223. Atlanta, GA: Society of Biblical Literature, 2009.

Seligman, Adam. "The American System of Stratification: Some Notes towards Understanding Its Symbolic and Institutional Concomitants." In *Centre Formation, Protests Movements, and Class Struggles in Europe and the United States*, edited by S.N. Eisenstadt, L. Roniger, and A. Seligman. 171–72. New York: New York University, 1987.

Shakir, Evelyn. *Bint Arab: Arab and Arab American Women in the United States*. Westport, CT: Praeger, 1997.

Shohat, Ella, and Robert Stam. *Unthinking Eurocentrism: Multiculturalism and the Media*. Sightlines. New York: Routledge, 1994.

Silva, Denise Ferreira da. *Toward a Global Idea of Race*. Minneapolis: University of Minnesota Press, 2007.

Smith, Andrea. *Conquest: Sexual Violence and American Indian Genocide*. Cambridge, MA: South End Press, 2005.

Smith, Andrea. *Native Americans and the Christian Right: The Gendered Politics of Unlikely Alliances*. Durham, NC: Duke University Press, 2008.

Smith, Craig. *Whiteman's Gospel*. Winnipeg: Indian Life Books, 1997.

Smith, Justine. "Resistance Disguised as Fundamentalism: Cherokee Nationalism, Racial Identity, and the Bible." Paper delivered at the American Academy of Religion Conference, 2000.

Smith, Linda Tuhiwai. *Decolonizing Methodologies*. London: Zed, 1999.

Solberg, S. E. "Sui Sin Far/Edith Eaton: First Chinese-American Fictionist." *MELUS* 8 (1981): 27–39.

Smith, W. C. *What Is Scripture? A Comparative Approach*. Minneapolis, MN: Fortress, 1993.

Steet, Linda. *Veils and Daggers: A Century of National Geographic's Representation of the Arab World*. Philadelphia, PA: Temple University Press, 2000.

Steinken, Ken. "Native Christians Reclaim Worship." *Christianity Today* 42 (October 26, 1998): 13.

Stendahl, Krister. "The Bible as a Classic and the Bible as Holy Scripture." *Journal of Biblical Literature* 103, no. 1 (March 1984): 3–10.

Stewart, Jimmy. "Native Praise." *Charisma* 26 (November, 2000): 91.

Stiffler, Matthew. "Authentic Arabs, Authentic Christians: Antiochian Orthodox and the Mobilization of Cultural Identity." PhD diss., University of Michigan, Ann Arbor, 2010.

Strauss, Anselm, and Juliet Corbin. *Basics of Qualitative Research: Ground Theory Procedures and Techniques*. Newbury Park, CA: Sage Publications, 1990.

Sugirtharajah, R. S. *The Bible and the Third World: Precolonial, Colonial, and Postcolonial Encounters*. New York: Cambridge University Press, 2001.

Suh, Sharon A. *Being Buddhist in a Christian World: Gender and Community in a Korean American Temple*. Seattle: University of Washington Press, 2004.

Suleiman, Michael W. "Introduction: The Arab Immigrant Experience." In *Arabs in America: Building a New Future*, edited by Michael W. Suleiman, 1–21. Philadelphia, PA: Temple University Press, 1999.

Suuqiina. "Cultural Restoration: It's Time, It's Here." *Inuit Ministries International Newsletter* (2000): 1–3.

Taussig, Michael. *Mimesis and Alterity: A Particular History of the Senses*. New York: Routledge, 1993.

Taussig, Michael. *The Nervous System*. New York: Routledge, 1992.

Thomas, David. "Arab Christianity." In *The Blackwell Companion to Eastern Christianity*, edited by Ken Parry, 1–22. Oxford: John Wiley & Sons, 2007.

Thurman, Howard. "On Viewing the Coast of Africa." In *A Strange Freedom: the Best of Howard Thurman on Religious Life and Public Service*, edited by Walter E. Fluker and Catherine Tumber, 301–302. Boston: Beacon Press, 1998.

Tiénou, Tite. "Indigenous Theologizing from the Margins to the Center." *NAIITS Journal* 3 (2005): 5–17.

Torreglosa, Eleazar. *En la Escritura*. Translated by S. T. Kimbrough Jr. New York: GBGMusik, 2004.

Townes, Emile M., ed. *A Troubling in My Soul: Womanist Perspectives on Evil and Suffering*. Maryknoll, NY: Orbis Books, 1995.

Tran, Scott G. "Vietnamese Refugees Finally Find Home." *Los Angeles Times*, April 24, 2000, PA, A–1.

Treat, James. *Around the Sacred Fire*. New York: Palgrave, 2003.

Tsing, Anna Lowenhaupt. *In the Real of the Diamond Queen*. Princeton, NJ: Princeton University Press, 1993.

Twiss, Richard. "Culture, Christ and the Kingdom Seminar." Vancouver, WA: Wiconi International, 1996.

Twiss, Richard. "Indian Uprising." *Charisma* 26 (October, 2000a): 51.

Twiss, Richard. "Out of Sight, Out of Mind." *Mission Frontiers* 22 (September, 2000b): 12–13.

Twiss, Richard. *Sanctification, Syncretism and Worship*. Vancouver, WA: Wiconi International, 1998.

US Census Bureau, "State and County Quickfacts: Hartford City, Connecticut." http://quickfacts.census.gov/qfd/states/09/0937000.html.

Volpp, Leti. "The Citizen and the Terrorist." In *September 11 in History: A Watershed Moment?* Edited by Mary L. Dudziak, 147–62. Durham, NC: Duke University Press, 2003.

Walker, David. "Our Wretchedness in Consequence of the Preachers of Religion." In *Afro-American Religious History A Documentary Witness*, edited by Milton C. Sernett, 193–201. Durham, NC: Duke University Press, 1985.

Warren, Rick. *The Purpose Driven Life: What on Earth Am I Here For?* Grand Rapids, MI: Zondervan, 2002.

Warrior, Robert. *Tribal Secrets*. Minneapolis: University of Minnesota Press, 1994.

Weaver, Jace. *That the People Might Live: Native American Literatures and Native American Community*. New York: Oxford University Press, 1997.

Weber, Samuel. *Institution and Interpretation*. Palo Alto, CA: Stanford University Press, 2001.

Whitt, Laurie Anne. "Cultural Imperialism and the Marketing of Native America." In *Natives and Academics: Researching and Writing about American Indians*, edited by Devon Mihesuah, 139–71. Lincoln: University of Nebraska Press, 1998.

Wilkinson, Bruce. *Secrets of the Vine: Breaking through to Abundance*. Sisters, OR: Multnomah, 2001.

Wilson, Waziyatawin Angela. *Remember This!* Lincoln: University of Nebraska Press, 2005.

Wimbush, Vincent L. "Introduction: Reading Darkness, Reading Scriptures." In *African Americans and the Bible: Sacred Texts and Social Textures*, edited by V. L. Wimbush, with the assistance of R. C. Rodman, 1–43. New York: Continuum International, 2000.

Wimbush, Vincent L. *The Bible and African Americans: A Brief History*. Minneapolis, MN: Fortress Press, 2003.

Wimbush, Vincent L. "The Bible and African Americans: An Outline of an Interpretive History?" In *Stony the Road We Trod: African American Biblical Interpretation*, edited by Cain Hope Felder, 81–97. Minneapolis, MN: Fortress Press, 1991.

Wimbush, V. L. ed. *Theorizing Scriptures: New Critical Orientations to a Cultural Phenomenon*. Signifying [on] Scriptures Series. New Brunswick, NJ: Rutgers University Press, 2008.

Woodley, Randy. "Putting It to the Test." *Mission Frontiers* 22 (2000): 18–19.

Wrone, David, and Russel Nelson, eds. *Who's the Savage?* Malabar. FL: Robert Krieger Publishing, 1982.

Yamamoto, Hisaye. *Seventeen Syllables and Other Stories*. New Brunswick, NJ: Rutgers University Press, 2001.

Yang, Fenggang. *Chinese Christians in America: Conversion, Assimilation, and Adhesive Identities*. University Park: Pennsylvania State University Press, 1999.

Yates, Joshua J., and James Davison Hunter, "Fundamentalism: When History Goes Awry." In *Stories of Change: Narrative and Social Movements*, edited by Joseph E. Davis, 123–48. Albany: State University of New York, 2002.

INDEX

abortion, 74–81, 112
acculturation, 65, 126–27
African Hebrew Israelites, 6, 87, 89
  of Jerusalem, 99–102, 111
African American Lectionary, 89, 97–98
African Americans, 5, 6, 93, 99, 102, 109,
  125, 153, 160, 247, 260
African Methodist Episcopal Church
  (AME), 95, 99
Afro-American Poetics (Baker), 15
afwaja, 267
Agosto, Efrain, 7, 117
Aircraft Stories (Law), 17
Al-Andalus, 157
Aldred, Ray, 52, 70, 77, 83
Alfred, Taiaiake, 58
al-Ghazali. *See* Ghazali, al-
alienated reading (*see also* Said, Edward),
  206
Alim, 250
Allah, 143, 159, 254, 263–67
Al-Nour, 216
ambivalence/double ambivalence, 7, 191,
  194, 197, 201, 206
America, 1
American Dream Act, 126
American Indian Movement (AIM), 51
American Muslim Council, 128
Americanism, 11
Americanization, 169, 219–21, 257
Ammerman, Nancy, 174, 178, 195
Ammi, Ben, 100–02, 107

Anaphora of St. James Brother of the
  Lord, 246
ancestor worship, 184
Angelou, Maya
  I Know Why the Caged Bird Sings, 92
antimiscegenation laws, 182
Antiochian Orthodox, 214–24, 228–31,
  233–35, 237–40, 247
Antiochian Orthodox Basilica of Saint
  Mary, 216
Appadurai, Arjun, 248
Arab Americans, 5, 7, 211–12, 225, 227,
  237, 243–44, 268
Arab American University Graduates, 212
Arnheim, Rudolf, 10
Around the Sacred Fire (Treat), 34
Asbury Theological Seminary, 34
Asian American Bible believers, 172,
  175–76, 178–81, 183–87, 189–90,
  198–201
Asian Americans, 5, 7, 165, 166–71, 176,
  178, 182–84, 189, 199–206
Asian Baptist Student Koinonia, 171
Asiatic Barred Zone, 167
assimilation, 7, 8, 57, 65, 82, 185, 208,
  268
Association for Hispanic Theological
  Education, 147
"Aunt Susan" and "My Friend Al"
  principle, 178
authenticity, 108, 216, 231, 233–35, 242,
  252

authority, 5, 7, 30, 50, 54, 58–59, 104,
    109, 118, 128, 136, 138, 140–42,
    144, 146, 148–50, 152, 159–161n2,
    163n57, 176, 178, 199–201, 203,
    205, 233–35, 238, 242, 249, 257
  of the Bible, 94, 104, 118, 136–37, 139,
    141, 149, 152, 158, 165, 173–74,
    185, 190–91, 195–96, 199–200,
    203–04
  of the government, 24
  of the Qur'an, 118, 136, 139, 249, 266
  of scriptures, 118–19, 135–41, 148–53,
    155, 158, 161n2

"bad" reading, 204, 206
Baker, Houston
  Afro-American Poetics, 15
Baptist
  American, 131
  Native Southern, 33
Baraka, Amiri, 19
Barber, Karin, 99
Barlas, Asma, 156
Barnett, Dicey, 37, 56, 66
Base Community Bible studies, 134
Batista, Fulgencio, 122
"Battle of the Bible," 60, 85n3
Bear, Cheryl, 40
Bee, Tom, 56
Begay, Art, 33, 37
Benjamin, Walter, 16
bet maroon, 216
Bible
  Cherokee, 65
  Creek, 65
  inerrancy of, 7, 60, 85n3, 173, 175,
    190, 194–96, 199, 201, 203–04
  King James, 47, 60, 61, 63, 169
Big Jim. *See* "Pondy Woods"
Bigpond, Negiel, 34
Bird, David, 44, 48, 69, 70, 76–78
Black Jews, 91
Black Power, 168
Blackburn, Julia
  White Man, The, 18
Bloom, Harold, 2

"boat people," 186–87
Boone, John, 32
Boyer, Roger, 55, 73, 75, 79
Briggs-Cloud, Marcus, 35, 46, 65, 71
Bureau of Indian Affairs (BIA), 24,
    51, 32
"burnt black," 205 (*see also* Yamamoto,
    Hisaye)
Busto, Rudy, 171, 184, 204
Buzzard. *See* "Pondy Woods"

Cainkar, Louise, 213
Canaanite woman, 150
canon/canonicity, 1, 11, 14, 17, 82, 159,
    238
capitalism, 21n22, 57, 169
Carlisle (boarding school), 31 (*see also*
    Pratt, Richard)
Castro, Fidel, 122–23
Catholic Charismatic Renewal groups,
    155
Cave, Albert, 31
center, the/centering, 8, 9, 10, 11, 14, 15,
    16, 19, 90, 93, 102, 167, 181, 182,
    184, 185, 187, 200, 246
  symbol(s) of, 15
  politics, 1
  practices, 25
  text, 187
"Chains of Babylon," 166 (*see also*
    Maeda, Daryl J.)
Chaldeans, 215
Chambers, Oswald
  My Utmost for His Highest, 185
Campus Crusade for Christ, 171
"Changing Faiths: Latinos and the
    Transformation of American
    Religion" (*see also* Pew Charitable
    Trusts), 127
Chapel of Our Lady of Guadalupe, 134
Charisma, 29, 37
charismatic movement(s), 33–35
charity, 165, 185–90, 200–01, 205–07
CHIEF, 29, 34
Christian and Missionary Alliance, 188
Christian missionization, 33

Maronite Catholic, 7, 208, 214–29,
    231–41, 243–47, 270n15, 270n18,
    270n22, 270n23
Martínez-Vázquez, Hjamil A., 142,
    162n26, 162n32
Masjid Omar ibn Al-Khattab, 133,
    163n42, 164n70
Mason, Virginia, 45
master's tools, 3, 82
matrilineal society, 61, 70
Mauldin, Margaret McKane, 36, 39, 47,
    62–63, 67
Mbari house, 18
McAdams, Dan P., 101
McClain, William B., 94
McClintock, Anne, 83–84
McDowell, Josh, 185
    More Than a Carpenter, 185
meaning-making, 6, 111, 135, 143, 145
    (*see also* scripture[s])
medicine men, 36, 38, 43, 51, 61, 81
Melkites, 215
mestizaje, 160
Mexican Americans, 121, 124, 130, 157
Mexican-American War, 121
    Treaty of Guadalupe Hidalgo, 121
Middle East/Middle Eastern culture, 133,
    157, 209, 211–16, 218, 221, 223–24,
    229–34, 237, 243, 245, 251, 269n7,
    269n9
Miller, Donald, 35
Mimesis and Alterity (Taussig), 17
"mimetic excess," 17, 19
mimicry, 1
minoritized communities, 1–2, 4, 8, 184,
    200–01
"*miseducation*," 4
"*misreadings*," 2–3, 20, 21n1 (*see also*
    signify (on))
missionary societies, 31
"misprision," 2 (*see also* "misreading")
"model minority," 4, 166, 200–01, 204–06
    (*see also* Busto, Rudy)
modernism, 17, 22n47
monoculturalism, 62
Moravians, 32

More Than a Carpenter (McDowell), 185
Morrison, Toni, 15–16
    Playing in the Dark, 16
mosque, 133, 144, 248–49, 260
mujerista theology, 140
Muhammad, 133, 137, 145, 254, 261
*Muhammad: His Life Based on the
    Earliest Sources* (Lings), 133
multiculturalism, 29
"My Blackness is the Beauty of this
    Land" (Jeffers), 20
My Daily Frybread, 29
My People International, 41, 43
My Utmost for His Highest (Chambers),
    185

Naber, Nadine, 7, 208, 211–13
*Narrative of the Life of Frederick
    Douglass, An American Slave,
    Written by Himself* (Douglass), 8
nasr, 267, 271n28
Nation of Islam, 91
National Association of Arab Americans,
    212
nationhood, 58–59
Native Americans/First Nations, 5–6,
    23–25, 28, 30–31, 33–34, 39–40, 43,
    49, 51, 56, 63, 84, 151, 168, 211
    Catawba, 46
    Cherokee, 32–33, 65
    Iroquois, 44, 56, 59
    Lakota, 51
    Mashpee, 46
    Micmac, 43, 57
    Mohawk, 44, 58
    Mohican, 47
    Muskogee, 36, 64–65, 71, 81
    Wabanaki, 43, 57
Native boarding schools, 31–32, 42, 84n1
Native communities, 5, 23, 25–35, 39,
    44, 57–59, 63–64, 71, 73–74, 79, 81,
    83–84
Native evangelicalism/evangelicals, 6, 23,
    25, 27–31, 33–37, 39, 43–45, 47, 49,
    52, 60, 66, 69, 73–74, 79, 82–84
Native feminism, 58–59, 66, 73

property
  cultural, 26
  intellectual, 26
Puritanism, 11
Purpose Drive Life, The (Warren), 185,
  200

Qaumaniq, 56
Qur'an, 118, 133, 136–37, 139, 141–43,
  145–46, 156, 158–59, 163n57,
  164n69, 248–53, 257–58, 260–67

race reconciliation movement, 29, 33
race/racism/racialization, 2–3, 7–8,
  24, 56, 78, 98, 112, 147, 166–69,
  208–09, 211, 243, 258–61,
  267–68
Ramadan, 133, 249, 254
reading formations, 1, 4
"redemptive enterprises," 101, 111 (*see
  also* African Hebrew Israelites)
redemptive story, 101 (*see also* African
  Hebrew Israelites)
Red Sea Ministries 33, 56 (*see also* Bee,
  Tom)
Reed, Ishmael, 15, 22n24
refugee, 187, 189, 210, 222–23,
  269n6
  camps, 187, 189
religious pluralism, 170
Renew International, 134
[re]orientation, 1–2
reversion/revert, 132, 136, 139, 142–43,
  145–46, 156–57, 162n32, 163n41,
  163n50
rhema, 138, 158, 162n37
Rhema Bible Training College,
  107
rhetoric, 83, 166, 186–87, 190, 200–01,
  217
Rijaloon Sadaq Allah Ma'Ahadoo Alai,
  264
ritual, 2, 5, 18, 30, 73, 89, 93, 128, 137,
  147–48, 154–55, 158, 170, 184, 240,
  246–47, 249
Roman Catholic Archdiocese of Los
  Angeles, 133

Rupert, Greenberry G., 168–69
  The Yellow Peril: Or, The Orient Vs.
    the Occident as Viewed by Modern
    Statesman and Ancient Prophets,
    168

Saliba, Philip, 218, 229, 271n28
Said, Edward, 206, 211
salah, 249
Sampson, L., 11
Schaeffer, Frank, 74
Schaeffer, Francis, 74
scripture(s)/scripturalizing practices, 1,
    4–8, 11, 13–15, 20, 22n25, 35, 40,
    42, 48, 56, 58, 60–64, 68, 72, 78–79,
    81, 86–94, 99–102, 107–08, 110–14,
    117–20, 126–29, 131, 135–56,
    158–60, 161n30, 169, 182, 200,
    208–09, 219, 236, 238–47, 250–56,
    258–59, 261–62, 265–68, 271n27
scriptural formations, 2
scripturalization, 117–19, 128
Secrets of the Vine (Wilkinson), 185
Segarra, Pedro, 123
Segovia, Fernando, 120, 161n4
Seligman, Adam, 11
Sermon on the Mount, 12
shahadah, 132
Shariah, 257
signification, 2, 138, 142, 148
signify (on), 2, 5, 66, 82, 111, 148, 158,
    160, 168
Silva, Denise Ferreira da, 29, 84
Simpson, Audra, 84
slavocracy, 10
Smith, Andrea, 6, 23, 28, 33, 59, 73, 84n1
Smith, Craig, 42
Smith, Justine, 65
Smith, Linda Tuhiwai, 26, 28
Smith, Wilfred Cantwell, 14
social and historical realities, 97
social environment, 86
social formation, 5–6, 10, 66, 99, 110–11,
    204
social hierarchy, 59
social movement, 10, 90
social order, 204